A Guide to the Sources of
United States Military History:
Supplement I

A Guide to the Sources of United States Military History: Supplement I

EDITED BY
ROBIN HIGHAM
AND
DONALD J. MROZEK

1981
ARCHON BOOKS

Library of Congress Cataloging in Publication Data
Main entry under title:

A Guide to the sources of United States military
history, supplement I.

1. United States—History, Military—Bibliog-
raphy. I. Higham, Robin D. S. II. Mrozek,
Donald J.
Z1249.M5G83 1975 Suppl. [E181] 016.355'00973 80-49
ISBN 0-208-01750-X

© 1981 Robin Higham and Donald J. Mrozek

First published 1981 as an Archon Book,
an imprint of The Shoe String Press, Inc.,
Hamden, Connecticut 06514

Printed in the United States of America

CONTENTS

EDITORIAL NOTE

Most of the authors contributing articles to this *Supplement* participated in the publication of the original *Guide to the Sources of the United States Military History* in 1975. All were asked to continue their files, collecting important bibliographic information in their fields, especially for the period between 1973 and 1978. In this way, a supplement could be readily assembled that would extend the coverage provided by the original volume. In a few cases, however, at the request of the original authors, new contributors entered the project, building on the basis of the 1975 volume.

The editors and publisher agreed that several significant areas that had not been treated directly in the original *Guide* merited coverage in complete chapters. Hence this *Supplement* includes extensive treatment of the United States Marine Corps, nuclear war and arms control, military law, martial law, and military government, and U.S. government documentation in chapters specifically devoted to each of those topics. These new essays were numbered so as to follow the sequence of the original nineteen chapters and thereby to minimize any difficulty in using the original *Guide* and the *Supplement* together.

With few exceptions, all essays and material included in this volume were written and received by 1979. The authors have been asked to continue their files with the intent of producing a succeeding quinquennial supplement.

R. H. and D. M.

Kansas State University

AUTHORS

Dean C. Allard, Head of the Operational Archives of the U.S. Naval History Division in Washington, served in the USN from 1955 to 1958, when he joined the Division. A graduate of Dartmouth, he received his Ph.D. from George Washington University and is a frequent panelist at professional meetings as well as a contributor to scholarly journals such as *The American Neptune.*

Daniel R. Beaver, professor of history at the University of Cincinnati, was educated at Heidelberg College and received his Ph.D. from Northwestern University. A former infantryman, he is the author of *Newton D. Baker* (1966) and of *Some Pathways in Twentieth Century History* (1969).

William R. Braisted, professor of history at the University of Texas at Austin, is a graduate of Stanford and received his Ph.D. from the University of Chicago. A military intelligence analyst for the U.S. Army in World War II, he has since been a Fulbright fellow in Japan. His publications include *The United States Navy in the Pacific, 1897–1909* (1958) and *The United States Navy in the Pacific, 1909–1922* (1971).

James O. Breeden is professor of history at Southern Methodist University. A graduate of the University of Virginia, he obtained his Ph.D. from Tulane University in 1967. He is the author of a number of articles and of *Joseph Jones, MD—Scientist of the Old South* (1974).

Calvin L. Christman, professor of history at Cedar Valley College in Dallas, Texas, received his A.B. from Dartmouth and his Ph.D. from The Ohio State University. His specialty is twentieth-century United States military history. He is cocompiler of the annual dissertation article in *Military Affairs,* serves as the Southwest Regional Coordinator of the Inter-University Seminar on Armed Forces and Society, and has contributed articles to *Mid-America, The Americas,* and *Diplomatic History.*

Robert W. Coakley, Deputy Chief Historian, Center for Military History, Department of the Army Washington, D.C., was graduated from William and Mary and received his Ph.D. from the University of Virginia. He was both a field artilleryman and a military historian in World War II. He is the coauthor of a number of official volumes including two on global logistics and strategy in World War II and is also with Stetson Conn responsible for the CMH study, *The War of the American Revolution: Narrative, Chronology and Bibliography* (1975).

B. Franklin Cooling III is both Assistant Director for Historical Services, U.S. Army Military History Institute, Carlisle Barracks, and member of the faculty,

U.S. Army War College. In the Army Reserve, 1956–63, he graduated from Rutgers University and received his Ph.D. from the University of Pennsylvania. He is past cocompiler of the annual dissertations in *Military Affairs*, past Vice President and Trustee of the American Military Institute, past Fellow of the Company of Military Historians, and currently Bibliography Committee Chairman for the U.S. Commission on Military History. His publications include: *Benjamin Franklin Tracy: Father of the Modern American Fighting Navy* (1973); *Symbol, Sword, and Shield: Defending Washington during the Civil War* (1975); (editor) *War, Business, and American Society* (1977); (editor) *The New American State Papers: Military Affairs* (1979); and *Gray Steel and Blue Water Navy: Formative Years of America's Military-Industrial Complex, 1881–1917* (1979).

Graham A. Cosmas received his B.A. from Oberlin and his M.S. and Ph.D. from the University of Wisconsin. A member of Phi Beta Kappa, he was selected as a Woodrow Wilson Fellow (1960–61) and a National Securities Group Fellow (1964–65). In 1966, he received the Moncado Award of the American Military Institute. He is the author of *An Army for Empire: The United States Army in the Spanish-American War* (1971) and of articles in journals such as *Military Affairs* and the *Wisconsin Journal of History*. He is currently with the Medical History Branch, Histories Division, U.S. Army Center of Military History.

Richard N. Ellis, professor of history at the University of New Mexico, received his Ph.D. from the University of Colorado in 1967. He has contributed a large number of articles to a variety of periodicals and is the author of *General Pope and the U.S. Indian Policy* (1970), *New Mexico, Past and Present* (1971), and *The Western American Indian: Case Studies in Tribal History* (1972).

Edward C. Ezell, a NASA contractor with the University of Houston, graduated from Butler University, had a Hagley Museum Fellowship, and received his Ph.D. from the Case Institute of Technology. He specializes in arms procurement and has contributed articles to a number of journals in the field. In 1975 he was awarded the AMI's Moncado Prize.

Robert T. Finney is Research Professor Emeritus of Military History, Air University. He was a member of the Office of Air Force History, 1944–58, contributing to the seven-volume *Army Air Forces in World War II* and writing a *History of the Air Corps Tactical School* and many background studies dealing with Air Force affairs, with special emphasis on Air Force doctrine. From 1959 until retirement in 1976, Mr. Finney was engaged in a program of writing and editing a wide variety of publications for use within Air University.

Dale E. Floyd, formerly with the Naval and Old Army Branch of the National Archives, is a historian with the U.S. Army Corps of Engineers. After study at Ohio University, he pursued graduate work at the University of Dayton. Among his publications is a "World Bibliography of Armed Land Conflict from Waterloo to World War I" (1979).

Robin Higham, professor of history at Kansas State University and Editor of both *Military Affairs* and of *Aerospace Historian,* has written a number of books and articles and has edited *A Guide to the Sources of British Military History* (1971) and *Bayonets in the Streets* (1969). He is the author of *Air Power: A Concise History* (1973) and of *The Compleat Academic* (1975). He served in the RAFVR, 1943–47.

Douglas Edward Leach received his A.B. from Brown University and his Ph.D. from Harvard. Currently professor of history at Vanderbilt University, he has been a Fulbright lecturer at the Universities of Liverpool and Auckland. His publications include *Flintlock and Tomahawk: New England in King Philip's War* (1958), *The Northern Colonial Frontier, 1607–1763* (1966), and *Arms for Empire: A Military History of the British Colonies in North America, 1607–1763* (1973).

Philip K. Lundeberg, Curator of Naval History at the Smithsonian Institution, received his A.B. from Duke and his Ph.D. from Harvard. He joined the Smithsonian staff in 1959, after serving in both World War II and the Korean War in the USN. He has contributed to numerous books and is the author of *The Continental Gunboat Philadelphia* (1966) and of *Samuel Colt's Submarine Battery* (1975). Since 1968 he has written the "Museums Perspective" in *Military Affairs.* He was president of the American Military Institute, 1971–73, and is president of the U.S. Military History Commission.

Christopher F. McKee is Librarian and Rosenthal Professor of History at Grinnell College. Educated at the University of St. Thomas (Texas) and at the University of Michigan, he has authored *Edward Preble: A Naval Biography, 1761–1807* (1972) and has edited and coedited works for the *American Neptune.* Professor McKee is affiliated with the American Military Institute, the American Historical Association, the American Library Association, and the Organization of American Historians.

Grady McWhiney received his B.S. from Centenary College and his Ph.D. from Columbia. He is Chairman of the Department of History at the University of Alabama and is the author of the prize-winning *Braxton Bragg and Confederate Defeat* (1969). Often a visiting professor, he is also the author of *Southerners and Other Americans* (1973), coeditor of *Robert E. Lee's Dispatches to Jefferson Davis* (1957) and of *To Mexico with Taylor and Scott* (1969), and editor of *Grant, Lee, Lincoln and the Radicals* (1964).

Donald J. Mrozek, associate professor of history at Kansas State University, received his undergraduate education at Georgetown University and took his Ph.D. at Rutgers University. He has published articles on the American military in the twentieth century in such journals as *Military Affairs, The Business History Review,* and various state and regional historical magazines. He is also active in the study of American cultural history.

Timothy K. Nenninger works in the Military Archives Division of the National Archives in Washington, D.C. He took his Ph.D. at the University of Wisconsin, Madison, in 1971, and is the author of *The Leavenworth Schools* *and the Old Army* (1978). He has also authored articles on military topics that have appeared in a variety of books and journals.

Roger L. Nichols, professor of history at the University of Arizona, graduated from Wisconsin State College, LaCrosse, and received his Ph.D. from the University of Wisconsin. He is the author of *The American Indian: Past and Present* (1971), *The Missouri Expedition, 1818–1820* (1969), and of *General Henry Atkinson: A Western Military Career* (1965), as well as of some fifty articles.

Donald Nieman received his B.A. from Drake University in 1970 and his Ph.D. from Rice University in 1975. Currently associate professor of history at Kansas State University, he is the author of *To Set the Law in Motion: The Freedmen's Bureau and the Legal Rights of Blacks* (1979).

Carroll W. Pursell, Jr. received both his A.B. and his Ph.D. from the University of California at Berkeley. Coeditor of *Technology and Western Civilization* (1968), he is the author of *Early Stationary Steam Engines in America* (1969) and editor of *The Politics of American Science* (1972). He is professor of history at the University of California, Santa Barbara and secretary of the Society for the History of Technology.

Hugh F. Rankin, professor of history at Tulane University, graduated from Elon College and received his Ph.D. from the University of North Carolina at Chapel Hill. A former superintendent of highway construction, he served in the Corps of Engineers, USA, in World War II. Coauthor of *Rebels and Redcoats* (1957) and author of *North Carolina in the American Revolution* (1959), *Pirates of Colonial North Carolina* (1950), *The American Revolution* (1964), and *Francis Marion: Swamp Fox* (1973), he is well known in his field.

Russell F. Weigley, professor of history at Temple University, graduated from Albright College and received his Ph.D. from the University of Pennsylvania. Editor of *Pennsylvania History,* 1962–67, he is the author of *Quartermaster-General of the Union Army: A Biography of M. C. Meigs* (1959), *Towards an American Army: Military Thought from Washington to Marshall* (1962), *History of the United States Army* (1967), and *The American Way of War* (1973), a multiple book-club selection.

I

INTRODUCTION

Robin Higham and
Donald J. Mrozek

The greater acceptance of military history as a legitimate scholarly enterprise and the dedication of many talented historians to the study of American military affairs have created a need for this volume, as planned, which supplements the 1975 edition of *A Guide to the Sources of United States Military History*. The outpouring of valuable books and articles since the 1972 cutoff date in the original volume is impressive; these, together with some works inadvertently omitted in 1975, are the meat of this supplement. The preponderance of chapters have been prepared by the authors of the corresponding chapters in the first volume, who have carried their fields forward for works made available from 1973 through 1978, inclusive. In addition, several topics not touched upon comprehensively in the original *Guide* have been given extensive treatment by new contributors: U.S. government documentation, nuclear war, arms control and disarmament, military law and justice, and a separate essay on the U.S. Marine Corps (which had been covered less thoroughly as a part of the essays on the U.S. Navy in the 1975 volume).

The decade of the 1970s stimulated interest in the U.S. military in a variety of wars, including reexamination of the American military tradition in the wake of Vietnam, renewed interest in security questions in the era of the SALT negotiations, and appraisal of American readiness sparked by military crises in Asia, Latin America, and the Middle East. Moreover, commemoration of the American Revolution and of the Second World War has brought on a sharpened interest in the history of the U.S. armed forces as a part of the broad sweep of development of American society. Hence, numerous works have appeared which, while general in scope, have important applications for the military historian. What follows supplements the introduction in the 1975 volume.

GENERAL REFERENCE AND BIBLIOGRAPHY. Various reference works touching upon American history in a broad framework can be exploited for leads in military history. In 1978, G.K. Hall & Co. released what proposed to be the first annual *Bibliographic Guide to North American History: 1977* (4), listing materials catalogued in that year by The Research Libraries of The New York Public Library and the Library of Congress. Published in 1977 in the

Gale Series, *History of the United States of America: A Guide to Information Sources* (8), edited by Ernest Cassara, includes a section devoted to the military. Edited by Donald F. Tingley, *Social History of the United States: A Guide to Information Sources* (55) has the benefit of an interdisciplinary perspective and can be used for information on the context of military policies and practice. Those studying specific campaigns and strategic questions may wish to consult the revised edition of *General World Atlases in Print: A Comparative Analysis,* published by R.R. Bowker. Also see Kenneth Winch, ed., *International Maps and Atlases in Print* (73). Among the many figures considered in John A. Garraty and Jerome L. Sternstein, eds., *Encyclopedia of American Biography* (22) are military personalities; and the student of many questions on civil-military relations, specific bases, and the like can take advantage of Robert Sobel, ed., *Biographical Directory of the Governors of the United States, 1789-1978* (48). For commentators or war correspondents, see John M. Harrison, ed., *American Newspapermen 1790-1933, Biographies and Autobiographies* (26). Seeking a comprehensive picture of the immense resources now available, the historian might consult the *Directory of Data Bases in the Social and Behavioral Sciences,* from Science Associates/ International (14). To translate the acronyms into English, see Ellen T. Crowley, ed., *Acronyms, Initialisms, and Abbreviations Dictionary,* sixth edition (1978) (11), with supplements scheduled for release in each of the following two years. To catch a hint of this work's utility, note that the first edition in 1960 had 12,000 entries; the new edition includes 178,949. For those more limited to the military, see the Joint Chiefs of Staff's "DoD Dictionary of Military Terms," available through the Superintendent of Documents.

For some topics, the military historian may seek basic information and leads from Gale Research Company's *Encyclopedia of Associations* (17). Greenwood Press has also instituted a series which will constitute an *Encyclopedia of American Institutions.* The first volume on *Labor Unions,* edited by Gary M. Fink, may be useful to certain military specialists, and historians should keep an eye on the promised volumes on *Government Agencies* as well as on *Foundations and Research Groups.* Researchers concerned with specific military leaders or with the reconstitution of groups in order to undertake social analysis should consult Kip Sperry, ed., *A Survey of American Genealogical Periodicals and Periodical Indexes* (50). For aiding a search through a "twilight zone," see *Irregular Serials and Annuals, An International Directory,* whose second edition was released by R. R. Bowker in 1972 (28).

An obvious starting point for checking resources available in a specific geographical area, the *Directory of Archives and Manuscript Repositories,* available through the Publication Sales Branch of the National Archives, provides concise descriptions of the holdings of some 3,200 institutions in the United States, arranged by state and town. The entries also give practical information on hours of operation, the availability of copying facilities, general restrictions on access, and the like. The catalogs of the National Historical Publications and Records Commission should be consulted for the growing numbers of volumes and microform publications useful to the military specialist. Typical are the papers of Henry Bouquet, the Swiss officer in British service at the time of the French and Indian War; the papers of Secretary of the Navy George Bancroft; the papers of Secretary of War Peter Porter; and the papers of Gen. William R. Shafter. The catalogue serves as a basic guide to these rich materials. Similarly, Charles E. South, ed., *Hearings in the Records of the U.S. Senate and Joint Committees of Congress* (49) helps take the researcher through the labyrinth of congressional paper.

Various volumes can aid the historian interested in those aspects of military history dealing with racial, ethnographic, and sectional questions. Among recent aids are Keith Irvine, ed., *Encyclopedia of Indians of the Americas* (29); Wilcomb Washburn, ed., *The American Indian and the United States* (72); Russell C. Brignano, *Black Americans in Autobiography, An Annotated Bibliography of Autobiographies and Autobiographical Books Written Since the Civil War* (5); and Jon Wakelyn, ed., with Frank E. Vandiver, *Biographical Dictionary of the Confederacy* (71).

GUIDES ON SELECTED MILITARY TOPICS. Research aids specifically pertinent to military history include T. N. Dupuy and Wendell Blanchard, *The Almanac of World Military Power* (15), which appeared in its second edition in 1972. Edited by Robert McHenry, *Webster's American Military Biographies* (36) offers over a thousand sketches on military figures from colonial to current times. For information on equipment and weapons systems, the researcher should continue to consult up-to-date editions of Jane's and Brassey's various reference volumes, and for the twentieth century the new Raintree *Illustrated Encyclopedia of Weapons and Warfare* in 24 volumes.

For information on blacks in the American military, consult Robert E. Greene, *Black Defenders of America, 1975-1973: A Reference and Pictorial History* (25). For the specialist on the Civil War or military cartography, *The Official Military Atlas of the Civil War* (12), edited by George B. Davis, Leslie J. Perry, and Joseph W. Kirkley, recently reissued with a new introduction by Richard Sommer, makes available the joint army and federal government effort after Appomattox to prepare a comprehensive history of the conflict and of its campaigns. Those interested in the rise of American naval power between the end of the nineteenth century and World War II should attend to *Strategic Planning in the U.S. Navy: Its Evolution and Execution, 1891-1945* (51), a set of microfilmed source materials from Scholarly Resources dealing with contingency war plans, naval preparedness, joint staff conversations in anticipation of World War II, and operational and administrative history.

In 1978, ABC-Clio added to its bibliographic series on war and peace with *The U.S. in World War I*, edited by Ronald Schaffer, which does not seek to be all-inclusive but is broadly comprehensive (46). Bridging that conflict and the succeeding worldwide fight, G. M. Bayliss has edited the *Bibliographic Guide to the Two World Wars* (3), while A. G. S. Enser has compiled *A Subject Bibliography of the Second World War* (19). To help in studying the interwar period, some will benefit from the thirty-volume set of daily and weekly intelligence summaries edited by Richard D. Challener, *United States Military Intelligence 1917-1927* (9). Edited by Thomas Parrish with S. L. A. Marshall as chief consultant editor, *The Simon and Schuster Encyclopedia of World War II* (41) includes 4,000 entries on a wide variety of topics concerning the European and Pacific theaters, such as weaponry, science, intelligence, conferences, strategies and campaigns, and personnel. Complementing the 1961 *Subject Catalog of the World War I Collection*, G. K. Hall & Co. released, in 1977, *The Subject Catalog of the World War II Collection* in the Research

Libraries of The New York Public Library (52), presenting in book form photographic reproductions of the estimated 47,671 cards in the catalog. For the 14th International Congress of the Historical Sciences in 1975, the American Committee on the History of the Second World War produced "A Select Bibliography of Books on the Second World War" published in English in the United States between 1966 and 1975. This continues the coverage provided in Janet Ziegler, ed., *World War II: Books in English, 1945-1965* (74), which also includes an essay on World War II bibliographies.

For the period since World War II, guides and sources are becoming steadily more available, as through the Joint Committee on Japanese Studies of the American Council of Learned Societies and the Social Science Research Council, which has undertaken a Joint Bibliographical Project on the Allied occupation of Japan. ABC-Clio Press continues its series on war and peace, edited by Richard Dean Burns, which produced *Songs of Protest, War, and Peace* (13) in 1973; *Arms Control and Disarmament, A Bibliography* (7) in 1977; *War, A Historical, Political and Social Study* (21) in 1978; and *World Treaty Index and Treaty Profiles* (45) in 1974. Also see Geoffrey Kemp et al., eds., *American Defense Policy Since 1945: A Preliminary Bibliography* (32). Meanwhile, important sources are becoming available, notably the *Records of the Joint Chiefs of Staff*, with a hundred thousand pages of JCS materials from 1942 to 1953.

SERVICE-PRODUCED BIBLIOGRAPHIES AND OTHER SOURCES. Through their various branches, the military services provide a wealth of bibliographic guides and other aids of great value to the historian of the American military. Merely to keep track of service-generated publications would be a mighty chore, as suggested by Bernadine M. Kopec in a 1971 article "The DoD Magazine Empire" (33), in which the author indicates that the number of periodical magazines sponsored by the Defense Department ranges anywhere between 78 and 371 (the difference in estimates depends upon the circulation level used as a cut off). Given the complexity implicit in such numbers, at least researchers into technical fields may win some relief through the "User's Guide to Defense Documentation Center" (64), released in August 1976 by DoD's Defense Supply Agency. This describes procedures for acquiring information on the department's research and development in most fields of science and technology.

The educational and training institutions of the services may provide both bibliographic and source materials. Some researchers may benefit from specific inquiries concerning syllabi for courses at the war colleges of the several services, or of the National War College. In addition, conferences at these institutions sometimes yield timely and interesting assessments of the recent military past and of defense prospects. See, for example, the *Proceedings of the 1977 Worldwide Strategic Mobility Conference* from the National War College (66).

The U.S. Army's Center for Military History (formerly OCMH) in Washington, D.C., continues to provide assistance to serious researchers who can identify topics with realistic limits. For example, bibliographic guides deal with areas such as small arms, coast artillery, and the development of tanks. In addition, the historian may profitably consult current listings of publications produced by the Center under the Office of the Chief of Military History.

Books are handled through the Superintendent of Documents, Government Printing Office; microfilmed materials should be purchased through the National Archives and Records Service.

As of 1978, several highly useful volumes in the Special Bibliographic Series of the U.S. Army Military History Institute (formerly the USAMH Research Collection) at Carlisle Barracks, Pennsylvania, had been added for sale through the Superintendent of Documents, Government Printing Office. These included Roy Barnard, *Oral History/Audio Archives* (62); Joyce Eakin, *Era of the American Revolution* (59); John Cornelius, *Military Forces of France* (61); Roy Barnard, Duane Ryan, and William Burns, *World War II,* volume 1 (63); and Lawrence James and Alexander Lentz, *God Save the Queen—A Bibliography of the British Commonwealth Holdings* (60). Scheduled for publication but not released as of 1978 were: Duane Ryan, *World War II,* volume 2; Laszlo M. Alfoldi, *World War II,* volumes 3, 4, 5; and Bruce Reber, *The Army and the Indian Wars, 1865-1890.* The institute also released in 1978 a revised and updated special bibliography on *United States Army Unit Histories*—originally prepared by George S. Pappas and revised by Elizabeth Snoke and Alexandra Campbell. All these volumes limit their entries, however, to the holdings at the USAMHI.

Elsewhere in the army, the Corps of Engineers Historical Division (moved in 1979 to Washington) has embarked on an extensive program of bibilographies and studies of field agencies. The geographical variety of the program is considerable, with special studies pertinent to such places as Alaska, Honolulu, Albuquerque, Galveston, Memphis, Baltimore, Philadelphia, and Savannah. Topics include topographical laboratories, nuclear cratering, river channeling, and many others. The Corps Historical Division's office in Washington provides information concerning the program as a whole, but a list of district histories was published in *Military Affairs* (October 1978) and in *Journal of the West* (October 1978).

Abbreviated bibliographies are included in syllabi for elective courses at the U.S. Army War College at Carlisle, Pennsylvania. Such syllabi, of course, may all serve as primary source materials for those interested in the recent history of military education. The same may be said of syllabi and special bibliographies prepared at the U.S. Army Command and General Staff College at Fort Leavenworth, Kansas. Researchers with appropriate serious interest might contact the college's Library Division for information on bibliographies listed since 1972, such as: 34, "Fort Leavenworth"; 35, "Military Intelligence"; 36, "Military Assistance to Chile"; 37, "Principles of War"; 38, "Selected Battles for Historical Study"; 39, "River Crossings"; 40, "Gettysburg"; 41, "Naval History"; 42, "1973 Middle East War"; 43, "Drug Abuse"; 46, "Battle of Antietam"; 48, "Peacekeeping"; 50, "Normandy Campaign"; 52, "Chosin Reservoir, Korea"; 54, "Efficiency Reports"; and 56, "Night Operations." Also of considerable interest is the Command and General Staff College's *Abstracts of Master of Military Art and Science MMAS Theses and Special Studies 1964-1976,* conceived and edited by L. L. Sims and A. D. Officer (58). The volume also benefits from a topical index employing key words. The USAF Air War College offers a similar annual guide.

In March 1976, the Department of the Navy's Naval History Division released an eighteen-page list of "Publications in Print," specifying works produced by the division and made available through the Superintendent of

Documents, Government Printing Office. Among interesting titles of recent date are: *The American Revolution, 1775-1783; An Atlas of 18th Century Maps and Charts: Theatres of Operations,* issued in 1972 (67); *United States Naval History: A Bibliography,* published in 1972 (70); and, through direct application to the Naval History Division rather than through the Superinten-dent of Documents, *Checklist: Unpublished Naval Histories in the "Z" File, Record Group 45, U.S. National Archives, 1911-1927* (68) and *Partial Check-list: World War II Histories and Historical Reports in the U.S. Naval History Division* (69), released in 1971 and 1973 respectively. Also see the Naval History Division's "Guide to United States Naval Administrative Histories of World War II," released through the Naval Historical Center in 1976.

The Department of the Air Force's *Friday Review of Defense Literature* intends to keep "key DoD personnel" aware of "current literature of interest to them in their official capacites." The newsletter includes brief abstracts of recent articles and short book reviews, as well as brief bibliographies on current issues such as military unionization. The *Friday Review* also has an annual index divided by country and, for the United States, subdivided by topic. The Air Force ROTC's *Education Journal,* published at Maxwell Air Force Base, carries articles on the development of doctrine and on selected topics in military history. Like other publications from military schools, it may constitute in its own right a source for the study of military education and training. One interesting aid omitted from the 1975 volume of the *Guide* is from the Air Force's Office of Scientific Research, *Annotated Bibliography of Prisoner Interrogation, Compliance and Resistance,* prepared in 1963 (57).

Eugene M. Emme's 1973 essay on "Space and the Historian" (18) provides helpful bibliographic leads into this realm, as well as suggesting areas in need of much more research. From a different perspective, B. Franklin Cooling III offers some insights into the occasionally uneasy relationship between military professionals and the history of their own enterprise in "Military History for the Professional" (10).

OTHER DOCUMENTARY SOURCES. As of 1977, the Superintendent of Documents reported that his office provided service for the sale of over twenty-four thousand different publications, periodicals, and subscription programs. Some three thousand new titles enter the sales inventory each year. To simplify screening of this vast set of publications, the researcher should consult the Government Printing Office's "Subject Bibliography Index" for listings such as "Civil Defense," "Civil War," "Military History," "Outer Space," "War," or "World War." As an example, the specific subject bibliography on "Military History" fills thirty pages of single-spaced type, with announcement of new titles and reprints. The historian should assume a broad perspective when approaching the office's bibliographic headings. "Military History," for exam-ple, includes works by the Armed Forces Institute of Pathology, the series on army lineage, specific studies of weapons development, information on chemi-cal warfare, and a wide range of other topics besides traditional combat histories.

Similarly, the researcher should consult recently issued titles in the National Archives and Records Service's Preliminary Inventories, such as the 1976 survey of the records of the United States Military Academy. Many a researcher will benefit from the regional branches of the National Archives system, and the historian should consult finding aids at and microfilm lists for the Federal Archives and Records Center in each region.

Providing greater access to known resources, various series of papers and diaries continue to emerge in printed form. In 1978 appeared the third volume of *The Diaries of George Washington,* edited by Donald Jackson. Louisiana State University Press has undertaken preparation of *The Papers of Jefferson Davis,* edited by Haskell M. Monroe, Jr., and James T. McIntosh. The Library of Congress, in 1977, made available a microfilm edition of the William Tecumseh Sherman Papers, half dealing with the period after his Civil War service. The Naval War College's series of historical monographs provides highly useful resources such as *The Writings of Steven B. Luce,* edited by John D. Hayes and John B. Hattendorf (27), and *Charleston Blockade: The Journals of John B. Marchand, USN, 1861-1862* (54). Such series deserve the historian's attention.

Now available through Chadwyck-Healey Ltd. in Cambridge, England, or Somerset House in Teaneck, New Jersey, the British Broadcasting Corporation's broadcast-newscripts from the Second World War offer the specialist in that period an opportunity to study the "home front" more closely. The full set, *The Home Service Nine O'Clock News 1939-1945,* consists of some 60,000 pages printed on 765 microfiches. The Macmillan Publishing Company has made a bold step in preparing audio materials for wide circulation in its set of twelve tape-cassettes *Voices of World War II,* produced and directed by Richard Lidz, with Marc Goldbaum, Patricia Dubin, and Mahlon Lovett (34). Released in 1975, the tapes include propaganda broadcasts, live reports of combat, and subsequent interviews.

Providing access to material from ancient and medieval through contemporary times, R. R. Bowker issued, in 1973, *A Documentary History of Arms Control and Disarmament,* compiled by T. N. Dupuy Associates (15). The same publisher has embarked on a Public Documents Series that may attract many students of the contemporary military, as evidenced in *The Intelligence Community: History, Organization, and Issues,* edited by Tyrus G. Fain, in collaboration with Katharine C. Plant and Ross Milloy, and introduced by Sen. Frank Church (20).

The U.S. Congress, of course, generates voluminous materials pertinent to military and national security issues; and the historian should regularly consult the holdings of any library designated as a government repository. Typical of recent reports are the Senate Armed Services Committee's *Achieving America's Goals: National Service or the All-Volunteer Armed Force?* and the Senate Committee on Foreign Relations' 1977 report on *United States/Soviet Strategic Options.*

POPULAR STUDIES. The decade of the 1970s has brought publication of the quarterly series *After the Battle,* edited by Winston G. Ramsey and distributed in North American through Sky Books International. Issues focus on specific battles and incidents of World War II, providing wartime and present-day photographs for purposes of comparison. Apart from detailing the physical impact of the battle on the site and suggesting the extent of the site's recovery, the issues include features on personalities, local interest in museums or other forms of historic preservation, hardware and equipment, and films. Also noteworthy for its combination of sensitive text and extensive use of American combat art is James Jones, *WW II* (30). Time-Life Books has generated a number of heavily illustrated sets, designed for a wide market, that have at least tangential pertinence to military or naval affairs. Among them is *The Seafarers,* which combines anecdotal information on pirates with legend and appraisals of dreadnoughts, and, of course, *World War II.*

Serious studies of the culture of war have been altogether too few. For a general overview, see Donald J. Mrozek's 1975 essay "The Army and Popular Culture" (39), in Robin Higham and Carol Brandt's *The United States Army in Peacetime.* Richard Polenberg's 1972 study of the American home front in World War II, *War and Society, The United States 1941-1945* (42), hints at some of the effects of the military on social institutions generally. Similarly, one may glean useful insights from the later documents in Warren I. Susman, ed., *Culture and Commitment, 1929-1945* (53), as also from Susman's highly suggestive introductory essay. A broad study covering the culture of several major participants in the conflict, Roger Manvell's *Films and the Second World War* (37) provides useful information about the propaganda films of the era, about documentary footage, and about feature films designed primarily for entertainment. Also, the recent publication of Peter G. Jones, *War and the American Novelist* (31) comes as welcome company to Peter Aichinger, *The American Soldier in Fiction* (1). Jones explores the themes of initiation, command, sexuality and violence, and the psychology of combat, while Aichinger seeks to use the development of American fiction as a mirror of public attitudes about warfare and the military. Edited by Jack G. Shaheen, *Nuclear War Films* consists of twenty-five essays on specific documentaries and feature films such as *The War Game* and *Dr. Strangelove* (47).

Numerous sources exist that could be mined for studies of the culture of American wars, as evidenced by the 1978 publication through the Library of Congress of a microfilm set of three hundred American posters of World War I and some twelve hundred posters from World War II, available through the library's Photoduplication Service in Washington. For shorter reference, the more casual researcher can refer to Maurice Rickards, ed., *Posters of the First World War* (44). A brief and intelligent essay by David Trask sets the standard for popular readings on American life during the "Great War" in Trask, ed., *World War I At Home* (56). However, various sources long available remain little exploited, and researchers may still profitably turn to the National Archives for aids such as a *List of World War I Signal Corps Films,* compiled by K. Jack Bauer and released in 1957. The corps filmed battle action, famous military and political figures, and many fascinating scenes of camplife and recreational activity.

New sources, it may be hoped, will also become available. Suggestive of future possibilities was the trial agreement by CBS News to provide the National Archives, the eleven regional branch archives, and the presidential libraries with video-cassettes of its regularly scheduled newscasts and of special broadcasts of hard news. To protect their copyright, CBS stipulated that the archives fill requests according to the interlibrary loan provisions of the American Library Association.

JOURNALS. Since the original volume of the *Guide* was assembled, several new publications have appeared which concentrate on the military experience and often provide studies of U.S. armed forces and their relationship to the social and political system. *Armed Forces and Society,* published by the Inter-University Seminar on Armed Forces and Society in Chicago, gives special emphasis to analyses by political scientists and sociologists, but has also devoted special issues to studies by historians. Its appearance in 1974 came close on the heels of the *Journal of Political and Military Sociology,* which began publication the previous year. Of special interest to buffs and popular historians, *Fusilier, A Quarterly for Military History* first appeared in 1977. Extensively illustrated with drawings and photographs, the magazine touches on broad subjects of interest such as occupation policies and on narrow, exhaustive consideration of hardware. Since 1973, the privately operated United States Strategic Institute has published a quarterly *Strategic Review* concentrating on current defense issues and, especially, on matters pertaining to the U.S.-Soviet military balance. The institute also releases Special Reports on selected topics.

Among new periodicals that may have selected information important to the military historians, is *Declassified Documents Quarterly Catalog* (1975-). The first volume, for example, included an extensive list of brief descriptions of documents recently declassified through the Department of Defense, the State Department, and the Central Intelligence Agency. Occasionally useful in military affairs, *Presidential Studies Quarterly* began publication in 1971. The researcher will also take advantage of such standard aids as the *General Indices* to the *American Historical Review.*

On an occasional basis, journals not traditionally devoted to military history carry pertinent articles. Typical is the *Journal of Interdisciplinary History* (1970-), which has featured studies of Cambrai, the American military experience, and the personality of Commander-in-Chief Richard Nixon. Similarly, the autumn 1976 *American Studies International,* the supplement to the *American Quarterly,* carried Martin K. Gordon's review of "American Military Studies" (24). In the same vein, Peter Paret contributed rather broad statements on "The History of War" to the spring 1971 issue of *Daedalus* (40).For the *Newsletter* of the North American Society for Oceanic History, K. Jack Bauer compiled a complete bibliography of the works of the late Samuel Eliot Morison, released in December 1977 (2).

Begun in 1973, *Reviews in American History* devotes some attention to selected works by historians of the U.S. military experience and should be appropriately consulted. Other sources of a somewhat more general nature, which may nonetheless provide valuable leads, include *Annotation,* the newsletter of the National Historical Publications Commission; *Overview,* providing current information on the Dwight D. Eisenhower Library; and *Whistle Stop,* the newsletter of the Harry S. Truman Library Institute.

LOCAL SOURCES. On a regular basis, the Council on Abandoned Military Posts (CAMP) continues to publish information about specific sites of interest to the military historian. Articles deal not only with the physical details of the abandoned posts but also with such matters as the operation of the posts, their commanding officers, and the life of then contemporary service personnel. The historian concerned with the military history of specific locales, then, would wisely keep current with *Periodical,* CAMP's journal, and with its newsletter, *Headquarters Heliogram.* For the period 1700-1900, the researcher may also now consult the convenient pamphlet issued in 1972 by the National

Archives, "Historical Information Relating to Military Posts and Other Installations." Prepared by David A. Gibson, the pamphlet briefly suggests how to use the records of the Adjutant General's Office (RG 94) to study such questions as the establishment of reservations, the missions performed at specific posts, and the like.

Local historical groups and officially sanctioned historical societies continue to provide detailed information about their areas' military past. Typical are publications describing Old Fort Mifflin, administered for the Recreation Department of Philadelphia by the Shackamaxon Society. In the wake of the celebration of the nation's bicentennial, the researcher interested in local or state military history will do well to check for guides or reports published in the mid-1970's, possibly under state auspices. The State Parks and Recreation Commission of Washington, for example, issued a booklet *Preserving Washington's History* in 1977, which includes some references to military sites. Moreover, the imaginative historian may be able to make use of the work of ethnologists and archaeologists.

Both customary and unexpected agencies of the federal government generate historical studies of some potential value to the military specialist. From the Office of Park Historic Preservation of the National Park Service, for example, came a handsome and neatly illustrated 1976 volume on *Fort Stanwix* (35). The volume includes an essay on "Construction and Military History" by John F. Luzader, "Historic Furnishing Study" by Louis Torres, and "Historic Structure Report" by Orville W. Carroll. But material of at least marginal value may also come from less likely sources. For example, the 2nd Psychological Operations Group at Fort Bragg, North Carolina, produced a study "Plank Road Revisited" with Capt. Perry J. Smith as project officer. The historical survey has more significance for civilian than military events; yet the volume suggests the disparateness of sources available to the more aggressive researcher.

BIBLIOGRAPHY

1. Aichinger, Peter. *The American Soldier in Fiction, 1880-1963.* Ames, Iowa: Iowa State University Press, 1975.
2. Bauer, K. Jack. "Samuel Eliot Morison (1887-1976): A Complete Bibliography." *North American Society for Oceanic History, Newsletter,* special edition, December 1977.
3. Bayliss, G.M. *Bibliographic Guide to the Two World Wars.* Ann Arbor, Mich.: R. R. Bowker, 1977.
4. *Bibliographic Guide to North American History: 1977.* Boston: G. K. Hall, 1978.
5. Brignano, Russell C. *Black Americans in Autobiography, An Annotated Bibliography of Autobiographies and Autobiographical Books Written Since the Civil War.* Durham, N. C.: Duke University Press, 1974.
6. Buchanan, A. Russell. *Black Americans in World War II.* Santa Barbara, Calif.: ABC-Clio Press, 1977.
7. Burns, Richard Dean. *Arms Control and Disarmament, A Bibliography.* Santa Barbara, Calif. ABC-Clio Press, 1977.

8. Cassara, Ernest, ed. *History of the United States of America: A Guide to Information Sources.* Detroit: Gale Research Co., 1977.

9. Challener, Richard D., ed. *United States Military Intelligence 1917-1927.* 39 vol. New York: Garland Publishing, Inc., 1977.

10. Cooling, Benjamin F., III. "Military History for the Military Professional." *Parameters: The Journal of the Army War College* 1, no. 3 (winter 1972): 28-35.

11. Crowley, Ellen T., ed. *Acronyms, Initialisms, and Abbreviations Dictionary.* 6th ed. Detroit: Gale Research Co., 1978.

12. Davis, George B., Leslie J. Perry, and Joseph W. Kirkley. *The Official Military Atlas of the Civil War.* New York: Crown Publishers, Inc., 1978.

13. Denisoff, R. Serge. *Songs of Protest, War, and Peace, A Bibliography and Discography.* Santa Barbara, Calif. ABC-Clio Press, 1973.

14. *Directory of Data Bases in the Social and Behavior Sciences.* New York: Science Associates/International, Inc.

15. Dupuy, T. N. and Wendell Blanchard. *The Almanac of World Military Power.* New York: R. R. Bowker Company, 1972.

16. Dupuy, T. N., Associates. *A Documentary History of Arms Control and Disarmament.* Ann Arbor, Mich.: R. R. Bowker Company, 1973.

17. *Encyclopedia of Associations.* Detroit: Gale Research Company, 1979.

18. Emme, Eugene M. "Space and the Historian." *Spaceflight* 15 (11 November 1973): 411-17.

19. Enser, A. G. S. *A Subject Bibliography of the Second World War.* Boulder, Colo.: Westview Press, 1977.

20. Fain, Tyrus G., with Katharine C. Plant and Ross Milloy. *The Intelligence Community: History, Organization, and Issues.* Ann Arbor, Mich.: R. R. Bowker Company, 1977.

21. Farrar, Lancelot L., Jr. *War, A Historical, Political and Social Study.* Santa Barbara, Calif.: ABC-Clio Press, 1978.

22. Garraty, John A., and Jerome L. Sternstein. *Encyclopedia of American Biography.* New York: Harper & Row, 1974.

23. *General World Atlases in Print: A Comparative Analysis.* Ann Arbor, Mich. R. R. Bowker, 1973.

24. Gordon, Martin K. "American Military Studies." *American Studies International* 15, no. 1(fall 1976): 3-16.

25. Greene, Robert E. *Black Defenders of America 1775-1973: A Reference and Pictorial History.* Chicago: Johnson Publishing Company, 1974.

26. Harrison, John M., ed. *American Newspapermen 1790-1933: Biographies and Autobiographies.* 32 vols. New York: Beekman Publishers, Inc., 1973.

27. Hayes, John D., and John B. Hattendorf, eds. *The Writings of Steven B. Luce.* Newport, R.I.: Naval War College, 1975.

28. *Irregular Serials and Annuals, An International Directory.* Ann Arbor, Mich.: R. R. Bowker, 1972.

29. Irvine, Keith, ed. *Encyclopedia of Indians of the Americas.* St. Clair Shores, Mich.: Scholarly Press, Inc., 1974- .

30. Jones, James. *WW II.* New York: Grosset & Dunlap, 1975.

31. Jones, Peter G. *War and the American Novelist.* Columbia, Mo.: University of Missouri Press, 1976.
32. Kemp, Geoffrey, Clark Murdock, and Frank L. Simonie. *American Defense Policy Since 1945: A Preliminary Bibliography.* Lawrence, Kan.: University Press of Kansas, 1973.
33. Kopec, Bernadine M. "The DoD Magazine Empire." *Armed Forces Journal,* (August 1971), 42–48.
34. Lidz, Richard, Marc Goldbaum, Patricia Dubin, and Mahlon Lovett. *Voices of World War II.* New York: Macmillan Publishing Co., 1975.
35. Luzader, John F., Louis Torres, and Orville W. Carroll. *Fort Stanwix: History, Historic Furnishing, and Historic Structure Reports.* Washington, D.C.: U.S. Government Printing Office, 1976.
36. McHenry, Robert. *Webster's American Military Biographies.* Springfield, Mass.: G. & C. Merriam Company, 1978.
37. Manvell, Roger. *Films and the Second World War.* New York: Dell Publishing Co., 1974.
38. Matthews, William. *American Diaries in Manuscript, A Descriptive Bibliography, 1580–1954.* Athens, Ga.: University of Georgia Press, 1974.
39. Mrozek, Donald J. "The Army and Popular Culture." In *The United States Army in Peacetime,* edited by Robin Higham and Carol Brandt. Manhattan, Kan.: Military Affairs/Aerospace Historian Publishing, 1975.
40. Paret, Peter. "The History of War." *Daedalus,* spring 1971, pp. 376–96.
41. Parrish, Thomas, and S. L. A. Marshall, eds. *The Simon and Schuster Encyclopedia of World War II.* New York: Simon and Schuster, 1978.
42. Polenberg, Richard. *War and Society, The United States 1941–1945.* Philadelphia: J. B. Lippincott Company, 1972.
43. *Records of the Joint Chiefs of Staff, 1943–1953.* Washington, D.C.: University Publications of America, 1978.
44. Rickards, Maurice, ed. *Posters of the First World War.* New York: Walker and Company, 1968.
45. Rohn, Peter H. *World Treaty Index* and *Treaty Profiles.* Santa Barbara, Calif.: ABC-Clio Press, 1974.
46. Schaffer, Ronald. *The U.S. in World War I.* Santa Barbara, Calif.: ABC-Clio Press, 1978.
47. Shaheen, Jack G., ed. *Nuclear War Films.* Carbondale, Ill.: Southern Illinois University Press, 1978.
48. Sobel, Robert. *Biographical Directory of the Governors of the United States, 1789–1978.* Westport, Conn.: Meckler Books, 1977.
49. South, Charles E. *Hearings in the Records of the U.S. Senate and Joint Committees of Congress.* Washington, D.C.: National Archives and Records Service, 1972.
50. Sperry, Kip, ed. *A Survey of American Genealogical Periodicals and Periodical Indexes.* Detroit: Gale Research Co., 1978.
51. *Strategic Planning in the U.S. Navy: Its Evolutions and Execution, 1891–1945.* Wilmington, Del.: Scholarly Resources Inc., 1977.
52. *The Subject Catalog of the World War II Collection.* [The Research Libraries of The New York Public Library]. Boston: G. K. Hall & Co., 1977.

53. Susman, Warren I. *Culture and Commitment, 1929–1945.* New York: G. Braziller, 1973.

54. Symonds, Craig L. *Charleston Blockade: The Journals of John B. Marchand, USN, 1861–1862.* Newport, R.I.: Naval War College, 1976.

55. Tingley, Donald F., ed. *Social History of the United States: A Guide to Information Sources.* Detroit: Gale Research Co., 1979.

56. Trask, David F. *World War I At Home, Readings on American Life, 1914–1920.* New York: John Wiley & Sons, Inc., 1970.

57. United States, Department of the Air Force, Office of Scientific Research. *Annotated Bibliography on Prisoner Interrogation, Compliance and Resistance.* Washington, D.C.: Air Force Office of Scientific Research, 1963 [AFOSR 68–1406].

58. United States, Department of the Army, U.S. Army Command and General Staff College. *Abstracts of Master of Military Art and Science (MMAS) Theses and Special Studies 1964–1976.* Edited by L. L. Sims and A. D. Officer. Fort Leavenworth, Kan.: U.S. Army Command and General Staff College [1976].

59. United States, Department of the Army, U.S. Army Military History Institute, Special Bibliographic Series. *Era of the American Revolution.* Edited by Joyce Eakin. Washington, D.C.: Government Printing Office, n.d.

60. United States, Department of the Army, U.S. Army Military History Institute, Special Bibliographic Series. *God Save the Queen—A Bibliography of the British and Commonwealth Holdings.* Edited by Lawrence James and Alexander Lentz. Washington, D.C.: Government Printing Office, n.d.

61. United States, Department of the Army, U.S. Army Military History Institute, Special Bibliographic Series. *Military Forces of France.* Edited by John Cornelius, Washington, D.C: Government Printing Office, n.d.

62. United States, Department of the Army, U.S. Army Military History Institute, Special Bibliographic Series. *Oral History/Audio Archives.* Vol. 1 and 2. Edited by Roy Barnard, Washington, D.C.: Government Printing Office, n.d.

63. United States, Department of the Army, U.S. Army Military History Institute, Special Bibliographic Series. *World War II.* Vol. 1. Edited by Roy Barnard, Duane Smith, and William Burns. Washington, D.C.: Government Printing Office, n.d.

64. United States, Department of Defense, Defense Supply Agency. *User's Guide to Defense Documentation Center.* Cameron Station, Alexandria, Va.: Defense Supply Agency, n.d.

65. United States, Department of the Navy, Naval History Division. *The American Revolution, 1775–1783. An Atlas of 18th Century Maps and Charts: Theatres of Operations.* Washington, D. C.: Government Printing Office, 1972.

66. United States, Department of the Navy, Naval History Division. *Checklist: Unpublished Naval Histories in the "Z" File, Record Group 45, U.S. National Archives, 1911–1927.* Washington, D.C.: Naval History Division, 1973.

67. United States, Department of the Navy, Naval History Division. *Partial Checklist: World War II Histories and Historical Reports in the U.S. Naval History Division.* Washington, D.C.: Naval History Division, n.d.

68. United States, Department of the Navy, Naval History Division. *United States Naval History: A Bibliography.* Washington, D.C: Government Printing Office [1973?].

69. United States, National Defense University. *Proceedings of the National Security Affairs Conference—1977.* Fort McNair, Washington, D.C.: National Defense University, 1977.

70. United States, National Defense University. *Proceedings of the 1977 Worldwide Strategic Mobility Conference.* Fort McNair, Washington, D.C.: National Defense University, 1977.

71. Wakelyn, Jon L., ed., with Frank E. Vandiver. *Biographical Dictionary of the Confederacy.* Westport, Conn.: Greenwood Press, 1977.

72. Washburn, Wilcomb, ed. *The American Indian and the United States, A Documentary History.* New York: Random House, 1973.

73. Winch, Kenneth, ed. *International Maps and Atlases in Print.* Ann Arbor, Mich.: R. R. Bowker Company, 1974.

74. Ziegler, Janet, ed. *World War II: Books in English, 1945–1965.* Stanford, Calif.: Hoover Institution Press, 1971.

II

EUROPEAN BACKGROUND OF

AMERICAN MILITARY AFFAIRS

Russell F. Weigley

Both the "new military history," the history not so much of battles and campaigns as of military institutions in relationship to society at large, and the older style of military antiquarianism continue in the later years of the twentieth century to offer illumination of the origins of American military thought and practice in the European military traditions of two centuries and more ago. Indeed, the "new military history," in the final quarter of the twentieth century no longer so new, at first tended to focus upon military institutions of the French Revolutionary and Napoleonic era and later, to the neglect of the earlier European military systems from which the original American modes of military organization derived. Only since the publication of *A Guide to the Sources of United States Military History* has it become possible to identify a distinct flourishing of studies of the military institutions of the ancien régime featuring something of the breadth of view, the relating of military tactics and technology to their social context, to which post-1945 studies of nineteenth- and twentieth-century soldiers and their states have accustomed us.

Hippocrene Books' series of army histories, directed to a somewhat popular audience but nevertheless soundly researched in addition to being generally well written, has now provided three excellent books on armies roughly contemporaneous with George Washington's: the Austrian army of Maria Theresa (329); the Prussian army of Frederick the Great, no doubt more influential than the Austrian in the shaping of the American army, if only because of General von Steuben (330); and the British army that was the most direct model for the Continental Army (335). The eighteenth-century British navy from which the American navy drew its earliest traditions is the subject of a new study by the indefatigable naval historian G. J. Marcus (332). David Chandler has given us two studies of the nature of military command and the practice of war in Europe in the age when the tactical and organizational preconceptions soon to mold the Continental Army were formed (324, 325); the second of these books is almost as essential to understanding the whole evolution of warfare in the Western world as Chandler's monumental survey of Napoleonic war (51). We also have a sound new history of the birth of the English professional army (326).

The medieval historians, inhabiting a scholarly world somewhat separate from that of either "new" or traditional military historians whose province is the modern age, continue to produce a steady flow of volumes on the more remote roots of the two, often conflicting principal lines of American military institutional development, professional armies and citizen-soldier armies (321, 322, 327, 338). The general tendency of these recent works is to reinforce the new direction of medieval military history remarked on in this *Guide* in 1975, toward pushing backward into time the emergence of something like professional armies and, with them, of discipline and coherence in medieval military forces, not the amorphous arrays depicted by some older historians.

When the military institutions of the United States were formed out of various borrowings of European traditions (influenced, but relatively slightly so, by distinctive New World experience), American republican ideology exalted a citizens' militia as the only type of military force capable of securing the liberties of a republic against despotism and corruption from within as well as against external foes. This ideology notwithstanding, the American colonies had been on their way toward substituting at least partially professional military forces for the part-time soldiery of the militia as their principal reliance on the French and Indian frontiers even before the Revolution. The Continental Army and the Regular Army of the United States promptly made a professional force the central military instrument of the new national government. Ideology and practice diverged. Nevertheless, the no-standing-army ideology retained a remarkably vigorous if somewhat disembodied life in America well into the nineteenth century, and its English origins are worth examining in the detail of Lois G. Schwoerer's *"No Standing Armies!" The Anti-army Ideology in Seventeenth-Century England* (336).

With the achievement of independence, the new United States government in developing a practical military policy paid less attention to the ideology of citizens' militias than to minimizing the prospective defensive labors of either professional or militia forces against possible foreign invaders, through coastal and border fortification. Seacoast fortification was the most consistent preoccupation of American military policy from the Revolution to the coming of nuclear weapons, which in the late 1940s assured the obsoleteness of the last sixteen-inch coast artillery to shadow the entrances of American bays and harbors. Military historians have not yet accorded seacoast fortifications the attention warranted by their long preeminence in American military policy. Perhaps excellent studies mainly of European fortress architecture (330, 331, 334) may encourage the Americans. Of these three books, Christopher Duffy's (330) especially succeeds in relating an era in the history of fortification to the whole history of war.

Two very specialized studies should be called to the student's attention despite the general absence from them of the wide horizons of the new military history: a history of the origins of French military publishing, and thus of much of the European military literature read by early American soldiers (333); and a history of the Medical Department of the British army to 1898, which both by implication and because of the historical relationship between the British and American armies offers much of relevance to American military history, even though only a relatively small proportion of the work deals with the period of American military beginnings before the French Revolution (323).

BIBLIOGRAPHY

321. Barnie, John. *War in Medieval English Society: Social Values in the Hundred Years War, 1337–98*. Ithaca: Cornell University Press, 1974.
322. Beeler, John. *Warfare in Feudal Europe, 730–1200*. Ithaca: Cornell University Press, 1971.
323. Cantlie, Sir Neil. *A History of the Army Medical Department*. 2 vols. Edinburgh: Churchill Livingstone, distributed New York: Longman, 1974.
324. Chandler, David. *The Art of Warfare in the Age of Marlborough*. New York: Hippocrene, 1976.
325. Chandler, David. *Marlborough as Military Commander*. New York: Scribner's, 1973.
326. Childs, John. *The Army of Charles II*. Toronto and Buffalo: University of Toronto Press, 1976.
327. Contamine, Philippe. *Guerre, état et société à la fin du moyen age: Ètudes sur les armées des rois de France, 1337–1494*. Paris: Mouton, 1972.
328. Duffy, Christopher. *The Army of Frederick the Great*. New York: Hippocrene, 1977.
329. Duffy, Christopher. *The Army of Maria Theresa*. New York: Hippocrene, 1974.
330. Duffy, Christopher. *Fire and Stone: The Science of Fortress Warfare, 1660–1860*. Newton Abbot, London, and Vancouver: David & Charles, 1975.
331. Hughes, Quentin. *Military Architecture*. New York: St. Martin's, 1974.
332. Marcus, G. J. *Heart of Oak: A Survey of British Sea Power in the Georgian Era*. New York: Oxford University Press, 1975.
333. Martin, Marc. *Les origines de la presse militaire en France à la fin de l'Ancien Régime & sous la Révolution (1770–1799)*. Château de Vincennes: Ministère de la Défense, État Major de l'Armée de Terre, Service Historique, 1975.
334. Rocolle, Pierre. *2000 ans de fortification française*. 2 vols. Paris: Charles-Lavauzelle, 1973.
335. Rogers, H. C. B. *The British Army of the 18th Century*. New York: Hippocrene, 1977.
336. Schwoerer, Lois G. *"No Standing Armies!" The Anti-army Ideology in Seventeenth-Century England*. Baltimore: Johns Hopkins Press, 1974.
337. Teitler, G. *The Genesis of the Professional Officers' Corps*. Sage Series on Armed Forces and Society, no. 11. Beverly Hills, Calif.: Sage Publications, 1977.
338. Verbruggen, J. F. *The Art of Warfare in Western Europe during the Middle Ages (From the Eighth Century to 1340)*. Amsterdam: North Holland, 1977.

III

COLONIAL FORCES, 1607-1776

Douglas Edward Leach

Constructive work in the field of American colonial military history has been continuing along diverse lines, with most of the significant advances being made by young scholars involved in writing their doctoral dissertations. It is these dissertations which suggest most clearly the kinds of approaches likely to yield the best results in the near future.

Primary sources recently made more readily accessible include Neville's abstracts of materials relating to Bacon's Rebellion (400), Gwyn's edition of previously unpublished papers of Adm. Sir Peter Warren (417), several memoirs from the Cherokee War of 1759-61 (392), and Williams's publication of Col. Henry Bouquet's orderly book of 1764 (420).

The important and still largely unexplored question of American colonial attitudes toward war has been addressed, for Puritan New England only, in Alexander's "Colonial New England Preaching on War as Illustrated in Massachusetts Artillery Election Sermons" (368).

Two articles and a dissertation deal with Anglo-Spanish rivalry in the Southeast: Matter's "Missions in the Defense of Spanish Florida, 1566-1710" (397), Pearson's "Early Anglo-Spanish Rivalry in Southeastern North America" (401) which comes down only to 1685, and Sanders's dissertation "The Spanish Defense of America, 1700-1763" (410).

New biographical studies of military leaders include Spalding's *Oglethorpe in America* (413), and Welch's dissertation "River God: The Public Life of Israel Williams, 1709-1788" (419). Beattie's "General Amherst and the Conquest of Canada, 1758-1760" (371), a doctoral dissertation, concentrates on the role of an important commander in a decisive sequence of campaigns. Helpful in assessing the competency of the British regular army in American campaigning is Russell's article "Redcoats in the Wilderness: British Officers and Irregular Warfare in Europe and America, 1740 to 1760" (409).

The colonial militia continues to intrigue scholars because of its roots in the Old World, its evolution in the different environment of the New World, and its significance as a social institution. Two recent dissertations deserving attention are Gates's "Disorder and Social Organization: The Militia in Connecticut Public Life, 1660-1860" (383), and Shea's "To Defend Virginia: The Evolution of the First Colonial Militia, 1607-1677" (411).

Relationships between government and the military, or the political process and war, provide continuing oportunities for study. Calmes's "The Lyttelton

IV

THE AMERICAN REVOLUTION

Hugh F. Rankin

There have been relatively few volumes published on the military history of the American Revolution since the bicentennial year of 1976. But those that have been published have generally been of good quality and are of significance.

GENERAL WORKS. Although Page Smith in his *New Age Now Begins* (328) only reaches the battle of Lexington on page 470, he devotes much of the remaining 1,362 pages in this two-volume work to battle on land and sea. And he displays a sound grasp of military strategy and tactics.

MILITARY BIOGRAPHY. On the American side, Paul David Nelson has written a biography of Horatio Gates in which Gates emerges as "neither genius nor fool but . . . a moderately gifted military officer with both commendable and damaging traits of character." In a like manner, Robert Champagne's study of Alexander McDougall (313) is a good one. For the British, James Lunt has written a biography of John Burgoyne (323) in which he readily admits that he has uncovered no new sources, but has based his conclusions upon his own experiences as a military man. In the light of some of the decisions made by Burgoyne, it is somewhat difficult to agree with the conclusion that he was unlucky rather than incompetent. And this seems to be a good spot in which to insert a mention of Robert Gross's study of the minutemen of Concord (320), in which he gives the social background of this group.

BATTLES AND CAMPAIGNS. Two of the books that have been published in this category are on the Saratoga campaign, one by Rupert Furneaux (319), the other by John R. Elting (315). While Furneaux sees Burgoyne's campaign as an honorable attempt to achieve the impossible, Elting sees the general as inept. Thomas Fleming's study (317) on the campaigns of 1776 is lively and knowledgeable.

UNIT HISTORIES AND PERIPHERAL STUDIES. One of the more important studies to have come out is the one on the logistics of the British Army in America by Bowler (310), in which he details the difficulties of that army. Other peripheral studies are Raoul F. Camus's definitive study of military music (311), and John R. Elting's volume on military uniforms (316), in which he has included sixty color plates covering American, British, French, and German units. A companion volume is Strachan's book on the uniforms of the British army (329). John Shy's collection of essays (327), although they cover a number of subjects, has much on the militia who were so able to control the Loyalists that the latter were never very effective. And Charles Lesser's study of the strength reports (322) of the Continental Army have been done with both care and imagination.

REGIONAL AND STATE HISTORIES. Wright's study of Florida (330) during the war is a welcome addition to the literature of the period in that it focuses on both the military and political operations in that province.

NAVAL AFFAIRS. Jonathan R. Dull (314) has written a volume on the participation of the French Navy in the American Revolution and has much to say about its size, ships, and operations. For the American Navy there is the volume by William M. Fowler, Jr. (318), which seems to be something of a synthesis of current scholarship on the subject. And John W. Jackson (321) details the defense of the Delaware River in his book on the Pennsylvania Navy.

CARTOGRAPHY. Douglas W. Marshal and Howard H. Peckham (324) have compiled an atlas of manuscript maps, over one-half of which have never been published before. Nebenzahl and Higginbotham (325) have prepared a volume reproducing maps that were published during the war. While a group of specially drawn maps are included in Lester J. Cappon's work (312), there are many fine maps in the Nebenzahl and Higginbotham work which, though expensive, is very useful.

BIBLIOGRAPHY

310. Bowler, R. Arthur. *Logistics and the Failure of the British Army in America, 1775–1783.* Princeton: Princeton University Press, 1975.
311. Camus, Raoul F. *Military Music of the American Revolution.* Chapel Hill: University of North Carolina Press, 1976.
312. Cappon, Lester J., ed. in chief. *Atlas of Early American History. The Revolutionary Era, 1760–1790.* Princeton: Princeton University Press, for the Newberry Library and the Institute for Early American History and Culture, 1976.
313. Champagne, Roger J. *Alexander McDougall and the American Revolution.* Schenectady: New York State Bicentennial Commission in conjunction with Union College Press, distributed by the Syracuse University Press, 1975.
314. Dull, Jonathan R. *The French Navy and American Independence: A Study in Arms and Diplomacy, 1774–1787.* Princeton: Princeton University Press, 1976.
315. Elting, John R. *The Battle of Saratoga.* Monmouth Beach, N.J.: Philip Freneau Press, 1978.
316. Elting, John R., ed. in chief. *Military Uniforms in America, the Era of*

the American Revolution, 1775-1795. San Rafael, Calif.: Presidio Press, 1975.

317. Fleming, Thomas. *1776: Year of Illusions*. New York: W. W. Norton & Company, 1975.

318. Fowler, William M., Jr. *Rebels Under Sail: The American Navy during the Revolution*. New York: Charles Scribner's Sons, 1976.

319. Furneaux, Rupert. *Saratoga, The Decisive Battle*. London: George Allen & Unwin, Ltd., 1971.

320. Gross, Robert A. *The Minutemen and Their World*. New York: Hill and Wang, 1976.

321. Jackson, John W. *The Pennsylvania Navy, 1775-1781: The Defense of the Delaware*. New Brunswick: Rutgers University Press, 1974.

322. Lesser, Charles H., ed. *The Sinews of Independence: Monthly Strength Reports of the Continental Army*. Chicago: University of Chicago Press, 1976.

323. Lunt, James. *John Burgoyne of Saratoga*. New York: Harcourt Brace and Jovanovich, 1975.

324. Marshal, Douglas W., and Howard H. Peckham. *Campaigns of the American Revolution: An Atlas of Manuscript Maps*. Ann Arbor, Mich. and Maplewood, N.J.: University of Michigan Press and Hammond, Inc., 1976.

325. Nebenzahl, Kenneth, and Don Higginbotham. *Atlas of the American Revolution*. Chicago: Rand McNally & Company, 1974.

326. Nelson, Paul David. *General Horatio Gates: A Biography*. Baton Rouge: Louisiana State University Press, 1976.

327. Shy, John. *A People Numerous and Armed: Reflections on the Military Struggle for American Independence*. New York: Oxford University Press, 1976.

328. Smith, Page. *A New Age Now Begins: A People's History of the American Revolution*. 2 vols. New York: McGraw Hill Book Company, 1976.

329. Strachan, Hew. *The Dress of the British Army from Official Sources*. New York: Hippocrene Books, 1975.

330. Wright, J. Leitch. *Florida in the American Revolution*. Gainesville: University of Florida Press for the American Revolution Bicentennial Commission of Florida, 1975.

V

FROM THE REVOLUTION TO THE MEXICAN WAR

Roger L. Nichols

Interest in the pre-Mexican War decades of American military history has remained steady during the past five years. Certainly the volume of scholarship on this era has not diminished significantly. Although most of what has been written deals with the same issues and topics considered previously, there are some books and articles which make solid contributions.

OFFICIAL AND PRIVATE PAPERS. The growing availability of primary material, both as manuscripts and in published forms, is of great assistance for the continuing study of the early army. A modest collection, the Randall-Bache letters (317), discusses life in the Corps of Artillery between 1816 and 1827. The John E. Wool Papers (318) are a source of major significance. General Wool's career stretched from the War of 1812 to the Civil War, and during that time he corresponded with presidents, governors, senators, and cabinet officers. Because of this his papers include much about issues which affected the army. Among recently published documents, two of Maj. Stephen Long's journals (295) dealing with his 1817 and 1823 explorations provide new data about army explorers. For the same period volumes eight and nine of W. Edwin Hemphill's edition of the John C. Calhoun Papers (275) complete the story of his administration of the War Department. We now have a thorough edition of the major documents related to Calhoun's entire tenure as secretary of war during the important years immediately following the War of 1812. Another set of documents, Ellen M. Whitney's three-volume edition of *The Black Hawk War* papers (272), provides all of the primary data anyone could use about that conflict. One of its major contributions is that one entire volume is devoted to the Illinois militia.

GENERAL MILITARY HISTORIES. Broad studies covering much or all of army history vary widely in the space they allot to the pre-Mexican War period. Jack Foner's *Blacks and the Military in American History* (279) devotes only one of nine chapters to the 1783-1865 years. He concludes that except in times of local crisis both the army and the state militias excluded blacks from military service. In *The Image of the Army Officer in America* (288), Charles Kemble focuses on the 1815-98 era. He devotes the first third of his study to the early years, and concludes that the public images of army officers changed with each generation in the nineteenth century. Usually, in the pre-Mexican War decades officers were seen first as gentlemen and later as soldier-engineers. This book offers valuable help for an understanding of contemporary thought about the army. Three recent articles by Joseph Holmes (286), Anthony Marro (296), and John B. B. Trussel, Jr. (310), deal with the militia system and its relationship to national defense needs. Essentially they agree that state militia forces did not function as expected, and that because of this there was a growing dependence on regular troops.

ESTABLISHING A PEACETIME ARMY, 1783-1812. The most comprehensive study of this process to appear in decades is *Eagle and Sword, The Federalists and the Creation of the Military Establishment in America, 1783-1802,* by Richard H. Kohn (290). The author questions Jeffersonian claims that military-minded Federalists created an army where none was needed. He shows that the growth of militarism as a set of ideas, and the birth of military institutions, were only a small part of the larger nation-building process then occurring. The author notes that prior to 1798 even the most rabid militarists depended upon the militia except for the 1794 Indian fighting. This excellent study blends military development and political thought carefully, and it is basic to understanding the complex story of creating a national army. Among the officers who played important roles in that army, Anthony Wayne stands out, as Glenn Tucker's recent biography (311) demonstrates. Although much of the book deals with the Revolutionary War era, Tucker shows how Wayne's forceful leadership and organizational skill helped bring victory over the Indians at Fallen Timbers. While the regulars campaigned in Indiana, the Whiskey Rebellion forced the Washington administration to call upon the militia to suppress this threat to the new government. Richard H. Kohn (291) examines the political dimensions of this decision carefully.

Throughout the years leading to the War of 1812, frontier issues were among those which kept Britain and the United States apart. J. Leitch Wright, Jr., *Britain and the American Frontier* (315), considers the points of conflict between the two nations. His study is chiefly diplomatic, but it deals with some military activity and places military quesions clearly within the economic and political context of that day. A careful biographer of William Clark, of Lewis and Clark fame, has long been needed, but unfortunately Jerome O. Steffen's *William Clark, Jeffersonian Man on the Frontier* (309) is not one. More an intellectual study than a biography, it is of only slight value for military historians.

Army activities helped the citizens in their quest for land and resources, and helped protect them from real and imagined dangers. An article by Powell A. Casey (276) considers army road building in frontier Louisiana, while Tommy R. Young (316) discusses the role soldiers played in protecting southerners from actual and potential slave revolts in the early decades of the nineteenth century.

THE WAR OF 1812. Interest in aspects of this conflict continues high. Clifford L. Egan brings together the latest trends in scholarship in "The Origins of the War of 1812" (278). The state militias continue to receive attention for their roles in the war. Robert L. Kerby, "The Militia System and the State Militias in the War of 1812" (289), shows how these units fit into wartime plans and operations. He distinguishes between the theoretical militia system established by Congress in 1792 and the actual condition of the troops called up for combat duty. He notes that with proper training, equipment, and leadership, the militiamen did well in combat.

Donald R. Hickey (284) shows the relationship between federal use of state troops and the growing opposition to the war in New England. He claims that the Hartford Convention grew out of dissatisfaction with federal handling of defense matters, the cost of equipping and supplying the militia by the states, and the overbearing actions of some federal officers sent to work with or to command the militia. Edward Brynn (273) and H. N. Muller III (299) also examine opposition to the war in New England. Two articles by C. Edward Skeen (304, 305) trace the administrative problems of the War Department under John Armstrong, and the rivalry between Armstrong and James Monroe, then secretary of state. The lack of cooperation between these two men and their mutual suspicion made prosecuting the war more difficult than it should have been.

Recently only slight attention has been given to the purely military aspects of the war. Articles by J. H. Alexander dealing with the Seminole-black defeat of a relief force entering north Florida in the 1812–13 campaign there (269), and by Maurice Melton on the Creeks in the Red Stick campaign a year later (297), provide some new information. Robin Reilly, *The British at the Gates* (303), is the only study of a major campaign during the war. A British historian, Reilly discusses the campaign activities from the invasion of the Chesapeake Bay region through the actions of British units along the Gulf Coast and at New Orleans. He used British sources carefully, and puts the blame for the New Orleans disaster on British commanders at several levels.

THE POSTWAR ARMY. When Americans decided that continuing military threats by the British seemed unlikely, Congressional budget-cutters concentrated most of their effort on the War Department. Much primary material on this issue is in the John C. Calhoun papers (275), which focus on the 1817–25 years. In addition to these documents, Carlton B. Smith (307) discusses military preparedness during those same years. Together, these two sources offer valuable insights into problems which faced the army for the following twenty years.

While struggling with reduced budgets and manpower, soldiers carried out a wide range of assignments throughout the country. Harold Kanarek (287) focuses on the work of the Corps of Engineers in Maryland. There they helped survey the Cumberland Road, the Chesapeake and Ohio Canal, the Baltimore and Ohio Railroad, and the Susquehanna Railroad during the 1820s and 1830s. In a related item Roger L. Nichols considers the role soldiers played in shaping American perceptions of the Great Plains between 1800 and 1835 (301). His new study, *Stephen H. Long and American Frontier Exploration* (302), considers Long's explorations of the Mississippi, Missouri, and Arkansas Rivers, and the Red River of the North as well as his trek across the central plains. Long later supervised snag-boat operations on the Ohio and Mississippi rivers, while other engineers labored at similar routine chores. A series of recent studies (319–23) of present army engineer districts traces many of these early nineteenth century activities.

Soldiers built, occupied, and served out of forts scattered across the nation, and studies of individual army posts continue to appear. Clearly Fort Leavenworth has received the most attention. George Walton's *Sentinel of the Plains: Fort Leavenworth and the American West* (314) is a competent popular history which devotes a third of its space to the pre-Mexican War period. Forrest R. Blackburn has two brief studies of Cantonment Leavenworth (270) and the later fort (271), while Arthur J. Stanley, Jr., offers yet another look at this frontier post (308). Fort Atkinson, farther up the Missouri River, is the center of Virgil Ney's study (300). Two articles by Daniel F. Littlefield, Jr., and Lonnie E. Underhill (293, 294) deal with Fort Wayne on the Arkansas frontier, and a third of theirs discusses Fort Coffee in the Indian Territory (292). Thomas Friggens (281) develops the story of Fort Wilkins in the Upper Michigan copper mining country during the 1840s.

THE ARMY AND THE INDIANS. The large amount of existing work on this topic appears to have inhibited scholars in recent years; only a few items have appeared. In a general article, William B. Skelton shows that "Army Officers' Attitudes Toward the Indians" (306) were generally negative even though the officers seemed to be sorry and even ashamed when American policies destroyed the Indians. Another noncombat article is Brad Agnew, "The Dodge-Leavenworth Expedition of 1834" (268), which examines the contributions of this effort to open relations with the tribes of the southern plains. Most of the other items focus on the Second Seminole War in Florida. George H. Walton, *Fearless and Free: The Seminole Indian War* (313) adds a little to earlier work. George E. Buker, *Swamp Sailors: Riverine Warfare in the Everglades* (274) considers an aspect of the conflict which has not received much previous attention. Gary E. Moulton, "Cherokees and the Second Seminole War" (298) shows that, although the Cherokee leaders tried to mediate between the Seminoles and American officials in Florida, the War Department refused to cooperate or even to deal honestly with either group of Indians.

SUGGESTIONS FOR FURTHER RESEARCH. Several of the issues which I suggested in the earlier *Guide* have not yet been dealt with adequately. In addition there are at least two other areas for continuing work. Biographies of regimental commanders such as Hugh Brady, Henry Leavenworth, and David Twiggs would be useful. Also enough work has now been done on state militia units that a general study of the problems surrounding the use of militiamen should be considered. This might include the actual state of the militia when it was offered for federal service, and the process by which states moved from the federally legislated militia system toward dependence on volunteer units by the middle of the nineteenth century.

BIBLIOGRAPHY

268. Agnew, Brad. "The Dodge-Leavenworth Expedition of 1834." *Chronicles of Oklahoma* 53 (fall 1975): 376–96.
269. Alexander, J. H. "The Ambush of Captain John Williams, U. S. M.C.: Failure of the East Florida Invasion, 1812–1813." *Florida Historical Quarterly* 56 (January 1978): 280–96.

270. Blackburn, Forrest R. "Cantonment Leavenworth: 1827–1832." *Military Review* 51 (December 1971): 57–66.

271. Blackburn, Forrest R. "Fort Leavenworth: Logistical Base for the West." *Military Review* 53 (December 1973): 3–12.

272. *The Black Hawk War 1831–1832.* Edited by Ellen M. Whitney. 2 vols., 3 parts. *Collections of the Illinois State Historical Library,* vols. 35–38. Springfield: Illinois State Historical Library, 1970–78.

273. Brynn, Edward. "Patterns of Dissent: Vermont's Opposition to the War of 1812." *Vermont History* 40 (winter 1972): 10–27.

274. Buker, George E. *Swamp Sailors: Riverine Warfare in the Everglades, 1835–1842.* Gainesville: University Presses of Florida, 1975.

275. Calhoun, John C. *The Papers of John C. Calhoun.* Edited by W. Edwin Hemphill. Vols. 8–9. Columbia: University of South Carolina Press, 1975–76.

276. Casey, Powell A. "Military Roads in the Florida Parishes of Louisiana." *Louisiana History* 15 (summer 1974): 229–42.

277. Dye, Dewey A., Jr. "The Indian Key Massacre." *United States Naval Institute Proceedings,* November 1973, pp. 74–78.

278. Egan, Clifford L. "The Origins of the War of 1812: Three Decades of Historical Writing." *Military Affairs* 38 (April 1974), 72–75.

279. Foner, Jack D. *Blacks and the Military in American History: A New Perspective.* New York: Praeger, 1974.

280. Font, Glen F. "Old Bugle Juice." *Infantry,* May-June 1975, pp. 42–45.

281. Friggens, Thomas. "Fort Wilkins: Army Life on the Frontier." *Michigan History* 61 (fall 1977): 220–50.

282. Froncek, Thomas. "I Once Was a Great Warrior: Tragedy of Black Hawk." *American Heritage* 24 (December 1972): 16–21.

283. Gordon, Roy. "Engineering For the People: Two-Hundred Years of Army Public Works." *Military Engineer* 68 (May-June 1976): 180–85.

284. Hickey, Donald R. "New England's Defense Problem and the Genesis of the Hartford Convention." *New England Quarterly* 50 (December 1977): 587–604.

285. Hickey, Donald R. "The United States Army Versus Long Hair: The Trials of Colonel Thomas Butler, 1801–1805." *Pennsylvania Magazine of History and Biography* 101 (October 1977): 462–74.

286. Holmes, Joseph J. "Decline of the Pennsylvania Militia, 1815–1870." *Western Pennsylvania Historical Magazine* 57 (April 1974): 199–217.

287. Kanarek, Harold. "The U.S. Army Corps of Engineers and Early Internal Improvements in Maryland." *Maryland Historical Magazine* 72 (spring 1977): 99–109.

288. Kemble, Charles R. *The Image of the Army Officer in America: Background for Current Views.* Westport, Conn.: Greenwood Press, 1973.

289. Kerby, Robert L. "The Militia System and the State Militias in the War of 1812." *Indiana Magazine of History* 73 (June 1977): 102–24.

290. Kohn, Richard H. *Eagle and Sword, The Federalists and the Creation of the Military Establishment in America, 1783–1802.* New York: Free Press, 1975.

291. Kohn, Richard H. "The Washington Administration's Decision to Crush the Whiskey Rebellion." *Journal of American History* 59

(December 1972): 567–84.

292. Littlefield, Daniel F., Jr., and Lonnie E. Underhill. "Fort Coffee and Frontier Affairs, 1834–1838." *Chronicles of Oklahoma* 54 (fall 1976): 314–38.

293. Littlefield, Daniel F., Jr., and Lonnie E. Underhill. "Fort Wayne and Border Violence, 1840–1847." *Arkansas Historical Quarterly* 36 (spring 1977): 3–30.

294. Littlefield, Daniel F., Jr., and Lonnie E. Underhill. "Fort Wayne and the Arkansas Frontier, 1838–1840." *Arkansas Historical Quarterly* 35 (winter 1976): 334–59.

295. Long, Stephen H. *The Northern Expeditions of Stephen H. Long: The Journals of 1817 and 1823 and Related Documents.* Edited by Lucile M. Kane, June D. Holmquist, and Carolyn Gilman. St. Paul: Minnesota Historical Society Press, 1978.

296. Marro, Anthony. "Vermont's Local Militia Units, 1815–1860." *Vermont History* 40 (winter 1972): 28–42.

297. Melton, Maurice. "War Trail of the Red Sticks." *American History Illustrated* 10 (February 1976): 32–42.

298. Moulton, Gary E. "Cherokees and the Second Seminole War." *Florida Historical Quarterly* 53 (January 1975): 296–305.

299. Muller, H. N., III. "A 'Traitorous and Diabolical Traffic': The Commerce of the Champlain-Richelieu Corridor During the War of 1812." *Vermont History* 44 (spring 1976): 78–96.

300. Ney, Virgil. "Prairie Generals and Colonels at Cantonment Missouri and Fort Atkinson." *Nebraska History* 56 (spring 1975): 51–76.

301. Nichols, Roger L. "The Army and Early Perceptions of the Plains." *Nebraska History* 56 (spring 1975): 121–35.

302. Nichols, Roger L. *Stephen H. Long and American Frontier Exploration, 1815–1824.* Newark: University of Delaware Press, 1980.

303. Reilly, Robin. *The British at the Gates: The New Orleans Campaign in the War of 1812.* New York: G. P. Putnam's Sons, 1974.

304. Skeen, C. Edward. "Mr. Madison's Secretary of War." *Pennsylvania Magazine of History and Biography* 100 (July 1976): 336–55.

305. Skeen, C. Edward. "Monroe and Armstrong: A Study in Political Rivalry." *New York Historical Society Quarterly* 50 (April 1973): 121–47.

306. Skelton, William B. "Army Officers' Attitudes Toward the Indians." *Pacific Northwest Quarterly* 67 (July 1976): 113–24.

307. Smith, Carlton B. "Congressional Attitudes Toward Military Preparedness During the Monroe Administration." *Military Affairs* 40, (February 1976): 22–25.

308. Stanley, Arthur J., Jr. "Fort Leavenworth: Dowager Queen of Frontier Posts." *Kansas Historical Quarterly* 42 (spring 1976): 1–23.

309. Steffen, Jerome O. *William Clark: Jeffersonian Man on the Frontier.* Norman: University of Oklahoma Press, 1977.

310. Trussell, John B. B., Jr. "The Role of the Professional Military Officer in the Preservation of the Republic." *Western Pennsylvania Historical Magazine* 60 (January 1977): 1–21.

311. Tucker, Glenn. *Mad Anthony Wayne and the New Nation.* Harrisburg, Pa.: Stackpole Books, 1973.

312. Wallace, Lee A., Jr. "The Petersburg Volunteers, 1812–1813." *Virginia Magazine of History and Biography* 82 (October 1974): 458–85.
313. Walton, George H. *Fearless and Free: The Seminole Indian War, 1835–1842.* Indianapolis: Bobbs-Merrill, 1977.
314. Walton, George H. *Sentinel of the Plains, Fort Leavenworth and the American West.* Englewood Cliffs, N.J.: Prentice-Hall, Inc., 1973.
315. Wright, J. Leitch. *Britain and the American Frontier, 1783–1815.* Athens: University of Georgia Press, 1975.
316. Young, Tommy R., II. "The United States Army and the Institution of Slavery in Louisiana: 1803–1835." *Louisiana Studies* 13 (fall 1974): 201–22.

PRIVATE PAPERS
317. Randall-Bache Letters. U.S. Army Military History Institute, Carlisle Barracks, Pennsylvania.
318. John Ellis Wool Papers. New York State Library, Albany.

SUPPLEMENTARY ITEMS
319. Dobney, Frederick J. *River Engineers on the Middle Mississippi: A History of the St. Louis District, U.S. Army Corps of Engineers.* Washington, D.C.: Government Printing Office, 1978.
320. Johnson, Leland R. *Engineers on the Twin Rivers: A History of the Nashville District Corps of Engineers United States Army.* Washington, D.C.: Government Printing Office, 1978.
321. Johnson, Leland R. *An Illustrated History of the Huntington District: U.S. Army Corps of Engineers 1754–1974.* Washington, D.C.: Government Printing Office, 1977.
322. Kanarek, Harold. *The Mid-Atlantic Engineers: A History of the Baltimore District, U.S. Army Corps of Engineers, 1775–1974.* Washington, D.C.: Government Printing Office, 1978.
323. Parkman, Aubrey. *Army Engineers in New England: The Military and Civil Work of the Corps of Engineers in New England 1775–1975.* Washington, D.C.: Government Printing Office, 1978.

VI

THE NAVY IN THE NINETEENTH CENTURY, 1789-1889

Christopher F. McKee

An overworked and worn-out field. Within the past ten years that character-ization was applied to the historiography of the navy in the sailing ship period by a leader of the historical profession. Not long thereafter a younger scholar announced the death of naval biography. The condolences may have been premature. Strong scholarly interest in nineteenth-century naval history gives no indication of abating. Although many of the published pieces are tradi-tional, and an occasional article most charitably described as mediocre slips into print in an unrefereed journal, there is a promising core of studies which are innovative in their sources, methodologies, or interpretations.

In surveying historical writing about the nineteenth-century navy since the publication of the original *Guide to the Sources of United States Military History,* the author has attempted to review all appropriate journal articles published between January 1974 and approximately September 1979, and books bearing imprint dates of 1975 through 1979. Of the mass of books and periodical articles thus examined, only those which appeared to make some original contribution to the field were selected for final inclusion in the bibliography. Four books published before 1975, but not included in the original *Guide,* and two pre-1974 articles are incorporated in the present essay. With one exception, no attempt was made to cite unpublished doctoral dissertations. Limited space to cover a long period of history was the primary reason for the decision; however, dissertations receive thorough bibliographic coverage elsewhere, and it can be assumed that the best of them will eventually reach print in book or article form.

The almost total seizure and continued occupation of the field of nineteenth-century naval history by academically trained or academically affiliated historians is the single most salient feature of recent writing. Taken as a whole, the journal articles listed focus on narrowly defined subjects, are based on a thorough exploitation of archival sources, give careful attention to detail, are more often narrative than analytical, and avoid either the integration of the specialized topic under consideration with a comprehensive view of the main currents of the time or the application to the particular of overarching historical theories or models. To reach publication, scholarly books must survive a more rigorous screening process than do periodical articles. Conse-quently, they are generally better written, and are more likely to represent fresh departures in research topics and techniques or to advance new interpretations of familiar facts. But, be it book or journal article, research in nineteenth-century naval history remains distressingly parochial. It is nearly fifty years since James Phinney Baxter published *The Introduction of the Ironclad Warship* (22), but there is today no significant body of scholarship systematically connecting nineteenth-century naval developments in the United States with those in other parts of the world. Comparative studies of even the United State's own army and navy are nowhere to be found.

While a small band of scholars, including Lance Buhl (296, 297, 314), Kenneth Hagan (91), Linda Maloney (314), and Christopher McKee (149), explicitly or silently questions the historical theses of Alfred T. Mahan (145, 146), the shadow of the admiral still falls across most of the pages written about the nineteenth-century navy. The pre-1890 period is seen as one in which the people of the United States blindly rejected the option of building a command-of-the-seas navy. Too often unasked are the questions: Did the United States actually need such a navy? Could a young, developing nation have afforded that institution?

Two other, more recent interpretations of nineteenth-century naval history have markedly influenced the scholarship of the past five years. Peter Karsten's masterwork, *The Naval Aristocracy* (116), with its view of the nineteenth-century naval officer as a self-serving militarist of narrow vision, shows some signs of becoming the new orthodoxy in naval historiography, as calls are heard in the land for someone to "do a Karsten-type study" on such and such a period or topic. Leonard F. Guttridge and Jay D. Smith in *The Commodores* (90) see an officer corps riddled with interpersonal feuds and conspiracies as the key to understanding the navy in its first half-century. The influence of *The Commodores* is paradoxical: it received no attention in the book review section of any major scholarly journal at the time of its publication (see *American Neptune* 30 (1970): 73–75 for the sole exception), yet its judgments can be found blended into the texts of many of the entries in the appended bibliography, and it is repeatedly cited in their notes. So far no scholar has systematically challenged Karsten or Guttridge and Smith on sources, methods, or conclusions. Indeed, naval historical scholarship lacks the lively debate between rival interpretations that characterizes other fields of historical study today.

GENERAL HISTORIES. In an attempt to fill the need for a new, one-volume survey history of the United States Navy, Kenneth J. Hagan assembled a panel of seventeen scholars and asked each of them to write an essay on the period of his or her special competence. The resulting volume, *In Peace and War* (314), includes seven chapters on the nineteenth-century navy, of which those by Linda Maloney, on the War of 1812, and Lance C. Buhl, covering the years 1865–89, are noteworthy for encapsulating stimulating new work and interpretation by younger scholars whose longer studies, on which these essays are based, have not yet reached publication. Robert E. Johnson's *Far China Station* (325) traces the history of U.S. naval activities in one particular part of the world, the western Pacific, throughout the nineteenth century. Especially useful to scholars of naval affairs in the first half of that century is Charles R. Fisher's article on naval guns and gunnery (311), which seeks to provide "a better understanding of the ordnance used in stirring sea fights during the early years of the United States Navy" through an account of the guns themselves, their ammunition, handling, and capabilities.

FROM THE QUASI WAR WITH FRANCE THROUGH THE WAR OF 1812. There has been a revival of scholarly interest in the naval side of the War of 1812 during the 1970s, with no fewer than sixteen of the seventy-three entries in the appended bibliography dealing with some aspect of the war. By contrast the earliest years of the federal navy, 1794-1811, are attracting less attention than they did a few years ago. Craig Symonds's succinct essay on the opposition to naval expansion in the early republic (350) summarizes a longer study due for publication in book form (351) in 1980. The Coast Guard and its predecessor organizations have been more neglected by historians than one might have expected from the civil/military duality of its mission. Irving H. King's *George Washington's Coast Guard* (326) is easily the best book to date on the 1789-1801 origins of the Revenue Cutter Service, but it does not by any means exhaust the sources or the possibilities for research on the early years of this force.

The most exciting new work on the War of 1812 has been directed towards privateering. Jerome R. Garitee's stunningly impressive *The Republic's Private Navy* (312), a study of the war-for-profit business of Baltimore, is one of the most significant contributions to United States naval history of the past five years; it is equally a contribution to the social and economic history of the period. Fred W. Hopkins has also made a strong addition to the history of Baltimore privateering with his biography of Thomas Boyle (324) and his companion article on Boyle's *Chasseur* (323).

Linda Maloney outlines a revisionist interpretation of the naval conflict in her essay "The War of 1812: What Role for Sea Power?" in Hagan's *In Peace and War* (314). In addition to the articles on operational aspects of the War of 1812 by Aimone (288) and Dunnigan (306), particular note should be made of William L. Calderhead's three excellent studies covering aspects of the career of Capt. Charles Gordon (301, 302, 303). Joseph A. Goldenberg's "Blue Lights and Infernal Machines: The British Blockade of New London" (313), an investigation of early attempts to use unconventional weapons, is a good example of the greater scholarly sophistication possible when War of 1812 students explore both British and American sources.

Graphic resources for the study of the early navy have been largely neglected by academic scholars. Edgar Newbold Smith's *American Naval Broadsides* (344) is a useful place to start, because its citations will guide the user to earlier collections of similar material.

FROM THE WAR OF 1812 TO THE CIVIL WAR. Though rich in potential subjects, the years between the Treaty of Ghent and the Mexican War remain one of the less-investigated periods in the navy's history. David Long's essay from Hagan's *In Peace and War* (314) covers the period 1815-42, when naval affairs were dominated by the Board of Navy Commissioners. The succeeding years are the subject of Geoffrey Smith's "An Uncertain Passage: The Bureaus Run the Navy, 1842-1861" in the same volume. One event falling within the era of the Board of Navy Commissioners—the selection of Pensacola as a site for a naval establishment—has been examined by George F. Pearce (338). Frances X. Holbrook relates the navy's responses to the filibustering activities of William Walker in the 1850s (320) and its role in the 1855-57 war with the Indian tribes in the Puget Sound area of Washington Territory (319). Naval aspects of another Indian conflict, the Second Seminole War of 1835-42, are the subject of a rather more important book and article by George E. Buker (298, 299). In *Swamp Sailors* (299), Buker argues that the conditions of warfare against the Seminoles in Florida forced the navy to break free from the confines of old strategic and tactical concepts and develop a new combat doctrine—riverine warfare.

CIVIL WAR. Neither scholarly nor lay enthusiasm for refighting the War Between the States shows any sign of diminishing. Dana Wegner surveys the Union navy, and Frank Merli the Confederate, in chapters six and seven of *In Peace and War* (314). The implications of Lincoln's decision to impose a formal blockade of the Confederate ports in 1861, thus granting the Confederacy the status of a belligerent, rather than declaring the ports closed by administrative action because of insurrection, are explored by Stuart Anderson (292). Acquisition of vessels for the Confederate States in Great Britain is examined by Richard I. Lester in two articles (327, 328) based in part on British sources. However, in the host of Civil War publications one major work stands out as a leading contribution of the years 1975-79 to nineteenth-century naval history: Rowena Reed's *Combined Operations in the Civil War* (340). To oversimplify greatly a rich and detailed work, Reed argues that Gen. George B. McClellan's amphibious or combined strategy was the one that would have brought Union victory most speedily and at the smallest human and material cost. McClellan proposed to capitalize on the Union's assets of larger industrial capacity, greater manpower, and command of the seas to move up the major waterways of the South and seize key points on rail lines, thus allowing the Confederacy to strangle for lack of internal rail and external seaborne communication, while its armies exhausted themselves in attacks on the strongly fortified Union enclaves with their gunboat- and cruiser-controlled water lifelines. One particular combined operation has been scrutinized in detail by Myron Smith in his "Gunboats in a Ditch: The Steele's Bayou Expedition, 1863" (346).

Unlike other periods of nineteenth-century naval history, strong interest in the Civil War years seems to assure the steady publication of letters, journals, memoirs, and other primary sources (293, 295, 321, 322, 329, 332a, 333). A less conventional primary source—this time a graphic one—is *The Civil War Sketchbook of Charles Ellery Stedman*, edited by Jim Dan Hill (349).

FROM THE CIVIL WAR TO THE NEW NAVY. Disappointingly little scholarly attention has been devoted to this still-misunderstood period in the navy's history. *In Peace and War* (314) contains Lance C. Buhl's essay "Maintaining 'An American Navy,' 1865-1889." This, together with his article "Mariners and Machines: Resistance to Technological Change in the American Navy, 1865-1869" (296), will serve to give the essence of Buhl's revisionist interpretation of these years until such time as his 1968 Harvard dissertation, "The Smooth Water Navy" (297), is published in book form, an event which all naval scholars must hope will occur in the none-too-distant future. A portion of the reports of the Austrian Vice Admiral Baron Wilhelm von Tegetthoff during his 1867 tour of naval installations in the United States has been published by Armin Mruck and Arnold Blumberg (334). The diplomatic and naval responses of the United States, 1868–74, to the international tensions created by the rebellion in Cuba, which culminated in the Spanish capture of the blockade-runner *Virginius* and the summary execution of U.S. citizens on board, are the subject of an article by Lawrence C. Allin (289).

BIOGRAPHIES. No scholarly life of a major naval figure of the nineteenth century has appeared in the last five years, although definitive biographies of Isaac Hull and William Bainbridge are known to be approaching publication. David Long's critical study of the latter's role in the Barron-Decatur duel (330) makes one the more anxious for the complete life story. *We Have Met the Enemy,* Richard Dillon's biography of Oliver Hazard Perry (305), is partly based on manuscript sources, but its usefulness is limited by the absence of any documentation and by the distortions produced through the author's lack of background in naval history. There is a well-researched short life of Charles Gordon by William L. Calderhead (302), which interprets Gordon's life story in the Guttridge and Smith (90) tradition. The naval career, 1831–39, of a future Confederate secretary of war is thoroughly covered in George G. Shackelford's "George Wythe Randolph, Midshipman, United States Navy" (342). In the Civil War period Dana Wegner's sketch of William D. ("Dirty Bill") Porter (356) is based on primary sources and makes this historian wish for a full biography of this compelling member of an always interesting family. Robert E. Owens has used a collection of family papers to follow the early Civil War career of John Prichett Gillis (337), a Union naval officer whose loyalty was questioned because of his outspoken political opinions. More important than either of these, however, is Royce G. Shingleton's narrative of the Civil War career of one of the Confederacy's most daring and successful combat leaders in *John Taylor Wood, Sea Ghost of the Confederacy* (343).

Secretaries of the navy continue to receive scholarly attention. John Niven has supplemented his biography of Gideon Welles (170) with a study of Welles as a naval administrator (335). Materials for a life of the first secretary of the navy, Benjamin Stoddert, appear to be scarce; Robert L. Scheina has marshalled the bulk of what can be found regarding his subject's post-1798 political opinions and activities in "Benjamin Stoddert, Politics, and the Navy" (341). Edward K. Eckert's misleadingly titled *The Navy Department in the War of 1812* (309) is in reality an account of William Jones's tenure as secretary. Both this small monograph and Eckert's two related articles (308, 310) are the prisoners of Jones's view of himself: they tell nothing of the arrogant man, so ill equipped to deal with people, that his contemporaries knew.

In a class by itself, as the only major documentary publication of the years 1975–79, is the Naval History Division's edition of the massive 925-page *Autobiography* of Charles Wilkes (357), he of Exploring Expedition and *Trent* Affair fame, which William Stanton (348) has neatly characterized as "written with an uncritical enthusiasm for its subject that is evident on every one of its . . . pages."

SOCIAL HISTORY. An argument can be made that the best original work currently being done in naval and military history is the application of the insights and techniques of the new social history to armed forces.

Thus far the seaman has received more attention than the officer. Perhaps the most innovative research reported in the appended bibliography is Ira Dye's "Early American Merchant Seafarers" (307). This demographic study investigates merchant seamen who sailed during the first two decades of the nineteenth century; however, naval seamen were recruited from the same population and served alternately in the navy and the merchant marine, so its findings are transferrable to the navy's sailors. Christopher McKee complements Dye's statistical analysis by exploring the psychology of the naval enlisted man of the same years in his "Fantasies of Mutiny and Murder" (331). A valuable article by Leon Basile (293) publishes a contemporary disciplinary record of the Civil War cruiser *Ethan Allen*. James E. Valle's *Rocks and Shoals: Order and Discipline in the Old Navy* (354) is announced for spring 1980 publication.

Recent research on the officer corps has centered on the development of professionalism. Wm. Ray Heitzmann's "In-Service Naval Officer Education in the Nineteenth Century" (316) surveys two voluntary associations, the Naval Lyceum and the United States Naval Institute, which the officers founded as agencies for professional self-development. A rather more sophisticated analysis of the intellectual milieu surrounding the establishment of the latter organization is provided by Lawrence C. Allin's "The Naval Institute, Mahan, and the Naval Profession" (290). In another, related article (291) Allin has studied the officer corps' response to perceived challenges in two comparable periods, 1870-90 and 1950-70.

Rental of slaves, both as sailors on shipboard and as workers at shore installations, was a widespread practice in the antebellum navy that has been largely ignored by historians. Ernest F. Dibble's pioneering and thorough study of the use of rented slaves at the Pensacola Navy Yard (304a) ought to inspire other and more extensive examinations of the relationship between slavery and the military establishment.

NAVAL DIPLOMACY. *Far China Station: The U.S. Navy in Asian Waters, 1800-1898,* by Robert Erwin Johnson (325), is a major work on the naval officer as diplomatic agent and leads the field among recent publications. A closely related study by Curtis Henson (318) surveys the navy's diplomatic and commerce-protection activities in China during the Taiping Rebellion of the 1850s and early 1860s. Although Donald Bishop's account of the relations between the Asiatic Squadron and the U.S. legation in Korea, 1882-97 (294), is published in a relatively obscure journal, it should not be overlooked for that reason. The use of force by naval commanders in the Pacific in punitive operations against primitive peoples without specific authorization from Washington is critically reviewed by E. Mowbray Tate (352). Paolo E. Coletta has summarized the work of French E. Chadwick as the first U.S. naval attaché posted to London (304). An account of Commodore Robert W. Shufeldt's 1879 information-gathering mission to South Africa, by Thomas J. Noer (336), offers interesting insights into the racial and economic attitudes of this prominent officer, even though Shufeldt's mission itself soon sinks from view in the author's general discussion of the United States's South African policy.

NAVAL EXPLORATION AND SCIENTIFIC ACTIVITY. The 1838–42 Wilkes Expedition continues to attract the principal scholarly attention. *The Great United States Exploring Expedition,* by William Stanton (348), complements David B. Tyler's earlier *The Wilkes Expedition* (353). Taken together the two books provide a comprehensive review of the expedition and its participants. Since that subject is so thoroughly covered, it is to be hoped that historians will turn their attention to some of the navy's other scientific ventures around the globe. "A Memento of the Northern Alaska Naval Exploring Expedition of 1885–86," by Edwin S. Hall (315), analyzes an incised walrus tusk which displays graphic material about, and otherwise unrecorded data on, the Arctic investigations of Lt. George Moss Stoney. Geoffrey Smith's "The Navy before Darwinism: Science, Exploration, and Diplomacy in Antebellum America" (345) is one of the three or four outstanding articles of the past five years and a superior piece of historical interpretation which seeks to place the navy's scientific activities in the broad context of the political, economic, humanitarian, and scientific movements of the times. The extensive naval involvement in the scientific activities of the federal government in the nineteenth century may be followed in Harold L. Burstyn's survey, "Seafaring and the Emergence of American Science" (300). Finally, in a detailed and well-researched article (339), Howard Plotkin recounts the effort by professional astronomers to remove the directorship of the U.S. Naval Observatory from the hands of navy officers and place that institution under the supervision of a civilian scientist.

SHIP CONSTRUCTION. Naval shipbuilding studies, once the hardy perennial of maritime history, still blossom occasionally. Philip C. F. Smith's much-too-little-noticed work on the construction of the frigate *Essex* (347) is the best available account of the building of one of the navy's early ships, and the most beautiful book reviewed in this essay. A famous polemicist's attempt to design a new system for mounting cannon on a gunboat is expertly investigated as "Thomas Paine's Short Career as a Naval Architect," by Joseph G. Henrich (317). In "A Naval Experiment" Linda Maloney (332) has examined the attempt to build a warship, the 1832 *Experiment,* without an interior frame, according to the principles promulgated by naval architect William Annesley. The navy's live oak reserves on the sea islands of Georgia receive attention in Virginia Steele Wood's edition of James Keen's journal of his 1817–18 tour to cut timber on Blackbeard Island (358). And, while not exactly about naval construction, Gordon P. Watts's article on the location and identification of the submerged wreck of the original *Monitor* (355) is a thorough account of this venture in underwater archaeology.

SELECTED SUGGESTIONS. For the nonspecialist who wishes an overview of the most significant research and writing on the nineteenth-century navy during the five years past, but who has no need to examine all seventy-three entries in the following bibliography, the author particularly commends these books and articles: Buhl (296), Buker (299), Burstyn (300), Dibble (304a), Dye (307), Garitee (312), Hagan (314), Johnson (325), McKee (331), Reed (340), Smith (345), Stanton (348), and Symonds (350).

BIBLIOGRAPHY

288. Aimone, Alan Conrad. "The Cruise of the U.S. Sloop *Hornet* in 1815." *Mariner's Mirror* 61 (1975): 377–84.

289. Allin, Lawrence Carroll. "The First Cubic War: The *Virginius* Affair." *American Neptune* 38 (1978): 233–48.

290. Allin, Lawrence Carroll. "The Naval Institute, Mahan, and the Naval Profession." *Naval War College Review,* summer 1978, pp. 29–48.

291. Allin, Lawrence Carroll. "The Naval Profession: Challenge and Response, 1870–1890 and 1950–1970." *Naval War College Review,* spring 1976, pp. 75–90.

292. Anderson, Stuart. "1861: Blockade vs. Closing the Confederate Ports." *Military Affairs* 41 (1977): 190–94.

293. Basile, Leon, ed. "Harry Stanley's Mess Book: Offenses and Punishments Aboard the *Ethan Allen.*" *Civil War History* 23 (1977): 69–79.

294. Bishop, Donald M. "Navy Blue in Old Korea: The Asiatic Squadron and the American Legation, 1882–1897." *Bulletin of the Korean Research Center; Journal of Social Sciences and Humanities* [Seoul: Hanguk Yongu Tosogwan], no. 42 (December 1975): 49–63.

295. Brayton, Abbott A., ed. "The South Atlantic Blockading Squadron: The Diary of James W. Boynton." *South Carolina Historical Magazine* 76 (1975): 112–17.

296. Buhl, Lance C. "Mariners and Machines: Resistance to Technological Change in the American Navy, 1865–1869." *Journal of American History* 61 (1974–75): 703–27.

297. Buhl, Lance C. "The Smooth Water Navy: American Naval Policy and Politics, 1865–1876." Ph.D. dissertation, Harvard University, 1968.

298. Buker, George E. "The Mosquito Fleet's Guides and the Second Seminole War." *Florida Historical Quarterly* 57 (1978–79): 308–26.

299. Buker, George E. *Swamp Sailors: Riverine Warfare in the Everglades, 1835–1842.* Gainesville: University Presses of Florida, 1975.

300. Burstyn, Harold L. "Seafaring and the Emergence of American Science." In *The Atlantic World of Robert G. Albion,* edited by Benjamin W. Labaree, pp. 76–109. Middletown, Conn.: Wesleyan University Press, 1975.

301. Calderhead, William L. "Naval Innovation in Crisis: War in the Chesapeake, 1813." *American Neptune* 36 (1976): 206–21.

302. Calderhead, William L. "A Strange Career in a Young Navy: Captain Charles Gordon, 1778–1816." *Maryland Historical Magazine* 72 (1977): 373–86.

303. Calderhead, William L. "U.S.F. *Constellation* in the War of 1812: An Accidental Fleet-in-Being." *Military Affairs* 40 (1976): 79–83.

304. Coletta, Paolo E. "French Ensor Chadwick: The First American Naval Attaché, 1882–1889." *American Neptune* 39 (1979): 126–41.

304a. Dibble, Ernest F. "Slave Rentals to the Military: Pensacola and the Gulf Coast." *Civil War History* 23 (1977): 101–13.

305. Dillon, Richard. *We Have Met the Enemy: Oliver Hazard Perry, Wilderness Commodore.* New York: McGraw-Hill, 1978.

306. Dunnigan, Brian Leigh. "The Battle of Mackinac Island." *Michigan History* 59 (1975): 239–54.

307. Dye, Ira. "Early American Merchant Seafarers." American Philosophical Society *Proceedings* 120 (1976): 331-60.

308. Eckert, Edward K. "Early Reform in the Navy Department." *American Neptune* 33 (1973): 231-45.

309. Eckert, Edward K. *The Navy Department in the War of 1812.* Gainesville: University of Florida Press, 1973.

310. Eckert, Edward K. "William Jones: Mr. Madison's Secretary of the Navy." *Pennsylvania Magazine of History and Biography* 96 (1972): 167-82.

311. Fisher, Charles R. "The Great Guns of the Navy, 1797-1843." *American Neptune* 36 (1976): 276-95.

312. Garitee, Jerome R. *The Republic's Private Navy: The American Privateering Business as Practiced in Baltimore during the War of 1812.* Middletown, Conn.: published for Mystic Seaport by Wesleyan University Press, 1977.

313. Goldenberg, Joseph A. "Blue Lights and Infernal Machines: The British Blockade of New London." *Mariner's Mirror* 61 (1975): 385-97.

314. Hagan, Kenneth J., ed. *In Peace and War: Interpretations of American Naval History, 1775-1978.* Westport, Conn.: Greenwood Press, 1978

315. Hall, Edwin S., Jr. "A Memento of the Northern Alaska Naval Exploring Expedition of 1885-86." *Alaska Journal* 7 (1977): 81-87.

316. Heitzmann, Wm. Ray. "In-Service Naval Officer Education in the Nineteenth Century: Voluntary Commitment to Reform." *American Neptune* 39 (1979): 109-125.

317. Henrich, Joseph George. "Thomas Paine's Short Career as a Naval Architect, August-October 1807." *American Neptune* 34 (1974): 123-34.

318. Henson, Curtis T., Jr. "The U.S. Navy and the Taiping Rebellion." *American Neptune* 38 (1978): 28-40.

319. Holbrook, Francis X., and John Nikol. "The Navy in the Puget Sound War, 1855-1857: A Documentary Study." *Pacific Northwest Quarterly* 67 (1976): 10-20.

320. Holbrook, Francis X. "The Navy's Cross, William Walker." *Military Affairs* 39 (1975): 197-202.

321. Hoole, William Stanley, ed. "Admiral on Horseback: The Diary of Brigadier General Raphael Semmes, February-May 1865." *Alabama Review* 28 (1975): 129-50.

322. Hoole, William Stanley, ed. "Letters from a Georgia Midshipman [Edward Maffitt Anderson] on the C.S.S. *Alabama.*" *Georgia Historical Quarterly* 59 (1975): 416-32.

323. Hopkins, Fred W. "*Chasseur:* The Pride of Baltimore." *Mariner's Mirror* 64 (1978): 349-60.

324. Hopkins, Fred W. *Tom Boyle, Master Privateer.* Cambridge, Md.: Tidewater Publishers, 1976.

325. Johnson, Robert Erwin. *Far China Station: The U.S. Navy in Asian Waters, 1800-1898.* Annapolis: Naval Institute Press, 1979.

326. King, Irving H. *George Washington's Coast Guard: Origins of the*

U.S. Revenue Cutter Service, 1789–*1801*. Annapolis: Naval Institute Press, 1978.

327. Lester, Richard I. "Construction and Purchase of Confederate Cruisers in Great Britain during the American Civil War." *Mariner's Mirror* 63 (1977): 71–92.

328. Lester, Richard I. "The Procurement of Confederate Blockade Runners and Other Vessels in Great Britain during the American Civil War." *Mariner's Mirror* 61 (1975): 255–70.

329. Littlepage, Hardin Beverly. "A Midshipman aboard the *Virginia*." *Civil War Times Illustrated,* April 1974, pp. 4–11, 42–47; May 1974, pp. 36–43; June 1974, pp. 19–26. Title varies.

330. Long, David F. "William Bainbridge and the Barron-Decatur Duel: Mere Participant or Active Plotter?" *Pennsylvania Magazine of History and Biography* 103 (1979): 34–52.

331. McKee, Christopher. "Fantasies of Mutiny and Murder: A Suggested Psycho-History of the Seaman in the United States Navy, 1798–1815." *Armed Forces and Society* 4 (1977–78): 293–304.

332. Maloney, Linda McKee. "A Naval Experiment." *American Neptune* 34 (1974): 188–96.

332a. Marchand, John B. *Charleston Blockade: The Journals of John B. Marchand, U.S. Navy, 1861*–1862. Edited with commentary by Craig L. Symonds. Newport, R.I.: Naval War College Press, 1976.

333. Minor, Hubbard Taylor, Jr. "'I Am Getting a Good Education . . . ': An Unpublished Diary by a Cadet at the Confederate Naval Academy." *Civil War Times Illustrated,* November 1974, pp. 24–32; December 1974, pp. 24–36. Title varies.

334. Mruck, Armin, and Arnold Blumberg. "An Austrian View of the United States Navy, 1867." *American Neptune* 34 (1974): 59–64.

335. Niven, John. "Gideon Welles and Naval Administration during the Civil War." *American Neptune* 35 (1975): 53–66.

336. Noer, Thomas J. "Commodore Robert W. Shufeldt and America's South African Strategy." *American Neptune* 34 (1974): 81–88.

337. Owens, Robert E., Jr. "John Prichett Gillis." *American Neptune* 37 (1977): 276–87.

338. Pearce, George F. "The United States Navy Comes to Pensacola." *Florida Historical Quarterly* 55 (1976–77): 37–47.

339. Plotkin, Howard. "Astronomers versus the Navy: The Revolt of American Astronomers over the Management of the United States Naval Observatory, 1877–1902." American Philosophical Society *Proceedings* 122 (1978): 385–99.

340. Reed, Rowena. *Combined Operations in the Civil War.* Annapolis: Naval Institute Press, 1978.

341. Scheina, Robert L. "Benjamin Stoddert, Politics, and the Navy." *American Neptune* 36 (1976): 54–68.

342. Shackelford, George Green. "George Wythe Randolph, Midshipman, United States Navy." *American Neptune* 38 (1978): 101–21.

343. Shingleton, Royce Gordon. *John Taylor Wood, Sea Ghost of the Confederacy.* Athens: University of Georgia Press, 1979.

344. Smith, Edgar Newbold. *American Naval Broadsides: A Collection of*

Early Naval Prints, 1745-1815. Philadelphia: Philadelphia Maritime Museum, 1974.

345. Smith, Geoffrey Sutton. "The Navy before Darwinism: Science, Exploration, and Diplomacy in Antebellum America." *American Quarterly* 28 (1976): 41-55.

346. Smith, Myron J., Jr. "Gunboats in a Ditch: The Steele's Bayou Expedition, 1863." *Journal of Mississippi History* 37 (1975): 165-88.

347. Smith, Philip Chadwick Foster. *The Frigate "Essex" Papers: Building the Salem Frigate, 1798-1799*. Salem, Mass.: Peabody Museum of Salem, 1974.

348. Stanton, William Ragan. *The Great United States Exploring Expedition of 1838-1842*. Berkeley: University of California Press, 1975.

349. Stedman, Charles Ellery. *The Civil War Sketchbook of Charles Ellery Stedman, Surgeon, United States Navy*. Biography and commentary by Jim Dan Hill. San Rafael, Calif.: Presidio Press, 1976.

350. Symonds, Craig L. "The Antinavalists: The Opponents of Naval Expansion in the Early National Period." *American Neptune* 39 (1979): 22-28.

351. Symonds, Craig L. *Navalists and Antinavalists: The Naval Policy Debate in the United States, 1785-1827*. Newark: University of Delaware Press, forthcoming.

352. Tate, E. Mowbray. "Navy Justice in the Pacific, 1830-1870: A Pattern of Precedents." *American Neptune* 35 (1975): 20-31.

353. Tyler, David Budlong. *The Wilkes Expedition: The First United States Exploring Expedition, 1838-1842*. Memoirs of the American Philosophical Society, vol. 73. Philadelphia: American Philosophical Society, 1968.

354. Valle, James E. *Rocks and Shoals: Order and Discipline in the Old Navy, 1800-1861*. Annapolis: Naval Institute Press, forthcoming.

355. Watts, Gordon P., Jr. "The Location and Identification of the Ironclad USS *Monitor*." *International Journal of Nautical Archaeology and Underwater Exploration* 4 (1975): 301-29.

356. Wegner, Dana M. "Commodore William D. 'Dirty Bill' Porter." United States Naval Institute *Proceedings*, February 1977, pp. 40-49.

357. Wilkes, Charles. *Autobiography of Rear Admiral Charles Wilkes, U.S. Navy, 1798-1877*. Edited by William James Morgan [and others]. Washington, D.C.: Naval History Division, Dept. of the Navy, 1978.

358. Wood, Virginia Steele. "James Keen's Journal of a Passage from Philadelphia to Blackbeard Island, Georgia, for Live Oak Timber, 1817-1818." *American Neptune* 35 (1975): 227-47.

The author particularly thanks Ms. Kay Elaine Wilson of the Metropolitan Periodical Service, Chicago, for supplying on painfully short notice photocopies of many of the articles cited in this essay.

VII

SCIENCE AND TECHNOLOGY IN
THE NINETEENTH CENTURY

Edward C. Ezell

During the past five years, quite a number of important new books, dissertations, and articles relating to science, technology, and the military in the nineteenth century have appeared. In addition to these new publications, some older works not included in the last edition have been cited in this update.

Taken together, the studies in this bibliography underscore the point that the nineteenth century was an era of change—technological, scientific, economic, and managerial. At the beginning of the century, armies fought with muzzle-loading flintlocks and bronze cannon. Navy wooden ships moved by the wind in their sails. By the end of the century, steel had replaced bronze and iron; machine guns and breech-loading rifles and cannon had increased firepower on land and sea. Navies had replaced wooden hulls with steel armor plate, and cloth sails with the power of steam engines. On the horizon was "the fractious horse" of Tom Crouch's dissertation (409), as Langley, Chanute, and the Wright brothers began to explore "the problem of heavier-than-air flight." The even more apparent rate of technological change of the twentieth century should not blur the impact of new technologies on the life and death of military man in the nineteenth century.

OVERVIEWS FOR THE HISTORY OF TECHNOLOGY AND SCIENCE. Given the limited space available here, the interested researcher is directed to the book review sections of *Technology and Culture* and *ISIS* (published by the History of Science Society) for further entries. Jack Goodwin's "Current Bibliography in the History of Technology" appears annually in the second issue of *Technology and Culture*. *The Business History Review, The Journal of Economic History,* and *The Journal of Modern History* are three other journals that military historians should consult, as they address a wide range of topics, including military technology, and help the military historian understand the world in which military events occur.

John Kasson, *Civilizing the Machine: Technology and Republican Values* (441), looks at the interplay between society and technology for the era 1776-1900. Arthur Belonzi's biography of Roger Burlingame (395) examines that historian's role "as a pioneer in American sociotechnological history."

Burlingame's work (56) "expounds upon the interrelationship between technological innovation and social change."

MILITARY ENGINEERING AND EDUCATION. Peter Molloy has examined the roots of American technological education and reports that they lie in the engineering schools of eighteenth-century France. He compares the U.S. Military Academy to the École Polytechnique in his stimulating dissertation, "Technical Education and the Young Republic" (456). A complementary work is the biography of Sylvanus Thayer (1784-1872) by James Kershner (446), who not only covers Thayer's career at West Point but also describes his activities as a military engineer in New England. Thayer's subsequent endowment of the Thayer School of Civil Engineering at Dartmouth is also chronicled.

West Point should also be remembered as a repository for historically useful source material about military technology. An interesting starting point is Lt. Col. Robert Hall's 1876 *Catalogue of the Library, U.S. Military Academy, West Point, N.Y.* (426). An "Analytical Table of Classification" introduces the researcher to the volume. In addition to key topics such as "Military Engineering, Fortification, Attack, Defence, and Mines" and "Artillery, and Artillery Tactics, Small Arms, and Target Firing," other subjects— from "Acoustics" to "Military History," "Swedenborgianism," and "Weight, Measure, and Finance"—are covered. For example, there were seventy-five copies of Louis de Tousard's relatively rare *American Artillerists Companion* (88) in the Military Academy Library in 1876. A useful bibliographical project would be the determination of how many of the titles listed in the 1876 catalog are still in the West Point collection a century later.

On the naval side, Lawrence Allin examines the establishment and evolution of "The United States Naval Institute: Intellectual Forum of the New Navy: 1873-1889" (386).

Several recent studies examine the contribution of military figures and institutions to nineteenth-century science and technology. Milford Allen's 1958 *United States Government Exploring Expeditions and Natural History, 1800-1840* (385) was overlooked in the earlier edition. John Kazar has written a companion piece, "The United States Navy and Scientific Exploration, 1837-1860" (445). Six biographies add to our understanding of men who pursued science and technology in nineteenth-century America. Michael Brodhead has published a biography of Elliot Coues, army surgeon and active ornithologist (399). William King has chronicled the career of George Davidson, who spent fifty years with the Geological Survey on the Pacific coast (447). Paul Clark has written a biography of George Owen Squier, who served as chief signal officer of the army during World War I. Squier was known equally well for his efforts to institutionalize scientific research and development in the army from 1895 to 1918 (404). B. Franklin Cooling's study of *Benjamin Franklin Tracy: Father of the Modern American Fighting Navy,* who served as secretary of the navy under Benjamin Harrison (1889-93), is very useful for understanding the changes that occurred in the naval service. Cooling's bibliographical essay is especially helpful to students of nineteenth-century naval renaissance (405). George Brooke's biography of "John Mercer Brooke, Naval Scientist" (400) should not be overlooked, nor should Edward Sloan's *Benjamin Franklin Isherwood, Naval Engineer* (482).

NATIONAL ARMORIES AND ARSENALS. The national armories continue to be a subject of considerable scholarly interest. Roe Smith's dissertation on Harpers Ferry Armory (298) has been turned into the Frederick Jackson Turner Prize-winning book *Harpers Ferry Armory and the New Technology: The Challenge of Change* (484). Paul Uselding (496, 500), Gene Cesari (402), and Russell Fries (419, 420) have examined various aspects of technological progress at Springfield Armory and the machine tool manufacturers for the American small arms industry. All of these works touch on the role of the "American System of interchangeable manufacture" and its diffusion, as does Edwin Battison in his two works (392, 393). It is becoming apparent that the American System was resisted by the employees at Harpers Ferry (484), accepted and exploited by the management at Springfield Armory (452, 500) and by Enfield Arsenal in England (419, 420, 423), and generally more suited to the needs of military manufacturing establishments than civilian arms-makers, who were producing smaller quantities (420, 433).

Whereas the United States had been a borrower of technology in the early part of the century (349, 397, 473, 488, 487, 498), by midcentury the American System was being transferred to the arsenals of Europe by men such as James Henry Burton, former master armorer at Harpers Ferry, chief engineer at Enfield, and commanding officer of the Richmond Armory for the Confederacy, and companies such as Greenwood & Batley, Ltd., of Leeds, Yorkshire (414). Greenwood & Batley was an important force in the British machine tool industry, as well (417).

Several new books about the European small arms industry point to the need for and usefulness of comparative studies of the military industries of Europe and America. L. G. Beskrovnyi's *Russkaya armii i flot v XIX veke* (396) studies the technological foundations of the imperial Russian army and navy in the nineteenth century, and it deserves to be translated. Claude Gaier's *Four Centuries of Liege Gunmaking* (422) is a typographical and illustrated treat, as well as being an excellent source of much information about the Belgian arms industry. Jaroslav Lugs's classic, *Firearms Past and Present,* published in Czechoslovakia in 1956, is now available in English (450). Other useful European works include C. H. Roads's *The British Soldier's Firearm, 1850–1864* (468), Otto Moraweitz's *Beiträge zur Geschichte und Technik der Handwaffen und Maschinengewehr* (457), and Gianfranco Simone and colleagues' *Il-91,* the story of the Italian Mannlicher Carcano Rifle (480).

The impact of rifles, rifled artillery, and the railroads upon warfare is the central theme of Dennis Showalter's *Railroads and Rifles: Soldiers, Technology, and the Unification of Germany* (479). This book is more significant than John Ellis's *A Special History of the Machine Gun,* which trades seriousness for cuteness (413). Both books reexamine the oft-stated theory that military men do not usually understand new weapons until it is too late. A corollary theme of failing to understand the tactical role of new weapons is explored by David Armstrong in "The Endless Experiment: The United States Army and the Machine Gun" (390). All three volumes are related to I. B. Holley's main concerns in *Ideas and Weapons* (158).

PRIVATE MANUFACTURERS OF SMALL ARMS. Thirteen entries are devoted to this topic (397, 408, 410, 424, 428, 435, 438, 439, 442, 443, 448, 458, 486). Together these studies cover the period from 1650 to 1945, and they indicate the need for a synthesizing study of the American firearms industry. What does it mean to American history? How did the shift from craft to factory tradition take place? How much of the American System did the private manufacturers assimilate (433)?

DOMESTICATING THE AMERICAN SYSTEM. In March 1978, the Museum of History and Technology of the Smithsonian Institution sponsored a symposium, "The Rise of the American System of Manufacture." Familiar names —Eugene Ferguson, Nathan Rosenberg, Merritt Roe Smith, A. E. Musson (460), Paul Uselding, and Alfred D. Chandler (403)—were joined by younger scholars in examining many aspects of the American System. Proceedings of the symposium were edited by Otto Mayr at the Museum of History and Technology and will be published by the Smithsonian. Much emphasis was given to the marketing of products made with the American System technology, and it was generally agreed that much of the magic of the new technology, in fact, came from the executive suite and not the production floor. David Hounshell, "From the American System to Mass Production" (432), explores this theme in some depth. A. D. Chandler's *The Visible Hand* (403) discusses the managerial revolution that accompanied the shift from craft production to mass production.

Not included in the first edition of this bibliography was the introduction of scientific management and its reception by factory workers. Hugh Aitken's classic, *Taylorism at Watertown Arsenal* (384), is the foremost book on this subject. Taylor's own thoughts on *Scientific Management* (493) should also be examined.

STEEL AND THE TECHNOLOGY OF WAR. Johannes R. Lischka's article on "Armor Plate" (449) in Cooling (406) offers a starting point for a broader study of the relationship between the American steel companies and the requirements for steel artillery pieces and steel armor. Several excellent contemporary sources exist for such a study (387, 388, 389, 434, 467), as well as more recent examinations (391, 398, 430, 444, 462, 502). A companion topic would be the examination of the resistance to technological change in this field. Using Smith (484) as a model, one could investigate the "persistence of old techniques," as exemplified by Lance Buhl (401), Charles Harley (427), and James Mak and Gary Walton (454). Professional attitudes toward the introduction of unconventional technology (e.g., the submarine) is the major theme of Alex Roland's *Underwater Warfare in the Age of Sail* (471), which is the published version of his dissertation (368). Stephen Shepard provides us with a comparative view in "The Introduction of Steam Technology in the French Navy, 1818–1852" (469). A reprint of John Fitch's autobiography (464) can be read in conjunction with these as a tale of woe and a classic example of the inventor's lament of the rocky road trod by those who introduce new technological concepts.

SUGGESTIONS FOR FURTHER RESEARCH. The more deeply one explores science, technology, and their relationship to the military institutions of the nineteenth century, the more obvious it becomes that in spite of all the research that has been done in this field there are still many opportunities for more work. I. B. Holley, Jr., of the Duke University History Department, noted that a brief review of the entries in this bibliography and the earlier edition illuminated some interesting gaps in research. Some possible areas for work include:

1. Military surveying, cartography, and related contributions to the topographic sciences by the U.S. Army Corps of Engineers.

2. Breeding of horses and mules for the army and the growth of veterinary medicine in the U.S.

3. Preventive maintenance for military equipment, from mules to muskets, a thought inspired by John Speedy's dissertation, "From Mules to Motors: Development of Maintenance Doctrine for Motor Vehicles by the U.S. Army, 1896-1918" (487).

4. Studies that examine certain technologies—food canning, horseshoeing, harness making, musket making, sail making—within the context of the impact military needs had on those industries.

5. The art and technology of fortification and the impact of new weapons on the construction of forts. Arthur Wade's "Artillerists and Engineers'" (501) introduces this topic, and Willard Robinson pursues it from an architectural point of view (470).

BIBLIOGRAPHY

384. Aitken, Hugh G. J. *Taylorism at Watertown Arsenal; Scientific Management in Action, 1908-1915*. Cambridge: Harvard University Press, 1960.

385. Allen, Milford F. "United States Government Exploring Expeditions and Natural History, 1800-1840." Ph.D. dissertation, University of Texas, 1958.

386. Allin, Lawrence Carroll. "The United States Naval Institute: Intellectual Forum of the New Navy: 1873-1889." Ph.D. dissertation, University of Maine, 1976. University microfilm no. 76-28670.

387. American Iron and Steel Association. *Statistics of the American and Foreign Iron Trade ... Annual Statistical Report of the American Iron and Steel Association . . . 1868, 1871-1911*. Philadelphia: American Iron and Steel Association, 1868-1911.

388. American Iron and Steel Association, comp. *History of the Manufacture of Armor Plate for the United States Navy December 1, 1899*. Philadelphia: American Iron and Steel Association, 1899.

389. American Society of Naval Architects and Marine Engineers. *Historical Transactions, 1893-1943*.

390. Armstrong, David A. "The Endless Experiment: The United States Army and the Machine Gun." Ph.D. dissertation, Duke University, 1976. University microfilm no. 76-18940.

391. Basiuk, Victor. "The Differential Impact of Technological Change on the Great Powers, 1870-1914: The Case of Steel." Ph.D. dissertation, Columbia University, 1956.

392. Battison, Edwin A. *Muskets to Mass Production*. Windsor, Vt.: American Precision Museum, 1976.

393. Battison, Edwin A. "A New Look at the Whitney Milling Machine." *Technology and Culture* 14 (October 1973): 592-98.

394. Beaver, Daniel R. "The Problem of American Military Supply, 1890-1920." In *War, Business and American Society: Historical Perspectives on the Military-Industrial Complex,* edited by B. Franklin Cooling, pp. 73-92. Port Washington, N.Y.: Kennikat Press, 1977.

395. Belonzi, Arthur A. "Roger Burlingame, 1889-1967: Historian." Ph.D. dissertation, St. John's University, 1975. University microfilm no. 76-2968.

396. Beskrovnyi, L. G. *Russkaya armii i flot v XIX veke: Voennoekonomichesky potensial Rossi* [The Russian army and navy in the nineteenth century: The military-economic potential of Russia]. Moscow: Izdatel'stvo "Nauka," 1973.

397. Blackmore, Howard L. "Colt's London Armoury." In *Technological Change: The United States and Britain in the Nineteenth Century,* edited by S.B. Saul, pp. 171-95. London: Methuen, 1970.

398. Brandt, Walter I. "Steel and the New Navy, 1882-1895." Ph.D. dissertation, University of Wisconsin, 1920.

399. Brodhead, Michael J. *A Soldier-Scientist in the American Southwest: Being a Narrative of the Travels of Brevet Captain Elliot Coues, Assistant Surgeon, U.S.A. . . ., 1864-1865.* Tucson: Arizona Historical Society, 1973.

400. Brooke, George M., Jr. "John Mercer Brooke, Naval Scientist." Ph.D. dissertation, University of North Carolina, 1955.

401. Buhl, Lance C. "Mariners and Machines: Resistance to Technological Change in the American Navy, 1865-1869." *Journal of American History* 61 (December 1974): 703-27.

402. Cesari, Gene S. "American Arms-Making Machine Tool Development, 1789-1855." Ph.D. dissertation, University of Pennsylvania, 1970. University microfilm no. 70-25663.

403. Chandler, Alfred D., Jr. *The Visible Hand: The Managerial Revolution in American Business.* Cambridge: Harvard University Press, 1977.

404. Clark, Paul Wilson, "Major General George Owen Squier: Military Scientist." Ph.D. dissertation, Case Western Reserve University, 1974. University microfilm no. 74-16480.

405. Cooling, B. Franklin. *Benjamin Franklin Tracy: Father of the Modern American Fighting Navy.* Hamden,Conn.: Archon Books, 1973.

406. Cooling, B. Franklin, ed. *War, Business and American Society: Historical Perspectives on the Military-Industrial Complex.* Port Washington, N.Y.: Kennikat Press, 1977.

407. Craig, Hardin, Jr. *A Bibliography of Encyclopedias and Dictionaries Dealing with Military, Naval and Maritime Affairs, 1517-1971.* 4th ed. Houston: Rice University History Dept., 1971.

408. Cromwell, Giles. *The Virginia Manufactory of Arms.* Charlottesville, Va.: University of Virginia Press, 1975.

409. Crouch, Tom D. "To Ride the Fractious Horse: The American Aeronautical Community and the Problem of Heavier-than-Air Flight, 1875-1905." Ph.D. dissertation, Ohio State University, 1976. University microfilm no. 76-17978.

410. Demeritt, Dwight B. *Maine Made Guns and Their Makers.* Maine Heritage Series, no. 2. Hallowell, Maine: Maine State Museum, 1973.

411. Detlefsen, Ellen Gay. "Printing in the Confederacy, 1861–1865: A Southern Industry in Wartime." Ph.D. dissertation, Columbia University, 1975. University microfilm no. 78-04357.

412. Duffy, Christopher. *Fire and Stone: The Science of Fortress Warfare: 1660–1860.* New York: Hippocrene, 1975.

413. Eillis, John. *A Social History of the Machine Gun.* New York: Pantheon Books, 1975.

414. Ezell, Edward C. "James Henry Burton et le trasfert du 'système américain' aux arsenaux du gouvernement impérial russe." *Le Musée d'Armes* 5 (June 1977): 13–20. Translation of "James Henry Burton and the Transfer of the 'American System' to the Armories of the Imperial Russian Government." Paper read at 20th Anniversary Conference of the Hagley Program, Eleutherian Mills, Hagley Foundation, University of Delaware, 1975.

415. Faulk, Odie B. *The U.S. Camel Corps: An Army Experiment.* Oxford: Oxford University Press, 1976.

416. Fitch, Charles H. "Rise of a Mechanical Ideal." *Magazine of American History* 11 (June 1884): 516–27.

417. Floud, Roderick. *The British Machine Tool Industry, 1850–1914.* London: Cambridge University Press, 1976.

418. Fox, Frank W. "The Genesis of American Technology, 1790–1860: An Essay in Long-Range Perspective." *American Studies* 17 (fall 1976): 29–48.

419. Fries, Russell I. "British Response to the American System: The Case of the Small-Arms Industry after 1850." *Technology and Culture* 16 (July 1975): 377–403.

420. Fries, Russell I. "A Comparative Study of the British and American Arms Industries, 1790–1890." Ph.D. dissertation, Johns Hopkins University, 1972. University microfilm no. 76-8485.

421. Gaier, Claude. *Belgian Gunmaking and American History; One of Belgium's Official Bicentennial Projects.* Liege: E. Wahle [ca. 1976].

422. Gaier, Claude. *Four Centuries of Liege Gunmaking.* F. J. Norris, trans. London: Sotheby Parke Bernet, 1976.

423. Gilbert, K. R. "The Ames Recessing Machine: A Survivor of the Original Enfield Rifle Machinery." *Technology and Culture* 4 (1963): 207–11.

424. Gill, Harold B., Jr. *The Gunsmith in Colonial Virginia.* Charlottesville, Va.: University of Virginia Press, 1973.

425. Guinn, Gilbert Sumter. "Coastal Defense of the Confederate Atlantic Seaboard States, 1861–1862: A Study in Political and Military Mobilization." Ph.D. dissertation, University of South Carolina, 1973. University microfilm no. 74-16183.

426. Hall, Robert H. *Catalogue of the Library, U.S. Military Academy, West Point, N. Y.* Newburgh, N.Y.: Charles Jannicky, Steam Book and Job Printer, 1876.

427. Harley, Charles K. "On the Persistence of Old Techniques: The Case of North American Wooden Shipbuilding." *Journal of Economic History* 33 (June 1973): 372–98.

428. Hartzler, Daniel D. *Arms Makers of Maryland.* York, Pa.: Shumway, 1975.

498.   Uselding, Paul J. *Studies in the Technological Development of the American Economy during the First Half of the Nineteenth Century.* New York: Arno Press, 1975.

499.   Uselding, Paul J. "Studies of Technology in Economic History." In *Recent Developments in the Study of Business and Economic History: Essays in Memory of Herman E. Kroos,* edited by Robert Gallman, pp. 159–219. Greenwich, Conn.: JAI Press, 1977.

500.   Uselding, Paul J. "Technical Progress at the Springfield Armory, 1820–1850." *Explorations in Economic History* 9 (spring 1972): 291–316.

501.   Wade, Arthur Pearson. "Artillerists and Engineers: The Beginnings of American Seacoast Fortifications, 1794–1815." Ph.D. dissertation, Kansas State University, 1977. University microfilm no. 77-18616.

502.   Wall, Joseph F. *Andrew Carnegie.* Oxford: Oxford University Press, 1970.

VIII

THE MEXICAN WAR AND THE CIVIL WAR

Grady McWhiney

There are good reaons to consider the sources on the military history of the Mexican War and the Civil War together. In many ways the Mexican War was, as one writer called it, a rehearsal for conflict. It was more than that, of course, and anyone who examines it from such a limited perspective is likely to miss much of importance. On the other hand, it would be equally shortsighted to ignore the relationship between these two wars. There was much continuity despite significant differences. What young Americans saw and did in Mexico in 1846-47 strongly influenced the way they fought each other in 1861-65. Indeed, many of the Union and Confederate officers who led large bodies of men in the Civil War learned much of what they knew about combat in Mexico. This continuity also extends to some of the sources. Many collections of primary material that are useful in studying one war are also valuable in studying the other. This is true not only of certain unpublished papers, but also of some published material as well—especially biographies, letters, and memoirs.

GENERAL WORKS. Since the first edition of this guide appeared, only one general account of the Mexican War and one of the Civil War have been published in which military activities are given more than nominal attention. *To Conquer a Peace* (414) by John E. Weems is a readable volume that devotes considerable space to the major campaigns of the war between Mexico and the United States, and focuses on ten principal characters—James K. Polk, Antonio Lopez de Santa Anna, Robert E. Lee, Ulysses S. Grant, John C. Frémont, Samuel G. French, Ethan Allen Hitchcock, John T. Hughes (a cavalry volunteer), Joseph Warren Revere (a naval lieutenant), and Ephraim Kirby Smith. Shelby Foote's three-volume narrative history of the Civil War (380), though undocumented and written only from printed sources, is an impressive achievement. In comprehensiveness and dramatic presentation, it ranks with Bruce Catton's *Centennial History of the Civil War.*

POLICY AND STRATEGY. There is still no comprehensive treatment of Mexican War or Civil War strategy, but two recent works focus on Union policy and strategy. In *Combined Operations in the Civil War* (402), Rowena Reed argues that Union leaders after McClellan failed to exploit their naval supremacy and made no use of their earlier captured coastal bases. Michael C.

C. Adams insists in a speculation on Union military failure in the East (363) that northerners had an "inferiority complex" that "handicapped the North in realizing its military potential."

BIOGRAPHIES. Though there are no new books on Mexican War leaders, several prominent Civil War participants have been the subjects of recent studies. Perhaps the most controversial of these is Thomas L. Connelly's *The Marble Man* (370), an analysis of Robert E. Lee's generalship, a psychobiography, and an account of the generally successful effort to canonize Lee after the war. Herman Hattaway has produced the first detailed biography of the Confederacy's youngest lieutenant general, Stephen D. Lee (387), who served in both the eastern and the western armies. Gen. Henry Jackson Hunt, the Army of the Potomac's chief of artillery and the man whose guns checked the Confederates at Gettysburg, is the hero of a volume by Edward G. Longacre (397). *Colonel Grenfell's Wars* (409) is Stephen Z. Starr's engrossing account of an English soldier of fortune who made contributions to Confederate cavalry operations. Charles M. Cummings has written a balanced, readable account of Confederate Gen. Bushrod R. Johnson, a military mediocrity (373). *Joseph Jones, M.D.* by James O. Breeden (367) is a study of a research scientist for the Confederate army's medical department who visited the major armies, hospitals, and prisoner-of-war camps and studied the most important diseases.

CAMPAIGNS AND BATTLES. Several useful works on various military operations have been published recently. William C. Davis has written excellent accounts of First Bull Run and New Market (376, 377). Two books—one by Wiley Sword (410) and another by James L. McDonough (400)—have appeared on Shiloh. Though neither offers much that is new, they competently review the events and controversies. McDonough does a better job than Sword of integrating the battle into the war as a whole. Lumir F. Buresh has published a detailed account of the battle of Mine Creek, the only formal action between Union and Confederate forces in Kansas (369). Civil War raiders are treated in two books. *Yankee Blitzkrieg* by James P. Jones (391) is an extensively researched account of Union Gen. James H. Wilson's raid through Alabama and Georgia in 1865—"the largest cavalry force mounted during the Civil War." *Mounted Raids* by Edward G. Longacre (396), which includes a good essay on cavalry theory and practice, examines twelve raids, but fails to assess their military value. The defense system of Washington, D.C., a neglected aspect of the war, is treated in *Symbol, Sword, and Shield* by B. Franklin Cooling (371). Marion B. Lucas deals with a narrow but carefully researched subject in *Sherman and the Burning of Columbia* (398).

SPECIAL STUDIES. Two recent works on the Confederacy are of interest to military historians. Emory M. Thomas's excellent synthesis of recent scholarship, *The Confederate Nation* (412), devotes considerable attention to military afairs; and Paul D. Escott's study of Jefferson Davis and southern nationalism (379) provides a good overview of the Confederacy's internal problems, including conscription and impressment.

Rank and File (405), a collection of essays in honor of Bell I. Wiley, contains useful pieces on Civil War military topics by James I. Robertson, Jr.; Richard M. McMurry; Willard E. Wight; and Michael Dougan.

Civil War units are receiving more attention than previously. *North Carolina Troops,* by Weymouth T. Jordan, Jr., and Louis H. Manarin (392), is the best state roster of Civil War soldiers ever published. So far seven of a projected thirteen volumes have appeared. Martin H. Hall's study of the Confederate army in New Mexico (385) supplements his work on Sibley's New Mexico campaign by giving extensive biographical essays on the commanders and their commands through the company level. *Yankee Artillerymen* by John W. Rowell (406) is an account of the Eighteenth Indiana Light Artillery Battery from 1862 to 1865, and is based upon the usual official documents as well as letters, journals, and material of seventeen members of the unit. Leslie Anders's history of the Twenty-first Missouri Regiment (364), though it contains no notes, is of considerable value because of sound research on the unit's personnel. Charles T. Loehr's account of the First Virginia Infantry Regiment (395) is based on the author's war diary and recollections as a member of that unit. Robert K. Krick's *Parker's Virginia Battery* (394), a meticulously researched book, is a scholarly treatment of an artillery unit.

Covert operations are covered in a reasonably well-documented account of Confederate military intelligence by John Bakeless (365), and in Oscar A. Kinchen's exciting treatment of Confederate operations in Canada and the North (393) that describes plans to raid cities around the Great Lakes, to free Confederate prisoners, to burn New York City, and to separate the West from the Union.

Ordnance is the subject of Carl L. Davis's informed and valuable book on Union small arms (374), a previously neglected topic, and Warren Ripley's work on artillery and ammunition (403), a curious volume that neglects as much as it explains but is nevertheless useful.

Two volumes by William A. Frassanito deal with photographs made on the battlefields of Gettysburg and Antietam, and of the soldiers who died there (382, 381).

PRINTED PRIMARY SOURCES. *The Papers of Jefferson Davis* (375) and *The Papers of Ulysses S. Grant* (384) are the two most important editing projects relating to Civil War military history now under way. Two volumes of Davis's papers, through July 1846, are available, and another is in press; six volumes of Grant's papers, through 8 December 1862, have appeared. All of these volumes are carefully edited and indispensable for an understanding of their subjects and the war.

The Southern Historical Society Papers (404), recently reissued, are a treasure house of letters, recollections, and other documents on Confederate military affairs. The usefulness of these volumes has been enhanced tremendously by a comprehensive index, never before available. That was prepared under the direction of James I. Robertson, Jr.

Two useful works on the Mexican War and the period immediately thereafter are the war diary of Thomas D. Tennery (411), which reveals some of the hardships of army life faced by an Illinois volunteer who was wounded at Cerro Gordo; and Col. George A. McCall's account of New Mexico in 1850 (399), which contained the most comprehensive information available at the time to the War Department on population, economic life, military activities, and Indian problems.

Civil War diaries and collections of letters continue to be published. Some of the better recent publications include: the delightful journal of Robert M. Holmes, a private in the Twenty-fourth Mississippi Volunteers (389); the diary of Jedediah Hotchkiss, Stonewall Jackson's topographer (390); Felix P. Poché's diary, one of the best kept by a Louisianian during the war (401); the letters of George Washington Whitman, the brother of Walt Whitman, who served in the Union army and was captured (415); the papers of Franklin A. Haskell, which include thirty letters or essays besides his classic account of Gettysburg (386); the diary of Rice C. Bull, a New Yorker who was wounded at Chancellorsville and later served with Sherman's forces in Georgia and the Carolinas (368); the diary of Catherine Ann Devereux Edmondston, "a Secesh Lady," whose journal is neither as interesting nor as important as Mrs. Chesnut's *Diary from Dixie,* but is nevertheless an extremely valuable document (378); the letters of J. F. Culver, a literate and observant Illinois soldier who participated in Sherman's campaigns (372); and John Good's seventy-five letters, the views of an officer in the First Texas Artillery on operations in Arkansas and the battle at Pea Ridge (383).

Useful compilations of documents and memoirs are: Charles Spurlin's excellent collection of records on the Thirteenth Texas Cavalry Battalion, including brief biographies of its officers, muster rolls and service records of its members, and a diary covering some of its operations (408); the reissue of Louisianian Willie H. Tunnard's recollections of service in the trans-Mississippi theater (413); the unique memoir of Alfred Bellard, a New Jersey volunteer, that combines prose with the author's colorful drawings of life and death in the Union army (366); the memoirs of mediocre Confederate Gen. Henry Heth that are full of stories about Indians, life in the old army, and such figures as Scott, Lee, Grant, Davis, Hancock, and Burnside (388); and the reminiscences of George B. Sanford, a Connecticut Yankee, which contain valuable glimpses of Sherman and Sheridan (407).

SUGGESTIONS FOR FURTHER RESEARCH. In an earlier edition of this guide it was suggested that much work remained to be done on the military history of both the Mexican War and the Civil War. That is still true, though fewer obvious gaps remain unfilled. The Mexican War continues to be a relatively neglected field. Besides biographies of such leaders as John A. Quitman, Persifor F. Smith, and a fresh study of Winfield Scott, more detailed examinations of operations and tactics would add to our understanding of that conflict. Civil War Gen. Don Carlos Buell deserves a biography, and better studies of Generals Philip H. Sheridan and James Longstreet are needed. Staff studies and analyses of military administration have been neglected too long. A call for more unit histories and accounts of battles and campaigns has been partly answered, but the history of many brigades and regiments as well as of several significant campaigns and battles in both the Mexican War and the Civil War need to be written or rewritten. To be worthwhile, such studies should combine exhaustive research in the published and unpublished sources with the techniques of quantification and the insights and concerns of the social and military historian.

BIBLIOGRAPHY

363. Adams, Michael C. C. *Our Masters the Rebels: A Speculation on Union Military Failure in the East, 1861-1865.* Cambridge: Harvard University Press, 1978.

364. Anders, Leslie. *The Twenty-first Missouri: From Home Guard to Union Regiment.* Contributions in Military History, No. 11. Westport, Conn.: Greenwood Press, 1975.

365. Bakeless, John. *Spies of the Confederacy.* Philadelphia: Lippincott, 1970.

366. Bellard, Alfred. *Gone for a Soldier: The Civil War Memoirs of Private Alfred Bellard.* Edited by David H. Donald. Boston: Little, Brown, 1975.

367. Breeden, James O. *Joseph Jones, M.D.: Scientist of the Old South.* Lexington: University Press of Kentucky, 1975.

368. Bull, Rice C. *Soldiering: The Civil War Diary of Rice C. Bull, 123rd New York Volunteer Infantry.* Edited by K. Jack Bauer. San Rafael, Calif.: Presidio Press, 1977.

369. Buresh, Lumir F. *October 25th and the Battle of Mine Creek.* Edited by Dan L. Smith. Kansas City, Mo.: The Lowell Press, 1977.

370. Connelly, Thomas Lawrence. *The Marble Man: Robert E. Lee and His Image in American Society.* New York: Alfred A. Knopf, 1977.

371. Cooling, B. Franklin. *Symbol, Sword, and Shield: Defending Washington During the Civil War.* Hamden, Conn.: Archon Books, 1975.

372. Culver, J. F. *"Your Affectionate Husband, J. F. Culver": Letters Written During the Civil War.* Edited by Leslie W. Dunlap. Iowa City, Iowa: Friends of the University of Iowa Libraries, 1978.

373. Cummings, Charles M. *Yankee Quaker Confederate General: The Curious Career of Bushrod Rust Johnson.* Rutherford, N.J.: Fairleigh Dickinson University Press, 1971.

374. Davis, Carl L. *Arming the Union: Small Arms in the Civil War.* Port Washington, N.Y.: Kennikat Press, 1973.

375. Davis, Jefferson. *The Papers of Jefferson Davis. Vol. 1, 1808-1840,* edited by Haskell M. Monroe, Jr., and James T. McIntosh. *Vol. 2, June 1841-July 1846,* edited by James T. McIntosh. 2 vols. to date. Baton Rouge: Louisiana State University Press, 1971–

376. Davis, William C. *Battle at Bull Run: A History of the First Major Campaign of the Civil War.* Garden City, N.Y.: Doubleday, 1977.

377. Davis, William C. *The Battle of New Market.* Garden City, N.Y.: Doubleday, 1975.

378. Edmondston, Catherine A. D. *"Journal of a Secesh Lady": The Diary of Catherine Ann Devereux Edmondston, 1860-1866.* Edited by Beth G. Crabtree and James W. Patton. Raleigh: North Carolina Division of Archives and History, 1979.

379. Escott, Paul D. *After Secession: Jefferson Davis and the Failure of Confederate Nationalism.* Baton Rouge: Louisiana State University Press, 1977.

380. Foote, Shelby. *The Civil War: A Narrative.* 3 vols. New York: Random House, 1958-74.

381. Frassanito, William A. *Antietam: The Photographic Legacy of America's Bloodiest Day.* New York: Scribner's, 1978.
382. Frassanito, William A. *Gettysburg: A Journey in Time.* New York: Scribner's, 1975.
383. Good, John J. *Cannon Smoke: The Letters of Captain John J. Good, Good-Douglas-Texas Battery, CSA.* Compiled and edited by Lester Newton Fitzhugh. Hillsboro, Tex.: Hill Junior College Press, 1971.
384. Grant, Ulysses S. *The Papers of Ulysses S. Grant.* Edited by John Y. Simon. 6 vols. to date. Carbondale: Southern Illinois University Press, 1967–
385. Hall, Martin Hardwick, with the assistance of Sam Long. *The Confederate Army of New Mexico.* Austin: Presidial Press, 1978.
386. Haskell, Franklin A. *Haskell of Gettysburg, His Life and Civil War Papers.* Edited by Frank L. Byrne and Andrew T. Weaver. Madison: State Historical Society of Wisconsin, 1970.
387. Hattaway, Herman. *General Stephen D. Lee.* Jackson: University Press of Mississippi, 1976.
388. Heth, Henry. *The Memoirs of Henry Heth.* Edited by James L. Morrison, Jr. Contributions in Military History, no. 6. Westport, Conn.: Greenwood Press, 1974.
389. Holmes, Robert Masten. *Kemper County Rebel: The Civil War Diary of Robert Masten Holmes, C.S.A.* Edited by Frank Allen Dennis. Jackson: University Press of Mississippi, 1973.
390. Hotchkiss, Jedediah. *Make Me a Map of the Valley: The Civil War Journal of Stonewall Jackson's Topographer.* Edited by Archie P. McDonald. Dallas: Southern Methodist University Press, 1973.
391. Jones, James Pickett. *Yankee Blitzkrieg: Wilson's Raid through Alabama and Georgia.* Athens: University of Georgia Press, 1976.
392. Jordan, Weymouth T., Jr., and Louis H. Manarin. *North Carolina Troops, 1861–1865: A Roster.* 7 vols. to date. Raleigh: State Department of Archives and History, 1966–
393. Kinchen, Oscar A. *Confederate Operations in Canada and the North: A Little-known Phase of the American Civil War.* North Quincy, Mass.: Christopher, 1970.
394. Krick, Robert K. *Parker's Virginia Battery, C.S.A.* Berryville, Va.: Virginia Book Company, 1975.
395. Loehr, Charles T. *War History of the Old First Virginia Infantry Regiment, Army of Northern Virginia.* Dayton, Ohio: Morningside Bookshop, 1970.
396. Longacre, Edward G. *Mounted Raids of the Civil War.* New York: A. S. Barnes, 1975.
397. Longacre, Edward G. *The Man Behind the Guns: A Biography of General Henry Jackson Hunt, Chief of Artillery, Army of the Potomac.* New York: A. S. Barnes, 1977.
398. Lucas, Marion B. *Sherman and the Burning of Columbia.* College Station: Texas A & M University Press, 1976.
399. McCall, George A. *New Mexico in 1850: A Military View.* Edited by Robert W. Frazer. Norman: University of Oklahoma Press, 1968.
400. McDonough, James Lee. *Shiloh—In Hell Before Night.* Knoxville: University of Tennessee Press, 1977.

401. Poché, Felix P. *Louisana Confederate: Diary of Felix Pierre Poché* Edited by Edwin C. Bearss. Translated by Eugenie W. Somdal. Natchitoches: Louisiana Studies Institute, Northwestern State University, 1972.

402. Reed, Rowena. *Combined Operations in the Civil War.* Annapolis: Naval Institute Press, 1978.

403. Ripley, Warren. *Artillery and Ammunition of the Civil War.* New York: Van Nostrand Reinhold, 1970.

404. Robertson, James I., Jr., ed. *Southern Historical Society Papers* and *Index-Guide to the Southern Historical Society Papers, 1876–1959.* 30 vols. to date. Millwood, N.Y.: Kraus, 1977–

405. Robertson, James I., Jr., and Richard M. McMurry, eds. *Rank and File: Civil War Essays in Honor of Bell Irvin Wiley.* San Rafael, Calif.: Presidio Press, 1976.

406. Rowell, John W. *Yankee Artillerymen: Through the Civil War with Eli Lilly's Indiana Battery.* Knoxville: University of Tennessee Press, 1975.

407. Sanford, George B. *Fighting Rebels and Redskins: Experiences in Army Life of Colonel George B. Sanford, 1861–1892.* Edited by E. R. Hagemann. Norman: University of Oklahoma Press, 1969.

408. Spurlin, Charles, ed. *West of the Mississippi with Weller's 13th Texas Cavalry Battalion, C.S.A.* Hillsboro, Tex.: Hill Junior College Press, 1971.

409. Starr, Stephen Z. *Colonel Grenfell's Wars: The Life of a Soldier of Fortune.* Baton Rouge: Louisiana State University Press, 1971.

410. Sword, Wiley, *Shiloh: Bloody April.* New York: William Morrow, 1974.

411. Tennery, Thomas D. *The Mexican War Diary of Thomas D. Tennery.* Edited by D. E. Livingston-Little. Norman: University of Oklahoma Press, 1970.

412. Thomas, Emory M. *The Confederate Nation, 1861–1865.* New York: Harper and Row, 1979.

413. Tunnard, Willie H. *A Soldier's Record: The Story of the 3rd Louisiana Infantry, C.S.A.* Edited by Edwin S. Bearss. Dayton, Ohio: Morningside Bookshop, 1970.

414. Weems, John Edward. *To Conquer a Peace: The War Between the United States and Mexico.* Garden City, N.Y.: Doubleday, 1974.

415. Whitman, George Washington. *Civil War Letters of George Washington Whitman.* Edited by Jerome M. Loving. Durham: Duke University Press, 1975.

IX

CIVIL-MILITARY RELATIONS, OPERATIONS,
AND THE ARMY, 1865-1917

Richard N. Ellis

The past several years have been marked by continued interest in the role of the army from 1865 to 1917, and a number of useful, scholarly works have appeared. These publications demonstrate the depth of interest by scholars and by the general public in the history of the frontier army, but they also reflect new interests as well. The increase of publications about the Spanish-American War, which became evident during the early 1970s, has continued, and a number of military biographies have appeared.

If we are to judge from the number of publications relating to the Indian-fighting army, it is probably safe to conclude that this topic will be of enduring interest, but while there have been studies of engagements with Indian tribes, there have also been new approaches to the study of the frontier army. This is particularly true of works relating to George Armstrong Custer and the battle of the Little Big Horn. Michael Sievers (324) has made a fresh study of the literature relating to that battle, but more significant are Brian W. Dippie's *Custer's Last Stand: The Anatomy of an American Myth* (295) and Bruce A. Rosenberg's *Custer and the Epic of Defeat* (323). Both analyze the development of the Custer myth, and Rosenberg in particular makes comparisons to epic myths in world literature.

New approaches can be seen in other books and articles. *Life and Manners in the Frontier Army* by Oliver Knight (314) is based largely upon the fiction of Clarence King, who had served in the army and was a prolific novelist. Marvin Kroeker's biography of William Hazen (315) does shed light on Hazen's views of the West, but unfortunately does not deal with other important aspects of his career. Thompson's *The Army and the Navajo* (329) is a detailed study of army management of the Navajos during their incarceration at Bosque Redondo. In periodical literature Clow (290) has analyzed the impact of the confiscation of Sioux ponies by Philip Sheridan, while others have studied the role of the Department of the Platte in western settlement (303) and the development of Fort Wallace in Kansas (310).

Interest in the frontier army was further shown in the selection of that topic for the seventh military history symposium at the United States Air Force Academy in 1976. The papers, including an overview by Robert Utley (334), dealt with the socializing role of the military (300), the political role of the military (296), enlisted men (336), army women (319), and a comparison of frontier military experiences in Canada and the United States (318).

Minority groups in the army have also attracted attention. Marvin Fletcher studied the black volunteers in the Spanish-American War (299), but more significant is his book, *The Black Soldier and Officer in the United States Army 1891–1971* (298), which describes army racism which can be seen in the army belief that black soldiers needed white officers and the army's attitude that black soldiers in the Brownsville affair were guilty until proven innocent. The history of black soldiers in this period remains a fruitful area for research. American Indian soldiers have been studied by Tate (327) and White (338). Of special importance is *A Night of Violence: The Houston Riot of 1917* by Robert Haynes (304), which involved the Twenty-Fifth Infantry and resulted in lengthy court-martial proceedings and the execution of nineteen soldiers. In this detailed account Haynes concludes that the army had different standards of justice for white officers and black soldiers and that Houston racism, the city administration, and the army were contributing factors in the riot.

While some of the works mentioned above relate to the Spanish-American war, others are more directly involved with that conflict and the years that immediately followed. Crouch describes the role of Frederick Funston during the Cuban Insurrection (294). Graham Cosmas continues his research in this era with an analysis of the army occupation of Cuba from 1898–99 (292), and Hitchman describes public works programs by the military government in Cuba from 1898 to 1902 (307), as does Gilbert (301). Perhaps most provoctive is *The Mirror of War: American Society and the Spanish-American War* by Gerald Linderman, which views the impact of the war on parts of American society and includes a fine essay on the popular press.

While no major publications about the National Guard have appeared, several useful articles on local topics have been published. Peckham describes the police duties of the Ohio National Guard in 1894 (321); Cooper looks at National Guard reform in Wisconsin and the Spanish-American War (291); Brinckerhoff compiled an excellent collection of photographs of the Arizona National Guard (289); and James Hudson (309) also describes the activities of the California National Guard during the San Francisco earthquake and fire in 1906. Several recent dissertations on the National Guard also should lead to future publications.

There are a variety of new publications dealing with domestic functions of the army between 1865 and 1919. Fischer's "Horse Soldiers in the Arctic" (297) deals with the Garlington expedition of 1883, a unique episode in cavalry history where mounted troops were involved in attempts to rescue the Greely expedition to Ellesmere Island. More attention has also focused on the history of the Army Corps of Engineers. Cowdrey (293) describes the early relationship of the corps to environmental law. A number of the district histories that were written for the corps have also appeared. Among those that have significant portions relating to the years from 1865 to 1917 are histories of the Louisville (311), Rock Island (331), New England (320), Galveston (287), and New York (313) districts. Others should be forthcoming.

Disparate topics in the period from 1900 to 1917 have been covered by several authors. Tyler (333) describes an expedition into Mexico in the Big Bend region in 1916, and Turcheneske (330) analyzes the role of the army and others in decisions regarding the Chiricahua Apache prisoners of war. Gilmore (302) looks at rifles; Howell (308) describes army headgear; Steffen (325) describes saddles; and Powers and Younger (322) discuss treatment of cholera in the West in the 1860s.

Administrative history also attracted scholarly attention. In *From Root to McNamara: Army Organization and Administration* (305), James Hewes looks at army management in central headquarters but only a small portion is devoted to pre-1917. Hewes covers that period in an administrative history of the General Staff (306), in which he argues that efforts made to reform the War Department were similar to those in industry that created the modern corporation. Weigley presents a thoughtful analysis in "Elihu Root, Reformers, and the Progressive Era" (337), and Thomas looks at Ambrose E. Burnside and army reform (328).

Three important biographies shed light on a broader period. Heath Twichell's *Allen: The Biography of an Army Officer, 1859-1930* (332) is a biography of Henry Allen (who served in the Philippines and commanded the Philippine constabulary, pursued Villa, and led a major exploring expedition in Alaska), and the author shows army professionalism and also army involvement in affairs that were not purely military. *The General* by Allan R. Millett (317) is a biography of Robert L. Bullard, whose career provides a vehicle for describing the growth of professionalism in the army. Frank E. Vandiver's two-volume biography of John Pershing (335) is outstanding and effectively deals with the man and his times. It is essential for a study of this period.

SUGGESTIONS FOR FURTHER RESEARCH. Despite continued work in this period there are ample opportunities for further research. A new history of the Spanish-American War that utilizes Spanish and Cuban sources is still needed, and a number of officers still await modern critical biographies. The role of Indian allies and Indian soldiers has been touched upon but has not been explored in sufficient depth. While a number of recent works have appeared on the Corps of Engineers, more needs to be done. Other potential topics include military justice, weaponry, recruitment, army life, the enlisted man, and the impact of the army on the economy. Work under way by Darlis Miller on the impact of the army upon the economy of the Southwest between 1865 and 1900 will be of considerable use and may stimulate additional work in that area.

BIBLIOGRAPHY

287. Alperin, Lynn M. *Custodians of the Coast: History of the United States Army Engineers at Galveston.* Galveston: Galveston District, 1977.

288. Berry, Mary F. *Military Necessity and Civil Rights Policy: Black Citizenship and the Constitution, 1861-1868.* Port Washington, N. Y.: Kennikat Press, 1977.

289. Brinckerhoff, Sidney B. "Not Without Glory: The Arizona National Guard in Photographs." *Journal of Arizona History* 16 (1975): 161-70.

290. Clow, Richmond. "General Philip Sheridan's Legacy: The Sioux Pony Campaign of 1876." *Nebraska History* 57 (1976): 461–77.

291. Cooper, Jerry M. "National Guard Reform, the Army, and the Spanish-American War: The View from Wisconsin." *Military Affairs* 42 (1978): 20–23.

292. Cosmas, Graham A. "Securing the Fruits of Victory: The U. S. Army Occupies Cuba, 1898–1899." *Military Affairs* 38 (1974): 85–91.

293. Cowdrey, Albert E. "Pioneering Environmental Law: The Army Corps of Engineers and the Refuse Act." *Pacific Historical Review* 46 (1977): 331–49.

294. Crouch, Thomas W. *A Yankee Guerrillo: Frederick Funston and the Cuban Insurrection, 1896–1897.* Memphis: Memphis State University Press, 1975.

295. Dippie, Brian W. *Custer's Last Stand: The Anatomy of an American Myth.* Missoula, Mont.: University of Montana Press, 1976.

296. Ellis, Richard N. "The Political Role of the Military." In *The American Military on the Frontier,* edited by James P. Tate. Washington, D.C.: Office of Air Force History, 1978.

297. Fischer, Lawrence J. "Horse Soldiers in the Arctic: The Garlington Expedition of 1883." *American Neptune* 36 (1976): 108–24.

298. Fletcher, Marvin. *The Black Soldier and Officer in the United States Army 1891–1917.* Columbia: University of Missouri Press, 1974.

299. Fletcher, Marvin. "The Black Volunteers in the Spanish-American War." *Military Affairs* 38 (1974): 48–53.

300. Foner, Jack D. "The Socializing Role of the Military." In *The American Military on the Frontier,* edited by James P. Tate. Washington, D.C.: Office of Air Force History, 1978.

301. Gilbert, Howard, Jr. "Military Occupation of Cuba, 1899–1902: Workshop for American Progressivism." *American Quarterly* 26 (1973): 410–25.

302. Gilmore, Russell. "The New Courage: Rifles and Soldier Individualism, 1876–1918." *Military Affairs* 40 (1976): 97–102.

303. Gruentzel, Richard. "The Department of the Platte and Western Settlement 1866–1877." *Nebraska History* 56 (1975): 389–417.

304. Haynes, Robert V. *A Night of Violence: The Houston Riot of 1917.* Baton Rouge: Louisiana State University Press, 1976.

305. Hewes, James E. *From Root to McNamara: Army Organization and Administration, 1900–1963.* Washington, D.C.: Center of Military History, U. S. Army, 1975.

306. Hewes, James. "The United States Army General Staff, 1900–1917." *Military Affairs* 38 (1974): 67–72.

307. Hitchman, James H. "Unfinished Business: Public Works in Cuba, 1898–1902." *Americas* 31 (1975): 335–59.

308. Howell, Edgar M. "United States Army Headgear 1855–1902: Catalog of United States Army Uniforms in the Collections of the Smithsonian Institution, II." *Smithsonian Studies in History and Technology,* no. 30, 1975.

309. Hudson, James. "The California National Guard in the San Francisco Earthquake and Fire of 1906." *California Historical Quarterly* 55 (1976): 137–49.

310. Hurt, R. Douglas. "The Construction and Development of Fort Wallace, Kansas, 1865-1882." *Kansas Historical Quarterly* 43 (1977): 44-55.

311. Johnson, Leland R. *The Falls City Engineers: A History of The Louisville District Corps of Engineers United States Army.* N.p., n.d.

312. Kemble, C. Robert. *The Image of the Army Officer in America: Background For Current Views.* Westport, Conn.: Greenwood Press, 1973.

313. Klawonn, Marion J. *Cradle of the Corps: A History of the New York District U.S. Army Corps of Engineers 1775-1975.* New York: New York District, 1977.

314. Knight, Oliver. *Life and Manners in the Frontier Army.* Norman: University of Oklahoma Press, 1978.

315. Kroeker, Marvin E. *Great Plains Command: William B. Hazen in the Frontier West.* Norman: University of Oklahoma Press, 1976.

316. Linderman, Gerald F. *The Mirror of War: American Society and the Spanish-American War.* Ann Arbor: University of Michigan Press, 1974.

316a. Miller, Darlis A. "Carleton's California Column: A Chapter in New Mexico's Mining History." *New Mexico Historical Review,* 53 (1978): 5-38.

317. Millett, Allan R. *The General: Robert L. Bullard and Officership in the United States Army, 1881-1925.* Westport, Conn.: Greenwood Press, 1975.

318. Morton, Desmond. "Comparison of U.S./Canadian Military Experience on the Frontier." In *The American Military on The Frontier,* edited by James P. Tate. Washington, D.C.: Office of Air Force History, 1978.

319. Myres, Sandra L. "The Ladies of the Army—views of Western Life." In *The American Military on the Frontier,* edited by James P. Tate. Washington, D.C.: Office of Air Force History, 1978.

320. Parkman, Aubrey. *Army Engineers in New England: The Military and Civil Work of the Corps of Engineers in New England 1775-1975.* Waltham, Mass.: New England District, 1978.

321. Peckham, Charles A. "The Ohio National Guard and its Police Duties, 1894." *Ohio History* 83 (1974): 51-67.

322. Powers, Ramon S., and Gene Younger. "Cholera and the Army in the West: Treatment and Control in 1866 and 1867." *Military Affairs* 39 (1975): 49-54.

323. Rosenberg, Bruce A. *Custer and the Epic of Defeat.* University Park, Pa.: The Pennsylvania State University Press, 1974.

324. Sievers, Michael A. "The Literature of the Little Big Horn: A Centennial Historiography." *Arizona and the West* 18 (1976): 149-76.

325. Steffen, Randy. *United States Military Saddles, 1812-1943.* Norman: University of Oklahoma Press, 1973.

326. Stohlman, Robert F., Jr. *The Powerless Position: The Commanding General of the Army of the United States.* Manhattan, Kans.: *Military Affairs,* 1975.

327. Tate, Michael. "Soldiers of the Line: Apache Companies in the U.S. Army 1891-1897." *Arizona and the West* 16 (1974): 343-64.

328. Thomas, Donna. "Ambrose E. Burnside and Army Reform, 1850–1881." *Rhode Island History* 37 (1978): 3–13.

329. Thompson, Gerald. *The Army and the Navajo.* Tucson: University of Arizona Press, 1976.

330. Turcheneske, John T., Jr. "My People Want to be Free: The United States Congress and the Release of the Apache Prisoners of War at Fort Sill." *Chronicles of Oklahoma* 54 (1976): 199–226.

331. Tweet, Roald. *A History of the Rock Island District Corps of Engineers.* Rock Island: Rock Island District, 1975.

332. Twichell, Heath. *Allen: The Biography of an Army Officer, 1859–1930.* New Brunswick, N.J.: Rutgers University Press, 1974.

333. Tyler, Ronnie C. "The Little Punitive Expedition in the Big Bend." *Southwestern Historical Quarterly* 78 (1975): 271–91.

334. Utley, Robert M. "The Contribution of the Frontier to the American Military Tradition." In *The American Military On the Frontier,* edited by James P. Tate. Washington, D.C.: Office of Air Force History, 1978.

335. Vandiver, Frank E. *Black Jack: The Life and Times of John J. Pershing.* 2 vols. College Station: Texas A & M Press, 1977.

336. Walker, Henry P. "The Enlisted Soldier—on the Frontier." In *The American Military on the Frontier,* edited by James P. Tate. Washington, D.C.: Office of Air Force History, 1978.

337. Weigley, Russell. "Elihu Root, Reformers and the Progressive Era." In *Command and Commanders in Modern Warfare,* edited by William Geffen. Washington, D.C.: Office of Air Force History, 1971.

338. White, W. Bruce. "The American Indian as Soldier, 1890–1919." *Canadian Review of American Studies* 7 (1975): 15–25.

X

SCIENCE AND TECHNOLOGY
IN THE TWENTIETH CENTURY

Carroll W. Pursell, Jr.

Introducing the first edition of this bibliographic essay in 1975, I noted that the field of science and technology in the military was still much in need of description and explication. The same, despite the additional citations listed here, can be said today. These additions represent a sampling of the entire literature of the field: the reminiscences of a prominent advisor, Kistiakowsky (271); two studies of specific chemical technologies which were developed for or shaped by the needs of war, DDT (272) and tear gas (265); a look at NACA, a prewar agency (275); the OSRD, the leading agency of World War II (273); and a new investigation of a postwar group, the Research Board for National Security (269). Hardware is represented by an investigation of the electronic battlefield of the Vietnam years (259) and incendiary weapons (278).

One area that is still woefully neglected is the reverse side of this coin—the impact of war on civilian technology. Nuclear technology is a signal case in point, represented here (264) as is our network of interstate highways (267). The fact remains, however, that war-related research and invention might well be the greatest single source of new technologies in our society and little is being done to investigate and explain that phenomenon.

Nevertheless, a corporal's guard of scholars, augmented by the reminiscences and evaluations of people once intimately involved in the process, continue to work at this subject, one of the most rewarding and significant available to the serious historian of our time.

BIBLIOGRAPHY

257. Beard, Edmund. *Developing the ICBM: A Study in Bureaucratic Politics.* New York: Columbia University Press, 1976.

258. Deitchman, Seymour J. *The Best-Laid Schemes: A Tale of Social Research and Bureaucracy.* Cambridge, Mass.: MIT Press, 1976.

259. Dickson, Paul. *The Electronic Battlefield.* Bloomington: Indiana University Press, 1976.

260. Ellis, John. *The Social History of the Machine Gun.* New York: Pantheon Books, 1975.

261. Ezell, Edward C. "Patterns in Small-arms Procurement since 1945: Organization for Development." In *War, Business, and American Society: Historical Perspectives on the Military-Industrial Complex,* edited by Benjamin Franklin Cooling, pp. 146–57. Port Washington, N.Y.: Kennikat Press, 1977.

262. Fishbein, Mayer H. "Archival Remains of Research and Development during the Second World War." In *World War II: An Account of Its Documents,* edited by James E. O'Neill and Robert W. Krauskopf, pp. 163–79. Washington, D.C.: Howard University Press, 1976.

263. Hallion, Richard P. *Legacy of Flight: The Guggenheim Contribution to American Aviation.* Seattle: University of Washington Press, 1977.

264. Hewlett, Richard G. "Beginnings of Development in Nuclear Technology." *Technology and Culture* 17 (July 1976): 465–78.

265. Jones, Daniel P. "From Military to Civilian Technology: The Introduction of Tear Gas for Civil Riot Control." *Technology and Culture* 19 (April 1978): 151–68.

266. Jones, Daniel P. "The Role of Chemists in Research on War Gases in the United States during World War I." Ph.D. dissertation, University of Wisconsin, 1969.

267. Kelly, Thomas E. "The Concrete Road to MIC: National Defense and Federal Highways." In *War, Business, and American Society: Historical Perspectives on the Military-Industrial Complex,* edited by B. Franklin Cooling III, pp. 133–45. Port Washington, N.Y.: Kennikat Press, 1977.

268. Kevles, Daniel J. *The Physicists: The History of a Scientific Community in Modern America.* New York: Alfred A. Knopf, 1978.

269. Kevles, Daniel J. "Scientists, the Military, and the Control of Postwar Defense Research: The Case of the Research Board for National Security." *Technology and Culture* 16 (January 1975): 20–47.

270. Killian, James R., Jr. *Sputnik, Scientists, and Eisenhower: A Memoir of the First Special Assistant to the President for Science and Technology.* Cambridge, Mass.: MIT Press, 1977.

271. Kistiakowsky, George B. *A Scientist in the White House.* Cambridge: Harvard University Press, 1976.

272. Perkins, John H. "Reshaping Technology in Wartime: The Effect of Military Goals on Entomological Research and Insect-Control Practices." *Technology and Culture* 19 (April 1978): 169–86.

273. Pursell, Carroll. "Alternative American Science Policies in the Second World War." In *World War II: An Account of Its Documents,* edited by James E. O'Neill and Robert W. Krauskopf, pp. 151–62. Washington, D.C.: Howard University Press, 1976.

273a. Pursell, Carroll. "Science Agencies in World War II; The ORSD and Its Challengers." In *The Sciences in the American Context: New Perspectives,* edited by Nathan Reingold, pp. 359–78. Washington, D.C.: Smithsonian Institution, 1979.

274. Roland, Alex. *A Guide to Research in NASA History.* 2d ed. Washington, D.C.: History Office, NASA Headquarters, 1977.

275. Roland, Alex. "The National Advisory Committee for Aeronautics." *Aeronautics* 10 (summer 1978): 69–81.

275a. Sapolsky, Harvey M. "Academic Science and the Military. The Years

Since the Second World War." In *The Sciences in the American Context: New Perspectives,* edited by Nathan Reingold, pp. 379-99. Washington, D.C.: Smithsonian Institution, 1979.

276. Science for the People, Madison Wisconsin Collective. *The AMRC Papers: An Indictment of the Army Mathematics Research Center.* Madison: Science for the People, 1973.

277. Smith, Thomas M. "Project Whirlwind: An Unorthodox Development Project." *Technology and Culture* 17 (July 1976): 447-64.

278. Stockholm International Peace Research Institute. *Incendiary Weapons.* Cambridge, Mass.: MIT Press, 1975.

279. Whittemore, Gilbert F., Jr. "World War I, Poison Gas Research, and the Ideals of American Chemists." *Social Studies of Science* 5 (May 1975): 135-63.

280. York, Herbert. *The Advisors: Oppenheimer, Teller, and the Super-bomb.* San Francisco: W. H. Freeman & Co., 1976.

281. York, Herbert F., and G. Allen Greb. "Military Research and Development: A Postwar History." *Bulletin of the Atomic Scientists* 33 (January 1977): 13-22, 24-26.

XI

WORLD WAR I AND THE PEACETIME ARMY, 1917-41

Daniel R. Beaver

There is as yet no comprehensive study of the American army in the twentieth century: nor have any major reinterpretations of American military affairs before the Second World War appeared since the original publication of this essay in 1975. The essential primary sources, available for years, were carefully analyzed in the first volume of this series. Concern about military domination of the state, the "Uptonian-Citizen-Soldier" debate over manpower policy, civil-military relations, the organization of supply and procurement, and the army's role as a vital institution in America continues to dominate the secondary literature. Thus, the great themes remain constant, and recent publications serve to enrich and deepen understanding of the "conventional wisdom" rather than to challenge its validity. There is a new general history of the War Department in the twentieth century. Several excellent biographies of American generals of the Great War have been published, and a number of interesting articles have appeared which illumine further the experience of the American army abroad during the conflict. Other important work has been undertaken by scholars who have sought to link more firmly the history of the army to the broad changes which occurred in American economic and social institutions during and after the war.

BIBLIOGRAPHIES. Three significant selective and topical bibliographies have recently appeared. All are well organized with appropriate comments. They are: Martin Anderson and Valerie Bloom, *Conscription: A Select and Annotated Guide* (251); Gwyn M. Bayliss, *Bibliographical Guide to the Two World Wars: An Annotated Survey of English Language Reference Materials* (253); and Ronald Schaffer, *The U. S. in World War I: A Selected Bibliography* (287). They supplement but do not replace the materials listed in the previous volume.

GENERAL WORKS. Three recent books enhance the understanding of certain interpretive lines in American military affairs. Arthur Meyer Schlesinger, Jr.'s *The Imperial Presidency* (290) explores the growth of the commander-in-chief's power in the twentieth century. James E. Hewes's fine study, *From Root to McNamara* (270), describes the changing relationships between civilian secretaries of war and the soldiers they theoretically command since the creation of the General Staff in 1902. Although not primarily directed

72

toward the American experience, Martin van Creveld's *Supplying War: Logistics from Wallenstein to Patton* (298) should be required reading for any student interested in the problem of military supply. Finally, Alfred D. Chandler's *The Visible Hand* (258), a long-awaited comprehensive study of the modern corporation and American society, adds substantially to an understanding of the linkages between the army and the American business community.

NATIONAL POLICY 1917–41: THE NATION, THE STATES, AND MANPOWER PROCUREMENT. The debate between the "Uptonian professionals" and the "Citizen-Soldiers" continues unabated. A new biography of Leonard Wood, *Armed Progressive* (275) by Jack C. Lane, analyzes Wood's career and particularly his view of a proper manpower policy for the United States. John Gary Clifford's *The Citizen Soldiers* (259), an excellent study of the Plattsburg movement, carries the history of the manpower debate beyond 1920 into the interwar period. John K. Ohl's fine article, "Hugh S. Johnson and the Draft 1917–1918" (285), adds a new dimension to a story previously seen only from the perspective of Provost Marshal Enoch H. Crowder.

NATIONAL POLICY 1917–41: THE PROBLEM OF COMMAND. The relationships between the president (the commander in chief), the secretary of war, and the chief of staff; between the chief of staff and the commanders in the field; and between the chief of staff and the heads of the various War Department bureaus has shaped the discussion of this important issue in American military history. Edward B. Parsons's study, *Wilsonian Diplomacy* (287), adds some support to the view that President Wilson was more active as commander in chief than has been previously stated. Frank E. Vandiver in *Black Jack* (299), a new two-volume biography of John J. Pershing, gives some attention to the relationship of the president to his commander in the field. Vandiver also discusses the conflict between Chief of Staff Peyton C. March in Washington and General Pershing in France. Implicit in the discussion is the understanding that the nineteenth-century tradition of the primacy of the "Commanding General" of the army had not disappeared despite the existence of a new corporate staff organization. Hewes, *From Root to McNamara* (270), should be consulted for internal War Department changes, while Mark B. Powe's essay, *The Emergence of the War Department Intelligence Agency 1885–1918* (288), examines that aspect of military affairs for the war period. Daniel R. Beaver's "The Problem of American Military Supply, 1890–1920" (254) in B. Franklin Cooling, ed., *War, Business and American Society* (261), discusses the growing issues of management involved in modernizing military procurement during the First World War. A clearer view of the office of the secretary of war and that of the chief of staff during the 1930s can be gained from reading Keith D. McFarland's *Harry H. Woodring* (277) and William Manchester's recent controversial biography of Douglas MacArthur, *American Caesar* (281).

NATIONAL POLICY 1917–41: THE PROBLEM OF SUPPLY. The important essays in Cooling *War, Business and American Society* (261), all contribute to a better general understanding of procurement and supply in war and peace. The editor's introduction and the historical introduction by Theodore Ropp are especially enlightening. James P. Johnson's "The Wilsonians As War Managers: Coal and the 1917–18 Winter Crisis" (273) is important for understanding the search for methods of allocating raw materials in the early months of the First World War. Bruce Frazer, *Yankees at War: Social Mobilization on the Connecticut Home Front* (267); Gerald Senn, "Molders of Thought, Directors of Action: The Arkansas Council of National Defense 1917–1918" (291); and David O. Demuth, "An Arkansas County Mobilizes: Saline County Arkansas, 1917–1918" (263), all break exciting new ground by examining conflicts between local and national political and economic power elites during the war.

STRATEGY, DOCTRINE, AND TECHNOLOGY 1917–41. American strategic thinking, doctrinal change, and technological development have received some attention recently, but much remains to be done before a clearer understanding of their interrelatedness appears. Thomas C. Leonard has published an excellent conceptual work, *Above the Battle: War Making in America from Appomattox to Versailles* (276), which makes the proper historical analogy by comparing the unique American Civil War experience with the nation's reaction to the challenge of the Great War. James P. Tate's *The Army and Its Air Corps* (295) adds institutional depth to the traditional works on the air arm by Hurley and Craven and Cate. Three excellent new studies, one on transport, John C. Speedy III, *From Mules to Motors* (294); and two on artillery, Janice McKenney, "More Bang for the Buck in the Inter-War Army" (279), and S. L. A. Marshall's last published work, "On Heavy Artillery, America's Experience in Four Wars" (282), attempt to link doctrine and technical change creatively within the framework of traditional military history.

THE AMERICAN ARMY AT WAR 1917–18. The general experience of the Great War continues to generate important scholarship. By far the best book to appear in years on the social and intellectual history of the war is Paul Fussell, *The Great War and Modern Memory* (266). If read with proper appreciation, William R. Majors, ed., "Letters from the AEF" (280), adds an American dimension to the essentially English orientation of Fussell's story. Frank Vandiver's *Black Jack* (299) is too uncritical and not a great improvement over Pershing's own wartime memoirs. Far better for understanding inter-Allied issues, including amalgamation and the use and misuse of American troops by the Allies during the war, are Donald Smythe, "General of the Armies John J. Pershing" in Field Marshal Sir Michael Carver's *The War Lords* (292), and John K. Ohl, "The Keystone Division in the Great War" (286). Two fine new biographies, Allan Millett, *The General: Robert Lee Bullard and Officership in the United States Army 1881–1925* (283), and Heath Twitchell, Jr., *Allen: The Biography of an Army Officer* (297), give good insights into American battlefield management and command during the war.

THE ARMY AND AMERICAN SOCIETY 1917–41. The most exciting work which has appeared since 1975 is in sociomilitary history. Although it is still considered a new and even suspect field by some traditionalists and much of it is still in the form of doctoral dissertations, its practitioners are already ending the isolation of military history and building pathways toward the larger American scholarly community. There is little in the field that compares with Robin Higham and Carol Brandt, eds., *The United States Army in Peacetime 1775-1975* (271), which makes easily accessible essays on the non-military and "nation-building" activities of American soldiers. Also significant is James L. Abrahamson, *The Military and American Society 1881-1922* (249). John Ellis, *The Social History of the Machine Gun* (265), is poorly conceived and suspect in many ways, but it still shows what might be done by a more expert author with the theme of weapons development and social change. Carol Gruber's flawed but still interesting *Mars and Minerva* (268) discusses the role of American university scholars in the First World War. Two good articles, Weldon B. Durham's "Big Brother and the Seven Sisters" (264) and Thomas M. Camfield's "Will to Win" (257), link the American progressive movement with the war effort and show how the social and political responsibilities of the army were expanded during the conflict. Donald Smythe, "Venereal Disease: The AEF's Experience" (293), shows similar linkages between changing social attitudes and the army's policy of disease control in France. Alfred W. Crosby, Jr.'s *Epidemic and Peace: 1918* (262) is certainly not the last word on the influenza pandemic, but it marks the recognition by medical historians that an event which cost as many lives as the war itself played a part, admittedly still unclear, in shaping the depressing immediate postwar international environment. Ernest C. Bolt, Jr., *Ballots before Bullets* (256), is the latest examination of pacifist and antimilitarist alternatives to war, while Anne Trotter, "Development of the 'Merchants of Death' Theory," in Cooling, ed., *War, Business and American Society* (261), is the newest look at "devil theories" of war which were so popular during the interwar period. For the activities of other antimilitarists, see Peggy Lamson, *Roger Baldwin, Founder of the American Civil Liberties Union* (274). Several scholars have explored some important social and intellectual aspects of interwar army life. Edward M. Coffman and Peter F. Henly provide a social analysis in "The American Regular Officer Corps between the Wars" (260), and Leslie Anders traces the career of a soldier-intellectual in "The Watershed: Forest Harding's *Infantry Journal*" (250). Donald S. Napoli examines the growing relationship between the scientific community and the army in "The Mobilization of American Psychologists 1938-1941" (284). The experience of American blacks has also received more attention. In *A Night of Violence* (269) Robert Y. Haynes studies the Houseton race riots of 1917. Arthur Barbeau and Florette Henri reexamine the history of black soldiers in the World War in *The Unknown Soldiers* (252). Charles Johnson, Jr.'s study, *Black Soldiers in the National Guard 1877-1949* (272), and Lowell D. Black's excellent local case history of the same phenomena, *The Negro Volunteer Militia Units of the Ohio National Guard 1870-1954* (255), break new ground in another important area of the black experience. Finally, Phillip McGuire explores the deployment of black soldiers during the preparedness period in "Judge William H. Hastie and Army Recruitment, 1940-1942" (278).

BIBLIOGRAPHY

249. Abrahamson, James L. *The Military and American Society*. Ph.D. dissertation, Ph. D. Stanford University, 1977.

250. Anders, Leslie. "The Watershed: Forest Harding's *Infantry Journal* 1934–1938." *Military Affairs* 40 (February, 1976): 12–16.

251. Anderson, Martin, and Valerie Bloom, eds., *Conscription: A Select and Annotated Guide.* Stanford, Calif.: Hoover Institute Press, 1976.

252. Barbeau, Arthur, and Florette Henri. *The Unknown Soldiers: Black American Troops in World War I.* Philadelphia: Temple University Press, 1974.

253. Bayliss, Gwyn M. *Bibliographical Guide to the Two World Wars: An Annotated Survey of English Language Reference Materials.* New York: Bowker, 1977.

254. Beaver, Daniel R. "The Problem of American Military Supply, 1890–1920." In *War, Businesss and American Society: Historical Perspectives on the Military-Industrial Complex,* edited by B. Franklin Cooling. Port Washington, N.Y.: Kennikat Press, 1977.

255. Black, Lowell D. *The Negro Volunteer Militia Units of the Ohio National Guard 1870–1954: The Struggle for Military Recognition and Equality in the State of Ohio.* Ph. D. dissertation, Ohio State University, 1976.

256. Bolt, Ernest C., Jr. *Ballots before Bullets, The War Referendum Approach to Peace in America 1914–1941.* Charlottesville: University of Virginia Press, 1977.

257. Camfield, Thomas M. "Will to Win—The U.S. Army Troop Morale Program of World War I." *Military Affairs* 41 (October, 1977): 125–28.

258. Chandler, Alfred D. *The Visible Hand: The Managerial Revolution in American Buisness.* Cambridge: Harvard University Press, 1977.

259. Clifford, John Gary. *The Citizen Soldiers: The Plattsburg Training Camp Movement 1913–1920.* Lexington: University of Kentucky Press, 1972.

260. Coffman, Edward M., and Peter F. Henly. "The American Regular Officer Corps between the World Wars: A Collective Biography." *Armed Forces and Society* 4 (fall, 1977): 55–73.

261. Cooling, B. Franklin, ed. *War, Business and American Society: Historical Perspectives on the Military-Industrial Complex.* Port Washington, N.Y.: Kennikat Press, 1977.

262. Crosby, Alfred W. Jr. *Epidemic and Peace, 1918.* Westport, Conn: Greenwood Press, 1976.

263. Demuth, David O. "An Arkansas County Mobilizes: Saline County Arkansas, 1917–1918." *Arkansas Historical Quarterly* 36, no. 3 (fall, 1977): 211–33.

264. Durham, Weldon B. "Big Brother and the Seven Sisters: Camp Life Reforms in World War I." *Military Affairs* 42 (April, 1978): 57–60.

265. Ellis, John. *The Social History of the Machine Gun.* New York: Pantheon Books, 1975.

266. Fussell, Paul. *The Great War and Modern Memory.* New York: Oxford University Press, 1975.

267. Frazer, Bruce. *Yankees at War: Social Mobilization on the Connecticut Home Front 1917–1918.* Ph.D. dissertation, Columbia University, 1976.

268. Gruber, Carol S. *Mars and Minerva: World War I and the Uses of*

Higher Learning in America. Baton Rouge: Louisiana State University Press, 1975.

269. Haynes, Robert Y. *A Night of Violence, The Houston Riots of 1917.* Baton Rouge: Louisiana State University Press, 1976.

270. Hewes, James E., Jr. *From Root to McNamara: Army Organization and Administration 1900-1963.* Washington, D.C.: Center for Military History, 1975.

271. Higham, Robin, and Carol Brandt, eds. *The United States Army in Peace time; Essays in Honor of the Bicentennial 1775-1975.* Manhattan, Kans.: Military Affairs/Aerospace Historian, 1977.

272. Johnson, Charles, Jr. *Black Soldiers in the National Guard 1877-1949.* Ph.D. dissertation, Howard University, 1976.

273. Johnson, James P. "The Wilsonians as War Managers: Coal and the 1917-18 Winter Crisis." *Prologue* 9, no. 4 (winter, 1977): 193-208.

274. Lamson, Peggy. *Roger Baldwin, Founder of the American Civil Liberties Union: A Portrait.* Boston: Houghton, Mifflin, 1976.

275. Lane, Jack C. *Armed Progressive: A Study of the Public and Military Career of Leonard Wood.* San Rafael, Calif. Presidio Press, 1976.

276. Leonard, Thomas C. *Above the Battle: War Making in America from Appomattox to Versailles.* New York: Oxford University Press, 1978.

277. McFarland, Keith D. *Harry H. Woodring: A Political Biography of FDR's Controversial Secretary of War.* Lawrence, Kans.: University Press of Kansas, 1975.

278. McGuire, Phillip. "Judge William H. Hastie and Army Recruitment 1940-1942." *Military Affairs* 42 (April, 1978): 75-79.

279. McKenney, Janice. "More Bang for the Buck in the Inter-War Army: The 105mm Howitzer." *Military Affairs* 42 (April, 1978): 80-86.

280. Majors, William R., ed. "Letters from the AEF." *Tennessee Historical Quarterly* 36, no. 3 (fall, 1977): 367-82.

281. Manchester, William. *American Caesar: Douglas MacArthur 1880-1964.* Boston: Little, Brown, 1978.

282. Marshall, S. L. A. "On Heavy Artillery: American Experience in Four Wars." *Parameters* 8 (June, 1978): 2-20.

283. Millett, Allan R. *The Gerneral: Robert L. Bullard and Officership in the United States Army 1881-1925.* Westport, Conn: Greenwood Press, 1975.

284. Napoli, Donald S. "The Mobilization of American Psychologists 1938-1941." *Military Affairs* 42 (February, 1978): 32-36.

285. Ohl, John K. "Hugh S. Johnson and the Draft 1917-1918." *Prologue* 8, no. 2 (summer, 1976): 85-96..

286. Ohl, John K. "The Keystone Division in the Great War." *Prologue* 10, no. 2 (summer, 1978): 83-99.

287. Parsons, Edward B. *Wilsonian Diplomacy: Allied-American Rivalries in War and Peace.* St. Louis: Forum Press, 1978.

288. Powe, Mark B. *The Emergence of the War Department Intelligence Agency 1885-1918.* Manhattan, Kans.: Military Affairs/Aerospace Historian, 1974.

289. Schaffer, Ronald. *The U.S. in World War I: A Selected Bibliography.* War/Peace Bibliography series #7. Santa Barbara, Calif: American Bibliographical Center, Clio Press, 1978.

290. Schlesinger, Arthur M., Jr. *The Imperial Presidency.* New York: Popular Library, 1974.
291. Senn, Gerald. "Molders of Thought, Directors of Action, The Arkansas Council of Defense 1917–1918." *Arkansas Historical Quarterly* 36, no. 3 (fall, 1977): 280–90.
292. Smythe, Donald. "General of the Armies John J. Pershing." In *The War Lords: Military Commanders of the Twentieth Century,* edited by Field Marshal Sir Michael Carver. Boston: Little, Brown, 1976.
293. Smythe, Donald, "Venereal Disease: The AEF's Experience." *Prologue* 9, no. 2 (summer, 1977): 65–74.
294. Speedy, John C., III. *From Mules to Motors: Development of Maintenance Doctrine for Motor Vehicles by the U.S. Army 1896–1918.* Ph.D. dissertation, Duke University, 1977.
295. Tate, James P. *The Army and Its Air Corps: A Study of the Evolution of Army Policy toward Aviation 1919–1941.* Ph.D. dissertation, Indiana University, 1976.
296. Trotter, Anne. "Development of the Merchants of Death Theory." In *War, Business and American Society: Historical Perspectives on the Military-Industrial Complex,* edited by B. Franklin Cooling. Port Washington N.Y.: Kennikat Press, 1977.
297. Twitchell, Heath, Jr. *Allen: The Biography of an Army Officer.* New Brunswick, N.J.: Rutgers University Press, 1974.
298. van Creveld, Martin. *Supplying War: Logistics from Wallenstein to Patton.* London: Cambridge University Press, 1977.
299. Vandiver, Frank E. *Black Jack, The Life and Times of John J. Pershing.* 2 vols. College Station, Tex.: Texas A. and M. Press, 1977.

XII

MILITARY AND NAVAL MEDICINE

James O. Breeden

In my contribution to the original edition of this guide, I bemoaned both the quantity and the quality of works in American military and naval medical history. Little has occurred in the last five years to warrant a revision of this unflattering assessment. Thus, a sizable and significant void continues to exist in the literature of the military history of the United States. The following pages analyze the limited scholarly activity in American military and naval medical medicine in the five years since this guide appeared.

GENERAL STUDIES. Much of the recent work in American military medical history has been of a general nature, cutting across time periods. *Two Hundred Years of Military Medicine* (319), an especially useful booklet, presents in chronological fashion the major milestones in the evolution of the U.S. Army Medical Department and lists its chief contributions to military and civilian science, medicine, and public health. My essay in *The United States Army in Peacetime: Essays in Honor of the Bicentennial, 1775–1975* (268) explores the latter in depth. The published guide to a 1976 exhibit on military medicine at the U.S. Military Academy (320) is both well done and informative. Although quite brief, Joseph Treuta's analysis of the surgical principles that have evolved in the treatment of war wounds (314) and Richard B. Stark's history of military plastic surgery (310) are worthy of mention. The surgeon general of the Air Force commissioned a concise, but helpful, history of aeromedical evacuation (315) from its beginnings in 1918. Two significant studies (274, 276) deal with aspects of military nursing, a topic of increasing scholarly interest. A particularly praiseworthy editorial (312) appeared in a recent number of the *Journal of the History of Medicine and the Allied Sciences,* a leading organ for the history of medicine. It commended the newly established Uniformed Services School of Medicine, founded to train armed-forces medical officers, for the inclusion of medical history in the required curriculum. Hopefully, the editorialist writes, the result will be not only a civilized and humane military physician, but also a historically aware one.

Although technically not of a scholarly nature but of considerable interest nonetheless is the growing body of popular literature devoted to military medicine. Typical of such publications is one, engagingly entitled "The Bugs Bit What the Bullets Bypassed in Bygone Battles" (297) which appeared in the Smithsonian Institution's journal of popular culture. Finally, several classics in military and naval medical history have reappeared in reprint editions. These include histories of the Medical Department of the army by Percy M. Ashburn (261), Harvey E. Brown (321), and James A. Tobey (313), and Louis H. Roddis's history of naval medicine (302).

THE AMERICAN REVOLUTION. The recently celebrated bicentennial sparked surprisingly little scholarly interest in the medical aspects of the American Revolution. But not so surprising, many of the studies that did appear are of an ephemeral nature at best. No attempt was made at producing a comprehensive history of medicine, either military or civilian. Of the monographs devoted entirely to or that deal significantly with military medicine, Maurice B. Gordon's *Naval and Maritime Medicine During the American Revolution* (281) contains much interesting material, but is noticeably superficial; *Physician Signers of the Declaration of Independence* (280), a collective exercise in trivia by a group of historians of medicine, is of little value to the student of military medical history; Morris H. Saffron's *Surgeon to Washington: Dr. John Cochran, 1730–1807* (303) admirably rescues a deserving patriot and able director general of the Medical Department of the Continental Army from obscurity; *The Toll of Independence* (299), edited by Howard H. Peckham, presents in tabular form the war's battle casualties; and the chapter dealing with military medicine in Louis A. Meier's amateurish bicentennial medical history of Montgomery County, Pennsylvania (294), includes many informative, but largely undigested, primary sources. Medical histories of battles have been prepared by Philip Cash (272) and Toby Gelfand (279). In a similar vein, J. Worth Estes has skillfully edited the letters of Dr. Hall Jackson from the siege of Boston (278). Morris H. Saffron (304) and A. C. Wooden (327) have examined aspects of the career of James Tilton, the Revolution's well-known proponent of preventive medicine. In a short, but perceptive, piece Harry Bloch (266) compares the downfalls of Dr. John Morgan, the harried first director general of the Medical Department of the Continental Army, and Dr. William A. Hammond, the controversial Union surgeon general of the Civil War. Rudolf Schmitz's account of the medical problems of the Hessian mercenaries (306) interestingly explores a different side of the war's military medicine.

FROM THE REVOLUTION TO THE CIVIL WAR. During the last five years, research in American military medical history in the period between the Revolution and the Civil War has been centered almost exclusively on the army in the West. My examination of the health of the soldiers in Texas during the 1850s (269) suggests the use of the military to gain insights into the medical problems of the region's settlers for whom reliable vital statistics are not available. A related study of the Indian Territory garrisons north of the Red River (287), which was inadvertently missed during the research for my original contribution to this guide, is still unsurpassed. Thomas B. Hall's *Medicine on the Sante Fe Trail* (283), also overlooked the first time around, is likewise an important work. Two instructive pieces on Dr. Albert J. Myer, best known as the father of the U.S. Army Signal Corps and the U.S. Weather Bureau, dominate a recent number of the *Southwestern Historical Quarterly*. Paul J. Scheips (305) examined Myers's tour of duty in Texas during the 1850s, the first of his long career, and David A. Clary (275) edited his valuable letters written there.

THE CIVIL WAR. The medical side of even the perennially popular Civil War has received little recent attention. Only two monographs of interest have been published. Paul E. Steiner, perhaps the most prolific student of Civil War medical history, has produced an excellent analysis of the impact of disease on a Union regiment which was carefully chosen for its pronounced poor health (311). My *Joseph Jones: Scientist of the Old South* (270) focuses on the Civil War career of an extraordinary Southern medical officer. Ordered by Surgeon General Samuel P. Moore to investigate the health problems of the Confederacy, Jones visited the principal southern armies, hospitals, and prisoner-of-war camps. His findings were embodied in several masterful reports to Moore. A most noteworthy contribution to Civil War medical historiography is Mark A. Quinones's excellent study of drug abuse among the rival armies (301). He convincingly argues that there is insufficient evidence to designate the war years a catalyst for the onset of drug addition in America. John D. Smith has called attention to the health of Vermont's Civil War recruits (307). The recollections and letters of medical officers continue to find their way into print. Those of Dr. John C. Gill of the 120th Ohio Volunteer Infantry (292,290, and 293) and Dr. Cyrus Bacon, Jr., a Union field surgeon at Gettysburg (326), are good cases in point. To their great credit, the Library of the New York Academy of Medicine and Scarecrow Press have made available the immensely important *Confederate States Medical and Surgical Journal* (277). Representative of the popular pieces on Civil War medicine is a Union surgeon's commentary on the hostilities (325) published in *Civil War Times Illustrated,* the leading mass culture journal devoted exclusively to this struggle.

CIVIL WAR TO WORLD WAR I. Throughout most of the latter third of the nineteenth century, the chief concern of the American military establishment was the promotion of western expansion. The experiences of surgeons William M. Notson at Fort Concho in central Texas (298) and Walter Reed at Fort Sidney in western Nebraska (273) are good firsthand accounts of military medicine on this last frontier. Ramon S. Powers and Gene Younger have analyzed the 1866 and 1867 visitations of cholera among the soldiers stationed in the West (300). Almost nothing has been forthcoming on the confrontations with the Indian. The single exception seems to be the battle of the Little Big Horn. Two recent studies explore medical aspects of Custer's tragic encounter with the Sioux: the first is a shallow, but useful, collective biography of the medical officers present at the battle (293); the second is the edited diary of Dr. Holmes O. Paulding, a surgeon with the Custer relief column (267). Not technically a study in American military medical history, but one of considerable importance, is Richard Aquila's splendid examination of Plains Indian war medicine (259). Reprint editions have appeared of several of the army surgeon general's valuable circulars on military medicine, most notably John Shaw Billing's *Report on Barracks and Hospitals* and *Report on the Hygiene of the United States Army with Descriptions of Military Posts,* which were first published in 1870 and 1875 respectively (322 and 323).

Along with protecting the settler from the Indian, the military spent a good deal of its time exploring the West. Elliott Coues is a good example of the soldier-explorer. Later a giant in natural science, Coues traveled throughout much of the trans-Mississippi West as a military surgeon and scientist at the beginning of this period and conducted extensive and significant studies of the region's flora, fauna, topography, indigenous population and settlers. Michael J. Brodhead has compiled a very informative account of these travels and investigations in Coues's own words painstakingly gleaned from his published works (271).

Nineteenth-century American military history ended on an upbeat note with the short but glorious Spanish-American War. Two periodical pieces examine disparate medical facets of the hostilities: one describes the state of medicine in the Florida camps (328); the other examines the sizable scandal that occurred over canned meat (289).

WORLD WAR I. Scant attention has been paid in recent years to the medical side of America's first military involvement on European soil. The altruistic American Field Service has received a popular treatment in *American Heritage* (282). Washington University's Base Hospital 21, a typical medical school volunteer hospital unit, which was organized in 1916 and activated the next year, has been the subject of a highly sympathetic treatment (295). Donald Smythe has thoroughly researched the AEF's experience with venereal disease (308). Robert H. Ivy, a prominent plastic surgeon, has briefly recorded his personal recollections of William R. Keller, the army's outstanding thoracic surgeon (285).

WORLD WAR II. Like that of its predecessor, the military medical history of World War II has generated little scholarly interest. The greatest activity has been on the part of the Army Medical Department, which continues to bring out in piecemeal fashion its monumental official history of World War II military medicine. At least three volumes have been published during the last five years (316, 317, 318). Although detailed and technical, they are nonetheless important contributions to the historiography of the hostilities.

E.H. Beardsley has recorded the experiences of American physician volunteers during the Battle of Britain (262). Donald S. Napoli has studied the preparations of America's psychologists for the indispensable role they came to play in the war effort (296). Philip J. and Beatrice A. Kalisch have called attention to the heroic service of the nurses on Bataan and Corregidor (288). Carlo Henze's recollections as a medical intelligence officer (284), his participation in the ALSOS Mission in particular, are both interesting and important.

WORLD WAR II TO PRESENT. Owing largely to the recently concluded conflict in Southeast Asia, a sizable number of publications on contemporary military and naval medical history have appeared. The sole piece pertaining to the Korean War era is Frank B. Berry's excellent personal account of the system that he devised in 1953, as assistant secretary of defense for health and medical affairs, for the drafting of young doctors (264). This highly successful scheme, which lasted until the end of the draft in 1974, became widely known as "the Berry Plan." Vietnam has understandably monopolized military medical scholarship. Much of this material is highly specialized and has not been included in this essay. For access to it, consult the *Index Medicus,* the standard guide to medical literature, which can be found in the reference room of any medical school library. Characteristic of this literature are the brief analysis of the causes of death among American military personnel compiled by army doctors Keith Arnold and Robert T. Cutting (260); the comparative study of the effects of captivity on injured prisoners of war by two members of the military's Center for Prisoner of War Studies (263); and examinations of the war's considerable psychological impact by Douglas R. Bey and Vincent A. Zecchinelli (265) and Franklin D. Jones and Arnold W. Johnson, Jr. (286). Problems in medical ethics raised by the hostilities, especially the tension between professional responsibility and military obligation, have been perceptively explored by E. A. Vastyan (324). Another piece sponsored by the Center for Prisoner of War Studies deals with the medical problems and health profile of the *Pueblo* crew at the time of their release from captivity (309).

SUGGESTIONS FOR FURTHER RESEARCH. Military and naval medical history remains a most inviting field for the scholar. Indeed, I contended five years ago much of the field was essentially virgin territory. Little has changed. There is a need for early studies and modern studies, comprehensive accounts and period pieces, analyses of events, and examinations of the lives of major figures. Naval and Air Force histories are especially needed.

The sources discussed in my earlier essay and updated above will, it is hoped, serve as a stimulus to research in military and naval medical history. Neither set is exhaustive; nor were they intended to be. Rather, my object in each case was to construct a broad cross section of the types of sources available, to note those of exceptional quality, and to call attention to gaps that need filling.

With one exception, the major repositories for unpublished primary material remain the same as they were five years ago. A short time ago the Army Historical Unit at Fort Detrick, Maryland, was merged with the Department of the Army's Center of Military History (Washington, D.C. 21314). Its holdings were divided between the Army Historical Collection at Carlisle Barracks, Pennsylvania, and a new archive, the Department of Military Medicine and History at the Uniformed Services School of Medicine (4301 Jones Bridge Road, Bethesda, Maryland 20014). The former received the Army Historical Unit's medical history collection, consisting primarily of the professional writings of army medical officers and the personal papers of the surgeons general during the period extending from the 1940s to the 1960s. The latter received its reprint and photographic archives. It should also be noted that the library of the Uniformed Services School of Medicine is in the process of building a collection, manuscript and bound, in world military medical history. There is good reason to believe that this newly established school will soon become a major center for the study of the subject.

BIBLIOGRAPHY

259. Aquila, Richard. "Plains Indian War Medicine." *Journal of the History of the West* 13 (1974): 19–43.

260. Arnold, Keith, and Robert T. Cutting. "Causes of Death in United

States Military Personnel Hospitalized in Vietnam." *Military Medicine* 143 (1978): 161–64.

261. Ashburn, Percy M. *A History of the Medical Department of the United States Army.* 1929. Reprint. New York: AMS, 1976.

262. Beardsley, E. H. "Doctors to the Barricades! American Physicians and the Battle of Britain." *Bulletin of the History of Medicine* 51 (1977): 278–92.

263. Berg, S. William, and Milton Richlin. "Injuries and Illnesses of Vietnam War POWs. IV. Comparison of Captivity Effects in North and South Vietnam." *Military Medicine* 143 (1977): 757–61.

264. Berry, Frank B. "The Story of 'the Berry Plan,'" *Bulletin of the N.Y. Academy of Medicine* 52 (1976): 278–82.

265. Bey, Douglas R., and Vincent A. Zecchinelli. "G.I.'s Against Themselves—Factors Resulting in Explosive Violence in Vietnam." *Psychiatry* 37 (1974): 221–28.

266. Bloch, Harry. "John Morgan, M.D. and William Alexander Hammond, M.D.: Ingredients of Their Downfall." *Military Medicine* 140 (1975): 785–800.

267. Boyes, W., ed. *Surgeon's Diary. With the Custer Relief Column.* Washington, D.C.: South Capitol Press, 1974.

268. Breeden, James O. "The Army and Public Health." In *The United States Army in Peacetime: Essays in Honor of the Bicentennial, 1775–1975,* edited by Robin Higham and Carol Brandt, pp. 83–105. Manhattan, Kans.: Military Affairs/Aerospace Historian Publishing, 1975.

269. Breeden, James O. "Health of Early Texas: The Military Frontier," *Southwestern Historical Quarterly* (1977): (80): 357–98.

270. Breeden, James O. *Joseph Jones: Scientist of the Old South.* Lexington: University Press of Kentucky, 1975.

270. Breeden, James O. "The Army and Public Health." In *The United States Army in Peacetime: Essays in Honor of the Bicentennial, 1775–1975,* edited by Robin Higham and Carol Brandt, pp. 83–105. Manhattan, Kans.: Military/Aerospace Historian Publishing, 1975.

271. Brodhead, Michael J. *A Soldier-Scientist in the American Southwest; Being a Narrative of the Travels of Brevet Captain Elliott Coues, Assistant Surgeon, U.S.A., through Kansas and the Territories of Colorado and New Mexico, to Arizona, and thence to the Coast of California; Together with his Observations upon the Natural History, especially the Avifauna, of the Regions Traversed, 1864–1865.* Tucson: Arizona Historical Society, 1973.

272. Cash, Philip. "The Canadian Military Campaign of 1775–1776: Medical Problems and Effects of Disease." *Journal of the American Medical Association* 236 (5 July 1976): 52–56.

273. Chappell, Gordon S. "Surgeon at Fort Sidney: Captain Walter Reed's Experiences, 1883–1884." *Nebraska History* 54 (1973): 419–43.

274. Chow, Rita, Ethel A. Nelson, Gloria S. Hope, James L. Sokoloski, and Ruth A. Wilson. "Historical Perspectives of the United States Air Force, Army, Navy, Public Health Service, and Veterans Administration Nursing Services." *Military Medicine* 143 (1978): 457–63.

275. Clary, David A., ed. "'I Am Already Quite a Texan': Albert J. Myer's

Letters from Texas, 1854–1856." *Southwestern Historical Quarterly* 82 (1978): 25–76.

276. Conde, Marlette. *The Lamp and the Caduceus: The Story of the Army School of Nursing.* [Washington, D.C.] Army School of Nursing Alumnae, 1975.

277. *Confederate States Medical and Surgical Journal.* Introduction by William D. Sharpe. Metuchen, N.J.: Scarecrow Press, 1976.

278. Estes, J. Worth. "'A Disagreeable and Dangerous Employment': Medical Letters From the Siege of Boston." *Journal of the History of Medicine and Allied Sciences* 31 (1976): 271–91.

279. Gelfand, Toby S. "Military Victory, Medical Stalemate: The Battle of Princeton." In *Bicentennial Programs, 1976,* pp. 14–37. Evansville, Ind.: Indiana Graduate Medical Center, 1976.

280. Gifford, George E., ed. *Physician Signers of the Declaration of Independence.* New York: Science History Publications, 1976.

281. Gordon, Maurice B. *Naval and Maritime Medicine During the American Revolution.* Ventnor, N.J.: Ventnor Publishers, 1978.

282. Gray, Andrew. "The American Field Service." *American Heritage* 26 (1974): 58–63, 88–92.

283. Hall, Thomas B. *Medicine on the Santa Fe Trail.* Dayton: Morningside Bookshop, 1971.

284. Henze, Carlo. "Recollections of a Medical Intelligence Officer in World War II." *Bulletin of the N.Y. Academy of Medicine* 49 (1973): 960–73.

285. Ivy, Robert H. "Personal Memories of Colonel William R. Keller, Army Officer and Master Surgeon." *Military Medicine* 140 (1975): 488–90.

286. Jones, Franklin D., and Arnold W. Johnson, Jr. "Medical and Psychiatric Treatment Policy and Practice in Vietnam." *Journal of Social Issues.* 31 (1975): 49–65.

287. Kalisch, Philip A., and Beatrice J. Kalisch. "Indian Territory Forts: Charnel Houses of the Frontier." *Chronicles of Oklahoma* 50 (1971): 65–81.

288. Kalisch, Philip A., and Beatrice J. Kalisch. "Nurses Under Fire: The World War II Experience of Nurses on Bataan and Corregidor." *Nursing Research* 25 (1976): 409–29.

289. Keuchel, Edward F. "Chemicals and Meat: The Embalmed Beef Scandal of the Spanish-American War." *Bulletin of the History of Medicine* 48 (1974): 249–64.

290. Lupold, Harry F., ed. "An Ohio Doctor Views Campaigning on the White River, 1864." *Arkansas Historical Quarterly* 34 (1975): 333–51.

291. Lupold, Harry F., ed. "A Union Surgeon Views the 'Texans.'" *Southwestern Historical Quarterly* 77 (1974): 481–86.

292. Lupold, Harry F., ed. "A Union Surgeon Views the War from Kentucky, 1862." *Register of the Kentucky Historical Society* 72 (1974): 372–75.

293. McGreevy, Patrick S. "Surgeons at Little Big Horn." *Surgery, Gynecology and Obstetrics* 140 (1975): 774–80.

294. Meier, Louis A. *Early Pennsylvania Medicine: A Representative Early*

American Medical History, Montgomery County, Pennsylvania, 1682 to 1799. Boyertown, Pa.: Gilbert Printing Co., 1976.

295. Munger, Donna B. "Base Hospital 21 and the Great War." *Missouri Historical Review* 70 (1976): 272–90.

296. Napoli, Donald S. "The Mobilization of American Psychologists, 1938–1941." *Military Affairs* 42 (1978): 32–36.

297. Nealon, Eleanor. "The Bugs Bit What Bullets Bypassed in Bygone Battles." *Smithsonian* 7 (1976): 76–81.

298. Notson, William M. "Fort Concho, 1868–1872: The Medical Officer's Observations." Edited by Stephen Schmidt. *Military History of Texas and the Southwest* 12 (1975): 125–49.

299. Peckham, Howard H. *The Toll of Independence: Engagements & Battle Casualties of the American Revolution.* Chicago: University of Chicago Press, 1974.

300. Powers, Ramon S., and Gene Younger. "Cholera and the Army in the West: Treatment and Control in 1866 and 1867." *Military Affairs* 39 (1975): 49–54.

301. Quinones, Mark A. "Drug Abuse During the Civil War (1861–1865)." *International Journal of the Addictions* 10 (1975): 1007–20.

302. Roddis, Louis H. *A Short History of Nautical Medicine.* 1941. Reprint. New York: AMS, 1976.

303. Saffron, Morris H. *Surgeon to Washington: Dr. John Cochran, 1730–1807.* New York: Columbia University Press, 1977.

304. Saffron, Morris H. "The Tilton Affair." *Journal of the American Medical Association* 236 (5 July 1976): 67–72.

305. Scheips, Paul J. "Albert James Myer, an Army Doctor in Texas, 1854–1857." *Southwestern Historical Quarterly* 82 (1978): 1–24.

306. Schmitz, Rudolf. "The Medical and Pharmaceutical Care of Hessian Troops During the American War of Independence." *American Institute for the History of Pharmacy* 3 (1977): 37–47.

307. Smith, John D. "The Health of Vermont's Civil War Recruits." *Vermont History* 43 (1975): 185–92.

308. Smythe, Donald. "Veneral Disease: The AEF's Experience." *Prologue* 9 (1977): 64–74.

309. Spaulding, Raymond C. "The Pueblo Incident: Medical Problems Reported During Captivity and Physical Findings at the Time of the Crew's Release." *Military Medicine* 142 (1977): 142681–84.

310. Stark, Richard B. "The History of Plastic Surgery in Wartime." *Clinics in Plastic Surgery* 2 (1975): 509–16.

311. Steiner, Paul E. *Medical History of a Civil War Regiment: Disease in the Sixty-Fifth United States Colored Infantry.* Clayton, Mo.: Institute of Civil War Studies, 1977.

312. "The Education of Military Physicians." *Journal of the History of Medicine and Allied Sciences* 33 (1978): 3–5.

313. Tobey, James A. *The Medical Department of the Army, Its History, Activities and Organization.* 1927. Reprint. New York: AMS 1976.

314. Treuta, Joseph. "Reflections on the Past and Present Treatment of War Wounds and Fractures." *Military Medicine* 141 (1976): 255–58.

315. U.S. Air Force. Office of the Surgeon-General. *A Concise History of*

the USAF Aeromedical Evacuation System. Washington, D.C.:
G.P.O., 1976.

316. U.S. Army Medical Dept. *Civil Affairs/Military Government Public
Health Affairs.* Washington, D.C.: G.P.O., 1976.

317. U.S. Army Medical Dept. *Medical Statistics in World War II.* Washington, D.C.: G.P.O., 1975.

318. U. S. Army Medical Dept. *Medical Training in World War II.*
Washington, D.C.: G.P.O., 1974.

319. U.S. Army Medical Dept. Historical Unit. *Two Hundred Years of
Military Medicine.* Edited by Rose C. Engleman and Robert J. T. Joy.
Washington, D.C.: G.P.O., 1975.

320. U.S. Military Academy. *Military Medicine and the Wound Man; an
Exhibition of Selected Landmark Books and Articles in the History of
Military Medicine Together with a Graphic Display of the Wound
Man through History.* Designed and edited by Elizabeth M. Lewis.
West Point, N.Y.: U. S. Military Academy, 1976.

321. U.S. Surgeon-General's Office. *The Medical Department of the United States Army from 1775 to 1873.* Compiled by Harvey E. Brown.
1873. Reprint. New York: AMS, 1976.

322. U.S. Surgeon-General's Office. *Report on Barracks and Hospitals,
with Descriptions of Military Posts by John S. Billings... and Chapter
on "Arrow Wounds" from Circular No. 3. Report of Surgical Cases
Treated in the Army of the United States, by George A. Otis.* 1870 and
1871. Reprint. New York: Lewis, 1974.

323. U. S. Surgeon-General's Office. *Report on Hygiene of the United
States Army with Descriptions of Military Posts, by John S. Billings
... and Report to the Surgeon General on the Transport of Sick and
Wounded by Pack Animals, by George A. Otis.* 1875 and 1877.
Reprint. New York: Lewis, 1974.

324. Vastyan, E. A. "Warriors in White: Some Questions about the Nature
and Mission of Military Medicine." *Texas Reports on Biology and
Medicine* 32 (1974): 327–39.

325. Walton, Claiborne F. "'One Continued Scene of Carnage': A Union
Surgeon's View of the War." *Civil War Times Illustrated* 15 (1976):
34–36.

326. Whitehouse, Walter M., and Frank Whitehouse, Jr. "The Daily
Register of Dr. Cyrus Bacon, Jr.: Care of the Wounded at the Battle of
Gettysburg." *Michigan Academician* 8 (1976): 373–86.

327. Wooden, A. C. "James Tilton, Outstanding Military Administrator."
Delaware Medical Journal 47 (1975): 421–41.

328. Wright, S. H. "Medicine in the Florida Camps during the Spanish-
American War. Great Controversies." *Journal of the Florida Medical
Association* 62 (1975): 19–26.

XIII

THE NAVY IN THE EARLY TWENTIETH CENTURY,

1890-1941

William R. Braisted

The years since the last volume of the *Guide* have witnessed a steady flow of serious and popular works on various aspects relating to the navy during its battleship age, 1890-1941. In addition to a number of major monographs, there have appeared important dissertations, most of them relating to the navy between the world wars. Noteworthy as a supplement to this *Guide* are the two new volumes in Myron J. Smith's monumental bibliography that cover the years 1865-1941 (465, 466).

SURVEY HISTORIES. Three recent survey naval histories include chapters on the period. *In Peace and War* edited by Kenneth J. Hagan (424), is a collection of seventeen essays that constitutes the most significant American naval history survey to appear in more than thirty years; Nathan Miller's magnificently illustrated history of the navy (443) is graced by a text several levels superior to what one commonly expects in so sumptuous a publication; and Paolo E. Coletta's *American Naval Heritage* (411) is a brief, concise compendium of basic historical facts.

ON THE NEW NAVY TO 1900. In Robert Seager II, Alfred Thayer Mahan has finally attracted a first-rate biographer, who portrays the navy's most famous historian "warts and all" down to the last detail (462). Seager and Doris D. Maguire have also collaborated in the publication of Mahan's *Letters and Papers* (463); and from Germany comes a European analysis of Mahan's work by Michael Hanke (426). Complementing these materials on Mahan are the recently collected writings by Stephen B. Luce (428), Mahan's mentor and founder of the Naval War College. The Naval War College itself has published Ronald Spector's *Professors of War* dealing with the college's early decades (467), as well as Gerald J. Kennedy's institutional history of the college between the world wars (438). The educational role of the United States Naval Institute during its first century is the theme of William Ray Heitzman's dissertation (430).

Moving more specifically into the 1890s, Jeffrey M. Dorwart's *Pigtail War* (420) includes the activities of American warships on the Asiatic Station during the Sino-Japanese War. Hugh B. Hammett's dissertation on Hilary A.

Herbert, President Cleveland's able second naval secretary (425), has recently been published as a full biography. Surely one of the most thought-provoking contributions to the literature on the Spanish-American War is Adm. Hyman Rickover's reexamination of *How the Battleship Maine Was Destroyed* (456), in which Rickover concludes that the famous ship was sunk by internal, not an external explosion. The heroic battleship *Oregon* is the subject of a popular, book-length biography by Sanford Sternlicht (469). David B. Chidsay's *Spanish-American War* (406) is still another popular account of the "little war," and Barbara B. Tomblin's review of the navy in the Philippine Insurrection (472) is operational history based largely on secondary sources.

FROM THEODORE ROOSEVELT THROUGH WORLD WAR I. Naval strategy diplomacy during Theodore Roosevelt's presidency continues to fascinate historians. Holger Herwig's *Politics of Frustration* (431) is a superb study, based on research in German as well as American archives, of the United States in German war planning and Germany in American war planning during the last twenty-five years of the German empire and the first eight years of Hitler. In his entertaining vignette on "Roosevelt and the Sultans" (434), William J. Hourihan views the American naval demonstration against Morocco and Turkey in 1904 as a reminder by TR to Europe that the United States claimed recognition as a great power. Ronald Spector (468) has argued persuasively that Roosevelt, his disclaimers notwithstanding, was actually bluffing during the Venezuelan Crisis of 1902, and there has been lively interplay between Richard W. Turk (474) and his critics (449) on whether Roosevelt "took" Panama in 1903. David G. McCullough's account of the *Creation of the Panama Canal* (440), though perhaps not strictly naval history, is significant for understanding the canal in the navy's two-ocean strategy. Gerald E. Thomas's dissertation on "William D. Leahy's Imperial Years, 1893-1917" (470) uncovers a contradiction between Leahy's compassion for the victims of American imperialism and his belief that the United States should enhance its strategic and economic positions in China, the Philippines, and the Caribbean.

The recent studies of the navy during Woodrow Wilson's administrations are far more concerned with diplomacy than with operations. David Healy's inquiry into *Gunboat Diplomacy* in Haiti, 1915-16 (429), is especially sympathetic toward the delicate handling of the Haitians by Adm. William S. Caperton and Capt. Edward L. Beach of the U.S.S. *Memphis*. Hans Schmidt, on the other hand, views the *United States Occupation of Haiti* (461) in terms of the conflict between American democratic impulses and racial, colonial realities. Omitted from the previous *Guide* was the younger Edward L. Beach's moving story of the *Wreck of the Memphis* (399) in the great storm off Santo Domingo in 1916. Richard E. Quirk has examined the American occupation of Vera Cruz as *An Affair of Honor* (454) exemplifying Wilson's use of the navy in moral diplomacy, while William S. Coker has uncovered the embarrassment at Vera Cruz in 1914 caused by Rear Adm. Frank Friday Fletcher's claim to seniority over the British Rear Adm. Sir Christopher Cradock (409).

Jeffrey J. Safford's *Wilsonian Maritime Diplomacy* (460) delves into the maritime rivalries, especially between the United States and Britain, that contributed significantly to American naval expansion during the Great War. Both Dean Allard (397) and Roland A. Bowling (401) have reexamined Adm.

William S. Sims's influence on American naval policy during the war. The amusing reflections of a naval reserve with subchasers during the First World War (445) and with the New England inshore patrol after 1939 (446) are the stuff of Alexander Moffett's volumes on the *Maverick Navy*.

Rear Adm. Newton A. McCully was surely the most fascinating American naval officer involved in Russian-American relations of the period. Charles J. Weeks's dissertation (478) records McCully's experiences in Russia during the Russo-Japanese War, World War I, and the Revolution. McCully's full *Report* on conditions at Port Arthur in 1904–05 (441) has also been published. Weeks and Joseph O.Baylen have shed some light on the role of American naval men in the still somewhat mysterious mission by Admiral Kolchak to the United States in 1917 (479).

THE NAVY DURING THE DISARMAMENT ERA. For his study of *Power in the Pacific* (419), Roger Dingman examined Japanese, British, and American records to conclude that domestic political factors brought the three great naval powers to agreement at the Washington Conference, 1921–22. Scholars remain of several minds as to why the three powers failed at the subsequent Geneva Conference in 1927: David Carlton (405) cites British materials to place a large share of the blame on British naval extremists; Adolph B. Clemenson (407) found the Americans and the British deadlocked on how to deal with Japan; and William F. Trimble (473) points to the inability of either Britain or the United States to satisfy the strategic requirements of the other. Insight into the strategies behind the Anglo-American naval rivalry is contributed by William R. Braisted's inquiry into the American War Plans Red (402). On individuals in the disarmament negotiations, there are Richard D. Glasow's dissertation on Hugh Gibson's naval diplomacy (423) and Meredith W. Berg's appreciation of Adm. William S. Standley at the last two London naval conferences (400).

In the sphere of gunboat diplomacy, Bernard D. Cole's carefully researched dissertation on the navy and the Chinese Nationalist Revolution of 1927 (410) has uncovered a clear split between naval officers and diplomats in China and their more patient superiors in Washington. Stephen S. Roberts sees in the Shanghai Incident of 1932 the end of the distant stations era as the United States and other Western powers ceased to direct their naval forces against local Chinese populations and turned to confront Japan (457). Edwin Hoyt's *Lonely Ships* (435) is a popular account of the Asiatic Station with emphasis on the decade prior to Pearl Harbor. Richard W. Millett has described the Special Service Squadron as the State Department's navy in Latin American waters during the interwar years (444).

THE NAVY DURING THE NEW DEAL AND THE COMING OF THE WORLD WAR II. His searches in the naval records and at Hyde Park have led John Walter to the rather startling conclusion that the New Deal naval programs to 1938 were forced on the reluctant President Franklin D. Roosevelt by Congress and the navy (477). Thomas C. Hones's studies of naval expenditures (433) point to the declining importance of the battle line during the decade prior to Pearl Harbor as the navy rounded out the fleet with carriers and other classes. Malcom Muir, on the other hand, has concluded from the post-1934 building programs that the fast battleships were powerful and viable in their day (448). Francis L. Keith has sought to trace the evolution of fleet doctrine during the early thirties by probing the Fleet Problems (437). And Michael D. Doyle's impressive doctoral research on the decade before Pearl Harbor traces the emergent agreement between the Navy and State Departments during the final London naval conferences and the transformation of American defense policies after 1938 (421). The second and final volume of Stephen Roskill's masterwork, *Naval Policy between the Wars* (459), is oriented toward the politics of British sea power but pays more than casual attention to the United States Navy.

The critical naval maneuverings on the eve of formal war are superbly illuminated by James C. Leutze's *Bargaining for Supremacy* (439), a study of Anglo-American naval relations between 1937 and 1941, and by Patrick Abbazia's *Mr. Roosevelt's Navy* (396) relating to the Atlantic Fleet's "private war," 1939–41. The *Cruise of the Lanikai* (471) into Annamese waters is cited by the little ship's skipper, Rear Adm. Kemp Tolley, as new proof that Roosevelt incited war in 1941. Glen St. John Barclay takes a distinctly critical Australian view of Britain's Singapore strategy as it related to the United States (398). The recent biographies of Chester Nimitz by E. B. Potter (453) and of Raymond A. Spruance by Thomas B. Buell (414) include considerable material on service life before the Second World War.

NAVAL AIR. Charles M. Melhorn's *Two Block Fox* (442) is a brief, well-documented study of the struggle for carrier air through the completion of the navy's first two genuine aircraft carriers, the famed sisterships *Lexington* and *Saratoga*. Other recent contributions to naval air history include George Van Deurs's affectionate biography of Theodore G. "Spuds" Ellyson, the navy's first aviator (476); Douglas H. Robinson's history of rigid airships (458); a new edition of Clark G. Reynolds's well-known *Fast Carriers* (455); and Edward Jablonski's *Atlantic Fever* (436), the story of naval men and others who sought to fly the Atlantic.

SHIP TYPES. The Naval History Division has completed seven of the projected eight volumes in its definitive *Dictionary of American Fighting Ships* (475). Nostalgia has encouraged a small surge of books on the mighty battleships, one of the more professional of which is Siegfried Breyer's *Battleships and Battle Cruisers* (403). On a somewhat contrary course to Breyer and Malcom Muir (448), Robert L. O'Connell argues in his dissertation (450) that even though battleships were failures as weapons, they survived because they fit naval officers' conceptions of what warships should be.

THE MARINES. Two recent survey histories of the Marine Corps by Brig. Gen. Edwin H. Simmons (464) and J. Robert Moskin (447) are popular, operational narratives in the proud marine tradition. Lt. Gen. Pedro A. Del Valle's *Semper Fidelis* (418) is the autobiography of a colorful marine of Spanish extraction who served in both world wars and in many lands before he retired to become a vice-president of I.T.&T. Norman V. Cooper's biography of Gen. Holland M. Smith includes noteworthy material on amphibious training before World War II (415). From its handsome new quarters in the old Washington Navy Yard, the Marine Corps History and Museums Division continues to issue studies of substantial merit, some recent examples being on

Marine Corps doctrines, techniques, and institutions from 1900 to 1970 (408); marine aviation to 1940 (416); women marines in World War I (432); and a descriptive catalog of the personal papers held by the division (480).

PERSONNEL, INSTITUTIONAL, AND MISCELLANEOUS. Surely one of the most significant contributions to naval historiography of the battleship age is Frederick S. Harrod's *Manning of the New Navy* (427), a superb study of the professionalization of naval enlisted personnel between 1899 and 1940. The recently declassified history of the Joint Chiefs of Staff by Vernon J. Davis (417) also surveys in some detail the record of the Joint Chiefs' predecessor, the Joint Army and Navy Board. Paolo E. Coletta has been inquiring into the adventures of Bradley A. Fiske in the realms of naval invention (413, 414). And there have been initial probes into the origins of the naval-industrial complex by John K. Ohl (451), and Benjamin F. Cooling and others (414). In his dissertation on the naval administration of Samoa, Frederick H. Olsen (452) portrays the navy as protector of native tradition against white encroachment.

SUGGESTIONS FOR RESEARCH. The recent work by historians notwithstanding, opportunities for further research on the navy between 1890 and 1941 remain as numerous as they were four years ago. There are promising studies under way on the Office of Naval Intelligence and on the Chiefs of Naval Operations, but the bureaus of the Navy Department and the other elements of the naval shore establishment remain largely unexplored. Apart from the bureaus themselves, historians should inquire further into the long and heated line-staff controversy, one product of which was the Office of Naval Operations. Not yet adequately explored are the rich archives of the Naval War College at Newport, which together with the records of the Navy Department, the General Board, and the Fleet Problems contain the stuff for a full understanding of how fleet doctrine actually developed. Nor have historians yet undertaken systematic studies of the navy's relations with the civilian sectors of society such as the press, business, and the scientific world. In the diplomatic sphere, now that the records of the Office of Naval Intelligence are being opened, it is possible to determine how the navy's relations with foreign powers were conducted by its attachés in Europe and Asia and by its missions in Latin America, especially those in Brazil and Peru. There are studies of the navy at particular arms conferences but no systematic examination of the navy's role in the entire naval arms limitation movement between the world wars. Congress has yet to open its committee records so that the navy's dealings with the legislative branch can finally be understood. Historians are still fascinated by the early history of naval air power, leaving largely untouched the post-heroic but crucial years of naval air history during the decade before Pearl Harbor. The history of the American submarine arm before 1941 remains largely a barren waste. Josephus Daniels is still one of the most fascinating and least understood of the significant naval secretaries during the navy's battleship age. The last full operational history of the navy during World War I was completed more than a half-century ago, and there is no study on how the Navy Department conducted its business during the war. Biographies of Thomas C. Hart, French E. Chadwick, and Harry E. Yarnell are underway, but a host of other naval men and marines deserve to be saved from historical oblivion, among them Henry C. Taylor, Washington I. Chambers, Joseph B. Reeves, Albert Gleaves, John A. Lejeune, Smedley D. Butler, William D. Leahy, Charles O'Neill, and Mark Bristol. Of the tools for research, naval historians still need an adequate guide to the public and private naval historical collections, a factual encyclopedia of naval history, and a distinguished dictionary of naval biography.

BIBLIOGRAPHY

396. Abbazia, Patrick. *Mr. Roosevelt's Navy: The Private War of the U.S. Atlantic Fleet, 1939-1942.* Annapolis: Naval Institute Press, 1975.

397. Allard, Dean C. "Admiral William S. Sims and United States Naval Policy during World War I." *American Neptune* 35 (April 1975): 97-110.

398. Barclay, Glen St. John. "Singapore Strategy: The Role of the United States in Imperial Defense." *Military Affairs* 39 (April 1975): 54-59.

399. Beach, Edward L. *The Wreck of the Memphis.* New York: Holt, Rinehart, and Winston, 1966.

400. Berg, Meredith W. "Admiral William H. Standley and the Second London Naval Treaty, 1934-1936." *Historian* 33 (February 1971): 215-36.

401. Bowling, Roland A. "Convoy in World War I: The Influence of Admiral William S. Sims, U.S. Navy." Master's thesis, San Diego State University, 1975.

402. Braisted, William R. "On the American Red and Red-Orange Plans." In *Naval Warfare in the Twentieth Century, 1900-1945,* edited by Gerald Jordan, pp. 167-86. New York: Crane Russak, 1977.

403. Breyer, Siegfried. *Battleships and Battle Cruisers, 1905-1970.* Garden City, N.Y.: Doubleday, 1973.

404. Buell, Thomas B. *The Quiet Warrior: A Biography of Admiral Raymond A. Spruance.* Boston: Little, Brown and Company, 1974.

405. Carlton, David. "Great Britain and the Coolidge Naval Disarmament Conference of 1927." *Political Science Quarterly,* 83 (December 1968): 573-98.

406. Chidsay, Donald B. *The Spanish American War: A Behind-the-Scenes Account of the War in Cuba.* New York: Crown Publishers, 1971.

407. Clemenson, Adolph B. "The Geneva Tripartite Conference of 1927 in Japanese-American Relations." Ph.D. dissertation, University of Arizona, 1975.

408. Clifford, Kenneth J. *Progress and Purpose: A Developmental History of the United States Marine Corps, 1900-1970.* Washington, D.C.: Marine Corps History and Museums Division, 1973.

409. Coker, William S. "Naval Diplomacy during the Mexican Revolution: An Episode in the Career of Admiral Frank Friday Fletcher." *North Dakota Quarterly* 40 (spring 1972): 51-64.

410. Cole, Bernard D. "The United States Navy in China, 1925-1928." Ph.D. dissertation, Auburn University, 1978.

411. Coletta, Paolo E. *The American Naval Heritage in Brief.* Washington, D.C.: University Press of America, 1978.

412. Coletta, Paolo E. "The 'Nerves' of the New Navy." *American Neptune* 38 (April 1978): 122–30.

413. Coletta, Paolo E. "The Perils of Invention: Bradley A. Fiske and the Torpedo Plane." *American Neptune* 37 (April 1977): 111–27.

414. Cooling, Benjamin F., ed. *War, Business, and American Society: Historical Perspectives on the Military-Industrial Complex.* Port Washington, N.Y.: Kennikat Press, 1977.

415. Cooper, Norman V. "The Military Career of General Holland M. Smith, U.S.M.C." Ph.D. dissertation, University of Alabama, 1974.

416. Cosmas, Graham A. *Marine Corps Aviation, 1912–1940.* Washington, D.C.: Marine Corps History and Museums Division, 1977.

417. Davis, Vernon E. *The History of the Joint Chiefs of Staff in World War II.* 2 vols. Washington, D.C.: Historical Division, Joint Secretariat, Joint Chiefs of Staff, 1972.

418. Del Valle, Lt. Gen. Pedro A. *Semper Fidelis: An Autobiography.* Hawthorne, Calif.: Christian Book Club of America, 1976.

419. Dingman, Roger. *Power in the Pacific: The Origins of Naval Arms Limitation, 1914–1922.* Chicago: University of Chicago Press, 1976.

420. Dorwart, Jeffrey M. *The Pigtail War: American Involvement in the Sino-Japanese War, 1894–1895.* Amhurst: University of Massachusetts Press, 1975.

421. Doyle, Michael K. "The U.S. Navy: Strategy, Defense, and Foreign Policy, 1932–1941." Ph.D. dissertation, University of Washington, 1977.

422. Fuller, Stephen M., and Graham A. Cosmas. *Marines in the Dominican Republic, 1916–1924.* Washington, D.C.: Marine Corps History and Museums Division, 1974.

423. Glasow, Richard D. "The Naval Diplomacy of Hugh Gibson, 1926–1929." Ph.D. dissertation, San Diego State University, 1972.

424. Hagan, Kenneth J., ed. *In Peace and War: Interpretations of American Naval History, 1775–1978.* Westport, Conn.: Greenwood Press, 1978.

425. Hammett, Hugh B. *Hilary Abner Herbert: A Southerner Returns to the Union.* Philadelphia: American Philosophical Society, 1976.

426. Hanke, Michael. *Das Werk Alfred T. Mahan's: Darstellung und Analyse.* Osnabruk: Biblio Verlag, 1974.

427. Harrod, Frederick S. *The Manning of the New Navy: The Development of a Modern Naval Enlisted Force, 1899–1940.* Westport, Conn.: Greenwood Press, 1978.

428. Hayes, John D., and John B. Hattendorff. *The Writings of Stephen B. Luce.* Newport: Naval War College Press, 1975.

429. Healy, David. *Gunboat Diplomacy in the Wilson Era: the U.S. Navy in Haiti.* Madison: University of Wisconsin Press, 1976.

430. Heitzmann, William R. "The United States Naval Institute's Contribution to the In-Service Education of Naval Officers." Ph.D. dissertation, University of Delaware, 1974.

431. Herwig, Holger H. *Politics of Frustration: The United States in German Naval Planning, 1889–1941.* Boston: Little, Brown and Company, 1976.

432. Hewitt, Linda L. *Women Marines in World War I.* Washington, D.C.: Marine Corps History and Museums Division, 1974.

433. Hone, Thomas C. "Battleships vs Aircraft Carriers: the Pattern of U.S. Navy Operating Expenditures, 1932-1941." *Military Affairs* 41 (October 1977): 133–42.

434. Hourihan, William J. "Roosevelt and the Sultans: The United States Navy in the Mediterranean, 1904." Ph.D. dissertation, University of Massachusetts, 1975.

435. Hoyt, Edwin P. *The Lonely Ships: The Life and Death of the Asiatic Fleet.* New York: David McKay Company, 1976.

436. Jablonski, Edward. *Atlantic Fever.* New York: Macmillan, 1972.

437. Keith, Francis L. "United States Navy Task Force Evolution: An Analysis of United States Fleet Problems, 1931-1934." Master's thesis, University of Maryland, 1974.

438. Kennedy, Gerald J. *The United States Naval War College, 1919-1941, An Institutional Response to Naval Preparedness.* Newport: U.S. Naval War College, Center for Advanced Research, 1975.

439. Leutze, James R. *Bargaining for Supremacy: Anglo-American Naval Collaboration, 1937-1941.* Chapel Hill: University of North Carolina Press, 1977.

440. McCullough, David G. *The Path between the Seas: The Creation of the Panama Canal, 1870-1914.* New York: Simon and Schuster, 1977.

441. McCully, Newton A. *The McCully Report: The Russo-Japanese War, 1904-1905.* Annapolis: Naval Institute Press, 1976.

442. Melhorn, Charles M. *Two Block Fox: the Rise of the Aircraft Carrier, 1911-1929.* Annapolis: Naval Institute Press, 1974.

443. Miller, Nathan. *The U.S. Navy: An Illustrated History.* Annapolis: Naval Institute Press, 1978.

444. Millett, Richard. "The State Department's Navy: A History of the Special Service Squadron, 1920-1940." *American Neptune* 35 (April 1975): 118–38.

445. Moffat, Alexander W. *Maverick Navy.* Middletown, Conn.: Wesleyan University Press, 1976.

446. Moffat, Alexander W. *A Navy Maverick Comes of Age, 1939-1945.* Middletown, Conn.: Wesleyan University Press, 1977.

447. Moskin, J. Robert. *The Marine Corps Story.* New York: McGraw-Hill Book Company, 1977.

448. Muir, Malcom. "The Capital Ship Program in the United States Navy, 1934-1945." Ph.D. dissertation, Ohio State University, 1976.

449. Nikol, John, and Francis X. Holbrook. "Naval Operations and the Panama Revolution, 1903." *American Neptune* 37 (October 1977): 353–62.

450. O'Connell, Robert L. "Dreadnought? The Battleship, the United States and the World Naval Community." Ph.D. dissertation, University of Virginia, 1974.

451. Ohl, John K. "The Navy, the War Industries Board, and the Industrial Mobilization for War, 1917-1918." *Military Affairs* 40 (February 1976): 17–22.

452. Olsen, Frederick H. "The Navy and the White Man's Burden: Naval

Administration of Samoa." Ph.D. dissertation, Washington University, St. Louis, 1976.

453. Potter, E. B. *Nimitz*. Annapolis: Naval Institute Press, 1976.

454. Quirk, Robert E. *An Affair of Honor: Woodrow Wilson and the Occupation of Vera Cruz*. Lexington: University of Kentucky Press, 1962.

455. Reynolds, Clark G. *The Fast Carriers: The Forging of an Air Navy*. 2d ed. Huntington, N.Y.: Robert E. Krieger, 1978.

456. Rickover, Hyman G. *How the Battleship "Maine" Was Destroyed*. Washington, D.C.: Naval History Division, U.S. Navy Department, 1976.

457. Roberts, Stephen S. "The Decline of the Overseas Station Fleets: The United States Navy and the Shanghai Crisis, 1932." *American Neptune* 37 (July 1977): 185–202.

458. Robinson, Douglas H. *Giants in the Sky. A History of the Rigid Airship*. Seattle: University of Washington Press, 1973.

459. Roskill, Stephen. *Naval Policy between the Wars*. Vol. 2, *The Period of Reluctant Rearmament, 1930*–1939. Annapolis: Naval Institute Press, 1976.

460. Safford, Jeffrey J. *Wilsonian Maritime Diplomacy, 1913-1921*. New Brunswick: Rutgers University Press, 1978.

461. Schmidt, Hans. *The United States Occupation of Haiti, 1915-1916*. New Brunswick, N.J.: Rutgers University Press, 1971.

462. Seager, Robert, II. *Alfred Thayer Mahan: the Man and His Letters*. Annapolis: Naval Institute Press, 1977.

463. Seager, Robert, II, and Doris D. Maguire. *The Letters and Papers of Alfred Thayer Mahan*. 3 vols. Annapolis: Naval Institute Press, 1975.

464. Simmons, Brig. Gen. Edwin H. *The United States Marines, 1775-1975: the First Two Hundred Years*. New York: Viking, 1976.

465. Smith, Myron J. *The American Navy, 1865-1918: A Bibliography*. American Naval Bibliography, vol. 4. Metuchen, N.J.: The Scarecrow Press, 1974.

466. Smith, Myron J. *The American Navy, 1918-1941: A Bibliography*. American Naval Bibliography, vol. 5. Metuchen, N.J.: The Scarecrow Press, 1974.

467. Spector, Ronald. *Professors of War: The Naval War College and the Development of the Naval Profession*. Newport: Naval War College Press, 1977.

468. Spector, Ronald. "Roosevelt, the Navy, and the Venezuelan Controversy, 1902-1903." *American Neptune* 32 (October 1972): 257–63.

469. Sternlicht, Sanford V. *McKinley's Bulldog, the Battleship Oregon*. Chicago: Nelson-Hall, 1977.

470. Thomas, Gerald E. "William D. Leahy's Imperial Years, 1893-1917." Ph.D. dissertation, Yale University, 1973.

471. Tolley, Kemp. *Cruise of the Lanikai: Incitement to War*. Annapolis: Naval Institute Press, 1973.

472. Tomblin, Barbara B. "The United States Navy in the Philippine Insurrection." *American Neptune* 35 (July 1975): 183–96.

473. Trimble, William F. "The United States Navy and the Geneva Con-

ference for the Limitation of Armament." Ph.D. dissertation, University of Colorado, 1974.

474. Turk, Richard W. "The United States Navy and the 'Taking' of Panama, 1901-1904." *Military Affairs* 38 (October 1974): 92-96.

475. U.S. Naval History Division. *Dictionary of American Fighting Ships.* 7 vols. to date. Washington, D.C.: Government Printing Office, 1959–   .

476. Van Deurs, George. *Anchors in the Sky: Spuds Ellyson, First Naval Aviator.* San Rafael, Calif.: Presidio Press, 1977.

477. Walter, John C. *The Navy Department and the Campaign for Expanded Appropriations, 1933-1938.* Ph.D. dissertation, University of Maine, 1972.

478. Weeks, Charles J., Jr. "The Life and Career of Admiral Newton D. McCully, 1867-1951." Ph.D. dissertation, Georgia State University, 1975.

479. Weeks, Charles J., Jr., and Joseph O. Baylen. "Admiral Kolchak's Mission to the United States, 10 September-9 November 1917." *Military Affairs* 40 (April 1976): 63-67.

480. Wood, Charles A., comp. *Marine Corps Personal Papers Catalog.* Washington, D.C.: Marine Corps History and Museums Division, 1974.

XIV

THE UNITED STATES ARMY IN WORLD WAR II

Robert W. Coakley

During the last five years, the volume of writing on the U.S. Army in the Second World War has not been proportionately as great as it was during the previous three decades. For instance only one volume (259) has been added to the U.S. Army in World War II Series, leaving six yet to come to complete the planned eighty volumes. Although interest in World War II has continued high both among historians and popular writers, the focus of most writers about the army has shifted to the Vietnam War. The revelation having the most impact for the history of army operations, that of the ULTRA secret, has not yet been thoroughly digested; and it was considered during the period far more in what might be called broadly histories of intelligence than in histories of the army's part in the war *per se*.

BIBLIOGRAPHIES. There are as yet no general bibliographies dealing solely with the army itself or with the military history of the war. Bayliss (244) and Ensor (257) have contributed, respectively, new bibliographies of reference materials and books in English on the war, in many ways similar to the work of Ziegler (240). The U.S. Army Military Institute (formerly the U.S. Army Military History Research Collection) has also provided bibliographical listings of its World War II holdings (291).

MANUSCRIPT SOURCES. Certainly the most significant development with regard to manuscript sources has been the declassification of practically all World War II records held by the National Archives and Records Service. This action has made both Army and Joint and Combined Chiefs of Staff records readily available to scholars. The material declassified includes previously classified manuscript histories of the Joint Chiefs of Staff in World War II prepared by their historical section. Some idea of the scope of these archival holdings and the problems of using them can be gained from the published record of the Archives Conference on World War II records held in 1973 (280). Benedict K. Zobrist, director of the Truman Library, has also described some of the resources of the presidential libraries for the history of World War II in one article in *Military Affairs* (300), and Stuart Anderson has dealt specifically with the Eisenhower Library in another (242). The U.S. Army Military History Institute has issued a second listing of its manuscript holdings (292), which include many papers on World War II. Most notable among the new acquisitions in this area are the papers of Charles L. Bolte, Russell L. Maxwell, Raymond G. Moses, and S. L. A. Marshall. The U.S. Army Center of Military History in Washington has issued, for limited distribution, the first two volumes of a catalog and index to its manuscript holdings (290) that include many World War II materials.

MILITARY PREPARATIONS AND THE OUTBREAK OF WAR. Capt. Tracy B. Kittredge's manuscript on "United States Defense Policies and Global Strategy, 1900–1914," a part of the history of the JCS in World War II (272), is now available on microfilm from the National Archives. While not a well-integrated narrative, it contains a wealth of material and many valuable insights as to the background of American entrance into the war. Melose has contributed a study of the long-range political impact of the Pearl Harbor disaster (279), and the Department of Defense has published the texts of the MAGIC intercepts of Japanese radio messages in 1940 and 1941 (293).

STRATEGY AND THE HIGH COMMAND. New British and Australian studies stress the divergent aims of the English-speaking allies in the war against Japan. Thorne's *Allies of a Kind* (289) is an impressive analytical study of British-American relations in the Pacific area, and Roger Bell's *Unequal Allies* (245) deals with the stresses and strains of the relationship between the United States and Australia. Grace Hayes's narrative in the *History of the Joint Chiefs* (263) is a straightforward account of the development of American strategy in the Pacific based on the records of the JCS and CCS. By the same token, the voluminous multi-author typescript "History of the Joint Chiefs of Staff in the War against Germany" (265) is a useful though less well integrated account of the development of Allied strategy in Europe. The incomplete manuscript of Mason and Morgenthal on landing craft in the same group (278) is also a useful introduction to one of the central resource problems in the development of that strategy. Of outside works on strategy in Europe, Stoler's *Politics of the Second Front* (287) is the most significant recent work. Stoler seeks to prove that the American military direction of the war in Europe was not nearly so apolitical as it has usually been portrayed. Funk deals more with the French side in *The Politics of Torch* (261), while Smith and Agarossi deal equally effectively with the interaction of political and military factors in the surrender of Italy (286).

MEMOIRS AND BIOGRAPHIES. The most notable biographies of army leaders in World War II that have appeared recently are two of Gen. Douglas MacArthur—one by William Manchester and the other by D. Clayton James. Manchester's *American Caesar* (277), though widely acclaimed, is badly flawed by historical inaccuracies and the distortion of source material to create reader interest. Volume 2 of D. Clayton James's *Years of MacArthur* (269) is a much more reliable work for the serious student of history. The British writer Hubert Essame has added to the Patton shelf not a biography but a very favorable study of Patton as commander (258). Gen. J. Lawton Collins devotes about one-half of his autobiography, *Lightning Joe* (251), to the Second World War. Gen. James Gavin, always controversial, has contributed his own firsthand account of the war in Europe with some telling criticism of its conduct (262). In *Front Line General* (250), William Chase, who served as a regimental and division commander in MacArthur's theater, recounts his combat experiences.

INTELLIGENCE. In 1974, Frederick Winterbotham, a former group captain in the Royal Air Force who had had the responsibility in World War II for the dissemination of what was then known as "special intelligence," revealed to the English-speaking world for the first time the fact than the British had broken the German code during World War II by duplicating the Enigma machine used by the Germans to transmit and receive encoded radio messages. Winterbotham's book, *The ULTRA Secret* (298), was based largely on memory, contained many inaccuracies, and claimed more for ULTRA, as this sort of special intelligence was designated, than the facts justified. This revelation of the most closely guarded secret of World War II nevertheless created a furor among World War II historians who had to face the prospect of revising existing accounts of the war to reflect ULTRA's influence. Winterbotham's book was followed closely by a far more massive tome by Anthony Cave Brown, *Bodyguard of Lies* (248), detailing the supposed effects of ULTRA on almost every operation in the war. Brown, in the opinion of knowledgeable reviewers, also was guilty of exaggeration. In any case, the net result of the publication of the two books was to stimulate a lively debate among historians as to how much of World War II history needed revision in the light of ULTRA, and to lead to serious endeavors to cover more adequately the intelligence history of the war. The debate on the effect on U.S. Army operations is reflected in articles in *Military Affairs* by Dunn (256) and Rosengarten (282), in *Army* by Blumenson (247), and in *Parameters* by Deutsch (253, 254). Critics of Brown and Winterbotham pointed out that ULTRA was a very important but not the only source of intelligence during World War II. The British announced an official history project devoted to the whole intelligence operation during the war, in which ULTRA would be given its proper place. The first volume, covering the period to mid-1941, appeared in 1979 (264). By that time the British government had also released some of the ULTRA transcripts. Ronald Lewin, using at least some of them, has given the best appraisal to date of the influence of ULTRA in the various phases of the war (275). None of these most recent efforts, however, dwelt long on the influence of ULTRA on U.S. Army operations in Europe, and the question of how much of the history of those operations needs to be rewritten remains open. But it is already apparent that ULTRA had more influence on air and naval operations than on those involving ground forces. Meanwhile, little has been written beyond David Kahn's *The Codebreakers* (270), published in 1967, on the influence of the MAGIC intercepts on the course of the Pacific war beyond the well-known instances of the Battle of Midway and the interception of Admiral Yamamoto's plane.

OPERATIONS. In any event, the full evaluation of the relationship of intelligence gathering and army operations in World War II still lies largely in the future. The original work of the last five years on these operations, in its entirety rather meager, has largely been along conventional lines. More has appeared on the war against Germany than on that against Japan. The only volume in the "Green Volumes," the U.S. Army in World War II Series, to be published, Fisher's *Cassino to the Alps* (259), deals with the last phase of

American operations in Italy. Allen has revisited the Anzio battlefield (241), and Crookenden deals in detail with the airborne operations of the British and Americans in Normandy (252).

Lucas and Barker treat the Normandy operations leading to the Falaise Gap in a work (276) one reviewer characterizes as "peculiarly organized and curiously fragmented" but "basically sound despite small errors." Ross sketches the Tarawa campaign in *Line of Departure* (283), and the Marine Corps historian Benis Frank has produced a small volume on the Okinawa battle (260). Bidwell analyzes the relationship between General Stilwell and Orde Wingate, the British pioneer in fighting behind Japanese lines (246). Romanus and Sunderland, the army's historians of the China-Burma-India Theater, have provided basic source material on Stilwell's controversial command by publishing his personal file of correspondence and cables between 1942 and 1944, (281), documents Barbara Tuchman apparently did not use in writing her biography of Stilwell. Some interesting sidelights on this tangled theater may be found in newsman Theodore White's memoirs *In Search of History* (297).

LOGISTICS. There has been practically nothing published on U.S. Army logistics in World War II in the last five years. The laggard volumes on the technical services in the U.S. Army in World War II Series, on the engineers in Europe and the Medical Service in both Europe and the Pacific, should be forthcoming soon. Meanwhile, in a general survey called *Supplying War* (294), van Creveld has presented some challenging conclusions about the "logistical pusillanimity" of the Allied forces under Eisenhower in the advance across Europe in 1944.

SPECIAL TOPICS. Some works of a reference nature deserve mention, notably Hunnicut's work on the Sherman tank (268), Ladd's on commandos and rangers (273), Devlin's on parachute and glider troops in two world wars (255), and Barker's description of American and British infantry weapons of the war (243). Some unit histories are likewise worth noting—Houston's of the Second Armored Division (267), Hoffman's of the Sixth Armored Division (266), and Walthall's treatment of separate infantry regiments (295). Weingartner has told the story of the Malmedy massacre and the subsequent trial in some detail (296). Ziemke has covered the beginnings of military government in Germany during the war in a volume in the Army Historical Series (299). Brown and MacDonald have dug out from archives the army's wartime history of the Manhattan District and published it as *The Secret History of the Atomic Bomb* (249). Suid treats of the cooperation between the military services and the motion picture industry in making war movies (288). Sherry tells how during the war the army planned for its future (284). Longmate's *G.I.'s* (275) is an interesting account of the interaction between American soldiers in England and the British people. A virtually unique study is that of Shibutani in *The Derelicts of Company K,* (285), a treatment of the progressive demoralization of a group of Nisei in training camps, a marked contrast to the standard picture of the Nisei who fought so heroically in Europe.

OPORTUNITIES FOR ADDITIONAL RESEARCH. The area that must be added to the list of those requiring additional research is obviously that of intelligence and its relation to operations in World War II—what David Kahn has called the "biggest hole" in World War II historiography (271). ULTRA is, of course, the prime example but certainly not the only one. The influence of the MAGIC intercepts of Japanese radio traffic on the war in the Pacific has not yet been treated in any comprehensive manner; the emphasis has always been on the background of Pearl Harbor. Certainly, the claims that the whole history of World War II must be rewritten in terms of ULTRA, MAGIC, and other intelligence are exaggerated. It is more a question of revision of detail. But the true place of all these intelligence methods and usages must be examined and placed in proper perspective. Clearly, to date they have been neglected, very largely because it has been impossible for scholars, including the authors of official histories, to get at the archival material. With the revelation of the ULTRA secret, most of these barriers are now being broken down and there should be much fruitful research and writing in this field in the next five to ten years.

BIBLIOGRAPHY

241. Allen, William Lusk. *Anzio: Edge of Disaster.* New York: E. P. Dutton, 1979.

242. Anderson, Stuart. "Abilene, Kansas, and the History of World War II: Resources and Research Opportunities at the Dwight D. Eisenhower Library." *Military Affairs* 41 (December, 1977): 195–200.

243. Barker, A. J. *British and American Infantry Weapons of World War II.* New York: Arco, 1978.

244. Bayliss, Gwynn M. *Bibliographic Guide to the Two World Wars: An Annotated Survey of English Language Reference Materials.* New York: Bowker, 1977.

245. Bell, Roger J. *Unequal Allies: Australian-American Relations and the Pacific War.* Melbourne: Melbourne University Press, 1977.

246. Bidwell, Shelford. *The Chindit War: Stilwell, Wingate, and the Campaign in Burma.* New York: Macmillan, 1980.

247. Blumenson, Martin. "Will 'ULTRA' Rewrite History?" *Army* 28, no. 8 (August, 1978): 42–48.

248. Brown, Anthony Cave. *Bodyguard of Lies.* New York: Harper & Row, 1975.

249. Brown, Anthony Cave, and Charles B. MacDonald. *The Secret History of the Atomic Bomb.* New York: Dial Press/James Wade, 1977.

250. Chase, William C. *Front Line General: The Commands of William C. Chase.* Houston: Gulf Publishing Co., 1977.

251. Collins, J. Lawton. *Lightning Joe: An Autobiography.* Baton Rouge: Louisiana State University Press, 1979.

252. Crookenden, Napier. *Dropzone Normandy.* New York: Charles Scribner's Sons, 1976.

253. Deutsch, Harold C. "The Historical Impact of Revealing the ULTRA Secret." *Parameters 7, no. 3 (1977): 16–32.*

254. Deutsch, Harold C. "The Influence of ULTRA on World War II." *Parameters 8, no. 4 (December, 1978): 2–15.*

255. Devlin, Gerard. *Paratrooper! The Saga of the Parachute and Glider Troops, 1914 to 1945.* New York: St. Martin's, 1975.

256. Dunn, Walter S., Jr. "The ULTRA Papers." *Military Affairs.* 42 (October, 1978): 134–35.

257. Ensor, A. G. S. *A Subject Bibliography of the Second World War: Books in English, 1939–1974.* Boulder: Westview Press, 1977.

258. Essame, Hubert. *Patton, A Study in Command.* New York: Charles Scribner's Sons, 1974.

259. Fisher, Ernest. *Cassino to the Alps.* U.S. Army in World War II Series, *Mediterranean Theater of Operations.* Washington, D. C.: GPO, 1977.

260. Frank, Benis M. *Okinawa: The Great Island Battle.* New York: Elsevier-Dutton, 1978.

261. Funk, Arthur L. *The Politics of TORCH: The Allied Landings and the Algiers Putsch, 1942.* Lawrence: University Press of Kansas, 1974.

262. Gavin, James. *On to Berlin: Battles of an Airborne Commander, 1943–46.* New York: Viking Press, 1978.

263. Hayes, Grace P. *History of the Joint Chiefs of Staff in World War II: The War against Japan.* 2 vols. Washington, D.C.: JCS Historical Section, 1953-54. Printed history in custody of National Archives.

264. Hinsley, F. H. *British Intelligence in the Second World War: Its Influence on Strategy and Operations.* London: Her Majesty's Stationery Office, 1979–198–. 3 vols. to date.

265. Historical Section, JCS. "History of the Joint Chiefs of Staff in World War II: The War against Germany." Ms. in National Archives.

266. Hofmann, George F. *Super Sixth: The History of the 6th Armored Division in World War II and its Post-War Association.* Louisville: The Association, 1975.

267. Houston, Donald E. *The 2d Armored Division.* San Rafael, Calif.: Presidio Press, 1979.

268. Hunnicut, R. P. *Sherman.* San Rafael, Calif.: Presidio Press, 1979.

269. James, D. Clayton. *The Years of MacArthur.* Vol. 2, *1941–1945.* Boston: Houghton Mifflin, 1975.

270. Kahn, David. *The Code-Breakers: The Story of Secret Writing.* New York: Macmillan, 1967.

271. Kahn, David. "World War II History: The Biggest Hole." *Military Affairs* 39 (April, 1975): 74–76.

272. Kittredge, Tracy B. "United States Defense Policies and Global Strategy, 1900–1914." Historical Section, JCS, 1946-63. Available in microfilm from National Archives.

273. Ladd, James D. *Commandos and Rangers of World War II.* New York: St. Martin's, 1978.

274. Lewin, Ronald. *ULTRA Goes to War.* New York: McGraw-Hill, 1979.

275. Longmate, Norman. *The G.I.'s: The Americans in Britain, 1942–1945.* New York: Charles Scribner's Sons, 1975.

276. Lucas, James, and James Barker. *The Battle of Normandy: The Falaise Gap.* New York: Holmes & Meier, 1979.

277. Manchester, William. *American Caesar: Douglas MacArthur, 1880–1964.* Boston: Little Brown, 1978.

278. Mason, A. T., and Nathaniel Morgenthal. "Special Monograph on Amphibious Warfare." Chapters 1–6, prewar through January 1943. Historical Section, JCS, 1949–51. Available at National Archives.

279. Melose, Martin V. *The Shadow of Pearl Harbor: Political Controversy over the Surprise Attack.* College Station, Tex.: Texas A & M University Press, 1977.

280. O'Neill, James E., and Robert W. Krauskopf, eds. *World War II: An Account of its Documents.* Washington, D.C.: Howard University Press, 1976.

281. Romanus, Charles F., and Riley Sunderland, eds. *Stilwell's Personal File, China, Burma, India, 1942–1944.* 5 vols. Wilmington: Scholarly Resources, 1976.

282. Rosengarten, Adolph G. "With ULTRA from Omaha Beach to Weimar, Germany—a Personal View." *Military Affairs* 42 (October, 1978): 127–32.

283. Ross, Martin. *Line of Departure.* New York: Doubleday, 1977.

284. Sherry, Michael S. *Preparing for the Next War: American Plans for Post-war Defense, 1941–1945.* New Haven: Yale University Press, 1977.

285. Shibutani, Tamotsu. *The Derelicts of Company K: A Sociological Study of Demoralization.* Berkeley: University of California Press, 1978.

286. Smith, Bradley F., and Elena Agarossi. *Operation SUNRISE: The Secret Surrender.* New York: Basic Books, 1979.

287. Stoler, Mark A. *The Politics of the Second Front: American Military Planning and Diplomacy in Coalition Warfare, 1941–1943.* Westport, Conn.: Greenwood Press, 1977.

288. Suid, Lawrence. *Guts and Glory: Great American War Movies.* Reading, Mass.: Addison-Wesley, 1978.

289. Thorne, Christopher. *Allies of a Kind: The United States, Britain, and the War against Japan, 1941–1945.* New York: Oxford University Press, 1978.

290. U.S. Army Center of Military History. *Catalog and Index to Historical Manuscripts.* Vol. 1, *Headquarters, War Department and Department of the Army.* Vol. 2, *Army Service Forces.* Compiled by Hannah M. Zeidlik. Washington, D.C.: U.S. Army Center of Military History, 1979.

291. U.S. Army Military History Institute. Special Bibliography Series no. 16, *The Era of World War II.* Vol. 1: *General Reference Works, Biography,* compiled by Roy Barnard, William Burns, and Duane Ryan. Vol. 2: *Pacific,* compiled by Duane Ryan. Vol. 4: *Mediterranean and European Theaters of Operations,* compiled by Louise Arnold. Carlisle Barracks, Pa.: U.S. Army Military History Institute, 1977–79.

292. U.S. Army Military History Research Collection. *Manuscript Holdings of the Military History Research Collection.* Compiled by Richard J. Sommers. Special Bibliography Series no. 6, vol. 2. Carlisle Barracks, Pa.: U.S. Army Military History Research Collection, 1975.

293. United States Department of Defense. *The Magic Background of Pearl Harbor.* 5 vols. Washington, D.C. GPO, 1977–78.

294. van Creveld, Martin. *Supplying War: Logistics from Wallenstein to Patton.* Cambridge: Cambridge University Press, 1977.

295. Walthall, Melvin Curtis. *We Can't All be Heroes: A History of the Separate Infantry Regiments of World War II.* Hicksville, N.Y.: Exposition Press, 1975.

296. Weingartner, James J. *Crossroads of Death: The Story of the Malmedy Massacre and Trial.* Berkeley: University of California Press, 1978.

297. White, Theodore H. *In Search of History: A Personal Adventure.* New York: Harper & Row, 1978.

298. Winterbotham, Frederick. *The ULTRA Secret.* London: Weidenfeld & Nicholson, 1974.

299. Ziemke, Earl F. *The Army in the Occupation of Germany.* Washington, D.C.: GPO, 1975.

300. Zobrist, Benedict K. "Resources of Presidential Libraries for the History of the Second World War." *Military Affairs* 39 (April, 1975): 82–85.

XV

THE U.S. ARMY AIR CORPS

AND

THE UNITED STATES AIR FORCE, 1909–78

Robert T. Finney

World War II has been over for more than thirty years, and the United States Air Force has engaged in two major conflicts and several international crises since since 1945. Yet, if one can judge by the flood of current publications, interest of professional military historians and popular writers still centers on the air effort of the Second World War. Although official studies, for the most part, deal with more current subjects, popular accounts are dominated by publications dealing with the Army Air Forces' activities and the aircraft flown in World War II. The surge of the latter may be the result of the declassification of virtually all War Department documents through 1945 and of Air Force documents through 1955. This declassification, however, seems to have attracted popular writers more than professional historians, and the resultant output has been more in the area of operational accounts of derring-do than scholarly appraisals and analyses of causes and effects, results, lessons learned, and philosophies of the employment of air power.

OFFICIAL HISTORIES AND GOVERNMNENT DOCUMENTS. Although interest in United States Air Force affairs continues to run high, no official, comprehensive history of the air force has yet appeared. Nevertheless, the Office of Air Force History and the Albert F. Simpson Historical Research Center collect and classify pertinent air force historical materials and produce source guides for researchers in air force matters and well-documented, authorative studies and edited works on selected aspects of the United States Air Force and its predecessors.

In the former category, the center has prepared two brief, but complete, bibliographies: one, by Robinson (375), covering the center's holdings on the history of manned balloons and airships; and the other, by Peets (374), on its holdings on the history of women in the armed forces. Jacob Neufeld's (370) *United States Air Force History: A Guide to Monographic Literature* is the third in the USAF history reference series; it supplements Paszek's (214) earlier guide and lists all of the monographs prepared within the air force on a wide range of subjects. Knaack's (353) *Encyclopedia* is a history of fighters from the

F-80 through the development of the F-15; it is the first of a proposed multivolume series of official descriptions of USAF weapons. Considerable time could also be saved in searching for air force records by referring to Cornett's (327) brief article in *Aerospace Historian.* The new aerospace bibliography by Miller (363) is larger and more detailed than the earlier Office of Air Force History annotated bibliography (56). For the statistically minded, the center has published *USAF Credits for the Destruction of Enemy Aircraft, World War II* (317).

In the category of edited works falls the impressive four-volume *U.S. Air Service in World War I,* edited by Maurer (362). With few exceptions, such as Patrick's (215) *Final Report,* these volumes present a vast array of previously unpublished material. Few historians are aware of the fact, for example, that a survey strangely reminiscent of the U.S. Strategic Bombing Survey following World War II was undertaken after World War I.

Mueller and Carter's (365) combat chronology of air events of World War II is not only extensive in coverage, but is made even more usable by the addition of an almost unbelievably detailed index. An aspect of recent military history that has been somewhat neglected in official writings is the subject of Osur's (372) *Blacks in the Army Air Forces During World War II: The Problem of Race Relations;* it is concerned more with the questions of segregation and training than with combat operations of black air units. Gropman (337) continues the story of blacks in the United States Air Force, covering the turbulent postwar period of race relations, 1945–61.

For some new thoughts on the strategic airwar in Europe, presented by eminent scholars in the field of military aviation, see the *Proceedings of the Second Military History Symposim,* held at the Air Force Academy in May 1968; published under the title *Command and Commanders in Modern Military History,* the volume is edited by Lt. Col. William Geffen (334). For an overall survey of air power, see *Airpower and Warfare, Proceedings of the Eighth Military Symposium,* edited by Hurley and Ehrhart (348).

Official studies of United States Air Force participation in the conflict in Southeast Asia have begun to appear. The first overall study is Berger's (319) *The United States Air Force in Southeast Asia, 1961–1973.* Definitive histories of air force involvement are in preparation but, pending their publication, this volume may be considered the official history. Other studies dealing with specific aspects of air force activity are available. Nalty's (368) *Air Power and the Fight for Khe Sanh* is a well-balanced account, though it tends to report results quantatively rather than qualitatively. Eastman's (330) *Aces and Aerial Victories* covers more than the title might indicate; it provides researchers with an overview of the USAF's involvement in the conflict, detailed accounts of each combat which resulted in the destruction of enemy aircraft, and a valuable statistical record of enemy losses. The Office of Air Force History has also published a pictorial history of the air force in Southeast Asia (371). Another volume concerning the air force in Southeast Asia, by Fox (332), was published in 1980.

Obvious sources of information on military history are the hearings and reports of congressional committees, especially the Committee on Appropriations and the Armed Services Committee of the Senate and House of Representatives. References are too numerous to list here, but this fertile field should be consulted by any serious student of military history. In addition to the

Monthly Catalogue of United States Government Publications (285), a valuable guide to federal government publications is the Congressional Information Service, *CIS/Annual* (325), which began publication in 1970.

GENERAL HISTORIES. The best current general history of the United States Air Force consists of two related volumes by Mackin (358) and Coard (324). Although falling short of filling the need for a single, scholarly, definitive history of the air force and its predecessors, this work is the most comprehensive air force history since the Goldberg (105) volume. Volume 1, *US Air Power: Ascension to Prominence* begins with the advent of flight and continues through the creation of the United States Air Force in 1947; volume 2, *US Air Power: Key to Deterrence,* takes the air force story through 1976. Of two other general histories, Mason (361) and Glines (335), Mason's is the better choice. Although by no means a complete history, it is a readable, short introduction to the air force; it includes an interesting series of appendices. Glines is an update of an earlier history, to which he has added two chapters, one on the war in Vietnam and the other on the air force in the space age.

A few studies deal with the long-range evolution of specific weapons or organizations. For the most part, they make a significant contribution toward filling out the story of the United States Air Force. The inference in the subtitle of Anderton's (318) *Strategic Air Command: Two-Thirds of the Triad* is misleading in that it implies that this is a study of the current SAC. Actually this better than usual popular account of a major command opens with the concepts of air power employment of Douhet, Mitchell, and Trenchard, and carries the SAC story from origin through 1973. Sims (380) presents a well-written, but not definitive, argument in defense of the fighter as more important than the bomber, tracing fighter tactics and strategy from 1914 through 1970. Clark (322) describes the changing strategic and tactical employment of the bomber from ballooning to the present. Campbell (321) has done an excellent job in presenting the origin and development of military aviation badges and insignia, subjects generally ignored by military historians; the Aviation Section of the Signal Corps, Air Service, Air Corps, and Army Air Forces are included.

EARLY DAYS AND WORLD WAR I. World War I remains a wide-open field for investigation. A definitive history of the air experience of that war has yet to be undertaken. Hopefully, Maurer's volumes, which demonstrate the availability of unexplored research material, will arouse new interest in the beginnings of military aviation. As an aid to research in that field, Myron Smith (382) has produced a comprehensive bibliography of items published through 1975; the chronology added at the end is sketchy. As another lead to records of the World War I air experience, the National Archives (369) has prepared an exhaustive guide to its holdings on the air service 1917–19.

BETWEEN THE WARS. The period of the 1920s and 1930s is one of the most fascinating in the history of the American air arm. It is also one of the most challenging to military historians. Yet this formative period of U.S. air power, when concepts of air force employment were being forged and achievements, not spectacular but highly significant, were occurring, has yet to receive the attention it deserves. Lt. Gen. Howard A. Craig (328) has added some details on the battleship bombings in 1923 and insight into the person of Mitchell, but the full significance of the period will not be understood or appreciated until historians devote the time and effort necessary to bring activities of the two decades into proper perspective.

WORLD WAR II. The seven-volume history of the Army Air Forces in World War II, edited by Craven and Cate (55), continues to be supplemented by narratives that are more in the nature of personal and popular accounts than interpretive, analytical history. Two exceptions might be noted. General Hansell has followed up his illuminating view of American strategic bombing theory in his *The Air Plan That Defeated Hitler* (120) with a penetrating apprasal of the air effort against Japan in his *Strategic Air War Against Japan* (342a). The perennial question of the viability of the U.S. theory of strategic bombardment during the early stages of AAF involvement in World War II is addressed again by Coffey (324), who basically presents General Eaker's views of the Schweinfurt mission. A companion piece to this account of the early days of the strategic air war against Germany is Sweetman's *Ploesti: Oil Strike* (383).

Unit histories and stories of special operations range in quality from very good to poor. Only those of considerable merit are noted here. Kenneth Rust (377, 378, 379), for example, is producing short but well-researched histories of most of the overseas air forces. Johnson's (350) story of the 365th Fighter-Bomber Group is one of the most comprehensive unit histories to be published (623 pages), but it is burdened with some distractions, such as overlong quotations. H. E. and E. M. Oyster (373) have written a better than average unit history.

The air war in the Far East and CBI has received considerable attention. Birdsall's (320) *Flying Buccaneers: The Illustrated Story of Kenney's Fifth Air Force* is not a scholarly history, but it is a readable account that emphasizes men and missions. Thomas and Witt's (384) record of the first use of the atomic bomb is marred somewhat by some errors. The first use of the atomic bomb is one of the better portions of Sinclair's (381) story of B-29 operations from both the CBI and the Mariannas. Koenig (354) has related the impressive story of the airlift over the Hump into China. Hess (344) has one of the better unit histories, which bears evidence of research into available archive materials.

Rose's (376) unofficial retelling of the story of blacks in the AAF in World War II should be consulted by anyone doing further research in this field.

It is worth noting that MacIsaac's (356) dissertation on the United States Strategic Bombing Survey is now in print. In addition, he has published the 31 most important reports of the original 321 separate reports (357). Air University has reprinted Futrell's *Ideas, Concepts, Doctrine* (333) in a much cleaner, one-volume format to which has been added an excellent index.

AFTER WORLD WAR II. The problem of security classification remains a barrier when military historians attempt in-depth research for the most recent period. For the most part, monographs and studies are based on the public press, official studies that have run through the declassification mill (such as Futrell's Korean War volume [97]), unclassified public information releases from the services, and items appearing in the public domain, such as those found in congressional committees' hearings and reports. An exception to this general condition is a series of unofficial but significant monographs relating to the United States Air Force activities in Southeast Asia. These studies, published under the overall title *USAF Southeast Asia Monograph Series,* began under the aegis of Gen. W. W. Momyer, USAF, Ret., who has himself written *Air Power in Three Wars* (355). The monographs have been written by participants in the conflict and are, generally, operational accounts designed "to . . . highlight the dedication, courage, and professionalism of the U.S. airmen in combat." They are not analytical studies of United States involvement in Southeast Asia. Authors, with few exceptions (such as General Momyer), wrote their monographs (in several cases, several authors to one monograph) while students at the Air University's Air War College or Air Command and Staff College, where they had access to the voluminous records in the Historical Research Center. The first four volumes were edited by Maj. A. J. C. Lavalle (355), but subsequent volumes will be published under the auspices of the Airpower Research Institute, Air War College. Additional monographs are in preparation.

Another account of the air force's post-World War II combat operations can be found in Jackson's popular *Air War Over Korea* (349).

BIOGRAPHIES AND AUTOBIOGRAPHIES. Most senior Air Force officers are strangely reticent about publishing their memoirs. As a result, the service and the country, to say nothing of military historians, are being denied the benefit of irreplaceable stores of knowledge and experience. General Hansell has added to his intimate knowledge of the evolution and trial of U.S. strategic bombardment in his retelling of the strategic air war against Japan (342a). Another addition to what one might hope would be an eventual outpouring of autobiographies is Howard A. Craig's (328) personal narrative of peace and war, which, although welcome, is hampered by its brevity. Two biographies of General Doolittle have appeared—by Glines (336) and Thomas and Jablonski (385). The latter was written in collaboration with General Doolittle and is the closest to a definitive biography to appear so far on him, but it deals almost entirely with his public life. Although not strictly an autobiography, General Momyer's work (364) spans three wars (World War II, Korea, and Vietnam) in presenting his preoccupations with the basics of tactical air force employment, strategy, command and control, counter air operations, interdiction, and close air support. Flint DuPre's (329) short sketch can scarcely be termed a biography of General Arnold.

PILOTS AND PLANES. Interest still abounds in the origin, development, characteristics, and employment of aircraft and in personal stories of the men who flew them. Elliott (332) paints an especially illuminating personal picture of a World War I pilot's experience from enlistment through the armistice. Higham and Siddall (345) and Higham and Williams (346) present accurate and authentic reports by current and past air force pilots on how principal AAF and USAF aircraft were flown. Hess (343) reveals what it was like to fly the P-47 in combat. Lloyd Jones (351, 352) is one of the best sources on the evolution and characteristics of U.S. fighters and bombers. Bryan Cooper and John Batchelor (326) have produced an exceptionally well illustrated history of fighter aircraft. The story of several individual aircraft has been told with varying degrees of competence and authenticity. Among the best are

Gunston's several volumes (339–42) in which he gives detailed accounts, from conception through employment of the F-4, F-100, F-102, F-4D, F-8, F-111, B-47, B-52, B-58, A-3, A-5, B-70, and the B-1. His explanation of the fate of the B-1 is especially interesting. Other works on individual aircraft include Holder (347) on the B-52 and Martin (360) on the C-141. In his two volumes, Munson (366, 367) describes aircraft since 1960.

SUGGESTIONS FOR FURTHER RESEARCH. Books, pamphlets, journals, and articles continue to appear dealing with various aspects of the United States Air Force and its predecessors. Included here is a sampling of the most significant and those of greatest value to future researchers in air force history. For, despite the profusion of literature appearing annually on the United States Air Force, the works being published leave gaps. In many cases, published works only scratch the surface of subjects that call for serious, analytical study; other subjects are waiting for initial research. A few specific areas deserving further investigation have been noted from time to time above. For example, at the risk of repetition, attention is invited to the need for a comprehensive history of the air service and the origins of the concepts of air power employment in World War I. Causes of the 1920s and 1930s myopia of the War Department General Staff in viewing the air weapon needs to be analyzed. Was it caused, at least in part, by the recognition on the part of some that the air weapon was a threat to certain entrenched arms and branches? Or was the lack of understanding of air power's potential genuine? Futrell (96), Hansell (120, 342a), and Finney (83) have introduced the evolution of air doctrine at the Air Corps Tactical School, but the definitive study of the subject remains to be done. Moreover, the significance of and the contribution to the Air Corps by the Air Corps Board has not been adequately evaluated. Analytical appraisals of mission objective and accomplishment of World War II are needed to supplemnent the operations-oriented (men, missions, air battles, statistics of tons dropped, etc.) accounts. Futrell (96) has explained and interpreted air force thinking through 1964, but after fifteen years, his study should be updated to indicate any changes in basic air force philosophy of mission and employment brought about by technological developments and constantly changing international affairs. What has been the impact of budgetary limitations on the air force since 1945? What new weapon system does the air force require? What is the story of the B-1? Readable accounts of air force logistic problems and solutions are long overdue. These questions and a host of others are awaiting the attention of military historians. Finally, biographies of outstanding airmen are woefully lacking.

BIBLIOGRAPHY

317. Albert F. Simpson Historical Research Center. *USAF Credits for the Destruction of Enemy Aircraft, World War II.* USAF Historical Study no 85. Maxwell Air Force Base, Ala.: Albert F. Simpson Historical Research Center, 1978.

318. Anderton, David A. *Strategic Air Command: Two-Thirds of the Triad.* New York: Scribner, 1976.

319. Berger, Carl, ed. *The United States Air Force in Southeast Asia, 1961-1973.* Washington, D.C.: Government Printing Office, 1977.
320. Birdsall, Steve. *Flying Buccaneers: The Illustrated Story of Kenney's Fifth Air Force.* Garden City, N.Y.: Doubleday, 1977.
321. Campbell, J. Duncan. *Aviation Badges and Insignia of the United States Army, 1913-1946.* Harrisburg, Pa.: Triangle Press, 1977.
322. Clark, Ronald W. *The Role of the Bomber.* New York: Crowell, 1978.
323. Coard, Edna A. *US Air Power: Key to Deterrence.* Maxwell Air Force Base: ROTC, 1976.
324. Coffey, Thomas M. *Decision Over Schweinfurt: The U.S. 8th Air Force Battle for Daylight Bombing.* New York: David McKay, 1977.
325. Congressional Information Service. *CIS/Annual.* Washington: Congressional Information Service, 1970- . 2 vols. to date. Vol. 1, *Abstracts of Congressional Publications and Legislative Histories;* vol. 2, *Index to Congressional Publications and Public Laws.*
326. Cooper, Bryan, and John Batchelor. *Fighter. A History of Fighter Aircraft.* New York: Scribner, 1974.
327. Cornett, Lloyd, Jr. "The Albert F. Simpson Historical Research Center." *Aerospace Historian* 25 (Fall/September 1978): 189.
328. Craig, Lt. Gen. Howard A., USAF, Ret. *Sunward I've Climbed. A Personal Narrative of Peace and War.* El Paso, Tex.: Texas Western Press, 1975.
329. DuPre, Flint. *Hap Arnold: Architect of American Air Power.* New York: Macmillan, 1972.
330. Eastman, James N., Jr., ed. *Aces and Aerial Victories: The United States Air Force in Southeast Asia, 1965-1973.* Washington, D.C.: Government Printing Office, 1977.
331. Elliott, Stuart E. *Wooden Crates and Gallant Pilots.* Philadelphia: Dorrance, 1974.
332. Fox, Lt. Col. Roger, USAF, Ret. *Air Base Defense in the Republic of Vietnam.* Washington, D.C.: Government Printing Office, 1980.
333. Futrell, Robert F. *Ideas, Concepts, Doctrine: A History of Basic Thinking in the United States Air Force.* Maxwell Air Force Base: Air University, 1974.
334. Geffen, Lt. Col. William. *Command and Commanders in Modern Military History: Proceedings of the Second Military History Symposium.* [Washington, D.C.] Office of Air Force History, 1971.
335. Glines, Carroll V. *The Compact History of the United States Air Force.* New and rev. ed. New York: Hawthorne, 1973.
336. Glines, Carroll V. *Jimmy Doolittle: Daredevil Aviator and Scientist.* New York: Macmillan, 1972.
337. Gropman, Lt. Col. Alan L., USAF. *The Air Force Integrates, 1945-1964.* Washington: Government Printing Office, 1978.
338. Gropman, Lt. Col. Alan L., USAF. *Airpower and the Airlift Evacuation of Khan Duc.* Maxwell Air Force Base: Airpower Research Institute, Air War College, 1979.
339. Gunston, William. *Bombers of the West.* New York: Scribner, 1973.
340. Gunston, William. *Early Supersonic Fighters of the West.* New York: Scribner, 1975.
341. Gunston, William. *F-4 Phantom.* New York: Scribner, 1977.

342. Gunston, William. *F-111.* New York: Scribner, 1978.

342 a. Hansell, Maj. Gen. Haywood S., Jr., Ret. *Strategic Air War Against Japan.* Maxwell Air Force Base: Airpower Research Institute, Air War College, 1980.

343. Hess, William N. *P-47 Thunderbolt at War.* Garden City, N.Y.: Doubleday, 1977.

344. Hess, William N. *Pacific Sweep: The 5th and 13th Fighter Commands in World War II.* New York: Doubleday, 1974.

345. Higham, Robin, and Abigail Siddall, eds. *Flying Combat Aircraft of the USAAF and USAF.* Vol. 1. Ames, Iowa: Iowa State University Press, 1975.

346. Higham, Robin, and Carol Williams, eds. *Flying Combat Aircraft of the USAAF and USAF.* Vol. 2. Ames, Iowa: Iowa State University Press, 1978.

347. Holder, William G. *Boeing B-52 "Stratofortress."* Fallbrook, Calif.: Aero, 1975.

348. Hurley, Col. Alfred F., USAF, and Robert C. Ehrhart. *Airpower and Warfare: Proceedings of the Eighth Military History Symposium, United States Air Force Academy.* Washington, D.C.: Office of Air Force History, 1979.

349. Jackson, Robert. *Air War Over Korea.* New York: Scribner, 1975.

350. Johnson, Charles R. *The History of the Hill Hawks.* Anaheim: Southcoast Typesetting, 1975.

351. Jones, Lloyd S. *U. S. Bombers.* Fallbrook, Calif.: Aero, 1974.

352. Jones, Lloyd S. *U. S. Fighters.* Fallbrook, Calif.: Aero, 1975.

353. Knaack, Marcelle, S. *Encyclopedia of US Air Force Aircraft and Missile Systems.* Vol. 1, *Post-World War II Fighters, 1945-1973.* Washington, D.C.: Government Printing Office, 1978.

354. Koenig, William J. *Over the Hump: Airlift to China.* New York: Ballantine, 1972.

355. Lavalle, Maj. Arthur J. C. *USAF Southeast Asia Monograph Series.* Vol. 1, *The Tale of Two Bridges and the Battle for the Skies over North Vietnam* (monographs 1 and 2); vol. 2, *Airpower and the 1972 Spring Invasion* (monograph); vol. 3, *The Vietnamese Air Force, 1951-1975: An Analyses of Its Role in Combat and Fourteen Hours at Kah Tang* (monographs 4 and 5); vol. 4, *Last Flight from Saigon* (monograph 6). Washington, D.C.: Government Printing Office, 1976-78.

356. MacIsaac, Lt. Col. David, USAF. *Strategic Bombing in World War II.* New York: Garland, 1976.

357. MacIsaac, Lt. Col. David, USAF, ed. *The United States Strategic Bombing Survey.* 10 vols. New York: Garland, 1976.

358. Mackin, Thomas E. *US Air Power: Ascension to Prominence.* Maxwell Air Force Base: Air Force ROTC, 1974.

359. McCarthy, Brig. Gen. James R., USAF, and Lt. Col. George B. Allison, USAF. *LINEBACKER II: A View from the Rock.* Maxwell Air Force Base: Airpower Research Institute, Air War College, 1979.

360. Martin, Harold H. *Starlifter: The C-141, Lockheed's Highspeed Flying Truck.* Brattleboro: Greene, 1972.

361. Mason, Herbert M., Jr. *The United States Air Force: A Turbulent History.* New York: Mason/Charter, 1976.

362. Maurer, Maurer, ed. *The U.S. Air Service in World War I.* Vol. 1, *The Final Report and A Tactical History.* Vol. 2, *Some Early Concepts of Military Aviation.* Vol. 3, *The Battle of St. Mihiel.* Vol. 4, *Postwar Review.* Washington, D.C.: Government Printing Office, 1978-79.

363. Miller, Duncan *United State Air Force History: An Aerospace Bibliography.* Washington, D.C.: Government Printing Office, 1979.

364. Momyer, Gen. William W., USAF, Ret. *Air Power in Three Wars.* Washington, D.C.: Government Printing Office, 1978.

365. Mueller, Robert, and Kit C. Carter. *The Army Air Forces in World War II: Combat Chronology, 1941-1945.* Washington, D.C.: Government Printing Office, 1976.

366. Munson, Kenneth G. *Bombers in Service: Patrol and Transport Aircraft Since 1960.* New York: Macmillan, 1975.

367. Munson, Kenneth G. *Fighters in the Service: Attack and Training Aircraft Since 1960.* New York: Macmillan, 1975.

368. Nalty, Bernard C. *Air Power and the Fight for Khe Sanh.* Washington, D.C.: Government Printing Office, 1974.

369. National Archives. *Gorrell's History of the American Expeditionary Forces Air Service, 1917-1919* (National Archives Microfilm Publication Pamphlet Describing M990). Washington, D.C.: General Services Administration, 1975.

370. Neufeld, Jacob. *United States Air Force History: Guide to Monographic Literature, 1943-1974.* Washington, D.C.: Government Printing Office, 1977.

371. Office of Air Force History. *The United States Air Force in Southeast Asia: An Illustrated Account.* Washington, D.C.: Government Printing Office, 1977.

372. Osur, Alan M. *Blacks in the Army Air Forces during World War II: The Problem of Race Relations.* Washington, D.C.: Government Printing Office, 1977.

373. Oyster, H. E., and E. M. Oyster, eds. *The 319th in Action.* Akron: Burch Directory Co., 1976.

374. Peets, Eleanor E. *United States Air Force History: Women in the Armed Forces, A Selected Bibliography.* Maxwell Air Force Base: Albert F. Simpson Historical Research Center, 1976.

375. Robinson, Deryl W. *United States Air Force History of Manned Balloons and Airships: A Selected Bibliography.* Maxwell Air Force Base: Albert F. Simpson Historical Research Center, 1976.

376. Rose, Robert. *Lonely Eagles: The Story of America's Black Air Force in World War II.* Glendale: Aviation Book Co., 1977.

377. Rust, Kenneth C. *Fifteenth Air Force Story.* Temple City, Calif.: Historical Aviation Album, 1976.

378. Rust, Kenneth C. *Twelfth Air Force Story in World War II.* Temple City, Calif.: Historical Aviation Album, 1975.

379. Rust, Kenneth C., and Stephen Muth. *Fourteenth Air Force Story.* Temple City, Calif.: Historical Aviation Album, 1977.

380. Sims, Edward H. *Fighter Tactics and Strategy, 1914-1970.* New York: Harper, 1972.

381. Sinclair, William B. *The Big Brothers: The Story of the B-29s.* San Antonio: Naylor, 1972.

382. Smith, Myron J., Jr. *World War I in the Air. A Bibliography and Chronology.* Metuchen, N.J.: Scarecrow Press, 1977.
383. Sweetman, John. *Ploesti: Oil Strike.* New York: Ballantine, 1974.
384. Thomas, Gordon, and Max M. Witts. *Enola Gay.* New York: Stein and Day, 1977.
385. Thomas, Lowell, and Edward Jablonski. *Doolittle: A Biography.* Garden City, N.Y.: Doubleday, 1976.

XVI

THE DEPARTMENT OF DEFENSE, DEFENSE POLICY, AND DIPLOMACY SINCE 1945

Calvin L. Christman

In reviewing the sources for postwar defense policy that have appeared since the first edition of this guide, one is impressed with the decline of the polemical tone in much of the writing, especially in the material published since 1975. The decline is understandable, for with the shift of the Vietnam War from the present to the past tense, much of the literature has moved toward reflective judgments of the United States role in the post-Vietnam world, the effect of the war on the American military, and the level of military strength needed in the future. Though the emotional tone has waned, the appearance of source material has not, as the citations in the chapter will attest.

This chapter is not a rewriting or reconsideration of material from the first edition, but an addition to it. Thus, there will be no effort to reevaluate material previously discussed. In addition, sources concerning nuclear war, theory, and weaponry, as well as arms control and disarmament, are now in chapter XXI.

Research for this chapter ended in the summer and fall of 1978. Studies appearing after that time will be covered in the next edition.

GENERAL SOURCES. Arthur D. Larson's *National Security Affairs* (1290) provides extensive coverage, with its subject listings ranging over all facets of this topic. It should be considered one of the basic starting points for any bibliographical search. Unfortunately, it lacks annotation and limits its coverage of journal articles to a few publications. Some annotation can be found in Alcalá and Rosenberg's bibliography of "The New Politics of National Security" (1266), an article especially thorough in its survey of magazine and journal articles. Cronon and Rosenof (1275) list dissertations, books, and articles, and include an author index, a feature lacking in the other two works. Additionally, a survey of national security literature can be found in a useful Army Library publication (1262). For annotated discussions of foreign affairs literature, the Council on Foreign Relations sponsors the *Foreign Affairs Bibliography* series, with the fifth volume (1289) describing approximately eleven thousand works published between 1962 and 1972. Important military topics also receive consideration in the subject catagories of this work, and there is an author index included. Researchers can find a listing of dissertations on military topics in the February issue of *Military Affairs*. This annual article, begun by Millett and Cooling, was taken over by Christman and Showalter (1273) in 1977. Christman initiated a similar list of foreign affairs dissertations in the spring 1979 issue of *Diplomatic History* (1272).

In the area of reference works, the researcher should be familiar with *World Armaments and Disarmament* (1309). Put out by the Stockholm International Peace Research Institute (SIPRI), this yearbook is authoritative. A valuable review of United States foreign and defense policy is contained in *Congress and the Nation: 1973–1976* (1274), published by the Congressional Quarterly. The Council on Foreign Relations has replaced its helpful publications, *The United States in World Affairs* and *Documents on American Foreign Relations*, with a single series, *American Foreign Relations* (1303), which combines commentary and documents. Also examining the area of foreign relations, Grenville (1282) provides both a history and texts of major international treaties since World War I.

Congress continues to be an invaluable source of information on national security issues. Through its various hearings, reports, documents, and laws, Congress generates paper at a rate that can both literally and figuratively bury a researcher; its committees publish over eight hundred thousand pages a year. As mentioned in the first edition, Congressional Information Service (CIS), with its *Annual* and monthly *Index*, is indispensable in its abstracting of all congressional hearings, publications, and laws, with almost all material listed in its two publications available on CIS microfiche. CIS has also published a *Cumulative Index, 1970–1974* (1362). Burt and Kemp offer a valuable annotated guide in their *Congressional Hearings on American Defense Policy, 1947–1971* (1270).

MANUSCRIPTS. The presidential libraries serve as important depositories of manuscripts, with the Gerald R. Ford Library anticipating the opening of its permanent building (1341) to researchers in late 1980 or early 1981. Moreover, the Kennedy Library is now in its permanent quarters (1342). As noted in the first edition, the researcher should be as specific as possible when writing the director of a library inquiring about the amount and availability of material, giving both subjects and names involved whenever possible. Donated historical material is not subject to the regulations of the Freedom of Information Act. Thus, access is determined by the original donor and not by government legislation. Any federal records held in a presidential library, however, come under the Freedom of Information Act.

At the present time, plans for a Richard M. Nixon Library are in limbo. His papers are held by the General Services Administration (1343) and are now open to the public. Once the legal questions have been resolved, the GSA hopes to have some of the papers available within six months in temporary quarters within the Washington, D.C. area. Although the University of Southern California has voiced an interest in housing the permanent library, no decision has been made.

Researchers planning to use the Modern Military or Diplomatic Branches in the National Archives are further urged to be specific when requesting the quantity and accessibility of material. As of late 1978, most military and diplomatic records up to early 1950 were available, and there is expectation that additional material will come forth soon under Executive Order 12065. Effective 1 December 1978, this order allows the National Archives to follow a twenty-year rule for declassification of records under guidelines provided by the security agencies. Additional information on the National Archives and areas of research which have been largely ignored is found in *The National Archives and Foreign Relations Research* (1283). Though somewhat dated, the information contained is still useful. Furthermore, the *Declassified Documents Quarterly Catalog* (1319) supplies access to documents previously classified confidential, secret, and top secret.

Manuscript collections of government officials who served in security positions are those of Donald H. Rumsfeld (1357), Elliot L. Richardson (1356), William F. Raborn, Jr. (1355), John A. McCone (1353), Louis Johnson (1348), and Henry A. Kissinger (1349). Collections of figures involved in early nuclear development include those of Bush (1344), Compton (1345), Conant (1346), Lilienthal (1352), Lawrence (1350), Fermi (1347), Szilard (1358), and Oppenheimer (1354). Other collections of note are those of Gen. L. L. Lemnitzer (1351) and Henry A. Wallace (1359). Since some of these collections have restrictions on their use, researchers should first check on their accessibility. William E. Colby, R. H. Hillenkoetter, and Richard Helms left all CIA-related material with the agency, while Paul H. Nitze, Melvin R. Laird, W. Averell Harriman, George Bush, and Robert S. McNamara have made no decision concerning public papers. Many oral history collections may be obtained through *The New York Times Oral History Program* (1295).

NEWSPAPERS AND PERIODICALS. *The Wall Street Journal* and *The Christian Science Monitor* both occasionally give important treatment to national security issues. Opinions of leading newspaper columnists nationwide are available through *Viewpoint* (1310), while complete transcripts of *Meet the Press* (1292) and *CBS News Television Broadcasts* (1271) are available since 1957 and 1975 respectively. Valuable publications on foreign policy are *World Affairs* (1334), *Journal of International Affairs (1325), International Studies Quarterly* (1324), *Headlines Series* (1321), *Atlantic Community Quarterly* (1315), and the new journal, *Diplomatic History* (1320). Journals often emphasizing strategic implications are *AEI Defense Review* (1313), *Comparative Strategy* (1317), *International Security* (1323), *Strategic Review* (1329), and *Washington Review of Strategic and International Studies* (1333). All these journals began publication during the 1970s and often contain articles by authors who are or were quite influential in shaping national security policy. Though an established publication, *Science and Public Affairs* has now turned back to its original and better-known title of the *Bulletin of the Atomic Scientists*. The views of sociologists and political scientists receive emphasis in the *Journal of Political and Military Sociology* (1326) and *Armed Forces and Society* (1314), while *History, Numbers and War* (1322) is interested in quantifying the results of military experience. Other publications which may be of use are *Strategy & Tactics* (1330), *Technology and Culture* (1331), *Military Law Review* (1327), and *Command* (1316), the last being a new publication of the Department of Defense. Magazines which are often critical of defense policy and decisions are *Washington Monthly* (1332), *Counter Pentagon* (1318), and *Recon* (1328). Noteworthy indexes to military and foreign policy are provided in *Current Bibliographic Survey of National*

Defense (1337); *Abstracts of Military Bibliography* (1335), published in English and Spanish; *Social Sciences Index* (1340), which has split off from the previous *Social Sciences and Humanitites Index; Social Sciences Citation Index* (1339), which emerged in 1973; and *Scientific American Cumulative Index, 1948-1971* (1338).

AUTOBIOGRAPHICAL AND BIOGRAPHICAL MATERIALS. There exists no full-scale biography of Harry Truman, though Richard Kirkendall is working on one. Hamby (885) and Donovan (836) have provided sympathetic studies of aspects of his presidency, with the latter offering a study of Truman's first term by a veteran Washington journalist. Though Donovan spends more time on foreign affairs than Hamby, each generally tends to support Truman's foreign policy decisions. A far less favorable view emerges from Cochran's study (803), which assays Truman as an important cause of the cold war and the domination of American life by big business. Though the study seizes the flavor of Truman's thoughts, Miller's *Plain Speaking* (1000) must be used cautiously, for Truman's recollections, though lively, do not necessarily coincide with historical fact. Incisive essays on the historiography of Truman's foreign policy by Robert Ferrell and Lloyd Gardner are found in the updated version of Kirkendall's *The Truman Period as a Research Field* (936). This edition furnishes an excellent bibliography of books, articles, and dissertations. To date, no similar work has appeared on any other postwar president.

Once seen as a kindly but ineffectual president, Eisenhower is now being viewed as a stronger, more skillful chief executive, as illustrated by DeSantis (828) and Reichard (1370). Recent studies of the man (972) and his era (738), support this more approving view, as do monographs of his defense policy (931, 739). Stapleton's select bibliography (1302) surveys the literature on Truman and Eisenhower.

Jim Heath discusses Kennedy and Johnson in his study (891) of the 1960s, a decade that began with high hopes and ended with bitterness. Though Paper (1035) and Lord (967) portray Kennedy with general sympathy, others have placed him in an increasingly critical light, blaming him for intensifying the cold war with his unreconstructed warrior mentality. Miroff (1003) and Fitzsimons (853) express this viewpoint. A Kennedy bibliography has been compiled by Newcomb (1294). Kearns delivers many fascinating insights in her psychological study (923) of Lyndon Johnson's political life and thought, and Richard Nixon (1022), despite a style that is on occasion marred by self-pity and weak analysis, presents one of the better presidential memoirs of this century.

The literature on Kissinger and his influence continues to grow. Stoessinger (1117) gives a concise study of the secretary's personality, philosophy, and actions, and Marvin and Bernard Kalb present a full-scale picture (918) of his diplomacy. Both books are friendly to Kissinger, the latter perhaps too much so, occasionally reading like a publicity release. Nevertheless, both are important efforts. Sheehan's *The Arabs, Israelis, and Kissinger* (1098) produces an inside account of Kissinger's "shuttle diplomacy." Bell (755) supports Kissinger's view of detente, and Morris (1007), despite some reservations about Kissinger's performance, has strong praise for the secretary's triumph over the foreign policy bureaucracy. Ball (746) mounts a sharp attack on Kissinger's policies; Mazlish (983) is less concerned with his policies than with his personality. Kissinger's own views are found in the third edition of his *American Foreign Policy* (937).

With a few exceptions, little new has appeared on other secretaries of state or defense. Campbell and Herring have edited *The Diaries of Edward R. Stettinius, Jr., 1943-1946* (788), which, though containing no surprises, do supply information on the early cold war period. Acheson's years in the State Department are ably covered in McLellan's gentle portrait (990), while the secretary's own collection of essays shows that he modified his beliefs very little after leaving the government (735). A newsy but superficial view of the Dulles family comes from Mosley (1010), while Gaddis Smith (1104) illustrates the continuity of the Truman-Eisenhower-Kennedy administrations that transcends the influence of Dulles or any one man. Forrest C. Pogue hopes to complete his multi-volume biography of George C. Marshall by 1980 or 1981, and Keith McFarland has started work on a study of Louis Johnson. Military memoirs include Admiral Zumwalt's important and candid *On Watch* (1163), which is especially acrimonious concerning Kissinger's views and performance, and General Westmoreland's restrained *A Soldier Reports* (1147). D. Clayton James plans to finish his three-volume biography of MacArthur by 1980, the final volume focusing on the occupation of Japan and the Korean War.

With both Vietnam and détente in mind, historians are taking a more benign look at the foreign policy views of Henry Wallace. Blum contributes a sympathetic editing of his diary (769), Walker a balanced judgment of his ideas (1139), and Walton a hero-worshipping portrait (1142) of this critic of early cold war policy. More is to come, with Theodore A. Wilson presently working on a full-scale biography of Wallace. Merli and Wilson have edited a set of excellent essays, *Makers of American Diplomacy* (994); this collection includes articles on Truman, Acheson, Kennan, Dulles, Kennedy, Fulbright, and Kissinger. Some of the same figures are discussed in a generally negative tone in Donovan's *The Cold Warriors* (835). Influenced by the writings of C. Wright Mills, Donovan sees the policy-making elite propelled by their insatiable appetite for foreign markets. Writing from a similar radical base, Radosh (1057) studies individuals who were antiimperialist critics of United States policy.

NATIONAL SECURITY POLICY. Two effective introductions to foreign policy, supported by a clear understanding of the role of military power in the contemporary world, are by Ziegler (1162) and Nathan and Oliver (1018). Broad discussions of United States policy as it moves away from the Vietnam years are by Bloomfield (768) and Kennan (926). The former stresses the need for the United States to regain its self-respect by following policies that are not only wise but humane, while the latter emphasizes the need to reevaluate and reduce commitments around the world. Aron's *The Imperial Republic* (742) reviews United States foreign policy since 1945, believing that a middle ground must be found between globalism and isolationism. The importance of a continued balance of power backed by United States military might is argued by Eugene Rostow (1071). A major attack on the United States as an imperialist nation comes from Magdoff (973), and both Cohen (806) and Slater (1103) question the validity of such charges. Other valuable studies of various aspects of foreign policy are by Etzold (848), Williams (1152), Fox (855), Wilcox (1150),

Nau (1019), Nuechterlein (1026), Vogelgesang (1138), and Rosecrance (1068). Congress, in its hearings and publications, has reviewed détente (1198, 1230), technology(1195, 1200), human rights(1193, 1209, 1210), and its own role (1196, 1191) in United States policy.

Cohen's *The Public's Impact on Foreign Policy* (807) is an important study and will likely become a standard by which to measure future works on the subject. Russett (1075) and Nathan (1017) examine segments of domestic opinion on security issues, while Bachrack's *The Committee of One Million* (744) describes the organization of one major lobby effort in the foreign policy field. Broad discussions of military intervention and its various aspects can be found in Tillema's *Appeal to Force* (1128) and Stern's *The Limits of Military Intervention* (1113). Gurtov (879) presents a radical critique of past cold-war attempts at intervention by the United States. Doenecke's *The Literature of Isolationism* (1277) is a useful guide to noninterventionist writings.

A comprehensive account of foreign policy in the Nixon years comes in Tad Szulc's massive *The Illusion of Peace* (1121), a work generally critical in tone. Lehman's *The Executive, Congress, and Foreign Policy* (962) favors executive control and views with concern the strong drift toward congressional dominance. Early assessments of the Nixon Doctrine are provided by Wu (1158), Jones (917), Kintner (933), Osgood (1031), and Holloway (900).

Broad security needs and issues as the United States moves into the 1980s are the subjects for Palmer (1033), Goodpaster (874), Wolf (1155), Taylor (1123, 1124), and Middleton (996); a pessimistic tone emerges from most of these. The topic of secrecy and national security is explored by Halperin and Hoffman (884) and Franck and Weisband (857). These authors call for reforms to curb excessive secrecy. There exist a number of important collections of current essays and documents on national security. Though Endicott and Stafford's *American Defense Policy* (844) and Pranger and Labrie's *Nuclear Strategy and National Security* (1049) are the most recent and probably the best, Rosi's (1069) and Johnson and Schneider's (915) are also valuable. Knorr's excellent collection of essays explores the historical dimensions of national security problems (941), and Knorr and Trager do the same in their *Economic Issues and National Security* (942), a subject that has assumed increased importance in the last few years. In addition, the researcher should be familiar with the *Annual Report* of the secretary of defense, mentioned in the first edition, and, since 1971, the annual statement by the chairman of the Joint Chiefs of Staff, *Defense Posture of the United States* (1264).

Michael Sherry's important *Preparing for the Next War* (1099) investigates military plans and thinking toward the postwar world and includes considerable coverage of the idea of universal military training and the growing military-scientific alliance that emerged from World War II. Eisenhower's management of defense policy is viewed favorably by Kinnard (931), who argues that Eisenhower was in firm control, not the Pentagon or the National Security Council. This same positive view of Eisenhower's ability surfaces in Aliano, *American Defense Policy from Eisenhower to Kennedy* (739), which reasons that domestic politics were primarily responsible for the shift from "Massive Retaliation" to "Flexible Response," a shift that had unfortunate and unforeseen consequences for the United States. Bureaucratic politics within defense policy-making receive emphasis in Beard's *Developing the ICBM* (753). The missile system's progress did not lag for technical or budgetary reasons, Beard argues, but because the air force saw the ICBM as a threat to the manned bomber and, therefore, sat on the project as long as possible. An excellent concise discussion of overall defense policy in the two decades following World War II is found in Morton Halperin's *Contemporary Military Strategy* (881).

Defense management is covered in Stockfish, *Plowshares into Swords* (1115); Sanders, *The Politics of Defense Analysis* (1082); and Murdock, *Defense Policy Formation* (1013). The first gives a sophisticated analysis of the various factors affecting the subject and calls for more civilian participation on the level of fundamental decisions and less involvement on the level of specific details. The last two concentrate on the innovations associated with McNamara's systems analysis approach, changes which both authors favor. Murdock's portrayal of Eisenhower's leadership as weak is in conflict with the views of Kinnard and Aliano.

The enlarged role of Congress in shaping defense policy since 1968 is the subject for Alton Frye's *A Responsible Congress* (861). Giving special coverage to the ABM and MIRV issues in Congress, Frye supports this greater role. His tendency, however, to see the arms race within a simple action-reaction mode appears questionable. Other discussions of Congress and defense policy are provided by Entin (846), Cannon (790), Cobb (802), and Laurance (956). Mrozek (1012) stresses continuity in the Truman-Eisenhower defense thinking, and the *Naval War College Review* has reprinted the complete text of that key security document of April 1950, NSC-68 (1024). Brown's *Drop Shot* (774) supplies some interesting insights into military contingency planning in the late 1940s, but this reprinting of a war plan prepared by a committee of the Joint Chiefs of Staff is damaged by Brown's poor editorial performance. Perspective on the defense policy of two close allies, Britain and Canada, can be found respectively in Gowing (876) and Eayrs (840), Preston (1051), and Roy (1074).

Broad discussions of power relationships in the postwar world are provided by Liska (966), Buchan (778, 779), and a series published in *Foreign Affairs* (1030), while Morgenstern (1006) and Cline (797) are interested in forecasting and measuring strategic power. Valuable works that deal specifically with military power are Martin's *Arms and Strategy* (981), Dupuy's *The Almanac of World Military Power* (1278), and the two authoritative annuals compiled by the International Institute for Strategic Studies, *Strategic Survey* (1288), which stresses strategic developments, and *The Military Balance* (1287), which surveys the world's armed forces.

Whereas the late 1950s produced a fear that a dangerous "missile gap" was opening between the United States and the Soviet Union, the growing concern of the late 1970s seems to be over a "strategic power gap" between the two nations. Both Kirk and Wessell, *The Soviet Threat* (935), and Draper, *Defending America* (838), assess the United States-Soviet strategic balance. The latter expresses particular concern over the growth of Soviet strategic power, its ability to project that power, and the resultant political implications for the world. Discussions of previous estimates of Soviet strength are the subject of studies by Lee (958) and Freedman (858). The first, written by a former Soviet specialist for the CIA, argues that past CIA estimates of Soviet military spending have been too low; and the second, written by a British defense specialist, discusses bureaucratic factors that affect intelligence estimates, with particular emphasis on how American perception of the issue of

United States ICBM vulnerability influences estimates of Soviet strength (see chapter XXI).

Specific projections of Soviet power have become quite controversial. Sen. John C. Culver (Democrat of Iowa) asked John M. Collins of the Congressional Research Service, Library of Congress, to prepare a comprehensive analysis of the military balance between the United States and the Soviet Union; the Senate Armed Services Committee published Collins' preliminary findings (1226) in early 1976, but declined to publish an enlarged and expanded version in 1977. This second version, quite pessimistic in its view of current strategic trends, concludes that the United States is losing its ability to deter Soviet aggression. Read into the *Congressional Record,* the Collins Report has now appeared in two commercial editions (810, 811). Other negative assessments of the United States position come from the Harvard historian Richard E. Pipes (1046), who chaired Team B's review of CIA estimates, and retired Maj. Gen. George J. Keegan, Jr. (1021), who once headed air force intelligence. The entire controversy over the various estimates of the late 1970s is traced in Petersen's concise article, "American Perceptions of Soviet Military Power" (1043).

DEFENSE ORGANIZATION AND OPERATION. The creation of the Department of Defense as seen by the navy, air force, and army is the subject for a series of articles in *Prologue* (809), while Trager looks back on the National Security Act of 1947 from the perspective of thirty years (1129). The text of this act as amended through 1973 may also be of interest (1174).

Bureaucratic operation of the national security organization is discussed by Halperin (880). He is particularly concerned with the way lower-level bureaucratic resistance can thwart higher-level decisions. Allison and Szanton's *Remaking Foreign Policy* (740) is a thorough review of the national security apparatus that emerged from the 1940s. Recent presidential use of this apparatus is critically discussed by Destler (830), while Estes and Lightner's *The Department of State* (847) sketches the basic organizational structure. The Council on Foreign Relations is attacked as the true center of policy making power by Shoup and Minter (1100) and Schlafly and Ward (1090); the former, writing from the political left, sees the council as representing the ruling capitalist class; the latter, coming from the political right, believes the council is betraying the nation into national surrender.

As the Vietnam War dragged into the 1970s, the opinion that presidential power had become bloated and unchecked increased markedly. Schlesinger's widely quoted *The Imperial Presidency* (1091) gives an example of this popular belief. Congress held extensive hearings (1187, 1188, 1245, 1246), finally passing the War Powers Act in 1973 over President Nixon's veto. Since that time, Congress (1202), Holt (902), and Hoxie (904) have reviewed the act's effectiveness and wisdom, with the last presenting a strongly worded, unapologetic defense of presidential supremacy in security affairs.

Greenberg (877) and Penick (1040) contribute broad discussions and documents dealing with the role of science in government policy. Both give consideration to defense issues. Primack's *Advice and Dissent* (1052) analyzes the roles played by scientific advisory groups, with considerable attention being given to the ABM issue. The president and science are discussed in recent studies by Katz (922), Killian (928), and Kistiakowsky (938). The first provides a significant overview of White House science policy since World War II, including a fine bibliography. The latter two authors provide inside accounts by men who served as special assistants for science and technology to President Eisenhower. Each gives valuable insights into Eisenhower's leadership and such contemporary scientific issues as arms control, missile developments, and the space program.

Since the mid-1970s, major criticism of defense organization and power has centered on the Central Intelligence Agency and the various parts of the intelligence network. Marchetti and Marks (978), Agee (737), Smith (1107), Prouty (1053), Cox (823), and Halperin (883) have all marshalled heavy attacks on this network, with some of these works displaying a heavy dose of emotionalism and sensationalism. An opposite view comes from Copeland (817), who is as biased for the CIA as some others are against. Cline (796), McGarvey (986), Phillips (1044), and Rositzke (1070), while basically supportive of the CIA, see areas of needed reform. Rositzke's study, *The CIA's Secret Operation,* gives an articulate defense of the necessity for covert operations, a subject also explored by Scoville (1093).

Two memoirs that are supportive of the CIA come from Vernon Walters (1140), who spent many years as a high-level interpreter and later as deputy director of the agency, and William Colby (808), who served as the director from 1973 to 1976. The first is entertaining and anecdotal, the latter frank and revealing. An important view of the entire question of intelligence, including valuable information and documents covering even as far back as the pre-World War II period, comes in William Corson's *The Armies of Ignorance* (819). It will be a basic starting point for future studies. In comparison, Jeffreys-Jones's *American Espionage* (914) falls woefully short and deserves to be neglected. An apparently successful CIA operation that gained considerable mention in the press, the raising of parts of a Soviet Golf-class submarine, provides the subject for a good journalistic treatment of the technical aspects of the salvage in *The Jennifer Project* (783).

Godfrey (872), Blackstock (763), and Ransom (1059) furnish helpful discussions of aspects of intelligence questions, and Borosage and Marks (770) have edited a collection of pro and con essays and remarks. Helpful reference and bibliographical materials are located in works by Blackstock and Schaf (1268), Buncher (1269), DeVore (1276), Fain (1280), Harris (1284), and Powe (1299); moreover, there are the major sources produced by the United States government (1176, 1189, 1206, 1229, 1253, 1255, 1256, 1259), including the Rockefeller report on CIA activities within the United States (1265) and the extensive Senate hearings headed by Frank Church (1257, 1258).

DEFENSE PROBLEMS. The Vietnam War doomed the draft. Political forces insisted upon another method for recruiting manpower, and the All-Volunteer Force (AVF) was seen as the solution. It went into effect in July 1973, despite troubled predictions concerning problems of numbers, cost, race, and ideology. Bliven (767) gives an early, timely look at the AVF and the academicians who have studied the concept. Recent assessments of the AVF, generally positive in tone, come from Cooper (814, 815), with his *Military Manpower and the All-Volunteer Force* being the most comprehensive study available. Sabrosky (1079) and Keeley (924) also furnish an appraisal, while Levitan and Alderman (964) concentrate on personnel management problems that must receive priority if the AVF is to compete successfully in the labor market. The racial composition of the AVF and the implications imbalance of race hold for both the military and American society are explored by Janowitz and Moskos (913), while Bachman, Blair, and Segal (743) study the ideology of the AVF. Their conclusions suggest a trend within the AVF toward a narrow, promilitary ideology that may tend to isolate the armed services and make them less responsive to civilian controls. Important additional information and assessments come from the Defense Manpower Commission (1165) and congressional publications (1167, 1179, 1217, 1223, 1224), including the extensive and pessimistic study (1224) completed by Congressman Robin Beard (Republican of Tennessee).

Though the AVF has generally been able to fill its manpower needs for the active forces, it has been far less successful in manning the reserve forces, a problem mentioned by Cooper (815) and stressed by Coffey (805) and Binkin (760). An additional problem intensified by the AVF is the growing numbers of military families, for no longer are the enlisted men young draftees with few family commitments. *Families in the Military System* (985) gives a wide discussion and includes an extensive annotated bibliography. Other bibliographies covering various segments of the manpower issue are provided by Nyberg and Snyder (1296), Slonaker (1301), the Army (1261), and the Department of Defense (1373).

With the coming sharp decline in the number of eighteen-year-old males available for military service in the mid-1980s, recent debate has centered on the possibility of increasing the number of women in the armed forces. Current Pentagon goals call for a thirteen to one male-female ratio by 1982, but manpower and political pressures may well push for a lower ratio. *Women and the Military* (761) provides discussion and data on most of the issues and concludes that there should be a greater utilization of women. Additional information can be found in *Armed Forces and Society,* which devotes an issue to "Women as New 'Manpower'" (899). Quester considers the issue of "Women in Combat" (1056), and Hunter, Rose, and Hamlin have compiled an annotated bibliography on "Women in the Military" (1286).

Along with the growing military role of women, the subject of unionization has attracted attention. *Military Unions: U. S. Trends and Issues* (1125), *Blue-Collar Soldiers?* (1078), and *Unionizing the Armed Forces* (947) furnish helpful explorations of the subject, with the last being rather optimistic toward military unionization and concluding that unionization will not bring the downfall of the armed services. Congressional hearings (1220) and an Army bibliography (1260) provide additional sources of information. Both Cooper (816) and Congress (1217) have explored the possibility of a national service draft as a means of easing manpower demands, and again the Army has put together a bibliography (1263).

With the close of the Vietnam War and continued heavy defense spending by the Soviet Union, criticism of defense expenditures has mellowed though not ceased, and expenditures for defense in terms of noninflated dollars began to move upward by the late 1970s, though it continued its decline with respect to budget and GNP percentages. Kennedy's *The Economics of Defense* (927) and Weidenbaum's *The Economics of Peacetime Defense* (1144) give introductions to the subject. Agapos (736) argues that defense spending has been beneficial to United States industrial and economic growth, while Seymour Melman (993), long a critic of defense spending, argues in *The Permanent War Economy* (992) that swollen defense budgets have led to waste, inefficiency, and declining industrial productivity. Johnson (916) questions Melman's views on defense economics.

Specific studies of security needs and costs can be found in the annual volume from the Brookings Institution, *Setting National Priorities* (1039), and in recent similar assessments from the American Enterprise Institute (1041). *Arms, Men, and Military Budgets* (897) concludes that United States defense spending is dangerously inadequate to meet its needs and that a larger proportion of the national budget should go toward security forces. Though not quite so pessimistic, Blechman's *The Soviet Military Buildup and U.S. Defense Spending* (765) comments that defense spending from 1968 to 1975 declined in terms of noninflated dollars and that funding for military hardware dropped well below the pre-Vietnam War levels, and agrees that a modest growth of the defense budget in terms of noninflated dollars is probably necessary. The researcher should always remember, in addition to the above studies, the massive amount of defense information contained in the annual congressional hearings relating to the defense budget. Amounting to thousands of pages and covering the Department of Defense (1168, 1173, 1177, 1214, 1219), military construction (1170, 1171, 1216), foreign assistance (1169, 1192, 1215), Energy Research and Development Administration (1205, 1218), and related items, this material includes charts, tables, and budget justification throughout, and provides a largesse of defense information.

Cahn's *Controlling Future Arms Trade* (785) and Harkavy's *The Arms Trade and International Systems* (886) present the best recent studies of the complexities of this subject. Sampson's *The Arms Bazaar* (1081) is a journalist's view, helpful in its detailed survey of conventional arms trade but lacking in analysis. Gervasi (869), unhappy with the United States role in the arms trade, provides a catalog of United States weaponry and sales data. Additional sources of major value are the publications of the Arms Control and Disarmament Agency (1164) and the Stockholm International Peace Research Institution (1304, 1305). Discussion of the benefits and liabilities of the military assistance program are covered by Pranger and Tahtinen (1050), Wolpin (1156), Lefever (959), and Louscher (969). Discussion of the military-industrial complex seems to have abated, with Cooling's *War, Business and American Society* (813) being the major recent effort. A collection of historical essays, it is especially valuable for its bibliography and suggestions for subsequent research.

Dickson (833) and Canan (789) give journalistic treatments of the newer electronic weaponry, the latter being a helpful layman's introduction to recent weapons technology. Political and strategic effects of this technology receive attention in *The Other Arms Race: New Technologies and Non-Nuclear Conflict* (925), and Morrison and Walker (1008) argue that the new "smart" weapons give a decisive edge to the defender, thus allowing the United States to reduce substantially the size of its defense force. Burt (1361) and Digby (1363) also discuss these weapons. Broad considerations of the impact of technology are found in Basiuk (752) and Beaumont and Edmonds (754). The role research and development (R & D) plays within the security structure is covered by Seitz (1094), while other aspects of R & D receive the attention of

Head (889), Reppy and Long (1063), Garwin (867), York (1161), and the Department of Defense (1372).

Fox's *Arming America: How the U.S. Buys Weapons* (856) presents a major study of weapons acquisition, with the author's attention centering on the management process. Congress has held extensive hearings on the subject (1212). *The Illusions of Choice* (822) details the problems of the acquisition process in its study of the F-111, concluding that the suborganizations necessary for implementation often tend to subvert high-level design decisions, thus precluding necessary design flexibility.

Chemical and biological warfare are discussed by Rose (1067), McCarthy (984), and Cookson and Nottingham (812), while Brown (775) gives an important study of its restraint. Recent coverage comes from a valuable set of papers edited by Meselson (995) and an article by Hoeber and Douglas (896). Congress (1185, 1186) and SIPRI (1308) yield additional information sources. Discussion of cluster bombs, weather modification as a weapon, and incendiary weapons can be found respectively by Krepon (948), Congress (1250), and SIPRI (1307). Such weapons as the neutron bomb, the B-1 bomber, the cruise missile, beam weapons, the antiballistic missile system, and multiple independently targeted reentry vehicles will be mentioned in chapter XXI.

CIVIL-MILITARY RELATIONS AND THE MILITARY ESTABLISH-MENT. In the immediate post-Vietnam environment, this subject has received heightened attention, much of it coming from active duty or retired military officers. Sarkesian's *The Professional Army Officer in a Changing Society* (1084) is one of the most valuable, presenting insights into the military establishment within its exploration of the proper place of today's military officer. Other general discussions of current civil-military relations are found with Clotfelter (798), Bletz (766), Moskos (1368), Cochran (804), and Goodpaster and Huntington (875), the last authors foreseeing less interaction between the military and society. Larson (955) contrasts the ideas of two leading scholars of the subject, Samuel Huntington and Morris Janowitz.

Richard Betts, *Soldiers, Statesmen, and Cold War Crises* (758), and Lawrence Korb, *The Joint Chiefs of Staff* (944), provide two key studies of civil-military relations at the policymaking levels. Betts finds that military leaders have been no more anxious to intervene militarily than civilian leaders; the resort to force has not been advice given by the military only. Once force has been used, however, the military has been more desirous of seeing the crisis through to a positive conclusion, hence being more willing to escalate. In gauging their influence, Betts concludes that the military has had the greatest impact when it has counseled against rather than for military intervention. The study is supported by very extensive notes. Korb's study concludes that the Joint Chiefs of Staff have not been innovators in the area of policy, even within military areas. And, far from wielding powerful influence, they too often have meekly followed political leaders and allowed intimidation to rule, resulting in their support of erroneous policies.

Kinnard's review essay, "For the Post-Vietnam Military: No End of Advice" (930), provides a helpful starting point for literature on that topic. *The United States Army in Transition* (771) and *Crisis in Command* (862) are two of the best studies, with the first written by officers on active duty, the latter by former officers. Both discuss the loss of traditional values within the officer corps, with *Crisis in Command* being markedly critical of the displacement of traditional leadership values by newer managerial values. Farris (851) gives added comments on the subject. Other studies of the military come from Sarkesian (1083, 1085), Margiotta (979), Mylander (1014), Walton (1141), and Petersen (1042), the last study attempting to rebut the antimilitary tone of some recent literature. Though somewhat polemical in tone, *Soldiers in Revolt* (821) sheds light on the dissension within the military during the Vietnam years. The author is a former enlisted man involved with the "G.I. Movement." Military academy education is the subject for Ellis and Moore (841), who present serious questions concerning the quality and thrust of West Point education. Additional educational information comes from a collection of essays by Korb (946) and the hearings (1178, 1225) on the system of honor codes at the academies.

Helpful introductions to the area of military law come from Bishop (762) and Byrne (784), while Moyer's *Justice and the Military* (1011) is the most extensive coverage of the subject, concentrating on developments since the passage of the Uniform Code of Military Justice in 1950. There are also studies by Jacobs (912), Generous (868), and the special issues devoted to military justice in the *Indiana Law Journal* (909, 910). Veterans' problems are covered by Starr (1112), Twentieth Century Fund (1135), and Congress (1254), while Abercrombie (734) discusses the role of the military chaplain, Olson (1029) the G.I. Bill, and Congress (1222) the military programs to deal with drugs and alcohol problems.

DIPLOMATIC PRACTICE: PAST AND PRESENT. The most important recent study of the early cold war period is Daniel Yergin's *Shattered Peace* (1160). Based on extensive research and centering on the 1945-48 period, Yergin examines the conflict within United States foreign policy between the "Yalta axioms," which saw the Soviet Union as a power ruled by reasonable self-interest and willing to negotiate, and the "Riga axioms," which saw the Soviet Union as a power ruled by an aggressive ideology of world revolution and unwilling to be turned from that path. With the ultimate ascendency of the "Riga axioms" by 1947, Yergin argues, the United States moved toward an emphasis on military perceptions and needs. Another major effort, massive in its coverage, comes from Wheeler-Bennett and Nicholls (1148). Their history of the cold war exemplifies an earlier view of the Soviet Union as implacably expansionist; holds up Churchill, Eden, Truman, and Acheson as the heroes for the West; and completely brushes aside the views of New Left historians. Other books relating to the cold war are by Rose (1065) and Lukacs (971), with each concentrating on 1945, and Miller and Pruessen (999), an edited collection of original essays.

Europe and the cold war are the topics for Paterson (1038) and Pruessen (1054), with both seeing economic motives as the primary force behind United States policy and a major cause of the cold war, a conclusion challenged by Davis (824). Herring (894) also downplays the handling of economic issues as a cause of the breakdown of the Soviet-American wartime understanding. Mee's popular *Meeting at Potsdam* (991) presents a poorly researched, anecdotal, and oversimplified account of that July 1945 meeting. Gaddis (863, 864) provides incisive essays on containment and the Truman Doctrine. Reid (1062) gives a firsthand account of the creation of NATO, and Arkes (741) and

Gimbel (871) study the Marshall Plan, with Arkes emphasizing the bureaucratic environment and Gimbel arguing that problems with Germany and France, and not with the Soviet Union, brought on the plan. Sharp (1096) and Backer (745) discuss the division of Germany, while Smith (1105) has edited the papers of Gen. Lucius D. Clay and is currently working on a full-scale biography of this key American in postwar Germany. Howard (903), Knight (940), and DeLuca (826) provide information on the Turkish Straits question of 1946.

Less has been published on Asia and the cold war. The best treatment comes from Iriye (911), who focuses on the decade of the 1940s and includes a fine bibliographical essay on English and non-English language sources. Other recent treatments are by Rose (1066), Fifield (852), and Nagai and Iriye (1015), the last being a collection of essays from a conference held in Japan. Woodward (1157) and Scalapino (1086) discuss the American occupation of Japan, while Ward (1311) has compiled an annotated bibliography of works on the occupation.

The heated debate from the mid-1960s through the early 1970s between orthodox or traditional historians and the revisionists or New Left historians as to whether the actions of Soviet expansionism or American capitalism were primarily responsible for the cause and intensity of the cold war seems largely to have run its course; little has been published on this historiographical controversy since 1975 (898, 929, 963, 974, 1064, 1102). Most recent studies, such as Yergin's (1160), have moved toward a balanced, scholarly, and detached synthesis using elements of the two views.

An increasing number of important sources are or will soon be open to researchers, including State Department records of the early 1950s. The important State Department series, *Foreign Relations of the United States,* has now reached the year 1950 in its coverage. In addition, commercially published collections of some State Department reports (1297) and Joint Chiefs of Staff records (1300) of the early postwar period are available, while Etzold and Gaddis (1279) have edited a collection of documents on containment, with much of the material being only recently declassified. Sources in the presidential libraries on American postwar occupation forces are surveyed by Zobrist (1312). Additionally, Congress began in 1973 to make available massive amounts of early cold war hearings originally held in executive session (1180, 1232, 1233, 1234, 1235, 1237, 1238, 1240, 1241, 1243, 1244). This material is vital for understanding the perceptions of United States policymakers. Until the Soviet Union takes similar steps, however, any studies of cold war origins must remain largely one-dimensional.

In comparison to World War II or the Vietnam War, the Korean War remains largely ignored. Detzer (832) and McGovern (987) provide readable accounts of military aspects of the war, as does Manchester in his generally sympathetic biography of MacArthur (975). Simmons's *The Strained Alliance* (1101) includes a chapter on the origins of the war in its valuable research on the difficult relationship between North Korea, China, and Russia. Noble (1023) gives a view of the war from the United States embassy in Seoul, LaFeber (950) focuses on the implications of the decision to cross the 38th parallel, Stairs (1111) discusses Canada's hopes to moderate United States policy, and Stueck and Kolko (1118, 943) debate the war's origins. Heller's *The Korean War* (1285) grew out of a 1975 conference held at the Truman Library; it contains an excellent essay on the available literature by Leopold (1291) that includes suggestions for further research. The complete texts of the MacArthur hearings (1293) are now available, and their previously secret portions are explored by Wiltz (1154).

Dinerstein's *The Making of A Missile Crisis* (834) gives the best available discussion of the origins of the Cuban episode. Stressing the assumptions and perceptions of the participants, it is especially valuable for its insights into the Soviet and Cuban views. Chayes (792) discusses and probably overemphasizes the influence of international law in the resolution of the crisis. Essays come from Bernstein (756, 757) and Nathan (1016), and a select bibliography from Gillingham and Roseman (1281).

There has been an extensive growth in the literature of the Vietnam War during the 1970s, despite the fact that the scholarly histories of the military campaigns and diplomatic efforts are still to be written. Introductions to the subject, though their approaches differ, can be found in Alastair Buchan's "The Indochina War and World Politics" (780), the special issue of *Armed Forces and Society* on "The Vietnam Experience" (1137), and Allan Millett's *A Short History of the Vietnam War* (1001), which includes a chronology of the war and a valuable bibliographical essay. Two important books on the American effort at counterinsurgency warfare are by Lansdale (954) and Blaufarb (764), both of whom were personally involved in this effort in Vietnam. Policymaking is discussed by Milstein (1002), Gallucci (865), and Schandler (1088), with the last describing the link between Tet and Johnson's decision not to run for reelection in 1968. Kinnard's *The War Managers* (932) surveys the quite heterogeneous views held by American generals who saw duty in Vietnam, while Admiral Sharp (1097) and General Westmoreland (1147) give the views of two top military leaders. Chen (793) analyzes key decisions coming from Hanoi prior to the commitment of United States combat troops. Early efforts at an overall history of the American role in the war come from Palmer (1034) and Brown (776, 777), the former more successful than the latter. Individual experiences of combat in Vietnam have produced stark memoirs by Caputo (791), Kirk (934), O'Brien (1027), Parrish (1037), and Herr (893).

The final collapse of Saigon in the spring of 1975 is discussed by Snepp (1108) and Dawson (825); both stress a human-interest style at the cost of hard analysis; both are critical of the way the United States dealt with events. Giap (870), Dung (839), and Burchett (782) present the collapse as seen from the view of the North Vietnamese, while Congress has also explored those events (1197, 1202). The seizure of the *Mayaguez,* which occurred a short while after the collapse of the Saigon government, is described in a competent but hurriedly produced journalistic piece by Rowan (1072); Head's *Crisis Resolution* (890), concentrating on the view of Washington policymakers, furnishes a more detailed and incisive analysis of the *Mayaguez* incident. There are also the four-part hearings (1201) held by Congress.

The Paris peace discussions are the subject of Porter's *A Peace Denied* (1048), which presents a very critical picture of United States policy. Further information comes from Sullivan (1119) and Congress (1184), while Kaplan discusses the question, *Vietnam Settlement: Why 1973, Not 1969?* (921), and Randle (1058) provides a detailed study of the earlier peace settlement at Geneva.

John Hubbell, *P.O.W.* (905), gives a comprehensive view of the American

POW experiences during the Vietnam War. Memoirs of prisoners include those by McGrath (988), who includes his own intense pen and ink sketches; Denton (827), one of the highest ranking prisoners; Dramesi (837); and Rowe (1073). Hunter (907) and Naughton (1020) explore resistance and motivation among the POWs, and Hunter (906) covers the separation of the POW from his family. Extensive discussions were conducted by Congress on the topics of POWs and missing servicemen (1172, 1184, 1207, 1208).

In his aforementioned *The War Managers,* Kinnard found that one of the few areas where the American generals demonstrated near universal agreement was their negative view of the media coverage during the war. Peter Braestrup, chief of the *Washington Post's* Saigon bureau at the time of the Tet offensive, explores news coverage in *Big Story* (772) and finds the press's reporting of Tet seriously flawed in that a complete military defeat for the Vietcong was presented to the United States as a disaster for the American military. Lefever's *TV and National Defense* (960) also questions the objectivity of segments of the media.

The draft and the Vietnam War are discussed by Baskir and Strauss (750, 751), while O'Sullivan (1298) and Anderson (1267) provide documents and an annotated bibliography on the overall subject of conscription. Veterans of the war are the subject for Helmer (892) and Ladinsky (949). John Moore furnishes an important and massive study, *Law and the Indo-China War* (1004), Richard Falk (850) compiles an even more comprehensive treatment in his four-volume edited collection on the same subject, while Trooboff demonstrates the variety of legal issues and the general lack of consensus among experts in his edited study, *Law and Responsibility in Warfare* (1131); all three are important works. The released portion of the Peers Commission investigation of the My Lai massacre is included in Goldstein, Marshall, and Schwartz's collection of articles, *The My Lai Massacre and Its Cover-Up* (873), while the classified congressional hearings (1175) on the incident were released in 1976. Efforts at assessing the war's legacy for the United States can be found in works by Lake (953), Corson (820), Stevens (1114), and Thompson and Frizzell (1127).

A readable but somewhat superficial introduction to the history of American diplomacy in Asia is by Hart (888), while May and Thomson (982) furnish an excellent collection of essays, as well as suggestions for additional research. Collections of papers highly critical of United States policies can be found in Friedman and Selden (860) and Selden (1095). An introduction to current and past relations with China comes from Sutter (1120), and valuable sets of essays are edited by Barnds (747) and Oksenberg and Oxnam (1028). Barnett's discussions (748, 749) of current and future policy include considerations of security issues, Clough (801) explores specific questions of future arms control measures between the United States and China, and Kalicki (919) relates past political-military interactions. Clough's *East Asia and U.S. Security* (800) concludes that only Japan holds vital security interests for the United States. Destler (831), Greene (878), and Weinstein (1374) explore American-Japanese security relations, while both Endicott (843) and Emmerson (842) agree that Japan is not likely to acquire nuclear weapons in the foreseeable future. President Carter's policy calling for a phased withdrawal of American ground troops in Korea may have been stimulated by Clough's conclusions in *Deterrence and Defense in Korea* (799), conclusions challenged by Lefever (961). The future strategic importance of Micronesia is explored by Webb (1143),

Louis (968), Mihaly (997), and Cameron (786); McHenry (989) is critical of United States policy in the area.

Recent consideration of United States security interests in Latin America has largely revolved around the Panama Canal, with the best historical treatment of the issues coming from LaFeber (952), who supports the 1978 treaties. Less sanguine views come from Ryan (1077) and Kitchel (939), who feel the treaties do not adequately protect American security needs, and Falk (849), who believes that the treaties are too imperialistic toward Panama, thus lessening their acceptance by the Panamanians. As would be expected, there is extensive material from Congress (1203,1204,1227,1242) on the subject. A balanced scholarly treatment of the 1965 Dominican intervention comes from Lowenthal (970), while Parkinson paints a broad picture in his *Latin America, the Cold War, and the World Powers, 1945*-1973 (1036). Treverton (1371) gives an overview of the coming decade.

With the 1973-74 Arab oil embargo, the high priority given to affairs in the Middle East became even higher. Mangold's *Superpower Intervention in the Middle East* (977) gives a recent introduction to security policy in the area, while Quandt (1055), Reich (1061), and Safran (1080) provide excellent and extensive coverage of United States-Israeli relations in the last decade and a half. Polk (1047) covers events through 1973 in his revised standard work, *The United States and the Arab World*, while Churba (795) castigates the increased strength of United States-Arab relations at the expense, in his opinion, of a weakened and betrayed Israel. Specific discussion of geopolitical security needs relating to energy and policy come from Miller (998), Krapels (1366), Campbell (787), and Maull (1367), while some consideration of the subject is also found in Willrich (1153), Vernon (1136), Yager (1159), and Schneider (1092). Tucker (1132,1133,1134) and Ignotus (908) explore the possibilities of United States military intervention to seize oil supplies, as does Congress (1194) in its various discussions (1251,1252) of the Middle East situation. Friedland, Seabury, and Wildavsky (859) give an emotional diatribe in their condemnation of the United States for not taking a tougher stand toward the Arab oil embargo. Comparisons of the United States-Soviet naval presence in the Mediterranean can be found in Lewis (965) and Whetten (1149), while sub-Sahara Africa is discussed in congressional hearings (1247), and by Stockwell (1116) in his disillusioned exposé of the CIA in Angola. Past policy toward Iran and current and future policy in the Indian Ocean are presented by Hess (895) and Bezboruah (759) and Tahtinen (1122) respectively, with the latter two supporting naval arms limitations in the area.

In the first half of the 1970s, much of the writing concerning United States security policy toward Europe examined the possibilities and implications of a reduced manpower commitment to NATO. In the second part of the decade, writings have shifted toward a concern for Soviet-Warsaw Pact power in the area and the need to strengthen United States forces, a shift in thought reflected by President Carter's increased emphasis on NATO's military needs. Coverage of various aspects of NATO's security requirements and strategy can be found in works by Schilling (1089), Fischer (1364), Schaetzel (1087), Pierre (1045), Holst and Nerlich (901), Foster (854), Williams (1151), and Bray (773). Specific treatments of NATO manpower size and organization come from Lawrence and Record (957), Enthoven (845), Cordier (818), and Congress (1166,1249). NATO, nuclear weapons, and the neutron bomb are discussed in chapter XXI. Anglo-American relations are surveyed by Alastair Buchan (781), while Manderson-Jones (976) examines their "special relationship" between 1947 and 1956. Treverton (1130) analyzes the discussions in 1966–67 between the United States and Germany to offset the costs of American troops stationed in West Germany, and Morgan (1005) describes alliance politics in his study, *The United States and West Germany, 1945–1973.*

RESEARCH NEEDED. By 1980, many of the records of the Korean War will be open for research. There is a need for a comprehensive military-diplomatic history of the war taking into account these new resources. And there are still no full biographical portraits of such important advisors of the early cold war period as Gen. Omar Bradley, George F. Kennan, and W. Averell Harriman. Additionally, the only biography of James Forrestal is somewhat dated and incomplete. Despite his long tenure, little exists on Dean Rusk, though this may be indicative of his lack of influence, and there are no studies of the institutional development and role of the secretary of defense similar to Korb's work on the Joint Chiefs of Staff. Though bits and pieces exist, there is no comprehensive analysis of the Kennedy-McNamara defense policy. Similarly, while there have been important monographs published on technology, doctrine, and the development of specific weapons, a full history of weapons and doctrine development since World War II would be helpful. In addition, the reader should note the earlier mention in this chapter of sources discussing further research needs.

BIBLIOGRAPHY

ARTICLES AND BOOKS
734. Abercombie, Clarence L., III. *The Military Chaplain.* Beverly Hills, Calif.: Sage, 1977.
735. Acheson, Dean. *This Vast External Realm.* New York: Norton, 1973.
736. Agapos, A. M. *Government-Industry and Defense: Economics and Administration.* University: University of Alabama, 1975.
737. Agee, Philip. *Inside the Company: CIA Diary.* New York: Stonehill, 1975.
738. Alexander, Charles C. *Holding the Line: The Eisenhower Era, 1952–1961.* Bloomington: Indiana University, 1975.
739. Aliano, Richard A. *American Defense Policy from Eisenhower to Kennedy: The Politics of Changing Military Requirements, 1957–1961.* Athens: Ohio University, 1975.
740. Allison, Graham, and Peter Szanton. *Remaking Foreign Policy: The Organizational Connection.* New York: Basic Books, 1976.
741. Arkes, Hadley. *Bureaucracy, the Marshall Plan and the National Interest.* Princeton, N.J.: Princeton University Press, 1973.
742. Aron, Raymond. *The Imperial Republic: The United States and the World, 1945–1973.* Translated by Frank Jellinek. Englewood Cliffs, N.J.: Prentice-Hall, 1974.
743. Bachman, Jerald G., John D. Blair, and David R. Segal. *The All-Volunteer Force: A Study of Ideology in the Military.* Ann Arbor: University of Michigan, 1977.

744. Bachrack, Stanley D. *The Committee of One Million: "China Lobby" Politics, 1953-1971.* New York: Columbia University, 1976.

745. Backer, John H. *The Decision to Divide Germany: American Foreign Policy in Transition.* Durham, N.C.: Duke University, 1978.

746. Ball, George W. *Diplomacy for a Crowded World.* Boston: Little, Brown, 1976.

747. Barnds, William J., ed. *China and America: The Search for a New Relationship.* New York: New York University, 1977.

748. Barnett, A. Doak. *China Policy: Old Problems and New Challenges.* Washington, D.C.: Brookings Institution, 1977.

749. Barnett, A. Doak. "Military-Security Relations between China and the United States." *Foreign Affairs,* April 1977.

750. Baskir, Lawrence M., and William A. Strauss. *Chance and Circumstance: The Draft, the War, and the Vietnam Generation.* New York: Knopf, 1978.

751. Baskir, Lawrence, and William A. Strauss. *Reconciliation after Vietnam: A Program of Relief for Vietnam-Era Draft and Military Offenders.* South Bend, Ind.: University of Notre Dame, 1977.

752. Basiuk, Victor. *Technology, World Politics and American Policy.* New York: Columbia University, 1977.

753. Beard, Edmund. *Developing the ICBM: A Study in Bureaucratic Politics.* New York: Columbia University, 1976.

754. Beaumont, Roger A., and Martin Edmonds, eds. *War in the Next Decade.* Lexington: University Press of Kentucky, 1974.

755. Bell, Coral. *The Diplomacy of Detente: The Kissinger Era.* New York: St. Martin, 1977.

756. Bernstein, Barton J. "The Cuban Missile Crisis." In *Reflections of the Cold War: A Quarter Century of American Foreign Policy,* edited by Lynn H. Miller and Ronald W. Pruessen. Philadelphia: Temple University, 1974.

757. Bernstein, Barton J. "The Week We Almost Went to War." *Bulletin of the Atomic Scientists* 32, no.2 (1976).

758. Betts, Richard K. *Soldiers, Statesmen, and Cold War Crises.* Cambridge: Harvard University, 1977.

759. Bezboruah, Monoranjan. *U.S. Strategy in the Indian Ocean: The International Response.* New York: Praeger, 1977.

760. Binkin, Martin. *U.S. Reserve Forces: The Problem of the Weekend Warrior.* Washington, D.C.: Brookings Institution, 1974.

761. Binkin, Martin, and Shirley J. Bach. *Women and the Military.* Washington, D.C.: Brookings Institution, 1977.

762. Bishop, Joseph W., Jr. *Justice under Fire: A Study of Military Law.* New York: Charterhouse, 1974.

763. Blackstock, Paul W. "The Intelligence Community under the Nixon Administration." *Armed Forces and Society,* winter 1975.

764. Blaufarb, Douglas S. *The Counterinsurgency Era: U.S. Doctrine and Performance, 1950 to the Present.* New York: Free Press, 1977.

765. Blechman, Barry M., et al. *The Soviet Military Buildup and U.S. Defense Spending.* Washington, D.C.: Brookings Institution, 1977.

766. Bletz, Col. Donald F. *The Role of the Military Professional in U.S. Foreign Policy.* New York: Praeger, 1972.

767. Bliven, Bruce, Jr. "All-Volunteer Armed Forces." *The New Yorker*, 24 November and 1 December 1975.

768. Bloomfield, Lincoln P. *In Search of American Foreign Policy: The Humane Use of Power*. New York: Oxford University, 1974.

769. Blum, John Morton, ed. *The Price of Vision: The Diary of Henry A. Wallace, 1942–1946*. Boston: Houghton Mifflin, 1973.

770. Borosage, Robert L., and John Marks, eds. *The CIA File*. New York: Grossman, 1976.

771. Bradford, Lt. Col. Zeb B., Jr., and Lt. Col. Frederic J. Brown. *The United States Army in Transition*. Beverly Hills, Calif.: Sage, 1974.

772. Braestrup, Peter. *Big Story: How the American Press and Television Reported and Interpreted the Crisis of Tet 1968 in Vietnam and Washington*. 2 vols. Boulder, Colo.: Westview, 1977.

773. Bray, Frank T. J., and Michael Moodie. *Defense Technology and the Atlantic Alliance: Competition or Collaboration?* Cambridge, Mass.: Institute for Foreign Policy Analysis, 1977.

774. Brown, Anthony Cave, ed. *Drop Shot: The U.S. Plan for War with the Soviet Union in 1957*. New York: Dial, 1978.

775. Brown, Frederic J. *Chemical Warfare: A Study in Restraints*. Princeton, N.J.: Princeton University, 1968.

776. Brown, Weldon A. *The Last Chopper: The Denouement of the American Role in Vietnam, 1963–1975*. Port Washington, N.Y.: Kennikat, 1976.

777. Brown, Weldon A. *Prelude to Disaster: The American Role in Vietnam, 1940–1963*. Port Washington, N.Y.: Kennikat, 1975.

778. Buchan, Alastair. *Change without War: The Shifting Structures of World Power*. New York: St. Martin, 1975.

779. Buchan, Alastair. *The End of the Postwar Era: A New Balance of World Power*. New York: Saturday Review, 1974.

780. Buchan, Alastair. "The Indochina War and World Politics." *Foreign Affairs*, July 1975.

781. Buchan, Alastair. "Mothers and Daughters (or Greeks and Romans)." *Foreign Affairs*, July 1976.

782. Burchett, Wilfred. *Grasshoppers & Elephants: The Viet Cong Account of the Last 55 Days of the War*. New York: Urizen, 1977.

783. Burleson, Clyde W. *The Jennifer Project*. Englewood Cliffs, N.J.: Prentice-Hall, 1977.

784. Byrne, Comdr. Edward M. *Military Law*. 2d ed. Annapolis, Md.: United States Naval Institute, 1976.

785. Cahn, Anne Hessing, et al. *Controlling Future Arms Trade*. New York: McGraw-Hill, 1977.

786. Cameron, Allan W. "The Strategic Significance of the Pacific Islands: A New Debate Begins." *Orbis* 19, no. 3 (1975).

787. Campbell, John C. "Middle East Oil: American Policy and Super-Power Interaction." *Survival* 15, no. 5 (1973).

788. Campbell, Thomas M., and George C. Herring, eds. *The Diaries of Edward R. Stettinius, Jr., 1943–1946*. New York: New Viewpoints, 1975.

789. Canan, James W. *The Superwarriors: The Fantastic World of Pentagon Superweapons*. New York: Weybright and Talley, 1975.

790. Cannon, Charles A. "The Politics of Interest and Ideology: The Senate Airpower Hearings of 1956." *Armed Forces and Society,* summer 1977.

791. Caputo, Philip. *A Rumor of War.* New York: Holt, Rinehart and Winston, 1977.

792. Chayes, Abram. *The Cuban Missile Crisis: International Crises and the Role of Law.* New York: Oxford University, 1974.

793. Chen, King C. "Hanoi's Three Decisions and the Escalation of the Vietnam War." *Political Science Quarterly,* summer 1975.

794. Chern, Kenneth S. "Politics of American China Policy, 1945: Roots of the Cold War in Asia." *Political Science Quarterly,* winter 1976-77.

795. Churba, Joseph. *The Politics of Defeat: America's Decline in the Middle East.* New York: Cyrco Press, 1977.

796. Cline, Ray S. *Secrets, Spies, and Scholars: Blueprint of the Essential CIA.* Washington, D.C.: Acropolis Books, 1976.

797. Cline, Ray S. *World Power Assessment 1977: A Calculus of Strategic Drift.* Boulder, Colo.: Westview, 1977.

798. Cloffelter, James. *The Military in American Politics.* New York: Harper & Row, 1973.

799. Clough, Ralph N. *Deterrence and Defense in Korea: The Role of U.S. Forces.* Washington, D.C.: Brookings Institution, 1976.

800. Clough, Ralph N. *East Asia and U.S. Security.* Washington, D.C.: Brookings Institution, 1975.

801. Clough, Ralph N., et al. *The United States, China, and Arms Control.* Washington, D.C.: Brookings Institution, 1975.

802. Cobb, Stephen. "Defense Spending and Defense Voting in the House: An Empirical Study of an Aspect of the Military-Industrial Complex Thesis." *American Journal of Sociology,* 82, no. 1 (1976).

803. Cochran, Bert. *Harry Truman and the Crisis Presidency.* New York: Funk and Wagnalls, 1973.

804. Cochran, Charles L., ed. *Civil-Military Relations: Changing Concepts in the Seventies.* New York: Free Press, 1974.

805. Coffey, Kenneth J. *Manpower for Military Mobilization.* Washington, D.C.: American Enterprise Institute, 1978.

806. Cohen, Benjamin J. *The Question of Imperialism: The Political Economy of Dominance and Dependence.* New York: Basic Books, 1973.

807. Cohen, Bernard C. *The Public's Impact on Foreign Policy.* Boston: Little, Brown, 1973.

808. Colby, William, and Peter Forbath. *Honorable Men: My Life in the CIA.* New York: Simon and Schuster, 1978.

809. Coletta, Paolo E., Richard F. Haynes, and Herman S. Wolk. "The Defense Unification Battle, 1947-50." *Prologue* 7, no. 1 (1975).

810. Collins, John M. *American and Soviet Military Trends since the Cuban Missile Crisis.* Washington, D.C.: Georgetown University, 1978.

811. Collins, John M., and Anthony H. Cordesman. *Imbalance of Power: Shifting U.S.-Soviet Military Strengths.* San Rafael, Calif.: Presidio, 1978.

812. Cookson, John, and Judith Nottingham. *A Survey of Chemical and Biological Warfare.* New York: Monthly Review, 1969.

813. Cooling, Benjamin Franklin, ed. *War, Business, and American Society: Historical Perspectives on the Military-Industrial Complex.* Port Washington, N.Y.: Kennikat, 1977.

814. Cooper, Richard V. L. "The All-Volunteer Force: Five Years Later." *International Security,* spring 1978.

815. Cooper, Richard V. L. *Military Manpower and the All-Volunteer Force.* Santa Monica, Calif.: RAND, 1977.

816. Cooper, Richard V. L. *A National Service Draft?* Santa Monica, Calif.: RAND, 1977.

817. Copeland, Miles. *Without Cloak or Dagger.* New York: Simon and Schuster, 1974.

818. Cordier, Sherwood S. *Calculus of Power: The Current Soviet-American Conventional Military Balance in Central Europe.* Washington, D.C.: University Press of America, 1977.

819. Corson, William R. *The Armies of Ignorance: The Rise of the American Intelligence Empire.* New York: Dial, 1977.

820. Corson, William R. *Consequences of Failure.* New York: Norton, 1974.

821. Cortright, David. *Soldiers in Revolt: The American Military Today.* Garden City, N.Y.: Doubleday, 1975.

822. Coulam, Robert F. *Illusions of Choice: The F-111 and the Problem of Weapons Acquisition Reform.* Princeton, N.J.: Princeton University, 1977.

823. Cox, Arthur M. *The Myths of National Security: The Peril of Secret Government.* Boston: Beacon, 1975.

824. Davis, Lynn Etheridge. *The Cold War Begins: Soviet-American Conflict over Eastern Europe.* Princeton, N.J.: Princeton University, 1974.

825. Dawson, Alan. *55 Days: The Fall of South Vietnam.* Englewood Cliffs, N.J.: Prentice-Hall, 1977.

826. DeLuca, Anthony R. "Soviet-American Politics and the Turkish Straits." *Political Science Quarterly,* fall 1977.

827. Denton, Rear Adm. Jeremiah A., Jr. *When Hell Was in Session: A Personal Story of Survival as a P.O.W. in North Vietnam.* New York: Reader's Digest, 1976.

828. DeSantis, Vincent. "Eisenhower Revisionism." *Review of Politics,* April 1976.

829. Destler, I. M. "National Security Advice to U.S. Presidents: Some Lessons from Thirty Years." *World Politics* 29, no. 2 (1977).

830. Destler, I. M. *Presidents, Bureaucrats, and Foreign Policy: The Politics of Organizational Reform.* Princeton, N.J.: Princeton University, 1972.

831. Destler, I. M., et al. *Managing an Alliance: The Politics of U.S.-Japanese Relations.* Washington, D.C.: Brookings Institution, 1976.

832. Detzer, David. *Thunder of the Captains: The Short Summer in 1950.* New York: Thomas Y. Crowell, 1977.

833. Dickson, Paul. *The Electronic Battlefield.* Bloomington: Indiana University, 1976.

834. Dinerstein, Herbert S. *The Making of a Missile Crisis: October 1962.* Baltimore: Johns Hopkins University, 1976.
835. Donovan, John C. *The Cold Warriors: A Policy-Making Elite.* Lexington, Mass.: D. C. Heath, 1974.
836. Donovan, Robert J. *Conflict and Crisis: The Presidency of Harry S. Truman, 1945-1948.* New York: Norton, 1977.
837. Dramesi, Lt. Col. John A. *Code of Honor.* New York: Norton, 1975.
838. Draper, Theodore, et al. *Defending America: Toward a New Role in the Post-Detente World.* New York: Basic Books, 1977.
839. Dung, Gen. Van Tien. *Our Great Spring Victory: An Account of the Liberation of South Vietnam.* New York: Monthly Review, 1977.
840. Eayrs, James. *In Defence of Canada: Peacemaking and Deterrence.* Toronto: University of Toronto, 1972.
841. Ellis, Joseph, and Robert Moore. *School for Soldiers: West Point and the Profession of Arms.* New York: Oxford University, 1974.
842. Emmerson, John K., and Leonard A. Humphreys. *Will Japan Rearm? A Study in Attitudes.* Washington, D.C.: American Enterprise Institute, 1974.
843. Endicott, Lt. Col. John E. *Japan's Nuclear Option: Political, Technical, and Strategic Factors.* New York: Praeger, 1975.
844. Endicott, Lt. Col. John E., and Maj. Roy W. Stafford, Jr., eds. *American Defense Policy.* 4th ed. Baltimore: Johns Hopkins University, 1977.
845. Enthoven, Alain C. "U.S. Forces in Europe: How Many? Doing What?" *Foreign Affairs,* April 1975.
846. Entin, Kenneth. "House Armed Services Committee: Patterns of Decision-Making during the McNamara Years." *Journal of Political and Military Sociology,* spring 1974.
847. Estes, Thomas S., and E. Allan Lightner, Jr. *The Department of State.* New York: Praeger, 1976.
848. Etzold, Thomas H. *The Conduct of American Foreign Relations: The Other Side of Diplomacy.* New York: New Viewpoints, 1977.
849. Falk, Richard A. "Panama Treaty Trap." *Foreign Policy,* spring 1978.
850. Falk, Richard A., ed. *The Vietnam War and International Law.* 4 vols. Princeton, N.J.: Princeton University, 1968-76.
851. Faris, John H. "An Alternative Perspective to Savage and Gabriel." *Armed Forces and Society,* spring 1977.
852. Fifield, Russell H. *Americans in Southeast Asia: The Roots of Commitment.* New York: Thomas Y. Crowell, 1973.
853. Fitzsimons, Louise. *The Kennedy Doctrine.* New York: Random House, 1972.
854. Foster, Richard B., André Beaufre, and Wynfred Joshua, eds. *Strategy for the West: American-Allied Relations in Transition.* New York: Crane, Russak, 1974.
855. Fox, Annette Baker. *The Politics of Attraction: Four Middle Powers and the United States.* New York: Columbia University, 1977.
856. Fox, J. Ronald. *Arming America: How the U.S. Buys Weapons.* Cambridge: Harvard Business School, 1974.
857. Franck, Thomas M., and Edward Weisband, eds. *Secrecy and Foreign Policy.* New York: Oxford University, 1974.

858. Freedman, Lawrence. *U.S. Intelligence and the Soviet Strategic Threat.* Boulder, Colo.: Westview, 1977.

859. Friedland, Edward, Paul Seabury, and Aaron Wildavsky. *The Great Détente Disaster: Oil and the Decline of American Foreign Policy.* New York: Basic Books, 1975.

860. Friedman, Edward, and Mark Selden, eds. *America's Asia: Dissenting Essays on Asian-American Relations.* New York: Pantheon, 1971.

861. Frye, Alton. *A Responsible Congress: The Politics of National Security.* New York: McGraw-Hill, 1975.

862. Gabriel, Richard A., and Paul L. Savage. *Crisis in Command: Mismanagement in the Army.* New York: Hill and Wang, 1978.

863. Gaddis, John Lewis. "Containment: A Reassessment." *Foreign Affairs,* July 1977.

864. Gaddis, John Lewis. "Reconsiderations: Was the Truman Doctrine a Real Turning Point?" *Foreign Policy,* January 1974.

865. Gallucci, Robert L. *Neither Peace Nor Honor: The Politics of American Military Policy in Viet-Nam.* Baltimore: Johns Hopkins University, 1975.

866. Gardner, Lloyd C. "Truman Era Foreign Policy: Recent Historical Trends." In *The Truman Period as a Research Field: A Reappraisal, 1972,* edited by Richard S. Kirkendall. Columbia: University of Missouri, 1972.

867. Garwin, Richard L. "Effective Military Technology for the 1980's." *International Security,* fall 1976.

868. Generous, William T., Jr. *Swords and Scales: The Development of the Uniform Code of Military Justice.* Port Washington, N.Y.: Kennikat, 1973.

869. Gervasi, Tom. *Arsenal of Democracy: American Weapons Available for Export.* New York: Grove Press, 1977.

870. Giap, Gen. Vo Nguyen, and Gen. Van Tien Dung. *How We Won the War.* Philadelphia: RECON Publications, 1976.

871. Gimbel, John. *The Origins of the Marshall Plan.* Stanford, Calif.: Stanford University Press, 1976.

872. Godfrey, E. Drexel, Jr. "Ethics and Intelligence." *Foreign Affairs,* April 1978.

873. Goldstein, Joseph, Burke Marshall, and Jack Schwartz. *The My Lai Massacre and Its Cover-up: Beyond the Reach of Law?* New York: Free Press, 1976.

874. Goodpaster, Gen. Andrew J. *For the Common Defense.* Lexington, Mass.: Lexington Books, 1977.

875. Goodpaster, Gen. Andrew J., and Samuel P. Huntington. *Civil-Military Relations.* Washington, D.C.: American Enterprise Institute, 1977.

876. Gowing, Margaret. *Independence and Deterrence: Britain and Atomic Energy, 1945-1952.* 2 vols. New York: St. Martin, 1975.

877. Greenberg, Daniel S. *The Politics of Pure Science.* New York: New American Library, 1971.

878. Greene, Fred. *Stresses in U.S.-Japanese Security Relations.* Washington, D.C.: Brookings Institution, 1975.

879. Gurtov, Melvin. *The United States against the Third World: Antinationalism and Intervention.* New York: Praeger, 1974.

880. Halperin, Morton H. *Bureaucratic Politics and Foreign Policy.* Washington, D.C.: Brookings Institution, 1974.

881. Halperin, Morton H. *Contemporary Military Strategy.* Boston: Little, Brown, 1967.

882. Halperin, Morton H. *National Security Policy-Making: Analyses, Cases, and Proposals.* Lexington, Mass.: Lexington Books, 1975.

883. Halperin, Morton H., et al. *The Lawless State: The Crimes of the U.S. Intelligence Agencies.* New York: Penguin Books, 1976.

884. Halperin, Morton H., and Daniel N. Hoffman. *Top Secret: National Security and the Right to Know.* Washington, D.C.: New Republic Books, 1977.

885. Hamby, Alonzo L. *Beyond the New Deal: Harry S. Truman and American Liberalism.* New York: Columbia University, 1973.

886. Harkavy, Robert E. *The Arms Trade and International Systems.* Cambridge, Mass.: Ballinger, 1975.

887. Harriman, W. Averell, and Elie Abel. *Special Envoy to Churchill and Stalin, 1941–1946.* New York: Random House, 1975.

888. Hart, Robert A. *The Eccentric Tradition: American Diplomacy in the Far East.* New York: Charles Scribner's Sons, 1976.

889. Head, Col. Richard G. "Technology and the Military Balance." *Foreign Affairs,* April 1978.

890. Head, Col. Richard G., Frisco W. Short, and Robert C. McFarlane. *Crisis Resolution: Presidential Decision Making in the Mayaguez and Korean Confrontations.* Boulder, Colo.: Westview, 1978.

891. Heath, Jim F. *Decade of Disillusionment. The Kennedy-Johnson Years.* Bloomington: Indiana University, 1975.

892. Helmer, John. *Bringing the War Home: The American Soldier in Vietnam and After.* New York: Free Press, 1974.

893. Herr, Michael. *Dispatches.* New York: Knopf, 1977.

894. Herring, George C., Jr. *Aid to Russia, 1941–1946: Strategy, Diplomacy, the Origins of the Cold War.* New York: Columbia University, 1973.

895. Hess, Gary R. "The Iranian Crisis of 1945–46 and the Cold War." *Political Science Quarterly,* March 1974.

896. Hoeber, Amoretta M., and Joseph D. Douglass, Jr. "The Neglected Threat of Chemical Warfare." *International Security,* summer 1978.

897. Hoeber, Francis P., David B. Kassing, and William Schneider, Jr. *Arms, Men, and Military Budgets: Issues for Fiscal Year 1979.* New York: Crane, Russak, 1978.

898. Hoffman, Stanley. "Revisionism Revisited." In *Reflections of the Cold War, A Quarter Century of American Foreign Policy,* edited by Lynn H. Miller and Ronald W. Pruessen. Philadelphia: Temple University, 1974.

899. Hoilberg, Anne, ed. "Women as New 'Manpower.'" *Armed Forces and Society,* summer 1978.

900. Holloway, Bruce K. "Reflections on Nuclear Strategy and the Nixon Doctrine." *Strategic Review,* spring 1973.

901. Holst, Johan J., and Uwe Nerlich, eds. *Beyond Nuclear Deterence: New Aims, New Arms.* New York: Crane, Russak, 1977.

902. Holt, Pat M. *The War Powers Resolution: The Role of Congress in U.S. Armed Intervention.* Washington, D.C.: American Enterprise Institute, 1978.

903. Howard, Harry N. *Turkey, the Straits and U.S. Policy.* Baltimore: Johns Hopkins University, 1975.

904. Hoxie, R. Gordon. *Command Decision and the Presidency: A Study of National Security Policy and Organization.* New York: Reader's Digest, 1977.

905. Hubbell, John G. *P.O.W.: A Definitive History of the American Prisoner-of-War Experience in Vietnam, 1964-1973.* New York: Reader's Digest, 1976.

906. Hunter, Edna J., ed. *Prolonged Separation: The Prisoner of War and His Family.* San Diego, Calif.: Center for Prisoner of War Studies, Naval Health Research Center, 1977.

907. Hunter, Edna J., et al. "Resistance Posture and the Vietnam Prisoner of War." *Journal of Political and Military Sociology,* fall 1976.

908. Ignotus, Miles [pseud.] "Seizing Arab Oil." *Harper's,* March 1975.

909. *Indiana Law Journal,* summer 1974. Issue devoted to military affairs since 1972.

910. *Indiana Law Journal,* fall 1976.

911. Iriye, Akira. *The Cold War in Asia: A Historical Introduction.* Englewood Cliffs, N.J.: Prentice-Hall, 1974.

912. Jacobs, James B. "Legal Change within the United States Armed Forces since World War II." *Armed Forces and Society,* spring 1978.

913. Janowitz, Morris, and Charles C. Moskos, Jr. "Racial Composition in the All-Volunteer Force." *Armed Forces and Society,* fall 1974.

914. Jeffreys-Jones, Rhodri. *American Espionage: From Secret Service to CIA.* New York: Free Press, 1977.

915. Johnson, David T., and Barry R. Schneider, eds. *Current Issues in U.S. Defense Policy.* New York: Praeger, 1976.

916. Johnson, Harry G. "Egregious Economics as Pacifist Propaganda: Melman's Methology of Defense Disbursements." *Armed Forces and Society,* summer 1975.

917. Jones, Alan M., Jr. *U.S. Foreign Policy in a Changing World: The Nixon Administration, 1969-1973.* New York: McKay, 1973.

918. Kalb, Marvin, and Bernard Kalb. *Kissinger.* Boston: Little, Brown, 1974.

919. Kalicki, J. H. *The Pattern of Sino-American Crises: Political-Military Interactions in the 1950's.* New York: Cambridge University, 1975.

920. Kanter, Arnold. "Congress and the Defense Budget." *American Political Science Review,* March 1972.

921. Kaplan, Morton A., et al. *Vietnam Settlement: Why 1973, Not 1969?* Washington, D.C.: American Enterprise Institute, 1973.

922. Katz, James Everett. *Presidential Politics and Science Policy.* New York: Praeger, 1978.

923. Kearns, Doris. *Lyndon Johnson and the American Dream.* New York: Harper & Row, 1976.

924. Keeley, John B., ed. *The All-Volunteer Force and American Society.* Charlottesville: University Press of Virginia, 1978

925. Kemp, Geoffrey, Robert L. Pfaltzgraff, Jr., and Uri Ra'anan, eds. *The Other Arms Race: New Technologies and Non-Nuclear Conflict.* Lexington, Mass.: Lexington Books, 1975.

926. Kennan, George F. *The Cloud of Danger: Current Realities of American Foreign Policy.* Boston: Little, Brown, 1977.

927. Kennedy, Galvin. *The Economics of Defense.* Totowa, N.J.: Rowman and Littlefield, 1975.

928. Killian, James R., Jr. *Sputnik, Scientists and Eisenhower: A Memoir of the First Special Assistant to the President for Science and Technology.* Cambridge, Mass.: M.I.T., 1977.

929. Kimball, Warren F. "The Cold War Warmed Over." *The American Historical Review,* October 1974.

930. Kinnard, Gen. Douglas. "For the Post-Vietnam Military: No End of Advice." *Polity* 8, no. 2 (1975).

931. Kinnard, Gen. Douglas. *President Eisenhower and Strategy Management: A Study in Defense Politics.* Lexington: University of Kentucky, 1977.

932. Kinnard, Gen. Douglas. *The War Managers.* Hanover, N.H.: University Press of New England, 1977.

933. Kintner, William R., and Richard B. Foster, eds. *National Strategy in a Decade of Change: An Emerging U.S. Policy.* Lexington, Mass.: Lexington Books, 1973.

934. Kirk, Donald. *Tell It to the Dead: Memories of a War.* Chicago: Nelson Hall, 1975.

935. Kirk, Grayson, and Nils H. Wessell, eds. *The Soviet Threat.* New York: The Academy of Political Science, 1978.

936. Kirkendall, Richard S. *The Truman Period as a Research Field: A Reappraisal, 1972.* Columbia: University of Missouri, 1974.

937. Kissinger, Henry A. *American Foreign Policy.* 3rd ed. New York: Norton, 1977.

938. Kistiakowsky, George B. *A Scientist at the White House: The Private Diary of President Eisenhower's Special Assistant for Science and Technology.* Cambridge: Harvard University, 1976.

939. Kitchel, Denison. *The Truth about the Panama Canal.* New Rochelle, N.Y.: Arlington House, 1978.

940. Knight, Jonathan. "American Statecraft and the 1946 Black Sea Straits Controversy." *Political Science Quarterly,* fall 1975.

941. Knorr, Klaus, ed. *Historical Dimensions of National Security Problems.* Lawrence: University Press of Kansas, 1976.

942. Knorr, Klaus, and Frank N. Trager, eds. *Economic Issues and National Security.* Lawrence: Regents Press of Kansas, 1978.

943. Kolko, Joyce, and Gabriel Kolko. "To Root Out Those among Them—A Response." *Pacific Historical Review,* November 1973.

944. Korb, Lawrence J. *The Joint Chiefs of Staff: The First Twenty-Five Years.* Bloomington: Indiana University, 1976.

945. Korb, Lawrence J. *The Price of Preparedness: The FY 1978–1982 Defense Program.* Washington, D.C.: American Enterprise Institute, 1977.

946. Korb, Lawrence J., ed. *The System for Educating Military Officers in the U.S.* Occasional Paper no. 9. Pittsburgh: International Studies Association, 1976.

947. Krendel, Ezra S., and Bernard Samoff, eds. *Unionizing the Armed Forces.* Philadelphia: University of Pennsylvania, 1977.

948. Krepon, Michael. "Weapons Potentially Inhumane: The Case of Cluster Bombs." *Foreign Affairs,* April 1974.

949. Ladinsky, Jack. "Vietnam, the Veterans, and the Veterans Administration." *Armed Forces and Society,* spring 1976.

950. LaFeber, Walter. "Crossing the 38th: The Cold War in Microcosm." In *Reflections on the Cold War: A Quarter Century of American Foreign Policy,* edited by Lynn H. Miller and Ronald W. Pruessen. Philadelphia: Temple University, 1974.

951. LaFeber, Walter. "Kissinger and Acheson: The Secretary of State and the Cold War." *Political Science Quarterly,* summer 1977.

952. LaFeber, Walter. *The Panama Canal: The Crisis in Historical Perspective.* New York: Oxford University, 1978.

953. Lake, Anthony, ed. *The Vietnam Legacy: The War, American Society and the Future of American Foreign Policy.* New York: New York University, 1976.

954. Lansdale, Gen. Edward G. *In the Midst of Wars: An American's Mission to Southeast Asia.* New York: Harper & Row, 1972.

955. Larson, Arthur D. "Military Professionalism and Civil Control: A Comparative Analysis of Two Interpretations." *Journal of Political and Military Sociology,* spring 1974.

956. Laurance, Edward J. "The Changing Role of Congress in Defense Policy-Making." *Journal of Conflict Resolution* 20, no. 2 (1976).

957. Lawrence, Richard D., and Jeffrey Record. *U.S. Force Structure in NATO: An Alternative.* Washington, D.C.: Brookings Institution, 1974.

958. Lee, William T. *The Estimation of Soviet Defense Expenditures, 1955-1975: An Unconventional Approach.* New York: Praeger, 1977.

959. Lefever, Ernest W. "The Military Assistance Training Program." *Annals of the American Academy of Political and Social Science* 424, March 1976.

960. Lefever, Ernest W. *TV and National Defense: An Analysis of CBS News, 1972-1973.* Boston, Va.: Institute for American Strategy, 1974.

961. Lefever, Ernest W. "Withdrawal from Korea: A Perplexing Decision." *Strategic Review,* winter 1978.

962. Lehman, John. *The Executive, Congress, and Foreign Policy: Studies of the Nixon Administration.* New York: Praeger, 1976.

963. Leigh, Michael. "Is There a Revisionist Thesis on the Origins of the Cold War?" *Political Science Quarterly,* March 1974.

964. Levitan, Sar A., and Karen Cleary Alderman. *Warriors at Work: The Volunteer Armed Force.* Beverly Hills, Calif.: Sage, 1977.

965. Lewis, Jesse W., Jr. *The Strategic Balance in the Mediterranean.* Washington, D.C.: American Enterprise Institute, 1976.

966. Liska, George. *Quest for Equilibrium: America and the Balance of Power on Land and Sea.* Baltimore: Johns Hopkins University, 1977.

967. Lord, Donald C. *John F. Kennedy: The Politics of Confrontation and Conciliation.* Woodbury, N.Y.: Barron's Educational Series, 1977.

968. Louis, William Roger, ed. *National Security and International Trusteeship in the Pacific.* Annapolis, Md.: United States Naval Institute, 1972.

969. Louscher, David J. "The Rise of Military Sales as a U.S. Foreign Assistance Instrument." *Orbis,* winter 1977.

970. Lowenthal, Abraham F. *The Dominican Intervention.* Cambridge: Harvard University, 1972.

971. Lukacs, John. *Nineteen Forty Five: Year Zero.* Garden City, N.Y.: Doubleday, 1978.

972. Lyon, Peter. *Eisenhower: Portrait of the Hero.* Boston: Little, Brown, 1974.

973. Magdoff, Harry. *The Age of Imperialism: The Economics of U.S. Foreign Policy.* New York: Monthly Review, 1969.

974. Maier, Charles S. "Revisionism and the Interpretation of Cold War Origins." *Perspectives in American History,* 4 (1970).

975. Manchester, William. *American Caesar: Douglas MacArthur, 1880-1964.* Boston: Little, Brown, 1978.

976. Manderson-Jones, R. B. *The Special Relationship: Anglo-American Relations and Western European Unity, 1947-56.* New York: Crane, Russak, 1972.

977. Mangold, Peter. *Superpower Intervention in the Middle East.* New York: St. Martin, 1977.

978. Marchetti, Victor, and John D. Marks. *The CIA and the Cult of Intelligence.* New York: Knopf, 1974.

979. Margiotta, Col. Franklin D., ed. *The Changing World of the American Military.* Boulder, Colo.: Westview, 1978.

980. Mark, Eduard. "The Question of Containment: A Reply to John Lewis Gaddis." *Foreign Affairs,* January 1978.

981. Martin, Laurence. *Arms and Strategy: The World Power Structure Today.* New York: David McKay, 1973.

982. May, Ernest R., and James C. Thomson, Jr., eds. *American-East Asian Relations: A Survey.* Cambridge: Harvard University, 1972.

983. Mazlish, Bruce. *Kissinger: The European Mind in American Policy.* New York: Basic Books, 1976.

984. McCarthy, Richard D. *The Ultimate Folly: War by Pestilence, Asphyxiation and Defoliation.* New York: Random House, 1969.

985. McCubbin, Hamiliton, Barbara B. Dahl, and Edna J. Hunter, eds. *Families in the Military System.* Beverly Hills, Calif.: Sage, 1976.

986. McGarvey, Patrick J. *CIA: The Myth and the Madness.* New York: Saturday Review, 1972.

987. McGovern, James. *To the Yalu: From the Chinese Invasion of Korea to MacArthur's Dismissal.* New York: William Morrow, 1972.

988. McGrath, Lt. Comdr. John M. *Prisoner of War: Six Years in Hanoi.* Annapolis, Md.: United States Naval Institute, 1975.

989. McHenry, Donald F. *Micronesia: Trust Betrayed. Altruism vs. Self Interest in American Foreign Policy.* Washington, D.C.: Carnegie Endowment for International Peace, 1976.

990. McLellan, David S. *Dean Acheson: The State Department Years.* New York: Dodd, Mead, 1976.
991. Mee, Charles L., Jr. *Meeting at Potsdam.* New York: Evans, 1975.
992. Melman, Seymour. *The Permanent War Economy: American Capitalism in Decline.* New York: Simon and Schuster, 1974.
993. Melman, Seymour. "Twelve Propositions on Productivity and War Economy." *Armed Forces and Society,* summer 1975.
994. Merli, Frank J., and Theodore A. Wilson, eds. *Makers of American Diplomacy.* Vol. 2, *From Theodore Roosevelt to Henry Kissinger.* New York: Scribner's Sons, 1974.
995. Meselson, Matthew, ed. *Chemical Weapons and Chemical Arms Control.* New York: Carnegie Endowment for International Peace, 1978.
996. Middleton, Drew. *Can America Win the Next War?* New York: Scribner's Sons, 1975.
997. Mihaly, Eugene B. "Tremors in the Western Pacific: Micronesian Freedom and U.S. Security." *Foreign Affairs,* July 1974.
998. Miller, Linda B. "Energy, Security and Foreign Policy: A Review Essay." *International Security,* spring 1977.
999. Miller, Lynn H., and Ronald W. Pruessen, eds. *Reflections of the Cold War: A Quarter Century of American Foreign Policy.* Philadelphia: Temple University, 1974.
1000. Miller, Merle. *Plain Speaking: An Oral Biography of Harry S. Truman.* New York: Putnam/Berkley, 1974.
1001. Millett, Allan R., ed. *A Short History of the Vietnam War.* Bloomington: Indiana University, 1978.
1002. Milstein, Jeffrey S. *Dynamics of the Vietnam War: A Quantitative Analysis and Predictive Computer Simulation.* Columbus: Ohio State University, 1974.
1003. Miroff, Bruce. *Pragmatic Illusions: The Presidential Politics of John F. Kennedy.* New York: David McKay, 1976.
1004. Moore, John Norton. *Law and the Indo-China War.* Princeton, N.J.: Princeton University, 1972.
1005. Morgan, Roger. *The United States and West Germany, 1945–1973: A Study in Alliance Politics.* New York: Oxford University, 1974.
1006. Morgenstern, Oskar, Klaus Knorr, and Klaus P. Heiss. *Long Term Projections of Power: Political, Economic, and Military Forecasting.* Cambridge, Mass. Ballinger, 1973.
1007. Morris, Roger. *Uncertain Greatness: Henry Kissinger and American Foreign Policy.* New York: Harper, 1977.
1008. Morrison, Philip, and Paul F. Walker. "A New Strategy for Military Spending." *Scientific American,* October 1978.
1009. Moskos, Charles C., Jr. "The American Combat Soldier in Vietnam." *Journal of Social Issues* 31. no. 4 (1975).
1010. Mosley, Leonard. *Dulles: A Biography of Eleanor, Allen, and John Foster Dulles and Their Family Network.* New York: Dial, 1978.
1011. Moyer, Homer E., Jr. *Justice and the Military.* Washington, D.C.: Public Law Education Institute, 1972.
1012. Mrozek, Donald J. "A New Look at 'Balanced Forces': Defense

Continuities from Truman to Eisenhower." *Military Affairs,* December 1974.

1013. Murdock, Clark A. *Defense Policy Formation: A Comparative Analysis of the McNamara Era.* Albany: State University of New York, 1974.

1014. Mylander, Maureen. *The Generals: Making It, Military Style.* New York: Dial, 1974.

1015. Nagai, Yonosuki, and Akira Iriye, eds. *The Origins of the Cold War in Asia.* New York: Columbia University, 1977.

1016. Nathan, James A. "The Missile Crisis: His Finest Hour Now." *World Politics* 27 (1975).

1017. Nathan, James A., and James K. Oliver. "Public Opinion and U.S. Security Policy." *Armed Forces and Society,* fall 1975.

1018. Nathan, James A., and James K. Oliver. *United States Foreign Policy and World Order.* Boston: Little, Brown, 1976.

1019. Nau, Henry R. *Technology Transfer and U.S. Foreign Policy.* New York: Praeger, 1976.

1020. Naughton, Robert J. "Motivational Factors of American Prisoners of War Held by the Democratic Republic of Vietnam." *Naval War College Review* January-February 1975.

1021. "New Assessment Put on Soviet Threat." *Aviation Week and Space Technology,* 28 March 1977.

1022. Nixon, Richard. *RN: The Memoirs of Richard Nixon.* New York: Grosset and Dunlap, 1978.

1023. Noble, Harold Joyce. *Embassy at War.* Edited by Frank Baldwin. Seattle: University of Washington, 1975.

1024. "NSC-68: A Report to the National Security Council." *Naval War College Review,* May-June 1975.

1025. "Nuclear Weapons Policy Questioned." *Aviation Week and Space Technology,* 6 November 1978.

1026. Nuechterlein, Donald E. *United States National Interests in a Changing World.* Lexington: University Press of Kentucky, 1973.

1027. O'Brien, Tim. *If I Die in a Combat Zone.* New York: Delacorte, 1973.

1028. Oksenberg, Michael, and Robert B. Oxnam, eds. *Dragon and Eagle: United States-Chinese Relations: Past and Future.* New York: Basic Books, 1978.

1029. Olson, Keith W. *The G.I. Bill, the Veterans, and the Colleges.* Lexington: University Press of Kentucky, 1974.

1030. "On Power." *Foreign Affairs,* October 1977.

1031. Osgood, Robert E., ed. *America and the World.* Vol. 2, *Retreat from Empire? The First Nixon Administration.* Baltimore: Johns Hopkins University, 1973.

1032. Owen, Henry, and Charles L. Schultze, eds. *Setting National Priorities: The Next Ten Years.* Washington, D.C.: Brookings Institution, 1976.

1033. Palmer, Gen. Bruce, Jr., ed. *Grand Strategy for the 1980's.* Washington, D.C.: American Enterprise Institute, 1978.

1034. Palmer, Dave Richard. *Summons of the Trumpet: U.S.-Vietnam in Perspective.* San Rafael, Calif.: Presidio, 1978.

1035. Paper, Lewis J. *The Promise and the Performance: The Leadership of John F. Kennedy.* New York: Crown, 1975.

1036. Parkinson, F. *Latin America, the Cold War, and the World Powers, 1945–1973: A Study in Diplomatic History.* Beverly Hills, Calif.: Sage, 1974.

1037. Parrish, John A. *12, 20 & 5: A Doctor's Year in Vietnam.* New York: Dutton, 1972.

1038. Paterson, Thomas G. *Soviet-American Confrontation: Postwar Reconstruction and the Origins of the Cold War.* Baltimore: Johns Hopkins University, 1973.

1039. Pechman, Joseph A., ed. *Setting National Priorities: The 1979 Budget.* Washington, D.C.: Brookings Institution, 1978.

1040. Penick, James L., Jr., et al. *The Politics of American Science: 1939 to the Present.* Chicago: Rand McNally, 1965.

1041. Penner, Rudolph G., with Lawrence J. Korb. *The 1978 Budget in Transition From Ford to Carter to Congress.* Washington, D.C.: American Enterprise Institute, 1977.

1042. Petersen, Lt. Col. Peter B. *Against the Tide: An Argument in Favor of the American Soldier.* New Rochelle, N.Y.: Arlington House, 1974.

1043. Petersen, Phillip A. "American Perceptions of Soviet Military Power." *Parameters 7, no. 4 (1977).*

1044. Phillips, David Atlee. *The Night Watch.* New York: Atheneum, 1977.

1045. Pierre, Andrew J. "Can Europe's Security Be 'Decoupled' from America?" *Foreign Affairs,* July 1973.

1046. Pipes, Richard. "Why the Soviet Union Thinks It Could Fight and Win a Nuclear War." *Commentary,* July 1977.

1047. Polk, William R. *The United States and the Arab World.* 3rd ed. Cambridge: Harvard University, 1975.

1048. Porter, Gareth. *A Peace Denied: The United States, Vietnam, and the Paris Agreement.* Bloomington: Indiana University, 1976.

1049. Pranger, Robert J., and Roger P. Labrie, eds. *Nuclear Strategy and National Security: Points of View.* Washington, D.C.: American Enterprise Institute, 1977.

1050. Pranger, Robert J., and Dale R. Tahtinen. *Toward a Realistic Military Assistance Program.* Washington, D.C.: American Enterprise Institute, 1975.

1051. Preston, Richard A. "Toward a Defence Policy and Military Doctrine for Canada." *Armed Forces and Society,* fall 1977.

1052. Primack, Joel, and Frank von Hippel. *Advice and Dissent: Scientists in the Political Arena.* New York: Basic Books, 1974.

1053. Prouty, L. Fletcher. *The Secret Team: The CIA and Its Allies in Control of the United States and the World.* Englewood Cliffs, N.J.: Prentice-Hall, 1973.

1054. Pruessen, Ronald W. "The Objectives of American Foreign Policy and the Nature of the Cold War." In *Reflections of the Cold War: A Quarter Century of American Foreign Foreign Policy,* edited by Lynn H. Miller and Ronald W. Pruessen. Philadelphia: Temple University, 1974.

1055. Quandt, William B. *Decade of Decisions: American Policy toward the*

Arab-Israeli Conflict, 1967N1976. Berkeley: University of California, 1977.

1056. Quester, George H. "Women in Combat." *International Security,* spring 1977.

1057. Radosh, Ronald. *Prophets on the Right: Profiles of Conservative Critics of American Globalism.* New York: Simon and Schuster, 1975.

1058. Randle, Robert F. *Geneva, 1954: The Settlement of the Indochinese War.* Princeton, N.J.: Princeton University, 1969.

1059. Ransom, Harry Howe, "Strategic Intelligence and Foreign Policy." *World Politics 27, no. 1 (1974).*

1060. Ravenal, Earl C. *Never Again: Learning from America's Foreign Policy Failures.* Philadelphia: Temple University, 1978.

1061. Reich, Bernard. *Quest for Peace: United States-Israel Relations and the Arab-Israeli Conflict.* New Brunswick, N.J.: Transaction, 1977.

1062. Reid, Escott. *Time of Fear and Hope: The Making of the North Atlantic Treaty, 1947-1949.* Toronto: McClelland & Stewart, 1977.

1063. Reppy, Judith, and F. A. Long. "U.S. Military R&D: A Set of Questions." *Bulletin of the Atomic Scientists, May 1978.*

1064. Richardson, James L. "Cold-War Revisionism: A Critique." *World Politics, July 1972.*

1065. Rose, Lisle A. *Dubious Victory: The United States and the End of World War II.* Kent, Ohio: Kent State University, 1973.

1066. Rose, Lisle A. *Roots of Tragedy: The United States and the Struggle for Asia, 1945-1953.* Westport, Conn.: Greenwood, 1976.

1067. Rose, Steven, ed. *CBW: Chemical and Biological Warfare.* Boston: Beacon, 1968.

1068. Rosecrance, Richard, ed. *America as an Ordinary Country: U.S. Foreign Policy and the Future.* Ithaca, N.Y.: Cornell University, 1976.

1069. Rosi, Eugene J., ed. *American Defense and Détente: Readings in National Security Policy.* New York: Dodd, Mead, 1973.

1070. Rositke, Harry. *The CIA's Secret Operation: Espionage, Counterespionage and Covert Action.* New York: Reader's Digest, 1977.

1071. Rostow, Eugene V. *Peace in the Balance: The Future of American Foreign Policy.* New York: Simon and Schuster, 1972.

1072. Rowan, Roy. *The Four Days of Mayaguez.* New York: Norton, 1975.

1073. Rowe, Maj. James N. *Five Years to Freedom.* Boston: Little, Brown, 1971.

1074. Roy, Reginald H. "Canadian Defense Policy, 1945-1976." *Parameters 1 (1976).*

1075. Russett, Bruce M., and Elizabeth C. Hanson. *Interest and and Ideology: The Foreign Policy Beliefs of American Businessmen.* San Francisco: W. H. Freeman, 1975.

1076. Russett, Bruce, and Miroslav Nincic. "American Opinion on the Use of Military Force Abroad." *Political Science Quarterly,* fall 1976.

1077. Ryan, Paul B. *The Panama Canal Controversy: U.S. Diplomacy and Defense Interests.* Stanford, Calif.: Hoover Institution, 1977.

1078. Sabrosky, Alan Ned, ed. *Blue-Collar Soldiers? Unionization and the U.S. Military.* Philadelphia: Foreign Policy Research Institute, 1976.

1079. Sabrosky, Alan Ned. *Defense Manpower Policy: A Critical Reappraisal.* Philadelphia: Foreign Policy Research Institute, 1977.

1080. Safran, Nadav. *Israel: The Embattled Ally.* Cambridge: Harvard University, 1978.

1081. Sampson, Anthony. *The Arms Bazaar: From Lebanon to Lockheed.* New York: Viking, 1977.

1082. Sanders, Ralph. *The Politics of Defense Analysis,* New York: Dunellen, 1973.

1083. Sarkesian, Sam C. "Political Soldiers: Perspectives on Professionalism in the U.S. Military." *Midwest Journal of Political Science,* May 1972.

1084. Sarkesian, Sam C. *The Professional Army Officer in a Changing Society.* Chicago: Nelson-Hall, 1975.

1085. Sarkesian, Sam C., and Thomas M. Gannon, eds. "Military Ethics and Professionalism." *American Behavioral Scientist,* May/June 1976.

1086. Scalapino, Robert A. "The American Occupation of Japan—Perspectives after Three Decades." *Annals,* November 1976.

1087. Schaetzel, J. Robert. *The Unhinged Alliance: America and the European Community.* New York: Harper & Row, 1975.

1088. Schandler, Herbert Y. *The Unmaking of a President: Lyndon Johnson and Vietnam.* Princeton, N.J.: Princeton University, 1977.

1089. Schilling, Warner R., et al. American Arms and a Changing Europe: Dilemmas of Deterrence and Disarmament. New York: Columbia University, 1973.

1090. Schlafly, Phyllis, and Chester Ward. *Kissinger on the Couch.* New Rochelle, N.Y.: Arlington House, 1975.

1091. Schlesinger, Arthur M., Jr. *The Imperial Presidency.* Boston: Houghton Mifflin, 1973.

1092. Schneider, William. *Food, Foreign Policy, and Raw Materials Cartels.* New York: Crane, Russak, 1976.

1093. Scoville, Herbert, Jr. "Is Espionage Necessary for Our Security?" *Foreign Affairs,* April 1976.

1094. Seitz, Frederick, and Rodney W. Nichols. *Research and Development and the Prospects for International Security.* New York: Crane, Russak, 1974.

1095. Selden, Mark, ed. *Remaking Asia: Essays on the American Uses of Power.* New York: Pantheon, 1974.

1096. Sharp, Tony. *The Wartime Alliance and the Zonal Division of Germany.* New York: Oxford University, 1975.

1097. Sharp, Adm. U. S. G. *Strategy for Defeat: Vietnam in Retrospect.* San Rafael, Calif.: Presidio, 1978.

1098. Sheehan, Edward R. F. *The Arabs, Israelis, and Kissinger: A Secret History of American Diplomacy in the Middle East.* New York: Reader's Digest, 1976.

1099. Sherry, Michael S. *Preparing for the Next War: American Plans for Postwar Defense, 1941–45.* New Haven, Conn.: Yale University, 1977.

1100. Shoup, Laurence H., and William Minter. *Imperial Brain Trust: The Council on Foreign Relations and United States Foreign Policy.* New York: Monthly Review, 1977.

1101. Simmons, Robert R. *The Strained Alliance: Peking, P'yŏngyang, Moscow and the Politics of the Korean Civil War.* New York: Free Press, 1975.

1102. Siracusa, Joseph M. *New Left Diplomatic Histories and Historians: The American Revisionists.* Port Washington, N.Y.: Kennikat, 1973.

1103. Slater, Jerome. "Is United States Foreign Policy 'Imperialist' or 'Imperial'?" *Political Science Quarterly, spring 1976.*

1104. Smith, Gaddis. "The Shadow of John Foster Dulles." *Foreign Affairs,* January 1974.

1105. Smith, Jean Edward, ed. *The Papers of General Lucius D. Clay: Germany 1945-1949.* 2 Vols. Bloomington: Indiana University, 1975.

1106. Smith, Jean Edward. "Selection of a Proconsul for Germany: The Appointment of Gen. Lucius D. Clay, 1945." *Military Affairs,* October 1976.

1107. Smith, Joseph B. *Portrait of a Cold Warrior.* New York: Putnam, 1976.

1108. Snepp, Frank. *Decent Interval: An Insider's Account of Saigon's Indecent End: Told by the CIA's Chief Strategy Analyst in Vietnam.* New York: Random House, 1977.

1109. Spector, Ronald. "Getting Down to the Nitty-Gritty: Military History, Official History and the American Experience in Vietnam." *Military Affairs,* February 1974.

1110. Srinivasachary, Mudumbhi S. "Sources for the Study of United States Mutual Security Policy towards South Asia, 1951-1960." *Military Affairs,* December 1975.

1111. Stairs, Denis. *The Diplomacy of Constraint: Canada, the Korean War, and the United States.* Toronto: University of Toronto, 1974.

1112. Starr, Paul. *The Discarded Army: Veterans after Vietnam.* New York: Charterhouse, 1974.

1113. Stern, Ellen P., ed. *The Limits of Military Intervention.* Beverly Hills, Calif.: Sage, 1977.

1114. Stevens, Robert Warren. *Vain Hopes, Grim Realities: The Economic Consequences of the Vietnam War.* New York: New Viewpoints, 1976.

1115. Stockfisch, J. A. *Plowshares into Swords: Managing the American Defense Establishment.* New York: Mason and Lipscomb, 1973.

1116. Stockwell, John. *In Search of Enemies: A CIA Story.* New York: Norton, 1978.

1117. Stoessinger, John G. *Henry Kissinger: The Anguish of Power.* New York: Norton, 1976.

1118. Stueck, William. "Cold War Revisionism and the Origins of the Korean Conflict: The Kolko Thesis." *Pacific Historical Review,* November 1973.

1119. Sullivan, Marianna P. "France and the Vietnam Peace Settlement." *Political Science Quarterly,* June 1974.

1120. Sutter, Robert G. *China-Watch: Toward Sino-American Reconciliation.* Baltimore: Johns Hopkins University, 1978.

1121. Szulc, Tad. *The Illusion of Peace: Foreign Policy in the Nixon Years.* New York: Viking, 1978.

1122. Tahtinen, Dale R. *Arms in the Indian Ocean.* Washington, D.C.: American Enterprise Institute, 1977.

1123. Taylor, Gen. Maxwell D. *Precarious Security.* New York: Norton, 1976.

1124. Taylor, Gen. Maxwell D., et al. *New Dynamics in National Strategy: The Paradox of Power.* New York: Crowell, 1975.

1125. Taylor, William J., Jr., Roger J. Arango, and Robert S. Lockwood. *Military Unions: U.S. Trends and Issues.* Beverly Hills, Calif.: Sage, 1977.

1126. Thompson, W. Scott. *Power Projection: A Net Assessment of U.S. and Soviet Capabilities,* New York: National Strategy Information Center, 1978.

1127. Thompson, W. Scott, and Donaldson D. Frizzell, eds. *The Lessons of Vietnam.* New York: Crane, Russak, 1977.

1128. Tillema, Herbert K. *Appeal to Force: American Military Intervention in the Era of Containment.* New York: Crowell, 1973.

1129. Trager, Frank N. "The National Security Act of 1947: Its Thirtieth Anniversary." *Air University Review,* November-December 1977.

1130. Treverton, Gregory G. *The "Dollar Drain" and American Forces in Germany: Managing the Political Economics of Alliance.* Athens: Ohio University, 1978.

1131. Trooboff, Peter D., ed. *Law and Responsibility in Warfare: The Vietnam Experience.* Chapel Hill: University of North Carolina, 1975.

1132. Tucker, Robert W. "Further Reflections on Oil and Force." Commentary, March 1975.

1133. Tucker, Robert W. "A New International Order." *Commentary,* February 1975.

1134. Tucker, Robert W. "Oil: The Issue of American Intervention." *Commentary, January 1975.*

1135. Twentieth Century Fund. *Those Who Served: Report of the Twentieth Century Fund Task Force on Policies toward Veterans.* New York: Twentieth Century Fund, 1974.

1136. Vernon, Raymond, ed. *The Oil Crisis.* New York: Norton, 1976.

1137. "The Vietnam Experience." *Armed Forces and Society,* spring 1976.

1138. Vogelgesang, Sandra. "What Price Principle? U.S. Policy on Human Rights." *Foreign Affairs,* July 1978.

1139. Walker, J. Samuel. *Henry A. Wallace and American Foreign Policy.* Westport, Conn.: Greenwood, 1976.

1140. Walters, Gen. Vernon A. *Silent Missons.* Garden City, N.Y.: Doubleday, 1978.

1141. Walton, Col. George. *The Tarnished Shield: A Report on Today's Army. New York: Dodd, Mead, 1973.*

1142. Walton, Richard J. *Henry Wallace, Harry Truman, and the Cold War.* New York: Viking, 1976.

1143. Webb, James H., Jr. *Micronesia and U.S. Pacific Strategy: A Blueprint for the 1980s.* New York: Praeger, 1974.

1144. Weidenbaum, Murray L. *The Economics of Peacetime Defense.* New York: Praeger, 1974.

1145. Weinstein, Franklin B. "U.S.-Vietnam Relations and the Security of Southeast Asia." *Foreign Affairs,* July 1978.

1146. West, Luther C. *They Call It Justice: Command Influences and the Court-Martial System.* New York: Viking, 1977.

1147. Westmoreland, Gen. William C. *A Soldier Reports.* Garden City, N.Y.: Doubleday, 1976.

1148. Wheeler-Bennett, Sir John, and Anthony Nicholls. *The Semblance of Peace, The Political Settlement after the Second World War.* New York: St. Martin, 1972.

1149. Whetten, Lawrence L. *The Canal War: Four-Power Conflict in the Middle East.* Cambridge, Mass.: M.I.T., 1974.

1150. Wilcox, Francis O., and Richard A. Frank, eds. *The Constitution and the Conduct of Foreign Policy.* New York: Praeger, 1976.

1151. Williams, Geoffrey. *The Permanent Alliance: The European-American Partnership, 1945-1984.* Leiden: Sijthoff, 1977.

1152. Williams, Phil. *Crisis Management: Confrontation and Diplomacy in the Nuclear Age.* New York: Halsted, 1976.

1153. Willrich, Mason. *Energy and World Politics.* New York: Free Press, 1976.

1154. Wiltz, John E. "The MacArthur Hearings of 1951: The Secret Testimony." *Military Affairs,* December 1975.

1155. Wolf, Joseph J. *The Growing Dimensions of Security.* Washington, D.C.: Atlantic Council, 1977.

1156. Wolpin, Miles D. *Military Aid and Counterrevolution in the Third World.* Lexington, Mass.: D. C. Heath, 1972.

1157. Woodward, William P. *The Allied Occupation of Japan, 1945-1952, and Japanese Religions.* Leiden: E. J. Brill, 1972.

1158. Wu, Yuan-li. *U.S. Policy and Strategic Interests in the Western Pacific.* New York: Crane, Russak, 1975.

1159. Yager, Joseph A., et al. *Energy and U.S. Foreign Policy: A Report to the Energy Policy Project of the Ford Foundation.* Cambridge, Mass.: Ballinger, 1974.

1160. Yergin, Daniel. *Shattered Peace: The Origins of the Cold War and the National Security State.* Boston: Houghton Mifflin, 1977.

1161. York, Herbert, and Allen Gerb. "Military Research and Development: A Postwar History." *Bulletin of the Atomic Scientists,* January 1977.

1162. Ziegler, David W. *War, Peace, and International Politics.* Boston: Little, Brown, 1977.

1163. Zumwalt, Adm. Elmo R., Jr. *On Watch: A Memoir.* New York: Quadrangle, 1976.

GOVERNMENT MATERIALS

1164. U.S. Arms Control and Disarmament Agency. *World Military Expenditures and Arms Transfers, 1967-1976.* Washington, D.C.: G.P.O., 1978. Title varies, 1966–   . Series.

1165. U.S. Commission on Manpower Defense. *Defense Manpower: Key to National Security.* Washington, D.C.: G.P.O., 1976.

1166. U.S. Congress. Congressional Budget Office. *Assessing the NATO/Warsaw Pact Military Balance.* 95th Cong., lst Sess. December 1977. Y 10.12: M59.

1167. U.S. Congress. Congressional Budget Office. *Costs of Defense Manpower: Issues for 1977.* 95th Cong., 1st Sess. January 1977. Y10.12: D36.

1168. U.S. Congress. House. Committee on Appropriations. Subcommittee on Defense Appropriations. *Department of Defense Appropriations for 1978: Hearings.* 7 Parts. 95th Cong., lst Sess. 8 February-21 September 1977. Y4. Ap6/1: D36/5/978/7 pts.

1169. U.S. Congress. House. Committee on Appropriations. Subcommittee on Foreign Operations. . . . *Foreign Assistance and Related Agencies Appropriations for 1978. Hearings.* 3 Parts. 95th Cong., 1st Sess. 16 February-21 April 1977. Y4. Ap6/1: F76/3/978/3 pts.

1170. U.S. Congress. House. Committee on Appropriations. Subcommittee on Military Appropriations. *Military Construction Appropriations for 1977. Hearings.* 94th Cong., 2nd Sess. 22 July-22 September 1976. Y4.Ap6/1: M59/6/977-2.

1171. U.S. Congress. House. Committee on Appropriations. Subcommittee on Military Construction Appropriations. *Military Construction Appropriations for 1978. Hearings.* 4 Parts. 95th Cong., 1st Sess. 7 February-20 April 1977. Y4.Ap6/1: M59/6/978/4 pts.

1172. U.S. Congress. House. Committee on Armed Services. *Full Committee Briefing on Project Egress Recap. Hearings.* 92nd Cong., 2nd Sess. 10 October 1972. Committee Serial No. 92-76. Y4.Ar5/2a: 971-72/76.

1173. U.S. Congress. House. Committee on Armed Services. *Hearings on Military Posture and H.R. 5068 (H.R. 5970). Hearings.* 6 Parts. 95th Cong., 1st Sess. 1 February-5 April 1977. Y4.Ar5/2a: 977-78/4/6pts.

1174. U.S. Congress. House Committee on Armed Services. *National Security Act of 1947 as Amended through September 30, 1973.* 93rd Cong., 1st Sess. October 1973. Committee Serial No. 93-21. Y4.Ar5/2a: 973-74.

1175. U.S. Congress. House. Committee on Armed Services. Armed Services Investigating Subcommittee. *Investigation of the My Lai Incident. Hearings.* 91st Cong., 2nd Sess. 15 April-22 June 1970. Y4.Ar5/2a: 975-76/47.

1176. U.S. Congress. House. Committee on Armed Services. Special Subcommittee on Intelligence. *Inquiry into the Alleged Involvement of the Central Intelligence Agency in the Watergate and Ellsberg Matters. Hearings.* 93rd Cong., 1st and 2nd Sess. 11 May 1973-2 July 1974. Y4.Ar5/2a: 975-76/4.

1177. U.S. Congress. House. Committee on Armed Services. Subcommittee on Intelligence and Military Application of Nuclear Energy. *Hearings on H. R. 6566. ERDA Authorization Legislation, Fy78 (National Security Programs). Hearings.* 95th Cong., 1st Sess. 28 February-27 April 1977. Committee Serial No. 95-15. Y4.Ar5/2a: 977-78/15.

1178. U.S. Congress. House. Committee on Armed Services. Subcommittee on Military Personnel. *U.S. Military Academy Honor Code. Hearings.* 94th Cong., 1st Sess. 25 August-1 September 1976. Y4.Ar5/2a: 977-78/3.

1179. U.S. Congress. House. Committee of the Budget. *Defense Manpower and the All-Volunteer Force. Hearings.* 95th Cong., 1st Sess. 12-13 July 1977. Y4.B85/3: D36/5.

1180. U.S. Congress. House. Committee on Foreign Affairs. *Selected Executive Session Hearings of the Committee, 1943-50.* 8 vols. 8 June 1943-2 February 1951. Y4.In8/16: H62/8 vols.

1181. U.S. Congress. House. Committee on Foreign Affairs. *Situation in Indochina. Hearings.* 93rd Cong., 1st Sess. 8 February-6 March 1973. Y4.F76/1: In2/9.

1182. U.S. Congress. House. Committee on Foreign Affairs. Subcommittee on Foreign Economic Policy. *Foreign Policy Implications of the*

Energy Crisis. Hearings. 92nd Cong., 1st Sess. 21 September-3 October 1972. Y4.F76/1: En2.

1183. U.S. Congress. House. Committee on Foreign Affairs. Subcommittee on Foreign Economic Policy. *U.S. Foreign Economic Policy: Implications for the Organization of the Executive Branch. Hearings.* 92nd Cong., 2nd Sess. 20 June-19 September 1972. Y4.F76/1: Ec7/4

1184. U.S. Congress. House. Committee on Foreign Affairs. Subcommittee on National Security Policy and Scientific Developments. *American Prisoners of War in Southeast Asia, 197- . Hearings.* 4 Parts. 92nd Cong., 1st and 2nd Sess.; 93rd Cong., 1st Sess. 23 March 1971-31 May 1973. Y4.F76/1: P93/4/973/4 pts.

1185. U.S. Congress. House. Committee on Foreign Affairs. Subcommittee on National Security Policy and Scientific Developments. *Chemical-Biological Warfare: U.S. Policies and International Effects. Hearings.* 91st Cong., 1st Sess. 18 November-19 December 1969.

1186. U.S. Congress. House. Committee on Foreign Affairs. Subcommittee on National Security Policy. . . . *U.S. Chemical Warfare Policy. Hearings.* 93rd. Cong., 2nd Sess. 1-14 May 1974. Y4: F76/1: W23/2.

1187. U.S. Congress. House. Committee on Foreign Affairs. Subcommittee on National Security Policy and Scientific Development. *War-Powers. Hearings.* 93rd Cong., 1st Sess. 7-20 March 1973. Y4.F76/1: W19/9.

1188. U.S. Congress. House. Committee on Foreign Affairs. Subcommittee on National Security Policy and Scientific Developments. *War Powers Legislation. Hearings.* 92nd Cong., 1st Sess. 1-2 June 1971.

1189. U.S. Congress. House. Committee on Government Operations. Subcommittee on Government Information. . . . *Central Intelligence Agency Exemption in the Privacy Act of 1974. Hearings.* 94th Cong., 1st Sess. 5 March-25 June 1975. Y4.G74/7: P93/6.

1190. U.S. Congress. House. Committee on International Relations. *Chronologies of Major Developments in Selected Areas of International Relations, January 197- .* 93rd Cong., 2nd Sess. Updated monthly. Y4.In8/16: In8/5.

1191. U.S. Congress. House. Committee on International Relations. *Congress and Foreign Relations: 19- .* Annual. First Issued 94th Cong., 1st Sess. 15 April 1975.

1192. U.S. Congress. House. Committee on International Relations. *Foreign Assistance Legislation for FY 78. Hearings.* 9 Parts. 95th Cong., 1st Sess. 16 March-4 May 1977. Y4.In8/16: F76/8/978/9pts.

1193. U.S. Congress. House. Committee on International Relations. *Human Rights in the International Community and in U.S. Foreign Policy, 1945-76.* 95th Cong., 1st Sess. 24 July 1977. Y4.In8/16: H88/20/945-76.

1194. U.S. Congress. House. Committee on International Relations. *Oil Fields as Military Objectives: A Feasibility Study.* 94th Cong., 1st Sess. 21 August 1975. Y4.In8/16: Oi5.

1195. U.S. Congress. House. Committee on International Relations. *Science, Technology, and American Diplomacy.* 94th Cong., 1st Sess. June 1975. Y4.In8/16: Sci Z.

1196. U.S. Congress. House. Committee on International Relations. Special

Subcommittee on Investigation. *Congress and Foreign Policy. Hearings.* 94th Cong., 2nd Sess. 17 June-22 September 1976. Y4.In8/16: F76/6.

1197. U.S. Congress. House. Committee on International Relations. Special Subcommittee on Investigations. *Vietnam-Cambodia Emergency, 1975. Hearings.* 4 Parts. 94th Cong., 1st and 2nd Sess. 6 March 1975- 5 May 1976. Y4.In8/16: V67/2/975 pts. 1-4.

1198. U.S. Congress. House. Committee on International Relations. Subcommittee on Europe. *Detente. Hearings.* 93rd Cong., 2nd Sess. 8 May-31 July 1974. Y4.F76/1: D48/2.

1199. U.S. Congress. House. Committee on International Relations. Subcommittee on Future Foreign Policy. . . . *Reassessment of U.S. Foreign Policy. Hearings.* 94th Cong., 1st Sess. 15-24 July 1975. Y4.In8/16: F76/2.

1200. U.S. Congress. House. Committee on International Relations. Subcommittee on International Security. . . . *Science, Technology, and American Diplomacy.* 94th Cong., 2nd Sess. June 1976. Y4.In8/16: Sci2/2.

1201. U.S. Congress. House. Committee on International Relations. Subcommittee on International . . . Affairs. *Seizure of the Mayaguez. Hearings.* 4 Parts 94th Cong., 1st and 2nd Sess. 14 May 1975-4 October 1976. Y4.In8/16: M45/pts. 1-4.

1202. U.S. Congress. House. Committee on International Relations. Subcommittee on International Security. . . . *War Powers: A Test of Compliance Relating to the . . . Evacuation of Saigon, and the Mayaguez Incident. Hearings.* 94th Cong., 1st Sess. 7 May-4 June 1975. Y4.In8/16: W19/2.

1203. U.S. Congress. House. Committee on Merchant Marine and Fisheries. *New Panama Canal Treaty. Hearings.* 95th Cong., 1st Sess. 17 August 1977. Y4.M53: 95-13.

1204. U.S. Congress. House. Committee on Merchant Marine and Fisheries. Subcommittee on Panama Canal. *U.S. Interest in Panama Canal. Hearings.* 95th Cong., 1st Sess. 25-27 July 1977. Committee Serial 95-10. Y4.M53: 95-10.

1205. U.S. Congress. House. Committee on Science and Technology. *1978 ERDA Authorization. Hearings.* 4 vols. 95th Cong., 1st Sess. 22 February 1977-10 June 1977. Y4.Sci2: 95.

1206. U.S. Congress. House. Select Committee on Intelligence. *U.S. Intelligence Agencies and Activities. Hearings.* 6 Parts. 94th Cong., 1st and 2nd Sess. 31 July 1975-10 February 1976. Y4.In8/18: In8/6 pts.

1207. U.S. Congress. House. Select Committee on Missing Persons in Southeast Asia. *Americans Missing in Southeast Asia. Hearings.* 5 Parts. 94th Cong., 1st and 2nd Sess. 23 September 1975-21 September 1976. Y4.M69/3: Am3/5pts.

1208. U.S. Congress. House. Select Committee on Missing Persons in Southeast Asia. *Americans Missing in Southeast Asia. Report.* 94th Cong., 2nd Sess. 13 December 1976. House Report 94-1764.

1209. U.S. Congress. Joint Commission on Security and Cooperation in Europe. *Basket III: Implementation of the Helsinki Accords. Hear-*

ings. 4 vols. 95th Cong., 1st Sess. 23 February-6 June 1977. Y4.Se2: B29/2/4 vols.

1210. U.S. Congress. Joint Commission on Security and Cooperation in Europe. *Implementation of the Final Act of the Conference on Security and Cooperation in Europe: Findings and Recommendations Two Years after Helsinki.* 95th Cong., 1st Sess. 1 August 1977.

1211. U.S. Congress. Joint Committee on Defense Production. *DOD-Industry Relations: Conflict of Interest and Standards of Conduct. Hearings.* 94th Cong., 2nd Sess. 2–3 February 1976. Y4.D36: C76/2.

1212. U.S. Congress. Joint Economic Committee. Subcommittee on Economy in Government. *The Acquisition of Weapons Systems. Hearings.* 6 Parts. 91st Cong., 1st and 2nd Sess.; 92nd Cong., 1st and 2nd Sess; 93rd Cong., 1st Sess. 29 December 1969–10 January 1973. Y4.Ec7: W37/4/6 pts.

1213. U.S. Congress. Joint Economic Committee. Subcommittee on Priorities and Economy in Government. *National Priorities: The Next Five Years. Hearings.* 92nd Cong., 1st Sess. 30 May-27 June 1972. Y4: Ec7: P93/15.

1214. U.S. Congress. Senate. Committee on Appropriations. Subcommittee on Defense Appropriations. *Department of Defense Appropriations. FY 78. Hearings.* 8 Parts. 95th Cong., 1st Sess. 31 January-11 May 1977. Y4.Ap6/2: D36/4/978/8 pts.

1215. U.S. Congress. Senate. Committee on Appropriations. Subcommittee on Foreign Operations Appropriations. *Foreign Assistance and Related Programs Appropriations, FY 78.* 95th Cong., 1st Sess. 10 February-27 April 1977. Y4.Ap6/2: F76/7/978.

1216. U.S. Congress. Senate. Committee on Appropriations. Subcommittee on Military Construction. *Military Construction Appropriations, FY 78.* Hearings. 95th Cong., 1st Sess. 22 February-7 April 1977. Y4.Ap6/1. M59/3/978.

1217. U.S. Congress. Senate. Committee on Armed Services. *All-Volunteer Armed Forces: Progress, Problems and Prospects.* 93rd Cong., 1st Sess. 1 June 1973. Y4.Ar5/3: V88/2.

1218. U.S. Congress. Senate. Committee on Armed Services. *Energy Research and Development Administration, FY 78 Authorization.* 95th Cong., 1st Sess. 25 March 1977. Y4.Ar5/3: En2/978.

1219. U.S. Congress. Senate. Committee on Armed Services. *FY78 Authorization for Military Procurement, Research and Development, and Active Duty, Selected Reserve, and Civilian Personnel Strengths. Hearings.* 11 Parts. 95th Cong., 1st Sess. 25 January-21 April 1977. Y4.Ar5/3. P94/6/978/11 pts.

1220. U.S. Congress. Senate. Committee on Armed Services. *Unionization of the Armed Forces.* Hearings. 95th Cong., 1st Sess. 18 March-26 July 1977. Y4.Ar5/3: Un3/3.

1221. U.S. Congress. Senate. Committee on Armed Services. *U.S./Soviet Military Balance: A Frame of Reference for Congress.* 94th Cong., 1st Sess. 21 January 1976. Y4.Ar5/3: So8/3.

1222. U.S. Congress. Senate. Committee on Armed Services. Subcommittee on Drug Abuse. . . . *Review of Military Drug and Alcohol Programs.*

Hearings. 93rd Cong., 1st Sess. 18–20 September 1973. Y4.Ar5/3: D84/5.

1223. U.S. Congress. Senate. Committee on Armed Services. Subcommittee on Manpower and Personnel. *Achieving America's Goals: National Service or the All-Volunteer Armed Force?* 95th Cong., 1st Sess. February 1977. Y4.Ar5/3: G53.

1224. U.S. Congress. Senate. Committee on Armed Services. Subcommittee on Manpower and Personnel. *All-Volunteer Armed Force. Hearings.* 95th Cong., 1st Sess. 2 March 1977. Y4.Ar5/3: V88/3.

1225. U.S. Congress. Senate. Committee on Armed Services. Subcommittee on Manpower and Personnel. *Honor Codes at the Service Academies. Hearings.* 2 Parts. 94th Cong., 2nd Sess. 21 June-22 October 1977. Y4.Ar5/3: Ac1/3/2 pts.

1226. U.S. Congress. Senate. Committee on Armed Services. Subcommittee on Manpower and Personnel. *Status of the All-Volunteer Armed Forces. Hearings.* 95th Cong., 2nd Sess. 20 June 1978. Includes *An Analysis and Evaluation of the United States Army: The Beard Study,* April 1.

1227. U.S. Congress. Senate. Committee on Foreign Relations. *Background Documents Relating to the Panama Canal.* 95th Cong., 1st Sess. November 1977. Y4. F76/2: P19/3.

1228. U.S. Congress. Senate. Committee on Foreign Relations. *Background Information Relating to Southeast Asia and Vietnam.* 7th Revised Edition. 93rd Cong., 2nd Sess. December 1974.

1229. U.S. Congress. Senate. Committee on Foreign Relations. *CIA Foreign and Domestic Activities. Hearings.* 94th Cong., 1st Sess. 22 January 1975. Y4.F76/2: C33.

1230. U.S. Congress. Senate. Committee on Foreign Relations. *Detente. Hearings.* 93rd Cong., 2nd Sess. 15 August-8 October 1974. Y4.F76/2: D48/2.

1231. U.S. Congress. Senate. Committee on Foreign Relations. *Economic Assistance to China and Korea: 1949-50. Historical Series.* 81st Cong., 1st and 2nd Sess. 11 March 1949-31 January 1950. Y4.F76/2: C44/11/949-50.

1232. U.S. Congress. Senate. Committee on Foreign Relations. *Executive Session of the Senate Foreign Relations Committee (Historical Series).* 4 vols. 80th-82nd Cong. 14 February 1947-27 June 1952. Y4.F76/2: Ex3/2/4 vols.

1233. U.S. Congress. Senate. Committee on Foreign Relations. *Executive Session of the Senate Foreign Relations Committee (Historical Series).* Vol. 5. 83rd Cong., 1st Sess. 19 January-23 July 1953. Y4.F76/2: Ex3/2/v.5.

1234. U.S. Congress. Senate. Committee on Foreign Relations. *Executive Sessions of the Senate Foreign Relations Committee (Historical Series).* Vol. 6. 83rd Cong., 2nd Sess. 7 January-18 November 1954. Y4.F76/2: Ex3/2/v.6.

1235. U.S. Congress. Senate. Committee on Foreign Relations. *Extension of the European Recovery Program: 1949. Hearings. Historical Series.* 81st Cong., 1st Sess. 16 February-7 March 1949. Y4.F76/2: Eu7/22.

1236. U.S. Congress. Senate. Committee on Foreign Relations. *Foreign*

Policy Choices for the Seventies and Eighties. Hearings. 2 vols. 94th Cong., 1st and 2nd Sess. 10 September 1975-20 September 1976. Y4.F76/2: F76/42/2 vols.

1237. U.S. Congress. Senate. Committee on Foreign Relations. *Foreign Relief Aid: 1947. Historical Series. Hearings.* 80th Cong., 1st Sess. 15 April-19 November 1947. Y4.F76/2: F76/34.

1238. U.S. Congress. Senate. Committee on Foreign Relations. *Foreign Relief Assistance Act of 1948: Historical Series. Hearings.* 80th Cong., 2nd Sess. 9 February-7 April 1948. Y4.F76/2: F76/33.

1239. U.S. Congress. Senate. Committee on Foreign Relations. *Legislation on Foreign Relations through 1976.* 2 vols. 95th Cong., 1st Sess. February 1977. Y4.F76/2: L52/976/2 vols.

1240. U.S. Congress. Senate. Committee on Foreign Relations. *Legislative Origins of the Truman Doctrine. Historical Series. Hearings.* 80th Cong., 1st Sess. 13 March-3 April 1947. Y4.F76/2: T77.

1241. U.S. Congress. Senate. Committee on Foreign Relations. *Military Assistance Program: 1949. Hearings.* 81st Cong., 1st Sess. 29 July-12 September 1949. Y4.F76/2: M59/949-2.

1242. U.S. Congress. Senate. Committee on Foreign Relations. *Panama Canal Treaties. Hearings.* Part 1. 95th Cong., 1st Sess. 26 September-19 October 1977. Y4.F76/2: P19/2/pt.1.

1243. U.S. Congress. Senate. Committee on Foreign Relations. *Review of the World Situation: 1949-1950. Historical Series.* 81st Cong., 1st and 2nd Sess. 19 May 1949-22 December 1950.

1244. U.S. Congress. Senate. Committee on Foreign Relations. *The Vandenburg Resolution and the North Atlantic Treaty. Historical Series. Hearings.* 80th Cong., 2nd Sess.; 81st Cong., 1st Sess. 11 May 1948-6 June 1949. Y4.F76/2: V28.

1245. U.S. Congress. Senate. Committee on Foreign Relations. *War Powers Legislation, 1973. Hearings.* 93rd Cong., 1st Sess. 11-12 April 1973. Y4.F76/2: W19/3/973.

1246. U.S. Congress. Senate. Committee on Foreign Relations. *War Powers Resolution. Hearings.* 95th Cong., 1st Sess. 13-15 July 1977. Y4.F76/2: W19/4.

1247. U.S. Congress. Senate. Committee on Foreign Relations. Subcommittee on African Affairs. *Angola. Hearings.* 94th Cong., 2nd Sess. 29 January-6 February 1976. Y4.F76/2: An4.

1248. U.S. Congress. Senate. Committee on Foreign Relations. Subcommittee on African Affairs. *U.S. Policy toward Africa. Hearings.* 94th Cong., 2nd Sess. 5 March-27 May 1976. Y4.F76/2: Af8/8.

1249. U.S. Congress. Senate. Committee on Foreign Relations. Subcommittee on Arms Control.... *U.S. Forces in Europe. Hearings.* 93rd Cong., 1st Sess. 25-27 July 1973. Y4.F76/2: Eu7/20.

1250. U.S. Congress. Senate. Committee on Foreign Relations. Subcommittee on ... International Environment. *Weather Modification . Hearings.* 93rd. Cong., 2nd Sess. 25 January-20 March 1974. Y4.F76/2: W37/4.

1251. U.S. Congress. Senate. Committee on Foreign Relations. Subcommittee on Near Eastern and South Asian Affairs. *Middle East Peace*

Prospects. Hearings. 94th Cong., 2nd Sess. 19 May-26 July 1976. Y4.F76/2: M58/14.

1252. U.S. Congress. Senate. Committee on Foreign Relations. Subcommittee on Near Eastern... Affairs. *Priorities for Peace in the Middle East. Hearings.* 94th Cong., 1st Sess. 23-24 July 1975. Y4.F76/2: M58/12.

1253. U.S. Congress. Senate. Committee on Government Operations. *Oversight of U.S. Government Intelligence Functions. Hearings.* 94th Cong., 2nd Sess. 21 January-6 February 1976. Y4.G74/6: In8/16.

1254. U.S. Congress. Senate. Committee on Veterans' Affairs. *Source Material on the Vietnam Era Veteran.* 93rd Cong., 2nd Sess. 12 February 1974. Committee Print No. 26. Y4.V64/4: V67/6.

1255. U.S. Congress. Senate. Judiciary Committee. Subcommittee on Constitutional Rights. *Military Surveillance. Hearings.* 93rd Cong., 2nd Sess. 9-10 April 1974. Y4.J89/2: M59/8.

1256. U.S. Congress. Senate. Select Committee to Study . . . Intelligence Activities, *Alleged Assassination Plots Involving Foreign Leaders. Report.* 94th Cong., 1st Sess. 20 November 1975. Senate Report 94-465.

1257. U.S. Congress. Senate. Select Committee . . . on U.S. Intelligence Agencies and Operations. *Intelligence Activities. Senate Resolution 21. Hearings.* [Church Committee]. 7 vols. 94th Cong., 1st Sess. 16 September-11 December 1975. Y4.In8/17: In8/7 vols.

1258. U.S. Congress. Senate. Select Committee . . . on U.S. Intelligence Agencies and Operations. *Report* [Church Committee]. 6 Parts [various titles]. 94th Cong., 2nd Sess. April 1976. Senate Report 94-755.

1259. U.S. Congress. Senate. Select Committee on Intelligence. *Whether Disclosure of Funds Authorized for Intelligence Activities Is in the Public Interest. Hearings.* 95th Cong., 1st Sess. 27-28 April 1977. Y4.In8/19: F96.

1260. U.S. Department of the Army. Army Library. *Military Unions: A Selective Bibliography.* Supplement 1. Washington, D.C.: U.S. Department of the Army, March 1978.

1261. U.S. Department of the Army. Army Library. *Modern Volunteer Army: A Selective Bibliography.* Washington, D.C.: U.S. Department of the Army, January 1977.

1262. U.S. Department of the Army. Army Library. *National Security, Military Power, and the Role of Force in International Relations: A Bibliographic Survey of Literature.* Washington, D.C.: G.P.O., 1976.

1263. U.S. Department of the Army. Army Library. *National Service: A Bibliography: A Selective Bibliography.* Washington, D.C.: U.S. Department of the Army, May 1977.

1264. U.S. Joint Chiefs of Staff. *Statement by Chairman... to the Congress on the Defense Posture of the United States for FY 19—.* Washington, D.C.: U.S. Department of the Army, 1971- . Annual.

1265. U.S. President's Commission on CIA Activities within the United States. *Report* [Nelson Rockefeller Report]. Washington, D.C.: G.P.O., 1975.

BIBLIOGRAPHIES AND REFERENCE WORKS

1266. Alcalá, Maj. Raoul H., and Douglas H. Rosenberg. "The New Politics of National Security: A Selected and Annotated Research Bibliography." *In Military Force and American Society,* edited by Bruce M. Russett and Alfred Stepan. New York: Harper & Row, 1973.

1267. Anderson, Martin, ed. *Conscription: A Select and Annotated Bibliography.* Stanford, Calif.: Hoover Institution, 1976.

1268. Blackstock, Paul W., and Frank L. Schaf, Jr. *Intelligence, Espionage, Counterespionage, and Covert Operations: A Guide to Information Sources.* Detroit: Gale, 1978.

1269. Buncher, Judith F., ed. *The CIA and the Security Debate: 1971–1975.* New York: Facts on File, 1976.

1270. Burt, Richard, and Geoffrey Kemp, eds. *Congressional Hearings on American Defense Policy, 1947–1971.* Lawrence: University Press of Kansas, 1974.

1271. *CBS News Television Broadcasts.* Glen Rock, N.J.: Microfilming Corporation of America, 1976– . Microfilm or microfiche.

1272. Christman, Calvin L. "Doctoral Dissertations in United States Foreign Affairs." *Diplomatic History,* spring 1979– . Annual article.

1273. Christman, Calvin L., and Dennis E. Showalter. "Doctoral Dissertations in Military Affairs." *Military Affairs,* February 1978– . Annual article.

1274. Congressional Quarterly Service. *Congress and the Nation.* Vol. 4, *1973–1976: A Review of Government and Politics.* Washington, D.C.: Congressional Quarterly, 1977.

1275. Cronon, E. David, and Theodore Rosenof. *The Second World War and the Atomic Age, 1940–1973.* Northbrook, Ill.: AHM Publishing, 1975.

1276. DeVore, Ronald M. *Spies and All That: Intelligence Agencies and Operations: A Bibliography.* Los Angeles: California State University, 1977.

1277. Doenecke, Justus D. *The Literature of Isolationism: A Guide to Non-Interventionist Scholarship, 1930–1972.* Colorado Springs, Colo.: Ralph Myles, 1972.

1278. Dupuy, Trevor N., John Andrews, and Grace P. Hayes. *The Almanac of World Military Power.* 3rd ed. New York: R. R. Bowker, 1975.

1279. Etzold, Thomas H., and John Lewis Gaddis, eds. *Containment: Documents on American Policy and Strategy, 1945–1950.* New York: Columbia University, 1978.

1280. Fain, Tyrus, G., ed. *The Intelligence Community: History, Organization, and Issues.* New York: R. R. Bowker, 1977.

1281. Gillingham, Arthur, and Barry Roseman. *The Cuban Missle Crisis: A Selected Bibliography.* Los Angeles: California State University, Los Angeles: California State University, 1976.

1282. Grenville, J. A. S. *The Major International Treaties, 1914–1973: A History and Guide with Texts.* New York: Stein and Day, 1974.

1283. Gustafson, Milton O., ed. *The National Archives and Foreign Relations Research.* Athens: Ohio University, 1975.

1284. Harris, William R. *Intelligence and National Security: A Bibliography with Selected Annotations.* 3 vols. Cambridge, Mass.: n.p., 1968.

1285. Heller, Francis H., ed. *The Korean War: A 25-Year Perspective.* Lawrence: The Regents Press of Kansas, 1977.

1286. Hunter, Edna J., Sharon J. Rose, and J. Bradley Hamlin. "Women in the Military: An Annotated Bibliography." *Armed Forces and Society,* summer 1978.

1287. International Institute for Strategic Studies. *The Military Balance, 1978-1979.* Boulder, Colo.: Westview, 1978.

1288. International Institute for Strategic Studies. *Strategic Survey 1977.* Boulder, Colo.: Westview, 1978.

1289. Kreslins, Janis A. *Foreign Affairs Bibliography: A Selected and Annotated List of Books on International Relations, 1962-1972.* New York: R. R. Bowker, 1976.

1290. Larson, Arthur D. *National Security Affairs: A Guide to Information Sources.* Detroit: Gale, 1973.

1291. Leopold, Richard W. "The Korean War: The Historian's Task." *In The Korean War: A 25-Year Perspective,* edited by Francis H. Heller. Lawrence: The Regents Press of Kansas, 1977.

1292. *Meet the Press.* Wooster, Ohio: Bell and Howell, 1976– . Microfiche.

1293. *The Military Situation in the Far East and the Relief of General Douglas MacArthur.* Washington, D.C.: University Publications of America, 1977. Microfilm.

1294. Newcomb, Joan I. *John F. Kennedy: An Annotated Bibliography.* Metuchen, N.J. Scarecrow, 1977.

1295. *The New York Times Oral History Program.* Glen Rock, N.J.: Microfilming Corporation of America, 1972– . Microfilm and microfiche.

1296. Nyberg, Kenneth L., and William P. Snyder. "Program Structure and Career Socialization in the ROTC: A Bibliographic Note." *Military Affairs,* December 1976.

1297. *O.S.S./State Department Intelligence and Research Reports.* 7 parts. Washington, D.C.: University Publications of America, 1977. Microfilm.

1298. O'Sullivan, John, and Alan M. Meckler, eds. *The Draft and Its Enemies: A Documentary History.* Urbana: University of Illinois, 1974.

1299. Powe, Marc B. "The History of American Military Intelligence—A Review of Selected Literature." *Military Affairs,* October 1975.

1300. *Records of the Joint Chiefs of Staff.* Part 2, *1946-53.* Washington, D.C.: University Publications of America, 1978. Microfilm.

1301. Slonaker, John. *The Volunteer Army.* Special Bibliography 5. Carlisle Barracks, Pennsylvania: U.S. Army Military History Research Collection, 1972.

1302. Stapleton, Margaret L. *The Truman and Eisenhower Years, 1945-1960: A Selective Bibliography.* Metuchen, N.J.: Scarecrow, 1973.

1303. Stebbins, Richard P., and Elaine P. Adam, eds. *American Foreign Relations 1971: A Documentary Record.* New York: New York University, 1976.

1304. Stockholm International Peace Research Institute. *Arms Trade Registers.* Cambridge, Mass.: M.I.T., 1975.

1305. Stockholm International Peace Research Institute. *The Arms Trade with the Third World.* Rev. ed. New York: Holmes & Meier, 1975.

1306. Stockholm International Peace Research Institute. *Arms Uncontrolled.* Cambridge: Harvard University, 1975.

1307. Stockholm International Peace Research Institute. *Incendiary Weapons.* Cambridge, Mass.: M.I.T., 1975.

1308. Stockholm International Peace Research Institute. *The Problem of Chemical and Biological Warfare.* 6 vols. to date. New York: Humanities Press, 1971– .

1309. Stockholm International Peace Research Institute. *World Armaments and Disarmament: SIPRI Yearbook 1978.* New York: Crane, Russak, 1978.

1310. *Viewpoint.* Glen Rock, N.J.: Microfilming Corporation of America, 1976– . Magazine/microform.

1311. Ward, Robert E., et al. *The Allied Occupation of Japan, 1945-1952: An Annotated Bibliography of Western-Language Materials.* Chicago: American Library Association, 1974.

1312. Zobrist, Benedict K. "Resources of Presidential Libraries for the History of Post World War II American Military Government in Germany and Japan." *Military Affairs,* February 1978.

PERIODICALS

1313. *AEI Defense Review.* Washington, D.C.: 1977– .

1314. *Armed Forces and Society: An Interdisciplinary Journal.* Chicago, Illinois: 1974– . Indexed: Curr. Cont.; Psych. Abstr.; Sociol. Abstr.

1315. *Atlantic Community Quarterly.* Washington, D.C.: 1963– . Index. Indexed: Hist. Abstr.; Amer. Hist.; Soc. Sci. & Hum. Ind.

1316. *Command.* Washington, D.C.: 1978– .

1317. *Comparative Strategy.* Arlington, Va.: 1977– .

1318. *Counter Pentagon.* Philadelphia: 1974– .

1319. *Declassified Documents Quarterly Catalog.* Arlington, Va.: 1975– .

1320. *Diplomatic History.* Wilmington, Del.: 1977– . Indexed: Hist. Abstr. Amer. Hist.

1321. *Foreign Policy Association Headline Series.* New York: 1935– . Indexed: P.A.I.S.; Soc. Sci. & Hum. Ind.

1322. *History, Numbers and War.* Dunn Loring, Va.: 1977– .

1323. *International Security.* Cambridge, Mass.: 1976– .

1324. *International Studies Quarterly.* Beverly Hills, Calif.: 1957– . Index.

1325. *Journal of International Affairs.* New York, 1947– . Index. Indexed: ABC Pol. Sci.; P.A.I.S.; Soc. Sci. & Hum. Ind.

1326. *Journal of Political and Military Sociology.* DeKalb, Ill.: 1973– . Cum. index. Indexed: P.A.I.S.; Hist. Abstr.; Amer. Hist.; ABC Pol. Sci.; Int. Pol. Sci. Abstr.

1327. *Military Law Review.* Charlottesville, Va.: 1958– . Indexed: P.A.I.S.; Leg. Per.; Ind. U.S. Gov. Per.; SSCI.

1328. *Recon.* Philadelphia: 1973– .

1329. *Strategic Review.* Cambridge, Mass.: 1973– .

1330. *Strategy & Tactics.* New York, 1966– . Indexed: Abstr. Mil. Bibl.

1331. *Technology and Culture.* Chicago: 1959– . Cum. index.

1332. *Washington Monthly.* Washington, D.C.: 1969– . Index. Indexed: Soc. Sci. Ind.

1333. *Washington Review of Strategic and International Studies.* New Brunswick, N.J.: 1977– .

1334. *World Affairs* (formerly under various titles). Washington, D.C.: 1928– . Indexed: ABC Pol. Sci.; P.A.I.S.; Curr. Cont.

INDEXES
1335. *Abstracts of Military Bibliography*. Buenos Aires, Argentina: 1967– .
1336. *Christian Science Monitor Index*. Ann Arbor, Mich.: 1960– .
1337. *Current Bibliographic Survey of National Defense*. Boulder, Colo.: 1975– .
1338. *Scientific American Cumulative Index, 1948–1971*. San Francisco: W. H. Freeman, 1972.
1339. *Social Sciences Citation Index*. Philadelphia: 1973– .
1340. *Social Sciences Index*. Bronx, N.Y.: 1974–.

MANUSCRIPT COLLECTIONS
1341. Gerald R. Ford Library
1000 Beal Avenue
Ann Arbor, Michigan 48109
1342. John F. Kennedy Library
Columbia Point
Boston, Massachusetts 02125
1343. Nixon Presidential Materials Project Staff
National Archives and Records Service
General Services Administration
Washington, D.C. 20408
1344. Bush, Vannevar. Library of Congress, Washington, D.C.
1345. Compton, Arthur H. Washington University Library, St. Louis, Missouri.
1346. Conant, James. Widener Library, Harvard University, Cambridge, Massachusetts.
1347. Fermi, Enrico. Regenstein Library, University of Chicago, Chicago, Illinois.
1348. Johnson, Louis. University of Virginia Library, Charlottesville, Virginia.
1349. Kissinger, Henry A. Library of Congress, Washington, D.C.
1350. Lawrence, Ernest O. Bancroft Library, University of California, Berkeley, California.
1351. Lemnitzer, Gen. L. L. National Defense University, Washington, D.C.
1352. Lilienthal, David. Seeley G. Mudd Library, Princeton University, Princeton, New Jersey.
1353. McCone, John A. Eisenhower Library, Abilene, Kansas.
1354. Oppenheimer, J. Robert. Library of Congress, Washington, D.C.
1355. Raborn, William F., Jr. Syracuse University Library, Syracuse, New York.
1356. Richardson, Elliot L. Library of Congress, Washington, D.C.
1357. Rumsfeld, Donald H. Library of Congress, Washington, D.C.
1358. Szilard, Leo. University of California, San Diego, Library, LaJolla, California.
1359. Wallace, Henry. University of Iowa Library, Iowa City, Iowa.

ADDITIONS TO BIBLIOGRAPHY

1360. Brown, Leslie H. "American Security Policy in Asia." *Adelphi Papers,* no. 132, spring 1977.

1361. Burt, Richard. "New Weapons Technologies: Debate and Directions." *Adelphi Papers,* no. 126, summer 1976.

1362. *CIS/Five-Year Cumulative Index, 1970–1974.* Washington, D.C.: Congressional Information Service, 1975.

1363. Digby, James F. "Precision-Guided Weapons." *Adelphi Papers,* no. 118, summer 1975.

1364. Fischer, Robert L. "Defending the Central Front: The Balance of Forces." *Adelphi Papers,* no. 127, autumn 1976.

1365. Grant, Bruce. "The Security of South-East Asia." *Adelphi Papers,* no. 142, spring 1978.

1366. Krapels, Edward N. "Oil and Security: Problems and Prospects of Importing Countries." *Adelphi Papers,* no. 136, summer 1977.

1367. Maull, Hanns. "Oil and Influence: The Oil Weapon Examined." *Adelphi Papers,* no. 117, summer 1975.

1368. Moskos, Charles C., Jr. "The Military." Annual Review of Sociology. Vol. 2. Edited by Alex Inkeles, et al. Palo Alto, Calif.: Annual Reviews, 1976.

1369. "New Conventional Weapons and East-West Security." *Adelphi Papers,* 2 parts, nos. 144 and 145, spring 1978.

1370. Reichard, Gary W. "Eisenhower as President: The Changing View." *The South Atlantic Quarterly,* summer 1978.

1371. Treverton, Gregory F. "Latin America in World Politics: The Next Decade." *Adelphi Papers,* no. 137, summer 1977.

1372. U.S. Department of Defense. *The FY19—Department of Defense Program for Research, Development and Acquisition.* Washington, D.C.: Department of Defense, 1959– . Annual.

1373. U.S. Department of Defense. *The Guard and Reserve in the Total Force: A Bibliographic Survey.* Washington, D.C.: Department of Defense, 1974.

1374. Weinstein, Franklin B. "The United States, Japan and the Security of Korea." *International Security,* fall 1977.

XVII

THE ARMY, 1945–78

B. Franklin Cooling III

The Institute for Social Research of the University of Michigan surveyed 1,444 Americans in the autumn of 1973, asking "how well they felt each of fifteen U.S. institutions was doing its job." Ironically, the military came out best. Antimilitarism supposedly governed the country as the trauma of Vietnam threatened to tear apart the fabric of American society. The army seemed to be the target for much of the radicalism, yet it was doing its job—fulfilling its mission. Five years later, while the nation seems to have slipped into a quasi neo-isolationism, and has largely put Southeast Asia behind it, the fires of self-doubt, the search for mission, even the agonies of personnel recruitment burn bright in the bowels of the institution we know as the United States Army.

The jury is still out as the decade of the eighties begins. The army wrestles with global mission in principle but bifurcation in fact as the foreign garrisons of Korea and NATO seem strangely detached from the continental home contingents. The officer corps deeply ponders questions of morality and ethics set against memories of Vietnam and their version of the Antichrist, the national press corps. Shrinking budgets, the need for almost complete rearmament of the nation's land forces with new generations of weaponry, and massive recruitment and training problems all plague the army as the nation wavers between détente with Russia and China, and the eternal democratic equation of guns or butter. Of one thing we may be sure, the army, like the other services, has become an interesting subject for study by political scientists, sociologists, historians, and other professionals determined to fathom the centrality of the military in modern American life.

PROBLEMS WITH ARCHIVAL SOURCES. Despite the importance of the army since 1945, very slow progress has been accomplished in opening official records past 1950. The problem is one of pace and focus in National Archives declassification programs. But the dedicated researcher would do well to consult, and periodically to prod, the principal repositories concerning declassification of records for the 1950s and 1960s. Professional staff will prove helpful at the army's Office of the Adjutant General as well as the Military Academy, Command and General Staff College, War College, Center of Military History and its branch, the Military History Institute at Carlisle, Pennsylvania, and the Institute of Heraldry. The CMH annual program summary is indispensable here (511). Then, too, National Archives and its presidential libraries must also be consulted.

POLICY AND STRATEGY. The army's story must be understood against the background of a changing world environment as well as general American security policies. Such broad treatments can be found in Bernstein, "Origins" (402); Endicott and Stafford's fourth edition (424); Gaddis (428); and Whelan (516). Akerman reflects upon the strategy of limited war (391), while the army's continued interface with strategic policymaking can be followed in Beaumont and Edmonds (401), Hamburg (433), and Owen and Schultze (474). Cortwright (415) suggests the usual postwar preoccupation with "lessons learned," and doomsday predictions after defeat. Also useful are Carpenter *et al* (409), Goodpaster (431), Rudoy (484), Taylor's *Precarious Security* (503), and the Army War College faculty anthology (508).

The perspective from the White House may be followed in Betts (403); Kirkendall (450) and Mueller (465) for the Truman period; and Aliano (392), Heath (436), Kinnard (448), for Eisenhower, Kennedy, and Johnson; while Hartley (434), Jones (443), and Morris (464) bring the picture into more recent focus. Clough (411) examines the role of U.S. presence in Korea while Srinivasachary (498) briefly treats military assistance as part of U.S. foreign policy.

MANAGEMENT, ORGANIZATION, AND DOCTRINE. Study of the army as an institution seems to appeal increasingly to scholars, mainly as part of the larger military canvas. Elzy (423), French (426), Sherry (491), and Swomley (501) are vital for understanding the army and the unification issue. Kinnard (449), Stockfish (499), Korb (452), and Poole (479) on the JCS are vital as is Hewes (439) in the army's historical publication series.

OPERATIONS. Despite the growth of a new ecological approach to military history, traditionalist operational history continues to provide most of the new works in print. For postwar occupation activities, consult Schmitt (487), Smith (495), Ziemke (518), and Zobrist (519). New works on Korea include O'Ballance (469), Eighth Army Historical Office (507), Detzer (420), Noble (466), and Simmons (492). But it is America's second land war in Asia which naturally gains the greatest new treatment. New works of great vitality on Vietnam include Galluci (429), Lang (454), Lewy (457), Millett (462), O'Ballance (470), and Palmer (475). Thompson contributes his British observations (504); Dung (422) gives the North Vietnamese perspective; while Brown (407), Corson (414), Dawson (419), Schandler (486), and Shaplan (490) see Vietnam in the guise of military defeat.

The official army Vietnamese history program continues to gain speed with new works by general officers connected with that war including Ewell and Hunt (425) on combat analysis, Larsen and Collins (455) on allied cooperation, McChristian (460) on intelligence, Ott (473) on field artillery, Pearson (476) on campaigns in the northern provinces, Prugh (480) on military jurisprudence, Rodgers (482) on Cedar Falls-Junction City, and Taylor (502) on financial management, with Allen (393) providing the first official medical history volume.

Baestrup dissects the role of the press and the Tet offensive (396). The outpouring of personal accounts include Daly (418), Downs (421), Grant (432), Herr (438), Lovy (459), Noell and Wood (467), and Yezzo (517), while the Calley case receives treatment in Peers (477). The war's dimly perceived long-range impact on the nation receives initial study in Kendrick (447), Lake (453), Riddell (481), and Stockholm International Peace Research Institute (500). See also Heath (435) and Helmer (437) for the war's impact on American fighting men.

CIVIL-MILITARY RELATIONS. The army has received other critical missions since World War II. The unpopularity of overseas expeditions to Korea and Vietnam may have simply overshadowed the more subtle, even insidious role of the military in contemporary American life. This phenomenon continues to gain attention in Clotfelter (410) and Sarkesian (485). But most encouraging of all the works appearing on the army since World War II is the new series about Corps of Engineers activities in national development. See, for example, Cowdrey (416), Dabney (417), Davis (418a), Johnson (441, 442), Kanarek (444), Klawonn (451), Settle (490), Snyder (497), and Turnhollow (505).

MANPOWER AND STAFFING. The critical area of traditional concern to the army as an institution has always been manpower. These policies have been brought into sharp focus since World War II by concern over volunteer versus conscription, antiwar protests and drug abuse, as well as the professional ethics issue surrounding "ticket-punching" by the officer corps and senior noncom corruption. Peterson (478) provides the defense, while more critical are Gabriel and Savage (427)—all essential for balanced understanding of army evolution in this period.

Basic manpower policy questions may be followed in AWC leadership study (509), Anderson (394), Barnes (397), Baskir and Strauss (398, 399), Kasinsky (445), O'Sullivan (472), and Useem (511) for conscription in particular. The All-Volunteer Forces (which necessarily mean mainly the army) receive scrutiny in Bachman (395), Bliven (406), Goffard (430), Keeley (446), Levitan and Alderman (456), Moore and Tuten (463), Singer (493), and Slonaker (494). The reserve components receive coverage in Binkin (404) and Colby (412), while Nyberg and Snyder on ROTC (468) and Bishop (405) on military justice are also important. Olson (471) and Ross (483) examine the veterans benefit issue.

ARMS AND BRANCHES. Organizational history continues to fascinate students of the army. One should continue to consult first with professional staff members of the Lineage Branch, Center of Military History, as well as the Military History Institute (Carlisle). Smith and Pelz (496) are essential for shoulder sleeve insignia and unit tradition since World War II. U'Ren (506) on West Point and Watkins and Reuss (514) on the Army Logistics Center point the way for much needed effort on the army's educational system. See Beaumont (400) on Special Forces.

WEAPONS, TECHNOLOGY, LOGISTICS. Another underworked area concerns scholarly treatment of ordnance and logistics. Too long the province of weapons collectors or antiquarians, the field is wide open for entrepreneurship. The ever-timely question of a military-industrial complex receives fresh attention in Canan (408); and Cooling (413). Jackson and Johnson (440) have given us a stimulating story of local history, technology, and the army.

MEN AND EVENTS. Continuing popularity of biographies and auto-biographies has not produced large numbers of works on contemporary army leaders. One should consult Walters (512) and Westmoreland (515). The oral history program at Carlisle (Military History Institute/Army War College) can be supplemented by similar activities at West Point, the Corps of En-gineers Historical Office, Transportation School at Fort Eustis, and Ser-geants-Major Academy at Fort Bliss.

SUGGESTIONS FOR FURTHER RESEARCH. The areas suggested for further scutiny in the initial edition of this chapter seem relatively untapped during the intervening five years. Perhaps only the Volunteer Army Program has received the attention first suggested for it 1973. The United States Army passed its two hundredth anniversary during the period just past, yet few Americans probably noted or appreciated the event. Like the nation as a whole, the army writhed in agonizing reappraisal of its last quarter-century. Nothing could be more helpful to this institution and the nation it serves than for more independent, scholarly research to be done leading to publications concerning the army from 1945 to 1978.

BIBLIOGRAPHY

391. Akerman, D., et al. *Effectiveness of the Modern Volunteer Army Advertising Program.* Menlo Park: Stanford Research Institute, 1971.

392. Aliano, Richard A. *American Defense Policy from Eisenhower to Kennedy; the Politics of Changing Military Requirements, 1957–1961.* Athens: Ohio University Press, 1975.

393. Allen, Alfred W. *Skin Diseases in Vietnam, 1965–72. Vol. 1, Internal Medicine in Vietnam, Medical Department, United States Army.* Washington, D.C.: Office of Surgeon General and Center of Military History, 1977.

394. Anderson, Martin, ed. *Conscription: A Select and Annotated Bibli-ography.* Stanford: The Hoover Institution Press, 1976.

395. Bachman, Jerald G., et al. *The All-Volunteer Force; A Study of Ideology in the Military.* Ann Arbor: University of Michigan Press, 1977.

396. Baestrup, Peter. *Big Story; How the American Press and Television Reported and Interpreted the Crisis of Tet 1968 in Vietnam and Washington.* Boulder: Westview Press, 1977.

397. Barnes, Peter. *Pawns; The Plight of The Citizen-Soldier.* New York: Knopf, 1972.

398. Baskir, Lawrence M., and William A. Strauss. *Chance and Circums-tance; The Draft, The War, and The Vietnam Generation.* New York: Knopf, 1978.

399. Baskir, Lawrence M., and William A. Strauss. *Reconciliation after*

Vietnam; A Program of Relief for Vietnam Era Draft and Military Offenders. South Bend: Notre Dame University Press, 1977.

400. Beaumont, Roger A. *Military Elites.* Indianapolis: Bobbs-Merrill, 1974.

401. Beaumont, Roger A., and Martin Edmonds, eds. *War in the Next Decade.* Lexington: University Press of Kentucky, 1974.

402. Bernstein, Barton J. "American Foreign Policy and the Origins of the Cold War." In *Politics and Policies of the Truman Administration,* edited by Barton J. Bernstein. Chicago: Quadrangle, 1970.

403. Betts, Richard K. *Soldiers, Statesmen, and Cold War Crises.* Cambridge: Harvard University Press, 1977.

404. Binkin, Martin. *U.S. Reserve Forces; The Problem of the Weekend Warrior.* Washington, D.C.: Brookings, 1974.

405. Bishop, Joseph W., Jr. *Justice Under Fire; A Study of Military Law.* New York: Charterhouse, 1974.

406. Bliven, Bruce. *Volunteers One and All.* New York: Readers Digest, 1976.

407. Brown, Weldon. *The Last Chopper; the Denouement of the American Role in Vietnam, 1963-1975.* Port Washington, N.Y. Kennikat Press, 1975.

408. Canan, James W. *The Superwarriors; The Fantastic World of Pentagon Superweapons.* New York: Weybright and Talley, 1975.

409. Carpenter, William M., et al. *Integrated Global Force Posture Analysis Guidelines for Planning.* Menlo Park: Stanford Research Institute, 1974.

410. Clotfelter, James. *The Military in American Politics.* New York: Harper and Row, 1973.

411. Clough, Ralph N. *Deterrence and Defense in Korea; The Role of U.S. Forces.* Washington, D.C.: Brookings Institution, 1976.

412. Colby, Elbridge. *The National Guard of the United States; A Half Century of Progress.* Manhattan, Kans.: Military Affairs/Aerospace Historian, 1977.

413. Cooling, B. Franklin, III, ed. *War, Business, and American Society; Historical Perspectives on the Military-Industrial Complex.* Port Washington, N.Y.: Kennikat, 1977.

414. Corson, William R. *Consequences of Failure.* New York: W. W. Norton, 1974.

415. Cortright, David. *Soldiers in Revolt; The American Military Today.* Garden City, N.Y.: Anchor/Doubleday, 1975.

416. Cowdrey, Albert E. *Land's End; A History of the New Orleans District, U.S. Army Corps of Engineers, and Its Lifelong Battle with the Lower Mississippi and Other Rivers Wending Their Way to the Sea.* Washington, D.C.: Government Printing Office, 1977.

417. Dabney, Frederick J. *River Engineers on the Middle Mississippi; A History of the St. Louis District U.S. Army Corps of Engineers.* Washington, D.C.: Government Printing Office, 1978.

418. Daly, James A., and Lee Bergman. *A Hero's Welcome; The Conscience of Sergeant James Daly Versus The United States Army.* Indianapolis: Bobbs-Merrill, 1975.

419. Dawson, Alan. *Fifty-Five Days; The Fall of South Vietnam.* Englewood Cliffs, N.J: Prentice-Hall, 1977.
420. Detzer, David. *Thunder of The Captains; The Short Summer in 1950.* New York: Crowell, 1977.
421. Downs, Frederick. *The Killing Zone: My Life in the Vietnam War.* New York: W. W. Norton, 1978.
422. Dung, Van Trien. *Our Great Spring Victory; An Account of the Liberation of South Vietnam.* New York: Monthly Review, 1977.
423. Elzy, Martin I. *The Origins of American Military Policy, 1945-1950.* Ann Arbor: University Microfilms, 1975.
424. Endicott, John E., and Roy W. Stafford, Jr. *American Defense Policy.* 4th ed. Baltimore: Johns Hopkins, 1977.
425. Ewell, Juluan, and Ira A. Hunt, Jr. *Sharpening the Combat Edge: The Use of Analysis to Reinforce Military Judgment.* Vietnam Studies. Washington, D.C.: Department of the Army, 1974.
426. French, Thomas A. *Unification and the American Military Establishment 1945-1950.* Ann Arbor: University Microfilms, 1973.
427. Gabriel, Richard A., and Paul L. Savage. *Crisis in Command.* New York: Hill and Wang, 1978.
428. Gaddis, John, ed. *Containment: Documents on American Policy and Strategy 1945-1951.* New York: Columbia University Press, 1978.
429. Galluci, Robert L. *Neither Peace Nor Honor; The Politics of American Military Policy in Vietnam.* Baltimore: Johns Hopkins, 1975.
430. Goffard, S. James, et al. *Attitudinal Studies of the VOLAR Experiment: Permanent Party Personnel, 1971.* Alexandria: Human Resources Research Organization, 1972.
431. Goodpaster, Andrew J. *For The Common Defense.* Lexington, Mass. D. C. Heath, 1977.
432. Grant, Zalin. *Survivors.* New York: W. W. Norton, 1975.
433. Hamburg, Roger. "Massive Retaliation Revisited." *Military Affairs* 38 (February 1974): 17-23.
434. Hartley, A. *American Foreign Policy in the Nixon Era.* Adelphi Papers, vol. 110. London: The International Institute for Strategic Studies, 1975.
435. Heath, G. Louis, ed. *Mutiny Does Not Happen Lightly; The Literature of the American Resistance to the Vietnam War.* Metuchen, N.J.: Scarecrow Press, 1976.
436. Heath, Jim F. *Decade of Disillusionment; The Kennedy-Johnson Years.* Bloomington: Indiana University Press, 1975.
437. Helmer, John. *Bringing The War Home; The American Soldier In Vietnam and After.* New York: The Free Press, 1974.
438. Herr, Michael. *Dispatches.* New York: Knopf, 1978.
439. Hewes, James E., Jr. *From Root to McNamara: Army Organization and Administration, 1900-1963. Special Studies.* Washington, D.C.: Center of Military Hisory, 1975.
440. Jackson, Charles O., and Charles W. Johnson. "The Urbane Frontier: The Army and the Community of Oak Ridge, Tennessee, 1942-1947." *Military Affairs* 41 (February 1977): 8-14.
441. Johnson, Leland R. *The Falls City Engineers: A History of the*

Louisville District Corps of Engineers, United States Army. Louisville: U.S. Army Corps of Engineers, 1974.

442. Johnson, Leland R. *An Illustrated History of the Huntington District, US Army Corps of Engineers, 1754-1974.* Washington, D.C. Government Printing Office, 1977.

443. Jones, Alan M., Jr, ed. *U.S. Foreign Policy in a Changing World; The Nixon Administration 1969-1973.* New York: David McKay, 1973.

444. Kanarek, Harold. *The Mid-Atlantic Engineers: A History of the Baltimore District U.S. Army Corps of Engineers, 1774-1974.* Washington, D.C.: Government Printing Office, 1977.

445. Kasinsky, Renee. *Refugees from Militarism; Draft-Age Americans in Canada.* New Brunswick: Transaction Books, 1976.

446. Keeley, John B., ed. *The All-Volunteer Force and American Security.* Charlottesville: University Press of Virginia, 1978.

447. Kendrick, Alexander. *The Wound Within; America in the Vietnam Years, 1945-1974.* Boston: Little, Brown, 1974.

448. Kinnard, Douglas. *President Eisenhower and Strategy Management: A Study in Defense Politics.* Lexington: University Press of Kentucky, 1977.

449. Kinnard, Douglas. *The War Managers.* Hanover, N.H.: University Press of New England, 1977.

450. Kirkendall, Richard S. *The Truman Period As A Research Field, A Reappraisal, 1972.* Columbia: University of Missouri Press, 1974.

451. Klawonn, Marion J. *Cradle of the Corps; A History of the New York District U.S. Army Corps of Engineers, 1775-1975.* Washington, D.C.: Government Printing Office, 1978.

452. Korb, Lawrence J. *The Joint Chiefs of Staff: The First Twenty-Five Years.* Bloomington: Indiana University Press, 1976.

453. Lake, Anthony, ed. *The Vietnam Legacy; The War, American Society and The Future of American Foreign Policy.* New York: New York University Press, 1976.

454. Lang, Daniel. *Patriotism Without Flags.* New York: W. W. Norton, 1974.

455. Larsen, Stanley R., and James Lawton Collins, Jr. *Allied Participation in Vietnam.* Vietnam Studies. Washington, D.C.: Department of the Army, 1975.

456. Levitan, Sar A., and Karen Cleary Alderman. *Warriors At Work: The Volunteer Armed Force.* Beverly Hills: Sage Publications, 1977.

457. Lewy, Guenther. *America in Vietnam.* New York: Oxford University Press, 1978.

458. Lifton, Robert J. *Home From the War; Vietnam Veterans; Neither Victims Nor Executioners.* New York: Simon and Schuster, 1973.

459. Lovy, Andrew. *Vietnam Diary October 1967-July 1968.* New York: Exposition, 1970.

460. McChristian, Joseph A. *The Role of Military Intelligence.* Vietnam Studies. Washington, D.C.: Department of the Army, 1974.

461. Manchester, William. *American Caesar.* Boston: Little, Brown, 1978.

462. Millett, Alan R., ed. *A Short History of the Vietnam War.* Bloomington: Indiana University Press, 1978.

463. Moore, Harold G., and Jeff M. Tuten. *Building A Volunteer Army;*

The Fort Ord Contribution. Modern Volunteer Army Series. Washington, D.C.: Department of the Army, 1975.

464. Morris, Roger. *Uncertain Greatness: Henry Kissinger and American Foreign Policy.* New York: Harper and Row, 1977.

465. Mueller, John E. *War, President, and Public Opinion.* New York: John Wiley, 1973.

466. Noble, Harold J. *Embassy at War.* Edited by Frank Baldwin. Seattle: University of Washington Press, 1975.

467. Noell, Chuck, and Gary Wood. *We Are All POWs.* Philadelphia: Fortress, 1975.

468. Nyberg, Kenneth L., and William P. Snyder. "Program Structure and Career Socialization in the ROTC; A Bibliographic Note." *Military Affairs* 30 (December 1976): 179–82.

469. O'Ballance, Edgar. *Korea: 1950–1953.* Hamden, Conn.: Archon, 1969.

470. O'Ballance, Edgar. *The Wars in Vietnam 1954–1973.* New York: Hippocrene, 1974.

471. Olson, Keith W. *The G.I. Bill, The Veterans, and the Colleges.* Lexington: University Press of Kentucky, 1974.

472. O'Sullivan, John O. *The Draft and Its Enemies; A Documentary History.* Urbana: University of Illinois Press, 1974.

473. Ott, D.E. *Field Artillery 1954–1973.* Vietnam Studies. Washington, D.C.: Department of the Army, 1974.

474. Owen, Henry, and Charles L. Schultze, eds. *Setting National Priorities; The Next Ten Years.* Washington, D.C.: Brookings, 1976.

475. Palmer, Dave Richard. *Summons of the Trumpet; U.S.-Vietnam in Perspective.* San Rafael: Presidio, 1978.

476. Pearson, William. *The War in the Northern Provinces 1966–1968.* Vietnam Studies. Washington, D.C.: Department of the Army, 1975.

477. Peers, William, et al. *The My Lai Massacre and Its Cover-up; Beyond the Reach of Law?* New York: Free Press, 1976.

478. Peterson, Peter B. *Against The Tide; An Argument in Favor of the American Soldier.* New Rochelle: Arlington House, 1974.

479. Poole, Walter S. "From Conciliation To Containment: The Joint Chiefs of Staff and the Coming of the Cold War, 1945–1946." *Military Affairs* 42 (February 1978): 12–17.

480. Prugh, George S. *Law at War; Vietnam 1964–1973.* Vietnam Studies. Washington, D.C.: Department of the Army, 1975.

481. Riddell, Thomas A. *A Political Economy of the American War in Indo-China: Its Cost and Consequences.* Ann Arbor: University Microfilms, 1975.

482. Rodgers, Bernard William. *Cedar Falls-Junction City; A Turning Point.* Vietnam Studies. Washington, D.C.: Department of the Army, 1974.

483. Ross, Davis R. B. *Preparing For Ulysses; Politics and Veterans During World War II.* New York: Columbia University Press, 1969.

484. Rudoy, Dean Wm. *Armed and Alone; The American Security Dilemma.* New York: George Braziller, 1972.

485. Sarkesian, Sam C. *The Professional Army Officer in a Changing Society.* Chicago: Nelson-Hall, 1975.

486. Schandler, Herbert Y. *The Unmasking of a President; Lyndon Johnson and Vietnam.* Princeton: Princeton University Press, 1977.

487. Schmitt, Hans A., ed. *U.S. Occupation in Europe After World War II.* Lawrence: Regents Press, 1978.

488. Schratz, Paul, ed. *Evolution of the American Military Establishment Since World War II.* Contoococh, N.H.: Select Press Book Service, 1978.

489. Settle, William A. *The Dawning; A New Day For The Southwest; A History of Tulsa District Corps of Engineers.* Tulsa: U.S. Army Corps of Engineers, 1975.

490. Shaplen, Robert. *Road From War; Vietnam 1965-1970.* New York: Harper and Row, 1970.

491. Sherry, Michael S. *Preparing for the Next War; American Plans for Postwar Defense, 1941-45.* New Haven: Yale University Press, 1977.

492. Simmons, Robert R. *The Strained Alliance; Peking, P'yongyang, Moscow and the Politics of the Korean Civil War.* New York: Free Press, 1975.

493. Singer, Max, et al. *Ideas and Trends For the Modern Volunteer Army.* Croton-on-Hudson, N.Y.: Hudson Institute, 1972.

494. Slonaker, John, comp. *The Volunteer Army.* Special Bibliography no. 5. Carlisle Barracks, Pa.: U.S. Army Military History Research Collection, 1972.

495. Smith, Jean Edward. "Selection of a Proconsul for Germany: The Appointment of General Lucius D. Clay, 1945." *Military Affairs* 30 (October 1976): 123-29.

496. Smith, Richard W., and Roy A. Pelz. *Shoulder Sleeve Insignia of the U.S. Army 1946-1976.* Evansville, Ind.: Evansville University Press, 1978.

497. Snyder, Frank E., and Brian H. Guss. *The District, A History of the Philadelphia District, U.S. Army Corps of Engineers, 1866-1971.* Philadelphia: U.S. Army Engineer District Office, 1974.

498. Srinivasachary, Mudumbhe. "Sources for the Study of United States Mutual Security Policy Towards South Asia, 1951-1960." *Military Affairs* 39 (December 1975): 208-9.

499. Stockfish, Jacob A. *Plowshares into Swords; Managing the American Defense Establishment.* New York: Mason and Lipscomb, 1973.

500. Stockholm International Peace Research Institute. *Ecological Consequences of the Second Indochina War.* Stockholm: Almquist and Wiksell International, 1976.

501. Swomley, John H., Jr. *A Study of the Universal Military Training Campaign 1944-1952.* Ann Arbor: University Microfilms, 1977.

502. Taylor, Leonard B. *Financial Management of the Vietnam Conflict 1962-1972.* Vietnam Studies. Washington, D.C.: Department of the Army, 1974.

503. Taylor, Maxwell D. *Precarious Security.* New York: W. W. Norton, 1976.

504. Thompson, Robert. *Peace Is Not At Hand.* New York: David McKay, 1974.

505. Turnhollow, Anthony F. *A History of the Los Angeles District, U.S.*

Army Corps of Engineers, 1898–1965. Los Angeles: U.S. Army Corps of Engineers, 1975.

506. U'Ren, Richard C. *Ivory Fortress; A Psychiatrist Looks at West Point.* Indianapolis: Bobbs-Merrill, 1974.

507. U.S. Army, Eighth, Historical Office. *Key Korean War Battles Fought in the Republic of Korea.* Seoul: Headquarters, U.S. Eighth Army, 1972.

508. U.S. Army War College. *New Dynamics in National Strategy, The Paradox of Power.* New York: Crowell, 1975.

509. U.S. Army War College. *Study on Leadership For The 1970s.* Carlisle Barracks, Pa.: Army War College, 1971.

510. U.S. Department of the Army. *Army Historical Program, FY 1978.* Washington, D.C.: Department of the Army, 1978.

511. Useem, Michael. *Conscription, Protest, and Social Conflict; The Life and Death of a Draft Resistance Movement.* New York: John Wiley and Sons, 1973.

512. Walters, Vernon A. *Silent Missions.* Garden City: Doubleday, 1978.

513. Warner, Denis. *Certain Victory; How Hanoi Won the War.* Kansas City: Sheed, Andrews and McMell, 1978.

514. Watkins, Jerry L., and Martin Reuss. *The Evolution of the U.S. Army Logistics Center.* Fort Lee: U.S. Army Logistics Center, 1977.

515. Westmoreland, William C. *A Soldier Reports.* Garden City: Doubleday, 1976.

516. Whelan, John T. *Some Conditions Affecting Continuity and Change in Congressional Committee Involvement in Defense Policy: The Case of the House Committee on Armed Services.* Ann Arbor: University Microfilms, 1973.

517. Yezzo, Dominick. *A GI's Vietnam Diary 1968–1969.* New York: Franklin Watts, 1974.

518. Ziemke, Earl F. *The U.S. Army in the Occupation of Germany, 1944–1946.* Army Historical Series. Washington, D.C.: Center of Military History, 1975.

519. Zobrist, Benedict K. "Resources of Presidential Libraries For the History of Post-World War II American Military Government in Germany and Japan." *Military Affairs* 42 (February 1978): 17–20.

XVIII

THE NAVY, 1941–78

Dean C. Allard

Since 1973, a number of volumes dealing with the operational and biographical aspects of World War II and, to a lesser extent, the postwar years, have appeared. Several notable studies dealing with naval strategy and policy, often within the context of more general assessments of national strategy, also are available. As usual institutional, scientific, technical, economic, and social aspects of the navy receive less attention. Nevertheless, some solid contributions in these areas can be noted.

REFERENCE WORKS. Among the bibliographies supplementing Myron Smith's comprehensive *World War II at Sea* (307) is an excellent selective volume covering both world wars by Bayliss (409), and catalogs by Burt and Kemp (419) and Greenwood (442) indexing congressional hearings and other materials on postwar defense policy. Specialized naval literature is described in works by Anderson dealing with submarines (407), Patterson and Winters on mine warfare (497), and a Naval History Division guide to a group of unpublished World War II administrative histories (446).

A useful biographical reference is Clark G. Reynolds's dictionary of prominent naval officers (501). Other collective biographies of interest to naval historians include the military volume in the *Who Was Who* series (537) and *Webster's American Military Biographies* (536). A new volume in the Chaplain Corps history (82) contains capsule accounts of postwar naval chaplains, while the annual *Register* of the Naval Academy Alumni Association (527) is valuable for locating many living officers.

New editions of the glossaries of ever-changing naval abbreviations and terms compiled by Wedertz (380) and Noel and Beach (243) are available, but Heinl's older dictionary of naval and military quotations (447) continues to be basic in its field.

Many reference works detailing the characteristics and use of naval weapons systems are being prepared. In addition to the ongoing series cited in this author's previous chapter recent contributions include informative volumes on World War II Anglo-American antisubmarine equipment and tactics by Anthony Watts (553) and a similar work on amphibious operations by Ladd (468). Norman Polmar has contributed an excellent handbook of strategic weapons since the end of the war (498). Among the best of many books dealing with specific classes of ships and aircraft are a thorough technical study of

American World War II battleships by Dulin and Garzke (431), and Tillman's fine operational account of the Dauntless dive bomber (524).

PERIODICALS. A new journal, *Diplomatic History* (429), often includes articles touching on the navy's role in foreign affairs. *Armed Forces and Society* (408), an interdisciplinary journal concentrating on recent military affairs, also is of interest. *Warship International* (532), which is oriented toward the ship buff community, includes some useful accounts of the material aspects of the American navy.

OPERATIONS, STRATEGY, AND POLICY OF THE WORLD WAR II ERA. Two general naval histories contributed by Hagan (444) and Reynolds (500) include informative interpretations of this period, while Riesenberg's overall history of the American merchant marine in World War II (502) now is available as a reprint. Several significant volumes offer insight into naval aspects of the war's strategy, including works by diplomatic historians Leutze (469), Thorne (523), and Louis (474), all of which stress tensions in Anglo-American wartime relations. The formulation of strategy within the U.S. Navy is discussed by Doyle's dissertation for the 1932–41 period (430). A number of the basic documents on policy and strategy in those years and during the war are available through a Scholarly Resources microfilm publication (519). Love's study of Admirals King and Cooke (475) and an older volume by Lobdell on Secretary of the Navy Frank Knox (472) also provide insight into naval policy. Limited but useful attention is given to the navy in Sherry's study of the posthostilities planning process under way during the war years (512). The diplomatic activities in France and the Soviet Union of two former chiefs of naval operations, Admirals Leahy and Standley, are covered in two additional titles (450, 515).

ATLANTIC THEATRE. Perhaps the most notable works on the Atlantic war are based on the recently released British, American, and German records describing the success of Allied and Axis authorities in decrypting or otherwise exploiting enemy communications. The most basic naval title appearing to date is by Patrick Beesly (410), an officer in the Admiralty's Operational Intelligence Centre, who was in close contact with his counterparts in the U.S. Navy. Ronald Lewin (470) provides an overall account of the British efforts against German communications. A superb analysis of the critical convoy battles of March 1943, which includes consideration of German and Allied radio intelligence, is by Jurgen Rohwer (504). Hughes and Costello (458) provide a more popular account of the Battle of the Atlantic, including its intelligence aspects.

Several other studies of the North Atlantic campaign contain useful tactical and human detail. A work by Martin Middlebrook (486) is based on extensive interviews with survivors of the same convoys analyzed by Rohwer, while a prominent British naval officer, Peter Gretton, assesses a subsequent convoy action in which he participated during the spring of 1943 (443). Abbazia's dissertation dealing with U.S. naval operations in 1939–42 (1) now is available as a Naval Institute publication. Two useful memoirs by a naval and a Coast Guard officer involved in the crucial antisubmarine campaign are by Alexander Moffat (489) and Roland T. Carr (423). George Washington Allen, a minesweeper commander in the Atlantic, also has contributed his reminiscences (405). Some of the basic documents on the sinking of the army transport *Dorchester,* in which four heroic chaplains perished, appear in a volume by Szymczak (522).

Several contributions assess the strategic and political background to the North African landings of November 1942, including studies by Sainsbury (508), Stoler (518), Funk (438), and Steele (517). The subsequent naval campaign by American and Allied forces in the Mediterranean came under the overall command of British Adm. Sir Andrew Brown Cunningham, who is the subject of a new biography by Pack (495). However, Cunningham's older memoir (426) is still essential. Pack also has published a special study on the Sicily invasion (496), while British Adm. B. B. Schofield discusses the Normandy operation (509), particularly from the point of view of his country's forces. The development and use of artificial harbors in the French landings are covered in a study by Hartcup (445), another British author. Considering the major role of U.S. naval forces in European campaigns and in the war against the U-boat, it is surprising that few Americans have turned to these subjects in recent years.

PACIFIC THEATER. Notable biographies of Fleet Admiral Nimitz by Potter (499) and of General MacArthur by James (460) give an excellent overview of the war from the perspective of the unified commanders of the two Pacific theaters. The colorful William F. Halsey is assessed in semipopular works by Merrill (485) and Frank (436). An older popular account of another famed combat commander, Arleigh A. Burke, is by Jones and Kelley (461).

As is true for the German side of World War II, titles are beginning to appear on intelligence programs aimed at Japanese communications. Capt. W.J. Holmes, who was a key participant at the navy's headquarters in Pearl Harbor in the exploitation of Japanese radio transmissions, has written an especially enlightening account (451). Edward Van Der Rhoer, an analyst of Japanese codes and ciphers at the naval communications intelligence office in Washington, has contributed his memoirs (530).

Other general titles include a fine analysis of American naval strategy in the Pacific during the first six months of the war, based on new Japanese and American materials, written by Paul Lundstrom (476). Paul Dull's study of the major fleet actions of the Pacific war (432), based on a detailed study of Japanese records and histories, provides corrections to previous accounts. Bert Webber uses local history and military sources in an unusual volume on Japanese naval actions and American defense efforts along the Pacific coast (535).

The central role of aircraft carriers in the early years of the Pacific war is developed by the Belote brothers (411) and in the second volume of a history by Brown (417), while Blair uses the official patrol reports and extensive interviews to describe American submarine operations (414). Blair's sources also provide considerable insight into the role of radio intelligence in that campaign. Richard O'Kane, the distinguished commander of the submarine *Tang,* has contributed his memoirs (493) and an unusual personal account by a Japanese submariner, Zenji Orita, also is available (494). A detailed study of the development of the fast battleship, including its operational use in the Pacific, has been written by Muir (490).

Numerous accounts of specific campaigns and a few personal memoirs also continue to appear. Many of these are popular efforts which add little new information. Among those contributions that do deserve notice are Schultz's volume on the loss of Wake Island (510), a description by the Dutch historian Van Oosten of the Battle of the Java Sea (531), assessments by the French writer Millot of the Coral Sea and Kamikaze campaigns (487, 488), an effective tactical account of the Battle of the Philippine Sea by Dickson (428), and Stratton's discussion of navy-army-OSS rivalries in the China Theater (520). Memoirs by Allen (405), who commanded minesweepers during the Okinawa operation, and by Nagatsuka (492), a fortunate survivor of the Japanese Kamikaze Corps, provide personal detail on specific actions.

OPERATIONS, STRATEGY, AND POLICY, 1945–78. Scholarly activity in the postwar years has increased with the opening of many basic records into the early 1950s. Overall accounts of the navy in this period appear in Hagan (444) and Reynolds (500). The first volume of the navy's official history of the Vietnam War (454) traces the navy in general during the 1945–59 era. The senior author of that volume, Vice Adm. Edwin B. Hooper, also has contributed two critical studies (452, 453) on the complexity of naval organization resulting from the postwar growth of the Department of Defense. A useful article on the navy and unification during the 1947–50 period is by Coletta (424). Adm. Elmo G. Zumwalt, the chief of naval operations during 1970–74, is the author of a frank, informative, and sometimes contentious memoir (540) concentrating on that period. An overall assessment of defense policy during the Eisenhower administration, including some of its naval aspects, is by Kinnard (463).

Much attention has been paid by historians and political scientists to the navy's role in international crises. General studies that are of interest both for their historical coverage and theoretical conclusions are by Betts (413), Blechman and Kaplan (416), Cable (420), and George and Smoke (440). Among the more specialized studies of naval operations is a dissertation by Houchins (456) recounting the role of the navy in the Chinese Civil War and a multivolume series on the Korean Conflict issued by the Republic of Korea (466) that includes the maritime aspects. Jackson's study of the Korean air war (459) gives limited attention to the U.S. Navy. A number of solid studies on the postwar development of the Sixth Fleet in the Mediterranean have appeared. These include an overall account through 1968 by Dur (433), and three special studies dealing with the formative 1945–47 era by Cane (422), Knight (464), and Alvarez (406). Starting in the mid-1960s, the Sixth Fleet and naval forces in other parts of the world faced a growing challenge from the Soviet navy. This theme receives attention in volumes edited by Michael McGwire and his associates (482, 483), Lewis (471), and the Zumwalt memoirs (540).

The origins of American participation in the Vietnam Conflict through 1959 are discussed in the navy's official history (454). Admiral Sharp, the Pacific unified commander during 1964–68, has contributed a sharp critique of national strategy in Vietnam (511). The Zumwalt memoirs (540) provide excellent material on events after 1968, including the Vietnamization process, the air offensive of 1972, and the eventual American withdrawal from Southeast Asia. Tregaskis is the author of a book (525) on the Navy's role as the manager of construction in Southeast Asia, while Tulich (526) provides a useful overview of Coast Guard operations. A moving, personal diary by Frank Elkins, a carrier aviator lost over North Vietnam, has been published (434), but the most numerous accounts describe the experiences of former prisoners of war. These include titles by Blakey (415), Denton (427), McDaniel (478), McGrath (480), and Rutledge (507). Collective accounts of the POWs of all services appear in *We Came Home* (534) and in a general work by Hubbell (457).

Throughout the postwar years, the aircraft carrier has been of central importance for the navy. The evolution of this weapon system in relation to national strategy, during the years before full American involvement in the Vietnam War, is the subject of informative studies by Rosenberg and Kennedy (505) and Wilson (538).

Additional facets of postwar operations are covered in a fine memoir by George Steele (516), *Seadragon's* commanding officer during that submarine's historic polar transit in 1962. A more controversial account of the capture of *Pueblo* in 1968 is by Murphy (491), who was one of the officers of that ill-fated ship. The navy's supervisor of salvage prepared a detailed account (528) of the U.S. minesweeping operations that allowed the reopening of the Suez Canal in 1974. Finally, a journalistic description of the recapture of *Mayaguez* from Cambodian forces in 1975 is contributed by Rowan (506).

OTHER ASPECTS OF NAVAL HISTORY. Fortunately, a number of recent publications add to an understanding of the social, economic, scientific, technical, and institutional aspects of the navy, although many research opportunities remain in these areas. For example, a good assessment of the investigations of the Pearl Harbor attack, in the context of American wartime politics, is provided by Melosi (484). His work can be supplemented by Brownlow's study of Husband E. Kimmel, the navy's Pacific commander in December 1941 (418). A detailed account of the postwar evolution of the military and naval justice system is by Generous (439). Two dissertations by Rilling (503) and Heitzmann (448), respectively, assess graduate education in the navy and the educational activities of the U.S. Naval Institute. Kolodziej discusses the postwar interaction of Congress with all of the military services (465), while McGovern's investigation of urbanization in the Pensacola area (479) indicates the navy's important role in that process.

As noted, Beesly (410), Holmes (451), Lewin (470), Rohwer (504), and Van der Rhoer (528), cover radio intelligence in World War II. Other intelligence operations are described in Walter Lord's outstanding study of the Solomons coastwatchers (473) and a volume on the same subject by Horton (455). Contacts between the navy's District Intelligence Office in New York City and underworld figures, especially in connection with the security of the New York port, are the subject of a book by Campbell (421).

Many titles touch on scientific and technical activities of the navy. A Booz-Allen study (529) offers a challenging critique of the complexities of the research and development process resulting from an overly elaborate defense organization. Considerable insight into the interaction of the navy and physical scientists, especially in World War II and the immediate postwar years, is contained in a study by Kevles (462). A second volume in the history of the Naval Weapons Center at China Lake, California (441) covers the remarkable development of that activity through 1948 despite the stringent budgetary limitations of the immediate postwar years. More specialized volumes describe research and development activities at the Dahlgren, Virginia ordnance laboratory (477), the underseas weapons center at White Oak, Maryland (514), and the Naval Research Laboratory (437). At least two works discuss the navy and the biological sciences: Shilling's account of the Medical Research Division (513), and Wood's journalistic treatment of the navy's use of porpoises and sea lions (539). Other technical programs are assessed in Hezlet's account of Anglo-American seagoing electronics which includes material on World War II and the postwar years (449), Coulham's study of the unsuccessful TFX project (425), and Bentley's controversial book (412) on the loss of the nuclear submarine *Thresher*. Since many pseudoscientific claims have been advanced regarding the forces at work in the Bermuda Triangle maritime region, Kusche's levelheaded volume on this subject (467) is worthy of note.

A large collection of documents on black naval and military history has been brought together by MacGregor and Nalty (481), and a general account of this subject is by Foner (435). For racial developments in the navy in the early 1970s, Zumwalt's memoirs (540) are important. Also in the area of social history is Suid's study (521) of the content of military and naval movies and discussion of the interaction of Hollywood and the military.

SUGGESTIONS FOR FURTHER RESEARCH. Most of the areas identified in this author's previous chapter continue to offer opportunities for fruitful research. For example, despite the work undertaken on strategy and policy, there are still a number of unstudied themes, including such subjects as naval policy in the Far East prior to the Korean War or naval shipbuilding programs during the first postwar decade. In the area of operations, few American scholars have taken advantage of the recently released radio intelligence documents, or the operational records that have long been available, to undertake original work on Atlantic naval warfare. Other examples of operational topics include the navy's numerous expeditions to polar regions after 1945, or various aspects of the service's participation in the Vietnam War.

Among the prominent figures that merit modern biographies are the two wartime secretaries of the navy, Frank Knox and James Forrestal; William D. Leahy, the chief of staff to the president from 1942 to 1949; and Adm. Forrest P. Sherman, who was an important postwar leader.

The logistics of World War II, ranging from the navy's efforts to promote an effective shipbuilding industry to its interaction with numerous other suppliers, offer useful topics for economic historians. In the area of social and cultural history, such subjects come to mind as the role of naval women or the service's extensive combat art program during World War II. Two of the many examples that could be offered of scientific or technical programs in need of study are the highly successful proximity (VT) fuse development effort, and the navy's pioneering work during World War II in developing the operational-research discipline.

The author wishes to thank the staff of the Navy Department Library for their generous assistance in the preparation of this chapter.

BIBLIOGRAPHY

405. Allen, George Washington. *Sails to Atoms: From Seaman to Admiral.* Philadelphia: Dorrance, 1975.
406. Alvarez, David J. "The *Missouri* Visit to Turkey: An Alternative Perspective on Cold War Diplomacy." *Balkan Studies,* 1974, pp. 225–36.
407. Anderson, Frank J., ed. *Submarines, Diving, and the Underwater World: A Bibliography.* Hamden, Conn.: Archon, 1975.
408. *Armed Forces and Society.* Chicago: Inter-University Seminar on Armed Forces and Society, 1974– .
409. Bayliss, Gwyn M. *Bibliographic Guide to the Two World Wars.* New York: Bowker, 1977.
410. Beesly, Patrick. *Very Special Intelligence: The Story of the Admiralty's Operational Intelligence Centre, 1939–1945.* Garden City, N.Y.: Doubleday and Co., 1978.
411. Belote, James H., and William M. Belote. *Titans of the Seas: The Development and Operations of Japanese and American Carrier Task Forces During World War II.* New York: Harper and Row, 1975.
412. Bentley, John. *The Thresher Disaster: The Most Tragic Dive in Submarine History.* Garden City, N.Y.: Doubleday and Co., 1974.
413. Betts, Richard K. *Soldiers, Statesmen, and Cold War Crises.* Cambridge: Harvard University Press, 1977.
414. Blair, Clay, Jr. *Silent Victory: The U.S. Submarine War Against Japan.* Philadelphia: J. B. Lippincott, 1975.
415. Blakey, Scott. *Prisoner at War: The Survival of Commander Richard Stratton.* Garden City, N.Y.: Doubleday and Co., 1978.
416. Blechman, Barry M., and Stephen S. Kaplan. *The Use of the Armed Forces as a Political Instrument.* Washington, D.C.: The Brookings Institution, 1976.
417. Brown, David. *Carrier Operations in World War II.* 2 vols. Annapolis: Naval Institute Press, 1974.
418. Brownlow, Donald G. *The Accused: The Ordeal of Rear Admiral Husband Edward Kimmel.* New York: Vantage Press, 1968.
419. Burt, Richard, and Geoffrey Kemp, comps. *Congressional Hearings on American Defense Policy, 1947–1971: An Annotated Bibliography.* Lawrence: University Press of Kansas, 1974.
420. Cable, James. *Gunboat Diplomacy: Political Applications of Limited Naval Force.* New York: Praeger Publishers, 1971.
421. Campbell, Rodney. *The Luciano Project: The Secret Wartime Collaboration of the Mafia and the U.S. Navy.* New York: McGraw Hill, 1977.
422. Cane, Guy. "The Build-Up of U.S. Naval Force in the Mediterranean as an Instrument of Cold War Policy." Mimeographed. Washington, D.C.: National War College, 1975.
423. Carr, Roland T. *To Sea in Haste.* Washington, D.C.: Acropolis Books, 1975.
424. Coletta, Paolo E. "The Defense Unification Battle, 1947-50: The Navy." *Prologue,* spring 1975, pp. 6–17.

425. Coulham, Robert F. *Illusions of Choice*. Princeton: Princeton University Press, 1977.
426. Cunningham, Andrew Browne. *A Sailor's Odyssey: The Autobiography of Admiral of the Fleet, Viscount Cunningham of Hyndhope*. New York: Dutton, 1951.
427. Denton, Jeremiah A., Jr. *When Hell Was in Season*. New York: Reader's Digest Press, 1976.
428. Dickson, W. D. *The Battle of the Philippine Sea*. London: Ian Allen, 1975.
429. *Diplomatic History*. Wilmington, Del.: Society for Historians of American Foreign Relations, 1977– .
430. Doyle, Michael Kedian. "The U.S. Navy: Strategy, Defense, and Foreign Policy, 1932–1941." Ph.D. dissertation, University of Washington, 1977.
431. Dulin, Robert O., Jr., and William H. Garzke, Jr. *Battleships: United States Battleships in World War II*. Annapolis: Naval Institute Press, 1976.
432. Dull, Paul S. *A Battle History of the Imperial Japanese Navy, 1941–1945*. Annapolis: Naval Institute Press, 1978.
433. Dur, Philip A. "The Sixth Fleet: A Case Study of Institutionalized Naval Presence, 1946–1968." Ph.D. dissertation, Harvard University, 1975.
434. Elkins, Frank C. *The Heart of a Man*. New York: Norton, 1973.
435. Foner, Jack D. *Blacks and the Military in American History*. New York: Praeger Publishers, 1974.
436. Frank, Benis M. *Halsey*. New York: Ballantine, 1974.
437. Friedman, Herbert. *Reminiscences of 30 Years of Space Research*. Washington, D.C.: Naval Research Laboratory, 1975.
438. Funk, Arthur L. *The Politics of Torch: The Allied Landings and the Algiers Putsch, 1942*. Lawrence: University Press of Kansas, 1974.
439. Generous, William T., Jr. *Swords and Scales: The Development of the Uniform Code of Military Justice*. Port Washington, N.Y.: Kennikat Press, 1973.
440. George, Alexander L., and Richard Smoke. *Deterrence in Foreign Policy: Theory and Practice*. New York: Columbia University Press, 1974.
441. Gerrard-Gough, J. D., and Albert B. Christman. *The Grand Experiment at Inyokern*. Vol. 2 of *History of Naval Weapons Center, China Lake, California*. Washington, D.C.: Naval History Division, 1978.
442. Greenwood, John, et al., comps. *American Defense Policy Since 1945: A Preliminary Bibliography*. Lawrence: University Press of Kansas, 1973.
443. Gretton, Peter. *Crisis Convoy: The Story of HX 231*. London: Peter Davis, 1975.
444. Hagan, Kenneth J., ed. *In Peace and War: Interpretations of American Naval History, 1775–1978*. Westport, Conn.: Greenwood Press, 1978.
445. Hartcup, Guy. *Code Name Mulberry: The Planning, Building and Operation of the Normandy Harbours*. New York: Hippocrene Books, 1977.

446. Heimdahl, William C., and Edward J. Marolda, comps. *Guide to United States Administrative Histories of World War II.* Washington, D.C.: Naval History Division, 1976.

447. Heinl, Robert D. *Dictionary of Military and Naval Quotations.* Annapolis: U.S. Naval Institute, 1966.

448. Heitzmann, William R. "The United States Naval Institute's Contributions to the In-Service Education of Naval Officers, 1873-1973." Ph.D. dissertation, University of Delaware, 1974.

449. Hezlet, Arthur. *Electronics and Sea Power.* New York: Stein and Day, 1975.

450. Holmes, James H. "Admiral Leahy in Vichy France, 1940-1942." Ph.D. dissertation, The George Washington University, 1974.

451. Holmes, W. J. *Double-Edged Secrets: U. S. Naval Intelligence in the Pacific During World War II.* Annapolis: Naval Institute Press, 1979.

452. Hooper, Edwin B. *The Navy Department: Evolution and Fragmentation.* Washington, D.C.: Naval Historical Foundation, 1978.

453. Hooper, Edwin B. "The Navy Department: From a Simpler to a More Complex State." In *Evolution of the American Military Establishment Since World War II,* edited by Paul Schratz. Lexington, Va.: George C. Marshall Foundation, 1978.

454. Hooper, Edwin B., Dean C. Allard, and Oscar P. Fitzgerald. *The United States Navy and the Vietnam Conflict: The Setting of the Stage 1959.* Washington, D.C.: GPO, 1976.

455. Horton, D. C. *Fire Over the Islands: The Coast Watchers of the Solomons.* London: Cooper, 1975.

456. Houchins, Lee S. "American Naval Involvement in the Chinese Civil War, 1945-1949." Ph.D. dissertation, American University, 1971.

457. Hubbell, John G. *POW: A Definitive History of the American Prisoner of War Experience in Vietnam, 1964-1973.* New York: The Readers Digest Press, 1976.

458. Hughes, Terry, and John Costello. *The Battle of the Atlantic.* New York: The Dial Press, 1977.

459. Jackson, Robert. *Air War Over Korea.* New York: Scribner, 1975.

460. James, Clayton D. *The Years of MacArthur.* Vol. 2, *1941-45.* Boston: Houghton Mifflin Co., 1975.

461. Jones, Ken, and Hubert Kelley, Jr. *Admiral Arleigh (31-Knot) Burke: The Story of a Fighting Sailor.* Philadelphia: Chilton Books, 1962.

462. Kevles, Daniel J. *The Physicists: The History of a Scientific Community in Modern America.* New York: Alfred A. Knopf, 1978.

463. Kinnard, Douglas. *President Eisenhower and Strategic Management.* Lexington, Ky.: University of Kentucky Press, 1977.

464. Knight, Jonathan. "American Statecraft and the 1946 Black Sea Straits Controversy." *Political Science Quarterly,* fall 1975, pp. 451-75.

465. Kolodziej, Edward A. *The Uncommon Defense and Congress, 1945-1963.* Columbus: Ohio State University Press, 1966.

466. Korea, Republic of, Ministry of National Defense. *The History of United Nations Forces in the Korean War.* 6 vols. Seoul: Ministry of National Defense, 1972-77.

467. Kusche, Lawrence D. *The Bermuda Triangle Mystery—Solved.* New York: Harper and Row, 1975.

468. Ladd, J. D. *Assault from the Sea, 1939-1945.* New York: Hippocrene Books, 1976.

469. Leutze, James R. *Bargaining for Supremacy: Anglo-American Naval Collaboration, 1937-1941.* Chapel Hill: University of North Carolina Press, 1978.

470. Lewin, Ronald. *Ultra Goes to War: The First Account of World War II's Greatest Secret Based on Official Documents.* New York: McGraw-Hill, 1978.

471. Lewis, Jesse W., Jr. *The Strategic Balance in the Mediterranean.* Washington, D.C.: American Enterprise Institute for Public Policy Research, 1976.

472. Lobdell, George H. "A Biography of Frank Knox." Ph.D. dissertation, University of Illinois, 1954.

473. Lord, Walter. *Lonely Vigil: Coastwatchers of the Solomons.* New York: The Viking Press, 1977.

474. Louis, William Roger. *Imperialism at Bay—the United States and the Decolonization of the British Empire: The Trusteeship Controversy, 1941-1945.* New York: Oxford University Press, 1978.

475. Love, Robert W., Jr. "Grand Strategists of Global War: A Dual Biography of Fleet Admiral Ernest J. King and Charles M. Cooke." Ph.D. dissertation, University of California, Davis, 1975.

476. Lundstrom, John B. *The First South Pacific Campaign: Pacific Fleet Strategy, December 1941-June 1942.* Annapolis: Naval Institute Press, 1976.

477. McCollum, Kenneth G., ed. *Dahlgren.* Washington, D.C.: GPO, 1977.

478. McDaniel, Eugene B. *Before Honor.* Philadelphia: A. J. Holman, 1975.

479. McGovern, James R. *The Emergence of a City in the Modern South: Pensacola, 1900-1945.* DeLeon Springs, Fla.: the author, 1976.

480. McGrath, John M. *Prisoner of War: Six Years in Hanoi.* Annapolis: Naval Institute Press, 1975.

481. MacGregor, Morris, and Bernard Nalty, eds. *Blacks in the United States Armed Forces: Basic Documents.* 13 vols. Wilmington, Del.: Scholarly Resources, Inc., 1977.

482. McGwire, Michael, and John McDonnell, eds. *Soviet Naval Influence: Domestic and Foreign Dimensions.* New York: Praeger Publishers, 1977.

483. McGwire, Michael, Ken Booth, and John McDonnell, eds. *Soviet Naval Policy: Objectives and Constraints.* New York: Praeger Publishers, 1975.

484. Melosi, Martin V. *The Shadow of Pearl Harbor: Political Controversy over the Surprise Attack, 1941-1946.* College Station, Tex.: Texas A and M University Press, 1977.

485. Merrill, James M. *A Sailor's Admiral: A Biography of William F. Halsey.* New York: Crowell, 1976.

486. Middlebrook, Martin. *Convoy: The Battle for Convoys SC.122 and HX.229.* London: Allen Lane, 1976.

487. Millot, Bernard. *The Battle of the Coral Sea.* Annapolis: Naval Institute Press, 1974.

488. Millot, Bernard. *Divine Thunder: The Life and Death of the Kamikazes.* New York: McCall Publishing Co., 1971.

489. Moffat, Alexander W. *A Navy Maverick Comes of Age, 1939-1945.* Middletown, Conn.: Wesleyan University Press, 1977.

490. Muir, Malcolm, Jr. "The Capital Ship Program in the United States Navy, 1934-1945." Ph.D. dissertation, Ohio State University, 1976.

491. Murphy, Edward R. *Second in Command: The Uncensored Account of the Capture of the Spy Ship Pueblo.* New York: Holt, Rinehart, 1971.

492. Nagatsuka, Ryuji. *I Was a Kamikaze.* New York: Macmillan, 1974.

493. O'Kane, Richard H. *Clear the Bridge: The War Patrols of the U.S.S. Tang.* Chicago: Rand McNally, 1977.

494. Orita, Zenji, and Joseph D. Harrington. *I-Boat Captain.* Canoga Park, Calif.: Major Books, 1976.

495. Pack, S. W. C. *Cunningham the Commander.* London: Batsford Books, 1974.

496. Pack, S. W. C. *Operation Husky: The Allied Invasion of Sicily.* New York: Hippocrene Books, 1977.

497. Patterson, Andrew, Jr., and Robert A. Winters, comps. *Historical Bibliography of Sea Mine Warfare.* Washington, D.C.: National Academy of Sciences, 1977.

498. Polmar, Norman. *Strategic Weapons: An Introduction.* New York: Crane, Russak and Co., 1975.

499. Potter, E. B. *Nimitz.* Annapolis: Naval Institute Press, 1976.

500. Reynolds, Clark G. *Command of the Sea.* New York: William Morrow and Co., 1974.

501. Reynolds, Clark G. *Famous American Admirals.* New York: Van Nostrand, 1978.

502. Riesenberg, Felix. *Sea War: The Story of the United States Merchant Marine in World War II.* Westport, Conn.: Greenwood Press, 1974.

503. Rilling, Alexander W. "The First Fifty Years of Graduate Education in the U.S. Navy, 1909-1959." Ph.D. dissertation, University of Southern California, 1972.

504. Rohwer, Jurgen. *The Critical Convoy Battles of March 1943: The Battle for HX 229/SC 122.* Annapolis: Naval Institute Press, 1977.

505. Rosenberg, David A., and Floyd D. Kennedy, Jr. *U.S. Aircraft Carriers in the Strategic Role.* Washington, D.C.: Lulejian Associates, 1975.

506. Rowan, Roy. *The Four Days of Mayaguez.* New York: W. W. Norton, 1975.

507. Rutledge, Howard and Phyllis. *In the Presence of Mine Enemies.* Old Tappan, N.J.: Fleming H. Revell, 1973.

508. Sainsbury, Keith. *The North African Landings, 1942: A Strategic Decision.* London: Davis-Poynter, 1976.

509. Schofield, B. B. *Operation Neptune.* Annapolis: Naval Institute Press, 1974.

510. Schultz, Duane. *Wake Island: The Heroic, Gallant Fight.* New York: St. Martin's Press, 1978.

511. Sharp, U. S. Grant. *Strategy for Defeat: Vietnam in Retrospect.* San Rafael, Calif.: Presidio Press, 1978.

512. Sherry, Michael S. *Preparing for the Next War: American Plans for Postwar Defense, 1941-45.* New Haven: Yale University Press, 1977.

513. Shilling, Charles W. *History of the Research Division, Bureau of Medicine and Surgery, U.S. Department of the Navy.* [Washington: n.p., 1977.]

514. Smaldone, Joseph P. *History of the White Oak Laboratory, 1945-1975.* Silver Spring, Md.: Naval Surface Weapons Center, 1977.

515. Standley, William H., and Arthur H. Ageton. *Admiral Ambassador to Russia.* Chicago: H. Regnery Co., 1955.

516. Steele, George P. *Seadragon Northwest Under the Ice.* New York: E.P. Dutton, 1962.

517. Steele, Richard W. *The First Offensive, 1942.* Bloomington: Indiana University Press, 1973.

518. Stoler, Mark A. *The Politics of the Second Front: American Military Planning and Diplomacy in Coalitition Warfare, 1941-1943.* Westport, Conn.: Greenwood Press, 1977.

519. *Strategic Planning in the U.S. Navy: Its Evolution and Execution, 1891-1945.* Wilmington, Del.: Scholarly Resources, Inc., 1978.

520. Stratton, Roy. *The Army-Navy Game.* Falmouth, Mass.: Volta Co., 1977.

521. Suid, Larry. *Guts and Glory: Great American War Movies.* Reading, Mass.: Addison-Wesley, 1978.

522. Szymczak, Chester J. *Sinking of the Dorchester.* Milwaukee: Great Lakes Publishing Co., 1976.

523. Thorne, Christopher. *Allies of a Kind: The United States, Britain, and the War Against Japan, 1941-1945.* New York: Oxford University Press, 1978.

524. Tillman, Barrett. *The Dauntless Dive Bomber of World War II.* Annapolis: Naval Institute Press, 1976.

525. Tregaskis, Richard. *Southeast Asia: Building the Bases.* Washington, D.C.: GPO, 1975.

526. Tulich, Eugene N. *The United States Coast Guard in Southeast Asia during the Vietnam Conflict.* Washington, D.C.: U.S. Coast Guard, 1975.

527. U.S. Naval Academy Alumni Association. *Register of Alumni.* Annapolis: The Association, 1886– .

528. U.S. Naval Sea Systems Command, Supervisor of Salvage. *Suez Canal Salvage Operations in 1974.* Washington, D.C.: GPO, 1975.

529. U.S. Navy Department. *Review of Navy R and D Management, 1946-1973.* 2 vols. Washington, D.C.: Booz, Allen and Hamilton, Inc., 1976.

530. Van der Rhoer, Edward. *Deadly Magic: A Personal Account of Communications Intelligence in World War II in the Pacific.* New York: Charles Scribner's Sons, 1978.

531. Van Oosten, F. C. *The Battle of the Java Sea.* Annapolis: Naval Institute Press, 1976.

532. *Warship International.* Toledo: International Naval Research Organization, 1964– .

533. Watts, Anthony. *The U-Boat Hunters*. London: Macdonald and Jane's, 1976.

534. *We Came Home*. Toluca Lake, Calif.: P.O.W. Publications, 1977.

535. Webber, Bert. *Retaliation: Japanese Attacks and Allied Counter-measures on the Pacific Coast in World War II*. Corvallis, Oreg.: Oregon State University Press, 1975.

536. *Webster's American Military Biographies*. Springfield, Mass.: G and C Merriam Co., 1978.

537. *Who Was Who in American History—The Military*. Chicago: Marquis Who's Who, 1975.

538. Wilson, Desmond P., Jr. *Evolution of the Attack Aircraft Carrier: A Case Study in Technology and Strategy*. Washington, D.C.: Center for Naval Analyses, 1965.

XIX

MUSEUMS AS HISTORICAL RESOURCES

Philip K. Lundeberg

As anticipated, the United States bicentennial celebration, gathering momentum early in 1974, generated a massive outpouring of historical works on the War for Independence, many related to commemorative exhibitions at museums and historic sites at home and abroad. The bicentennial celebration was by no means limited, however, to commemoration of the events of the American Revolution. At the Smithsonian Institution's National Museum of History and Technology, a unique and massively mounted exhibition, conceived by Daniel Boorstin under the rubric "A Nation of Nations," celebrated the successive contributions of varied ethnic groups during the two centuries of national development (128). The state of the nation's domestic arts, agriculture, and industrial technology after a century of independence was captured in the National Museum's other massive bicentennial offering, "1876: A Centennial Exhibition," which featured numerous military and naval specimens first exhibited at Philadelphia in 1876 (168). Under such broader historical rubrics, therefore, one may draw attention to a wide range of recent studies tracing the evolution of American military policy, technology, and service custom since the colonial era.

Such represents the rationale of Norman M. Cary's *Guide to U. S. Army Museums and Historic Sites* (78), a bicentennial offering of the U.S. Army's Center of Military History that covers much more than its title suggests. In addition to locating and describing some sixty-four regular army and nineteen Army National Guard museums, the *Guide* also provides a comprehensive introduction to the collections and archives of U.S. Air Force, Navy, Marine Corps, and Coast Guard museums. Remarkably, the *Guide* further affords comparable information on an array of other federal museums and historic sites, including the entire military component of the National Park System; historic sites on army property; and a number of state, municipal, and private repositories. Concluding sections that describe a variety of information centers dealing with military history round out this compact and useful compendium.

Particularly notable among those major exhibitions featuring the revolutionary era were those mounted, interestingly enough, at the British Library and at the National Maritime Museum at Greenwich. The documentary treasures exhibited in the venerable London institution are described with exceptionally informative detail in *The American War of Independence, 1775-1783* (74); the exhibition was subsequently presented at the Museum of

Our National Heritage at Lexington, Massachusetts. The Greenwich exhibit brought together the richest assemblage of revolutionary era weaponry, uniforms, and portraiture that appeared anywhere during the bicentennial celebration. Kenneth Pearson and Patricia Connor's exhibition catalog, *1776: The British Story of the American Revolution* (161) will remain of great permanent reference value, notwithstanding the devastatingly loyalist flavor of many captions and interpretive passages.

Especially outstanding among American exhibitions documenting the revolutionary era was "A Rising People" undertaken jointly by The American Philosophical Society, The Historical Society of Pennsylvania, and The Library Company of Philadelphia. Handsomely mounted at the Historical Society, this Philadelphia venture drew on a rich variety of books, pamphlets, manuscripts, maps, prints, portraits, and paintings contributed from the collections of those venerable institutions. The catalog for "A Rising People" (69), like those of the aforementioned British exhibitions, represents an invaluable resource for both American military and political historians.

Among those major studies that employ museum resources in providing substantial treatment of Revolutionary War weaponry, the following should receive particular notice: *General Washington's Military Equipment,* published by the Mount Vernon Ladies' Association (61); Theodore T. Belote, *American and European Swords in the Historical Collections of the United States National Museum* (70); Howard L. Blackmore, *British Military Firearms, 1650–1850* (71); Claude Blair, *European and American Arms, 1100–1850* (72); Sidney B. Brinckerhoff and Pierce A. Chamberlain, *Spanish Military Weapons in Colonial America, 1700–1821* (73); Rodney H. Brown, *American Polearms, 1526–1865* (75); Giles Cromwell, *The Virginia Manufactory of Arms* (83); John O. Curtis and William H. Guthman, *New England Militia Uniforms and Accoutrements: A Pictorial Survey* (84); Ernest M. Eller, *Naval Weapons of the American Revolution* (94); Claude Gaier, *Four Centuries of Liège Gunmaking* (98); Robert E. Gardner, *Small Arms Makers: A Directory of Fabricators of Firearms, Edged Weapons, Crossbows and Polearms* (99); Harold B. Gill, Jr., *The Gunsmith in Colonial Virginia* (101); Arcadie Gluckman and L. D. Satterlee, *American Gunmakers* (103); Stephen V. Grancsay, *American Engraved Powder Horns* (104); William H. Guthman, *March to Massacre: A History of the First Seven Years of The United States Army, 1784–1791* (106); O. F. G. Hogg, *English Artillery* (107); B. P. Hughes, *British Smooth-Bore Artillery: The Muzzle-Loading Artillery of the 18th and 19th Centuries* (110); Albert Manucy, *Artillery Through the Ages* (124); W. E. May and P. G. W. Annis, *Swords for Sea Service* (131); Michael J. McAfee, *Artillery of the American Revolution* (133); John J. McCusker, *"Alfred": The First Continental Flagship* (134); John Metschl, *The Rudolph J. Nunnemacher Collection of Projectile Arms* (135); numerous articles in the journal *Military Collector and Historian* (137); Military Service Institution of the States, *The Catalogue of the Museum* (138); Warren Moore, *Weapons of the American Revolution* (139); Robert Multhauf, "The French Crash for Saltpeter Production, 1776–1794," in *Technology and Culture* (140); James V. Murfin, *Historic Places of the American Revolution* (141); articles in the symposium at Greenwich in 1974, *The American Revolution and the Sea: The Proceedings of the 14th Conference of the International Commission of Maritime History* (144); articles in the *Nautical Research Journal* (147);

George C. Neumann, *Edged Weapons of the American Revolution* (152), *The History of Weapons of the American Revolution* (154), and *Firearms of the American Revolution* (153); Peter Padfield, *Guns at Sea* (160); Harold L. Peterson, *American Indian Tomahawks* (162), *The American Sword, 1775–1945* (163), *A History of Firearms* (164), and *Round Shot and Rammers* (165); Mendel L. Peterson, *The Last Cruise of H.M.S. "Looe"* (164); Robert H. Rankin, *Small Arms of the Sea Service* (173); Ray Riling, *The Powder Flask Book* (175); H. C. B. Rogers, *Weapons of the British Soldier* (178); Alex Roland, *Underwater Warfare in the Age of Sail* (179); and George F. G. Stanley, *Canada Invaded, 1775–1776* (188).

During the bicentennial, museums and historical societies in the United States systematically enlarged, recatalogued, and exhibited important documentary and graphic collections relating both to the revolutionary era and the longer course of the nation's history, evidencing a sophistication of interpretation that will both benefit and challenge the military historian. A notable traveling exhibition of the National Portrait Gallery is catalogued in Lillian B. Miller's *"The Dye is Cast": The Road to American Independence, 1774–1776* (136). As part of its bicentennial program, the Naval Historical Foundation published *The Naval Historical Foundation Manuscripts Collection* (149), providing a most useful guide to its major deposits in the Manuscripts Division of the Library of Congress. Of particular importance to biographers is Linda T. Neumaier's *National Portrait Gallery Permanent Collections Illustrated Checklist* (151). The graphic resources of the Philadelphia Maritime Museum and related institutions are illustrated in Edgar N. Smith, *American Naval Broadsides: A Collection of Early Naval Prints (1745–1815)* (181), a work that recalls Raymond Corry's earlier compilation, *The Old Navy, 1776–1860: A Catalogue of an Exhibit of Prints and Watercolors from the Naval Collection of Franklin D. Roosevelt* (182). In this genre is a bicentennial offering from the U.S. Naval Academy Museum, Roger B. Stein's *American Naval Prints from the Beverley R. Robinson Collection* (189). A decade earlier, the Annapolis institution had published its *Catalogue of Manuscripts* (200), *Catalogue of the Christian A. Zabriskie Manuscript Collection* (201), and *Catalogue of the Rosenback Collection of Manuscripts* (202). In 1964, the Mariners' Museum of Newport News issued a comprehensive accounting of its graphic and manuscript resources in its *Catalogue of Maps, Ship Papers and Log Books* (125), five-volume *Catalogue of Marine Photographs* (126), and three-volume *Catalogue of Marine Prints and Paintings* (127). In addition to the Brewingtons' previously noted catalogs of graphic holdings at the Peabody Museum of Salem, Philip C. F. Smith has applied notable analytic skill in his *Fired by Manley Zeal: A Naval Fiasco of the American Revolution* (184), recounting the occasion for the commissioning of four unique combat art paintings of that era recently acquired by the Peabody Museum. Smith has further illuminated that Salem institution's notable holdings in his recent *The Artful Roux: Marine Painters of Marseilles* (183), a handsome account of the work of an exceptional dynasty of marine painters ifn the age of sail. Many an intriguing surprise awaits scholars who explore the recent publication of the Smithsonian Institution Archives, *Guide to Manuscript Collections in the National Museum of History and Technology* (187), and of Roger J. B. Knight, *Guide to the Manuscripts in the National Maritime Museum* (117).

The approach of the bicentennial celebrations also prompted widespread renewed interest in the evolution of the United States national flag. Particularly noteworthy among recent additions to this literature are Boleslaw and Marie Louise Mastai, *The Stars and Stripes: The American Flag as Art and as History, from the Birth of the Republic to the Present* (129); Milo M. Quaife, Melvin J. Weig, and Roy E. Appleman, *A History of the United States Flag* (172); and Whitney Smith, *The Flag Book of the United States* (186). Not far distant is the publication of William Rhea Furlong's lifelong study of the national flag, utilizing the techniques of textile analysis pioneered in Grace Rogers Cooper's previously noted *Thirteen Star Flags: Keys to Identification* (21).

Significant and comprehensive contributions have also been made to the history of American military decorations and heraldic art. In the more particularly bicentennial vein is Vladimir and Elvira Clain-Stefanelli, *Medals Commemorating Battles of the American Revolution* (80). Notable among the broader surveys are Bauman L. Belden, *United States War Medals* (68); Evan E. Kerrigan, *American War Medals and Decorations* (116); and the Treasury Department, *Medals of the United States Mint* (197). More specialized studies are found in Francis P. Prucha, *Indian Peace Medals in American History* (171); and John Swettenham, *Valiant Men: Canada's Victoria Cross and George Cross Winners* (193).

Surviving remnants of Revolutionary War uniforms and insignia are rarely found, and museum-related publications on such equipage tend perforce to span longer periods in the life of the republic. Beyond the aforementioned *General Washington's Military Equipment* (61) and Curtis and Guthman's *New England Militia Uniforms and Accoutrements* (84), students will turn to the richly illustrated issues of *Military Collector and Historian*. John R. Elting's two-volume *Military Uniforms in America* (95) traces development from the Revolution to 1851, while James C. Tily's *The Uniforms of the United States Navy* (194) covers the entire history of that service to World War II. More specialized works include J. Duncan Campbell, *Aviation Badges and Insignia of the United States Army, 1913–1946* (77); Ralph W. Donnelly, *The History of the Confederate States Marine Corps* (92); John A. Driscoll, *The Eagle, Globe and Anchor, 1868–1968* (93); Fred and Liliana Funken, *L'Uniforme et les Armes des Soldats de la Guerre, 1914–1918* (97); William C. Gavin, *Accoutrement Plates: North and South, 1861–1865* (100); Edgar M. Howell, *United States Army Headgear, 1855–1902* (109); James S. Hutchins, *Boots and Saddles at the Little Bighorn* (111); Sidney C. Kerksis, *Plates and Buckles of the American Military 1795–1874* (115); Frederick P. Todd, *American Military Equipage, 1851–1872* (194); and Frederick P. Todd and Frederick T. Chapman, *Cadet Gray: A Pictorial History of Life at West Point as Seen Through its Uniforms* (196). For minute detail, one may refer to Luis F. Emilio, *The Emilio Collection of Military Buttons: American, British, French, Spanish* (96); and David F. Johnson, *Uniform Buttons: American Armed Forces, 1794–1948* (112).

Numerous additional references to selected aspects of nineteenth-and twentieth-century American military technology will be found in the supplemental bibliography, in whose critical compilation my esteemed colleague Craddock Goins of the Smithsonian Institution's Division of Military History has generously assisted. In concluding, the author would draw particular attention to an important new contribution to the study of American military architecture, Willard Robinson's *American Forts: Architectual Form and Function* (177), a work that significantly establishes the connection between American military engineers and their European predecessors.

BIBLIOGRAPHY

59. Albaugh, William A., III, and Edward N. Simmons. *Confederate Arms.* Harrisburg: Stackpole, 1975.
60. Anon. *The Canadian War Museum.* Ottawa: Evergreen Press, n.d.
61. Anon. *General Washington's Military Equipment.* Mount Vernon, Va.: Mount Vernon Ladies Association, 1963.
62. Anon. *Imperial War Museum Handbook.* London: H.M.S.O., 1972.
63. Apple, Nick, and Gene Gurney. *The Air Force Museum.* New York: Crown, 1975.
64. Archibald, E. H. H. *The Wooden Fighting Ship in the Royal Navy, A.D. 897-1860.* New York: Arco, 1970. See also Archibald's *Metal Fighting Ships* sequel, published by Arco in 1971.
65. *Army Museum Newsletter.* Washington, D.C.: Center of Military History, USA.
66. Barnett, J. P. *The Lifesaving Guns of David Lyle.* South Bend, Ind.: South Bend Replicas, 1976.
67. Bearss, Edwin C. *Hardluck Ironclad.* Baton Rouge: Louisiana State University Press, 1965. Account of the recovery of the U.S.S. *Cairo.*
68. Belden, Bauman L. *United States War Medals.* 1916. Reprint. New Milford, Conn.: Flayderman, 1962.
69. Bell, Whitfield, James E. Mooney, and Edwin Wolf, II. *A Rising People: The Founding of the United States, 1765 to 1789.* Philadelphia: American Philosophical Society, 1976.
70. Belote, Theodore T. *American and European Swords in the Historical Collections of the United States National Museum.* Washington, D.C.: G.P.O., 1932.
71. Blackmore, Howard L. *British Military Firearms, 1650-1850.* London: Hubert Jenkins, 1961.
72. Blair, Claude. *European and American Arms, 1100-1850.* London: B. T. Batsford, 1961.
73. Brinckerhoff, Sidney B., and Pierce A. Chamberlain. *Spanish Military Weapons in Colonial America, 1700-1821.* Harrisburg: Stackpole, 1972.
74. The British Library. *The American War of Independence, 1775-1783.* London: British Museum Publications Ltd., 1975.
75. Brown, Rodney H. *American Polearms, 1526-1865.* New Milford, Conn.: Flayderman, 1967.
76. Calver, William L., and Reginald P. Bolton. *History Written with Pick and Shovel.* New York: New York Historical Society, 1950.
77. Campbell, J. Duncan. *Aviation Badges and Insignia of the United States Army, 1913-1946.* Harrisburg: Triangle Press, 1977.
78. Cary, Norman M., Jr. *Guide to U.S. Army Museums and Historic Sites.* Washington, D.C.: Center of Military History, U.S.A., 1975.

79. Chinn, George M. *The Machine Gun.* 5 vols. Washington, D.C.: G.P.O., 1951-55. A sixth volume is under preparation.

80. Clain-Stefanelli, Vladimir and Elvira. *Medals Commemorating Battles of the American Revolution.* Washington, D.C.: Smithsonian Institution Press, 1973.

81. Clifford, Kenneth J. *Progress and Purpose: A Developmental History of the United States Marine Corps, 1900-1970.* Washington, D.C.: History and Museums Division, 1973.

82. Corry, Raymond, comp. *The Old Navy, 1776-1860: A Catalogue of an Exhibit of Prints and Watercolors from the Naval Collection of Franklin D. Roosevelt.* Washington, D.C.: National Archives, 1962.

83. Cromwell, Giles. *The Virginia Manufactory of Arms.* Charlottesville: University of Virginia Press, 1975.

84. Curtis, John O., and William H. Guthman. *New England Militia Uniforms and Accoutrements: A Pictorial Survey.* Sturbridge, Mass.: Old Sturbridge Village, 1971.

85. Cutter, Donald C., et al. *The Malaspina Expedition.* Santa Fe: Museum of New Mexico Press, 1977.

86. Darracott, Joseph, and Belinda Loftus. *First World War Posters.* London: Imperial War Museum, 1972.

87. Darracott, Joseph, and Belinda Loftus. *Second World War Posters.* London: Imperial War Museum, 1972.

88. Davis, Doris S. *John Lloyd Broome, 1849-1898.* Quantico: U.S.M.C. Museum, 1972.

89. Davis, Doris S. *Register of the Levi Twiggs Papers, 1834-1850.* Quantico: U.S.M.C. Museum, 1971.

90. Davis, Doris S., Richard A. Long, and Tyson Wilson. *Register of the George C. Reid Papers, 1898-1960.* Quantico: U.S.M.C. Museum, 1970.

91. Dillon, Lester R. *American Artillery in the Mexican War, 1846-1847.* Austin, Tex.: Presidial Press, 1975.

92. Donnelly, Ralph W. *The History of the Confederate States Marine Corps.* New Bern, N.C.: privately printed, 1976.

93. Driscoll, John A. *The Eagle, Globe and Anchor, 1868-1968.* Quantico: U.S.M.C. Museum, 1971.

94. Eller, Ernest M. *Naval Weapons of the American Revolution, 1775-1783.* Washington, D.C.: American Defense Preparedness Association, 1976.

95. Elting, John R. *Military Uniforms in America.* 2 vols. San Rafael, Calif.: Presidio Press, 1977. Period of coverage, 1775-1851.

96. Emilio, Luis F. *The Emilio Collection of Military Buttons: American British, French, Spanish.* Salem: Essex Institute, 1911.

97. Funken, Liliana and Fred. *L'Uniforme et les Armes des Soldats de la Guerre, 1914-1918.* Tournai, Belgium: Casterman, 1970.

98. Gaier, Claude. *Four Centuries of Liège Gunmaking.* New York: Sotheby Parke Bernet, 1976. See his related exhibition catalog, *Belgian Gunmaking and American History* (Liège: E. Wahle, 1976).

99. Gardner, Robert E. *Small Arms Makers: A Directory of Fabricators of Firearms, Edged Weapons, Crossbows and Polearms.* New York: Crown, 1963.

100. Gavin, William G. *Accoutrement Plates: North and South, 1861–1865.* Philadelphia: Riling and Lentz, 1963.

101. Gill, Harold B., Jr. *The Gunsmith in Colonial Virginia.* Williamsburg: Colonial Williamsburg Foundation, 1974.

102. Gluckman, Arcadie. *Identifying Old United States Muskets, Rifles and Carbines.* Harrisburg: Stackpole, 1965.

103. Gluckman, Arcadie, and L. D. Satterlee. *American Gunmakers.* Harrisburg: Stackpole, 1965.

104. Grancsay, Stephen V. *American Engraved Powder Horns.* Philadelphia: Riling, 1965.

105. Griffin, J. A. *Canadian Military Aircraft.* Ottawa: Queens Printer, 1969.

106. Guthman, William H. *March to Massacre: A History of the First Seven Years of the United States Army, 1784–1791.* New York: McGraw-Hill, 1970.

107. Hogg, O. F. G. *English Artillery.* London: Royal Artillery Institution, 1963.

108. Horgan, Thomas P. *"Old Ironsides": An Illustrated History of U.S.S. "Constitution".* Dublin, N.H.: Yankee Magazine, 1972.

109. Howell, Edgar M. *United States Army Headgear, 1855–1902.* Washington, D.C.: Smithsonian Institution Press, 1975.

110. Hughes, B. P. *British Smooth-Bore Artillery: The Muzzle-Loading Artillery of the 18th and 19th Centuries.* London: Arms and Armour Press, 1969.

111. Hutchins, James S. *Boots and Saddles at the Little Bighorn.* Ft. Collins, Colo.: Old Army Press, 1976.

112. Johnson, David F. *Uniform Buttons, American Armed Forces, 1784–1948.* 2 vols. Watkins Glen, N.Y.: Century House, 1948.

113. Johnson, Edward C. *Marine Corps Aviation: The Early Years, 1912–1940.* Washington, D.C.: History and Museums Division, USMC, 1977.

114. Johnson, George B., and Hans Bert Lockhaven. *International Armament.* 2 vols. Cologne: International Small Arms Publishers, 1965.

115. Kerksis, Sidney C. *Plates and Buckles of the American Military, 1795–1874.* Kennesaw, Ga.: Gilgal Press, 1974.

116. Kerrigan, Evans E. *American War Medals and Decorations.* New York: Viking, 1971.

117. Knight, Roger J. B. *Guide to the Manuscripts in the National Maritime Museum. Vol. 1, The Personal Collections.* London: Mansell, 1977.

118. Larkins, William T. *U.S. Marine Corps Aircraft, 1914–1959.* Concord, Calif.: Aviation History Publications, 1959.

119. Larkins, William T. *U.S. Navy Aircraft, 1921–1941.* Concord, Calif.: Aviation History Publications, 1961.

120. Latham, R. J. Wilkinson. *British Military Swords; From 1800 to the Present Day.* London: Hutchinson, 1966. See also this author's *British Military Bayonets* (1967).

121. Lewis, Berkeley R. *Small Arms Ammunition at the International Exposition, Philadelphia, 1876.* Washington, D.C.: Smithsonian Institution Press, 1972.

122. Lundeberg, Philip K. *Samuel Colt's Submarine Battery: The Secret*

and the Enigma. Washington, D.C.: Smithsonian Institution Press, 1974.

123. Madaus, Howard M., and Robert D. Needham. *The Battle Flags of the Confederate Army of Tennessee.* Milwaukee: Milwaukee Public Library, 1976.

124. Manucy, Albert. *Artillery Through the Ages.* Washington, D.C.: G.P.O., 1949.

125. The Mariners' Museum. *Catalogue of Maps, Ship Papers and Log Books.* Boston: G. K. Hall, 1964.

126. The Mariners' Museum. *Catalogue of Marine Photographs.* 5 vols. Boston: G. K. Hall, 1964.

127. The Mariners' Museum. *Catalogue of Marine Prints and Paintings.* 3 vols. Boston: G. K. Hall, 1964.

128. Marzio, Peter, ed. *A Nation of Nations.* New York: Harper & Row, 1976.

129. Mastai, Boleslaw and Marie Louise. *The Stars and Stripes: The American Flag as Art and as History, from the Birth of the Republic to the Present.* New York: Knopf, 1973.

130. Mathews, J. Howard. *Firearms Identification.* 2 vols. Madison: University of Wisconsin Press, 1962.

131. May, W. E., and P. G. W. Annis. *Swords for Sea Service.* 2 vols. London: H.M.S.O., 1970.

132. Mayr, Otto. *Feedback Mechanisms in the Historical Collections of the National Museum of History and Technology.* Washington, D.C.: Smithsonian Institution Press, 1971.

133. McAfee, Michael J. *Artillery of the American Revolution, 1775–1783.* Washington, D.C.: American Defense Preparedness Association, 1974.

134. McCusker, John. J. *"Alfred": The First Continental Flagship.* Washington, D.C.: Smithsonian Institution Press, 1976.

135. Metschl, John. *The Rudolph J. Nunnemacher Collection of Projectile Arms.* 2 vols. Milwaukee: Milwaukee Public Library, 1928.

136. Miller, Lillian B., et al. *"The Dye is Cast": The Road to American Independence, 1774–1776.* Washington, D.C. National Portrait Gallery, 1975.

137. *Military Collector and Historian.* Quarterly of the Company of Military Historians. Washington, D.C.

138. Military Service Institution of the United States. *The Catalogue of the Museum.* New York: Putnams, 1884.

139. Moore, Warren. *Weapons of the American Revolution . . . and Accoutrements.* New York: Funk and Wagnalls, 1967.

140. Multhauf, Robert. "The French Crash Program for Saltpeter Production, 1776–1794." *Technology and Culture* 12 (1971): 163–81.

141. Murfin, James V. *Historic Places of the American Revolution.* Washington, D.C.: National Park Service, 1974.

142. Murphy, Lynn C., comp. *Rockets, Missiles and Spacecraft of the National Air and Space Museum.* Washington, D.C.: Smithsonian Institution Press, 1976.

143. Musgrove, Daniel D., and Smith Hempstone Olliver. *German Machine Guns.* Washington, D.C.: MOR Associates, 1971.

144. National Maritime Museum. *The American Revolution and the Sea: The Proceedings of the 14th Conference of the International Commission of Maritime History, 1974.* Greenwich: National Maritime Museum, 1976.

145. National Maritime Museum. *The Proceedings of the First International Congress of Maritime Museums..., 1972.* Greenwich: National Maritime Museum, 1974.

146. National Trust for Historic Preservation. *The "Monitor": Its Meaning and Future.* Washington, D.C.: National Trust for Historic Preservation, 1978.

147. *Nautical Research Journal.* Quarterly of the Nautical Research Guild. Washington, D.C.

148. Naval Historical Foundation. *The First Fifty Years of the Naval Historical Foundation.* Washington, D.C.: Naval Historical Foundation, 1978. Lists all previous pamphlet publications and lectures of the foundation.

149. Naval Historical Foundation. *The Naval Historical Foundation Manuscripts Collection.* Washington, D.C.: G.P.O., 1975. Combines the registers of naval manuscript collections deposited by the foundation in the Manuscripts Division, Library of Congress.

150. Nelson, Thomas B., and Hans B. Lockhoven. *The World's Submachine Guns.* Cologne: International Small Arms Publishers, 1963.

151. Neumaier, Linda T., comp. *National Portrait Gallery Permanent Collection Illustrated Checklist.* Washington, D.C.: National Portrait Gallery, 1978.

152. Neumann, George C. *Edged Weapons of the American Revolution, 1775-1783.* Washington, D.C.: American Defense Preparedness Association, 1973.

153. Neumann, George C. *Firearms of the American Revolution, 1775-1783.* Washington, D.C.: American Defense Preparedness Association, 1976.

154. Neumann, George C. *The History of Weapons of the American Revolution.* New York: Harper and Row, 1967.

155. Norsk Sjofartsmuseum. *Proceedings from the Second Conference [of the International Congress] of Maritime Museums, 1975.* Oslo: Norsk Sjofartsmuseum, 1976.

156. Norton, Bettina. *The Boston Naval Shipyard, 1800-1974.* Boston: Bostonian Society, 1975.

157. Oakes, Claudia, comp. *Aircraft of the National Air and Space Museum.* Washington, D.C.: Smithsonian Institution Press, 1976.

158. Ogorkiewicz, Richard M. *Armor: A History of Mechanized Forces.* New York: Praeger, 1960.

159. *Organization of Military Museums of Canada Journal.* Publication of the OMMC, headquartered at the College militaire royale, Saint-Jean, Quebec.

160. Padfield, Peter. *Guns at Sea.* New York: St. Martin's Press, 1974.

161. Pearson, Kenneth, and Patricia Connor. *1776: The British Story of the American Revolution.* London: Times Newspapers, 1976.

162. Peterson, Harold L. *American Indian Tomahawks.* New York: Museum of the American Indian, 1965.

163. Peterson, Harold L. *The American Sword, 1775-1945*. New Hope, Pa.: River House, 1954.
164. Peterson, Harold L. *A History of Firearms*. New York: Scribners, 1961.
165. Peterson, Harold L. *Round Shot and Rammers*. Harrisburg: Stackpole, 1969.
166. Peterson, Mendel L. *The Funnel of Gold*. Boston: Little, Brown, 1975.
167. Peterson, Mendel L. *The Last Cruise of H.M.S. Looe*. Washington, D.C.: Smithsonian Institution Press, 1955.
168. Post, Robert C., ed. *1876: A Centennial Exhibition*. Washington, D.C.: National Museum of History and Technology, 1976.
169. Preston, Anthony. *Battleships of World War I*. London: Arms and Armour Press, 1972.
170. Prucha, Francis Paul *A Guide to the Military Posts of the United States, 1789-1895*. Madison: State Historical Society of Wisconsin, 1964.
171. Prucha, Francis Paul *Indian Peace Medals in American History*. Madison: State Historical Society of Wisconsin, 1971.
172. Quaife, Milo M., Melvin J. Weig, and Roy E. Appleman. *A History of the United States Flag*. New York: Harper and Row, 1961.
173. Rankin, Robert H. *Small Arms of the Sea Service*. New Milford, Conn.: Flayderman, 1972.
174. Reilly, Robert M. *United States Military Small Arms, 1816-1865: The Federal Firearms of the Civil War*. Baton Rouge: Eagle Press, 1970.
175. Riling, Ray. *The Powder Flask Book*. Philadelphia: Halter, 1953.
176. Ripley, Warren. *Artillery and Ammunition of the Civil War*. New York: Van Nostrand Reinhold, 1970.
177. Robinson, Willard. *American Forts: Architectual Form and Function*. Urbana: University of Illinois Press, 1977.
178. Rogers, H. C. B. *Weapons of the British Soldier*. London: Seeley Service & Co., 1960.
179. Roland, Alex. *Underwater Warfare in the Age of Sail*. Bloomington: Indiana University Press, 1978.
180. Sellers, Frank M., comp. *The William M. Locke Collection*. East Point, Ga.: Antique Armory, Inc., 1973.
181. Smith, Edgar N. *American Naval Broadsides: A Collection of Early Naval Prints (1745-1815)*. Philadelphia: Philadelphia Maritime Museum, 1974.
182. Smith, Merritt R. *Harpers Ferry Arsenal and the New Technology: A Challenge of Change*. Ithaca: Cornell University Press, 1977.
183. Smith, Philip C. F. *The Artful Roux: Marine Painters of Marseille*. Salem: Peabody Museum, 1978.
184. Smith, Philip C. F. *Fired by Manley Zeal: A Naval Fiasco of the American Revolution*. Salem: Peabody Museum, 1977.
185. Smith, Philip C. F. *The Frigate "Essex" Papers: Building the Salem Frigate, 1798-1799*. Salem: Peabody Museum, 1974.
186. Smith, Whitney. *The Flag Book of the United States*. New York: Morrow, 1971.
187. Smithsonian Institution Archives. *Guide to Manuscript Collections in*

the National Museum of History and Technology. Washington, D.C.: Smithsonian Institution Press, 1978.

188. Stanley, George F. G. *Canada Invaded, 1775-1776.* Toronto: Hakkert, 1973.

189. Stein, Roger B. *American Naval Prints from the Beverley R. Robinson Collection, U.S. Naval Academy Museum. . . .* Richmond: International Exhibitions Foundation, 1976.

190. Swanborough, F. G. *United States Military Aircraft since 1909.* New York: Putnam, 1963.

191. Swettenham, John. *Canada and the First World War.* Ottawa: Canadian War Museum, 1968.

192. Swettenham, John. *D-Day.* Ottawa: Canadian War Museum, 1969.

193. Swettenham, John, ed. *Valiant Men: Canada's Victoria Cross and George Cross Winners.* Toronto: Hakkert, 1973.

194. Tily, James C. *The Uniforms of the United States Navy.* New York: Yoselof, 1964.

195. Todd, Frederick P. *American Military Equipage, 1851-1872.* 2 vols. Providence: Company of Military Historians, 1974.

196. Todd, Frederick P., and Frederick T. Chapman. *Cadet Gray: A Pictorial History of Life at West Point as Seen Through its Uniforms.* New York: Scribners, 1955.

197. Treasury Department. *Medals of the United States Mint.* Washington, D.C.: G.P.O., 1972.

198. Tyson, Carolyn A., ed. *Guantanamo Bay, Cuba, 1898: The Journal of Frank Keeler.* Quantico: U.S.M.C. Museum, 1970.

199. Ulanoff, Stanley. *Illustrated Guide to U.S. Missiles and Rockets.* Garden City, N.Y.: Doubleday, 1959.

200. U.S. Naval Academy Museum. *Catalogue of Manuscripts.* Annapolis: U.S. Naval Academy Museum, 1957.

201. U.S. Naval Academy Museum. *Catalogue of the Christian A. Zabriskie Manuscript Collection.* Annapolis: U.S. Naval Academy Museum, 1956.

202. U.S. Naval Academy Museum. *Catalogue of the Rosenbach Collection of Manuscripts.* Annapolis: U.S. Naval Academy Museum, 1956.

203. Vichot, Jacques. *Répertoire d'Identité des Navires de Guerre Français des Origines à Jours.* Paris: Musée de la Marine, 1967.

204. Von Senger und Etterlin, F. M. *The World's Armored Fighting Vehicles.* Garden City, N.Y.: Doubleday, 1962.

205. Wadsworth Athenaeum. *Samuel Colt Presents.* Hartford: Wadsworth Athenaeum, 1961.

206. Wahl, Paul, and Donald R. Toppel. *The Gatling Gun.* New York: Arco, 1965.

207. White, B. T. *German Tanks and Armoured Vehicles, 1914-1945.* New York: Arco, 1966.

208. White, B. T. *Tanks and Other Armored Vehicles, 1855-1939.* New York: Macmillan, 1970.

209. Wiley, Irving Bell *The Common Soldier in the Civil War.* New York: Scribners, 1973.

210. Zienert, J. *Unsere Marineuniform.* Hamburg: Helmut G. Schultz, 1970.

XX

THE UNITED STATES MARINE CORPS, 1775–1978*

Graham A. Cosmas

From the two small battalions called for by the Continental Congress in 1775, the United States Marine Corps has evolved into a force of 190,000 men and women in three divisions and three aircraft wings, within the Navy Department but with the legal status and organizational characteristics of a separate service. The Marine Corps has survived repeated attempts to abolish it or incorporate it in other services, and it has been remarkably successful in discovering new missions as its old ones became obsolete. Marine courage and tenacity in combat have won for the Corps a heroic place in American folklore and a reputation as the nation's elite force in readiness. The Marine Corps saga has inspired a large amount of writing, much of it romantic, sensational, or polemical. Scholarly studies of this unique military force are limited in number and uneven in coverage.

GENERAL HISTORIES. The older histories of Collum (50), Abbott (1), McClellan (176), and Metcalfe (188) are still of value. They include much significant, if often undigested and uninterpreted, detail and extensive quotations from documents. Among more recent histories, the late Col. Robert D. Heinl, Jr.'s *Soldiers of the Sea* (119) is indispensable, as well as lively and unabashedly pro-Marine Corps. Briefer and less opinionated in tone is the concise official survey by Parker (236), which draws heavily from Heinl and the earlier general histories. The recent short account by Brig. Gen. Edwin H. Simmons, Director of Marine Corps History and Museums, (284) is a useful overview. J. Robert Moskin's longer volume (204) is vivid and anecdotal. Both Simmons and Moskin carry the Marine Corps story through the Vietnam conflict into the 1970s. In contrast to the heavily operational emphasis of the above-mentioned histories, Allan R. Millett's volume (192) in the Macmillan Wars of the United States series promises to be the first general survey of the institutional development of the Marine Corps. Thomas G. Roe's *History of Marine Corps Roles and Missions* (254) provides a brief but useful introduction to that perennially debated topic. James A. Donovan's *The United States Marine Corps* (79) is a primer on marine organization and doctrine in the mid-1960s. Short official histories have been published of most of the active

*This chapter supplements the sections concerning the Marine Corps in chapter XVIII of the *Guide to the Sources of United States Military History* on naval history.

regiments of the Marine Corps (28,53,85,94,144,145,263,264,287,299,361). Lynn Montross's pictorial history (197) covers the Marine Corps from its beginnings through the Korean War.

CHRONOLOGIES. The official chronology published by the Marine Corps History and Museums Division (324) is now undergoing revision and expansion. Harry A. Ellsworth's *One Hundred Eighty Landings* (84) fulfills many of the functions of a chronology, as it lists that number of marine landings by country, with a brief account of each.

ATLASES. The *West Point Atlas of American Wars* (87) includes maps of most major Marine campaigns. Others are to be found in the official histories published by the Corps Historical Division.

JOURNALS. *Military Affairs* (189) and the *U.S. Naval Institute Proceedings* (329) include much material on Marine Corps topics and related naval history. The *Army and Navy Journal* (4) is a useful primary source on late nineteenth and early twentieth century marine matters. Together, the two major marine professional publications, the *Marine Corps Gazette* since 1916 (170) and *Leatherneck* since 1917 (154) provide a running account of marine activities, opinion, and folklore.

BIBLIOGRAPHIES. The Marine Corps History and Museums Division's *Marine Corps Historical Bibliographies* (322) includes volumes on most periods and topics in Marine Corps history. As a general survey, Hilliard and Bivins's annotated reading list (128) from this series may be supplemented by the unofficial bibliographies by Dollen (75) and Moran (198). Strobridge (298) surveys marines in American fiction. Millett and Cooling's (since 1977, Christman and Showalter's) listing of doctoral dissertations in military affairs (193) also should be consulted.

PRIMARY SOURCES: THE MARINE CORPS HISTORICAL CENTER. The Marine Corps History and Museums Division, now housed in the Marine Corps Historical Center (366) in the Washington Navy Yard, is the most comprehensive single repository of unpublished Marine Corps documentation. Its Archives Section contains most Marine Corps operational records of the Vietnam Conflict, as well as extensive general materials on the post–World War II period, many World War II operational records, and smaller holdings on other periods. The Personal Papers Collection, for which a catalog (359) is available and is being revised and enlarged, covers the entire span of Marine Corps history. Its many collections include bodies of papers for Generals George Barnett, Joseph H. Pendleton, Alexander A. Vandegrift, Clifton B. Cates, Smedley D. Butler, and Wallace M. Greene. The Marine Corps Museum, now part of the History and Museums Division, has published registers of the papers of Henry Clay Cochrane (47), John Lloyd Broome (68), Levi Twiggs (69), George C. Reid (70), Samuel Miller (71), Joseph H. Pendleton (104), Louis McCarty Little (105), and Wilburt S. Brown (106). Eunice M. Lyon (166) has calendared the extensive Smedley D. Butler papers in the historical center.

Especially valuable to researchers on the post-1920 Marine Corps is the historical center's Oral History Collection, the published catalog (96) for which also is being revised and expanded. This collection includes transcripts and tapes of interviews with over two hundred retired senior marine officers, whose careers collectively span the period from the end of World War I to Vietnam. The collection also contains over six thousand taped field interviews and debriefings made during the Vietnam Conflict with both officers and enlisted men. These tapes cover all aspects of Marine operations and activities. The oral history program regularly interviews Marines involved in current trouble spots, for, for example, Marine security guards from the U.S. embassies in Nicosia and Beirut.

Besides these three major collections, the biographical and subject files of the reference section contain a miscellany of documents, photographs, and studies. The Historical Center Library possesses volumes on Marine Corps and general military history, as well as complete runs of the *Marine Corps Gazette, Leatherneck,* post and station newspapers, and other marine newspapers and journals. The center has large collections of Marine Corps combat art and military music and extensive still photograph and motion picture resources. Most pre-1945 Marine Corps still photographs, however, have been transferred to the National Archives.

PRIMARY SOURCES IN OTHER REPOSITORIES. Most pre-World War II records of Headquarters Marine Corps and of marine field commands, and most Marine administrative records of World War II, are in Record Group 127, U.S. National Archives (367), for which there is a preliminary inventory and guide (142). Record Group 80, the general records of the Department of the Navy, and other groups of navy records in the archives, contain much material on Marine Corps affairs. The U.S. Naval History Divison's Operational Archives (368) also possess important collections bearing on the marines, including the records of the General Board of the Navy. For detailed information on these and other naval history sources, researchers should consult the guide by Allard and Bern (2). The Library of Congress Manuscript Division (365) contains, among others, the papers of John A. Lejeune; and the Hoover Institution (363) holds papers of Gen. David M. Shoup and other cold war-era marines. The James C. Breckinridge Library (364) at the Marine Corps Development and Education Command, Quantico, Virginia, contains extensive reports of early marine amphibious exercises and other documents on the development of marine amphibious doctrine and tactics.

PUBLISHED OFFICIAL DOCUMENTS. Among printed government documents, the starting points for research are the annual reports of the Commandant of the Marine Corps, which are included in the Navy Department Annual Reports (330). Especially for the late nineteenth and early twentieth centuries, these documents are voluminous and detailed. Congressional committee hearings, especially those of the Senate and House naval affairs and appropriations committees, regularly contain testimony from commandants and other senior Marine officers on Marine Corps strength, activities, and policy.

BEGINNINGS, 1775-83. The American Marine Corps initially was patterned on that of Great Britain, the history of which is recounted by Field in *Britain's Sea-Soldiers* (90). In the 1740s, the British raised American colonial regiments which performed marine functions, as Alfred Jones demonstrates in his account of the American regiment at Cartagena (148).

Among studies of the Continental Marines, Charles R. Smith's *Marines in the Revolution* (288) supersedes all others. It includes an exhaustive bibliography and reprints diaries, muster rolls, and other contemporary documents. It is profusely illustrated with both contemporary artwork and specially commissioned paintings. Still useful short works by the Marine Corps Historical Section (323) and Lynn Montross (196) deal with Samuel Nicolas, the first commandant. C. C. Hanks (111), John J. McClusker (181), and Malcolm Lloyd (162) cover the Marines' first amphibious operation in the Bahamas. McClellan and Craige (179) describe Marine participation in the battles of Trenton and Princeton. Chester M. Colby (48) and Henry I. Shaw, Jr. (271) have published accounts of the ambitious, but unsuccessful, amphibious operation at Penobscot in 1779. The annotated bibliography by Tyson and Gill (310) is largely overshadowed by Charles R. Smith's work (288).

REBIRTH AND GROWTH, 1798-1871. Disbanded at the end of the War of Independence, the Marine Corps was reestablished in the 1790s as part of the Federalist naval building program. This crucial event, as well as marine operations in the Quasi-War with France and the Barbary Wars, has yet to find a historian and so must for now be followed in the general Marine Corps histories cited above. Smelser's *Congress Founds the Navy* (286), the *American State Papers* (311), and the navy documentary series on the Quasi-War (334) and the Barbary Wars (335) should be consulted for background and details. The Marine Corps role in the War of 1812 also lacks detailed scholarly treatment, although Wilburt S. Brown (26) covers amphibious aspects of the New Orleans campaign. The career of Lucy Brewer, allegedly the first woman to serve in the U.S. Marine Corps, is recounted in West's *The Female Marine* (347). Brewer claimed to have spent three years as a marine in the U.S.S. *Constitution* "without a discovery of her sex being made."

From 1835 to 1842, Marines received an early education in guerrilla warfare fighting the Florida Seminoles. Pierce and Myers (240) present a brief tactical analysis of these operations. George E. Buker in *Swamp Sailors* (27) analyzes Navy and Marine riverine warfare in the Everglades.

During the Mexican War, Marines participated in small-scale amphibious operations on the east and west coasts of Mexico and assisted army forces in the conquest of California and on the march to Mexico City. Neufeld's *Marines in the Mexican War* (220) is a detailed official overview of Marine activities. K. Jack Bauer, in *Surfboats and Horse Marines* (12), covers amphibious operations against Mexico. Marti (172) traces the controversial role of Lt. Archibald Gillespie, USMC, in the Bear Flag Revolt and the American takeover of California. Devlin's *The Marine Corps in Mexico* (74) and Reynolds's *Conclusive Exculpation of the Marine Corps in Mexico* (251) are contemporary views of Marine operations at Mexico City and the bitter intracorps quarrels resulting from them.

Besides helping open the way for continental expansion, early nineteenth century Marines took part in far-flung operations to enforce respect for the flag and protect American commerce around the world. Marines early assisted other Western contingents in forcing China open to Western penetration, as Nalty recounts in *The Barrier Forts* (211). Marines helped Commodore Perry overawe the Japanese, but no specialized scholarly study of their activities has been produced. The researcher must refer to such general accounts as Samuel Eliot Morison's *Old Bruin* (200) and Neumann's *America Encounters Japan* (221). The first Marine landing in Korea is described by Bauer (11) and the letters and reports of the detachment commander are published in Tyson (309). Ellsworth's *One Hundred Eighty Landings* (84) is a convenient summary of the smaller Marine forays of this period.

In 1859, Marines under Army command stormed the engine house at Harper's Ferry to capture John Brown. During the Civil War, Marines formed part of warships' crews, made amphibious landings on the Confederate coast, and occasionally operated with the army. Nalty's "*. . . At All Times Ready*" (210) surveys Marine participation in these events. It is supplemented by O'Quinlivan's official bibliography (229). The details of Marine activities can be extracted from the voluminous *Official Records of the Union and Confederate Navies* (332). Simmons (283) and King (151) describe the Marines' part in the large-scale amphibious attacks on Fort Fisher in late 1864 and early 1865. The diary of Frank Church (43) contains information on the life of Marines on board vessels of a Navy riverine squadron. Ella Lonn (164) covers Marine participation in Navy raids on Confederate salt works in Florida.

The Confederacy formed its own Marine Corps, the history of which is meticulously and lovingly reconstructed in Ralph W. Donnelly's *History of the Confederate States Marine Corps* (78). Nalty, in his article "Blue and Gray" (212), covers operations in which both Union and Confederate marines took part.

MARINES IN THE NEW NAVY, 1880-1917. As the Navy built battleships and sought command of the sea, the Marine Corps began developing its amphibious mission and doctrine. Its officers, like their Army and Navy counterparts, displayed growing professionalism as the Corps became institutionalized.

No full scholarly account of this crucial period has been written. The Navy background is surveyed in a number of works, including the two classic studies by the Sprouts (294,295). O'Connor's "Marines in the 20th Century" (227) and Clifford's *Progress and Purpose* (45) are useful general surveys of Marine Corps developments. William H. Russell's examination (261) of late nineteenth century amphibious doctrine in the U.S. Navy and John G. Miller's study (190) of Capt. William F. Fullam, USN, a persistent critic of the Marines in this era, shed light on the complex relationship between Navy and Marine Corps reform and modernization. Karsten's *Naval Aristocracy* (149), a social and intellectual examination of late nineteenth century Annapolis graduates, has value for study of the Marine Corps, since an increasing number of Marine officers came from the Naval Academy. Frances, in *History of the Marine Corps Schools* (93), outlines the development of this key institution for Marine officer professionalization. Wiegand, in "The Lauchheimer Controversy" (352), explores an episode in Marine Corps officer politics and relations with Congress. Officers' reminiscences, notably those of Lejeune (159), Barnett (8), Butler (303), and Wise (357) evoke much of the atmosphere of the corps of this period, as well as furnishing details on personalities and politics. Hans

Schmidt's biography of Butler (266) pays much attention to Marine Corps and congressional politicking.

EXPEDITIONARY SERVICE IN THE ERA OF IMPERIALISM. As American worldwide interests and military and diplomatic activity expanded, marines repeatedly were committed to expeditions and interventions, activities which often disrupted the Corps' effort to organize amphibious forces for wartime duty with the fleet. Marine operations in the Spanish-American War, during which a Marine battalion seized Guantanamo as an advance base for the squadron blockading Santiago de Cuba, are summarized sketchily by Nalty (218). Chadwick's detailed general history of the war (38) remains the best overall account of Marine and Navy operations, while the journal of Frank Keeler, edited by Tyson (308), presents a participant's view of the Guantanamo landing. Marine operations in the Philippines, against both Spaniards and Filipino nationalists, are described by Niblack (223), while the controversial Maj. Littleton W. T. Waller's campaign receives detailed coverage in Schott's *Ordeal of Samar* (268). O'Quinlivan and Nalty (233) cover minor Marine actions in Samoa in 1899.

During the 1900 Boxer Rebellion in China, Marines helped defend the Peking legations and fought their way into the capital with the international relief column. Aside from a master's thesis by Glickert (103) and an annotated bibliography by O'Quinlivan (230), the Marine role in this episode must be followed in general accounts, such as Tan's *Boxer Catastrophe* (301), Fleming's *Siege at Peking* (91), and O'Connor's *Spirit Soldiers* (228). Capt. John T. Myers, who commanded the legation detachment, wrote a firsthand *USNIP* article, "Military Operations and Defenses of the Siege of Peking" (207). Graves, in "And Saint David" (107), recounts British Army-American Marine camaraderie resulting from the Relief Expedition.

The early years of the twentieth century again saw numerous small-scale, short-duration Marine landings, summarized in Ellsworth (84), in which marines even penetrated the remote heartland of Ethiopia, as recounted by Nalty in *Guests of the Conquering Lion* (213).

Increasingly, the Caribbean became the center of Marine expeditionary activity, in support of the United States attempt to exercise hegemony without direct annexation under the Roosevelt Corollary, Taft's "Dollar Diplomacy," and Wilson's crusade to "teach the Latin Americans to elect good men." Marines, as well as Army troops, took part in the occupation of Vera Cruz in 1914, as described in Sweetman (300) and Quirk (243), but the most extensive Marine commitments occurred in Nicaragua, the Dominican Republic, and Haiti. An official Marine Corps bibliography (321) on operations in these three countries is available, as is one on Marines in guerrilla warfare (146), which focuses largely on these so-called "Banana Wars." The annual reports of the commandant (330) contain details of organization and troop movements. The State Department Foreign Relations series (338) is indispensable for both military detail on the interventions and information on policymaking, as are the two volumes (205,206) on United States-Caribbean relations by Dana G. Munro.

The first Nicaraguan intervention of 1912 is well covered in Nalty's *Marines in Nicaragua* (217), Megee's *Intervention in Nicaragua* (186), and MacCaulay's *Sandino Affair* (167). David F. Healy, in *Gunboat Diplomacy* (114), admirably chronicles the first months of the Haiti occupation in 1915, with much detail on the command relations between the navy, the State Department, and the marines. Hans Schmidt, in *Occupation of Haiti* (267), takes a thorough, largely unfavorable look at the entire intervention, with much attention to the marine role. James McCrocklin's *Garde d' Haiti* (182), compiled from an official Marine Corps report, contains useful detail on the formation of a native constabulary, a major marine activity in Nicaragua and the Dominican Republic, as well as Haiti. Fuller and Cosmas, in an official Marine Corps monograph (99), tell the story of the occupation of the Dominican Republic, while Bruce Calder, in "*Caudillos* and *Gavilleros*" (30), analyzes the motives for Dominican guerrilla resistance to the marines. The hearings and report of the 1921 United States Senate investigation of the occupations of Haiti and the Dominican Republic (313) contain testimony by marine commanders and much other information on marine activities, including real and alleged atrocities. Personal narratives of marine participants are numerous. Among the most worthwhile are the reminiscences of Smedley Butler (303), John H. Craige (59,60), Frederic M. Wise (357), and Faustin Wirkus (356). The Marine Corps oral history collection (96) includes reminiscences of retired marine generals who began their careers as lieutenants in Haiti and the Dominican Republic.

MARINES IN WORLD WAR I, 1917-19. During the United States participation in World War I, the Marine Corps, under the astute, determined leadership of Maj. Gen. Commandant George Barnett, expanded to seventy-five thousand men and deployed two brigades and an aviation group to France. Jack Shulimson, in his article "First to Fight" (280), chronicles the marines' political and bureaucratic battle for a major war role. For general coverage of marine wartime organization and operations, McClellan's official history (178) is the most thorough and detailed. Hilliard's annotated bibliography (127) is a useful guide to the literature.

Belleau Wood, the marines' first and bloodiest battle in France, is described vividly in Robert Asprey's *At Belleau Wood* (5). Lejeune's memoirs (159) tell of his war. The writings of marines John W. Thomason (305), Thomas Boyd (22,23), Frederic M. Wise (357), and Albertus W. Catlin (37) are a few of the best of many eyewitness narratives of combat.

The growth and activities of Marine Corps aviation in World War I are described in Johnson's *Marine Aviation: the Eary Years* (140), Cosmas's *Marine Flyer in France* (58), and Emmons's "The 1st Marine Aviation Force" (86). Women made their first official appearance in marine uniform in World War I. Linda Hewitt's official monograph (124), based heavily on survivors' reminiscences, describes their experiences.

BETWEEN THE WARS, 1919-41. During the 1920s and 1930s, Marine Corps strength remained at about twenty thousand officers and men. Expeditionary activity continued to tie up most Marine tactical units until 1934, when the last troops left Haiti. The Marines maintained a legation guard in Peking and in the late 1920s had a brigade deployed at Tientsin and Shanghai. Marine activities in China in this period have not yet found a historian, although Schmidt's biography of Butler (266) contains much information on his tactics as brigade commander. Louis Morton (202) explores Army-Marine rivalry on the "China Station."

During the late 1920s and early 1930s, the Marines fought the last and most difficult of their "Banana Wars" in Nicaragua, against their most formidable Central American opponent, Gen. Augusto C. Sandino. MacCaulay's *Sandino Affair* (167) is the most thorough study of this campaign available, and draws on both Marine and *Sandinista* primary sources. Nalty's (217) and Megee's (186) accounts supplement MacCaulay's, as does Lejeune Cummins's *Quixote on a Burro* (64). Julian C. Smith's voluminous report on the *Guardia Nacional de Nicaragua* (290) includes a wealth of detail and documents. Richard Millett, in *Guardians of the Dynasty* (194) recounts the disappointment of American hopes that the *Guardia* would remain a nonpolitical mainstay of constitutional government. Rowell's "Aircraft in Bush Warfare" (257) and Johnson's history of early Marine aviation (140) describe the origins in this campaign of the Marine air-ground team.

With the advent of the "Good Neighbor Policy" and the withdrawal of the last Marines from Haiti and Nicaragua in the early 1930s, the era of Caribbean police actions ended for the Marines. As it did so, the Marine Corps Schools distilled its lessons into the *Small Wars Manual* (317), a comprehensive textbook on military pacification. Ronald Schaffer (265) describes the development of this manual and the failure to apply its precepts in recent counterinsurgency operations.

The atmosphere of the expeditionary Marine Corps of the 1920s is evoked in the writings of John W. Thomason, notably—*And a Few Marines* (304).The Marine Corps oral history collection (96) contains a number of detailed recollections of life in the "Old Corps" in Nicaragua and China.

Beginning in 1933, with the creation of the Fleet Marine Force, the Marine Corps concentrated on preparation for amphibious warfare, with Japan the probable enemy. The outlines of amphibious assault tactics as practiced in World War II and of the "island-hopping" offensive strategy first received full articulation in the early 1920s in the writings of Maj. Earl H. Ellis, whose tormented career and mysterious death are described by John J. Reber (247). The standard account of amphibious development in the 1930s and of the implementation and modification of the doctrine in the war against Japan remains Isely and Crowl's *The U.S. Marines and Amphibious War* (138). *Progress and Purpose* (45) and the first volume of the Marine Corps official World War II history (325a) also contain informative discussions of the development of amphibious doctrine and technique, as does Norman Cooper's biography of Gen. Holland M. Smith (56). Bivins's bibliography of naval gunfire support (17) lists articles, mostly from naval and marine professional journals, on this key element of the amphibious assault.

WORLD WAR II. In contrast to other periods of Marine Corps history, the operations of the corps in World War II have been extensively and well chronicled. Flagship of the general accounts is the five-volume official *History of Marine Corps Operations in World War II* (325), which is comprehensive and detailed. It is paralleled by an older but still useful series of campaign monographs. The bibliography by O'Quinlivan and Hilliard (232) is a convenient listing of sources and is now undergoing revision by the Marine Corps History and Museums Division.

One-volume surveys of the marines' war abound. Among the more useful are Hough's *Island War* (133), Pratt's *The Marines' War* (241), and Leckie's *Strong Men Armed* (158). Hayashi in *Kogun* (113) describes Pacific operations from the Japanese army viewpoint. Morison's *History of Naval Operations in World War II* (199) and its one-volume condensation, *The Two-Ocean War* (201), are indispensable for the background and context of marine campaigns. Parrish's *Encyclopedia of World War II* (238) is a useful reference on weapons, material, and tactics.

The strategic decisions that shaped Marine campaigns are covered in the official Marine volumes and in the Army histories by Morton (203), Matloff (173, 174), and Conn (54). Marine command relations with other services are considered in Smith's *Coral and Brass* (289), Halsey's memoirs (109), and Creswell's *Generals and Admirals* (62). Furer, in *Administration of the Navy Department* (100), discusses many Marine administrative matters. George C. Dyer's *The Amphibians Came to Conquer* (83), a biography of Adm. Richmond Kelly Turner, describes the operations of Navy amphibious forces.

The Marine occupation of Iceland at the beginning of the war is treated in Byron Fairchild's account (89) of the decision and Clifford's official monograph (46) on the operation, as well as in the first of the official Marine volumes (325a). The same volume covers the early Marine defensive operations in the Pacific and the Marine role in the decisive battle of Midway. Heinl, in two official monographs, describes the defense of Wake (115) and Midway (116). The Marine commander at Wake, James S. Devereux (73), and his Navy superior, Cunningham, (65) both have written their personal accounts of this heroic but unsuccessful action.

Guadalcanal, the Marines' first offensive of the war, is described in the Marine Corps volume by Hough, Ludwig, and Shaw (325a), and in Zimmerman's official monograph (362). Among nonofficial accounts, that by Samuel B. Griffith (108) is the most nearly definitive. Robert Leckie's *Challenge for the Pacific* (155) is a popular history by a Marine World War II veteran. Tregaskis, in *Guadalcanal Diary* (306), presents a war correspondent's view from the front lines. Subsequent operations in the Solomons are recounted in Shaw's and Kane's *Isolation of Rabaul* (325b), and in monographs by Rentz (249, 250) and Hough and Crown (134).

The Marines' Central Pacific drive through the Gilberts, Marshalls, and Marianas is chronicled in the official Marine Corps volume by Shaw, Nalty, and Turnbladh (325c). Robert Sherrod's *Tarawa* (278), the official monograph by Stockman (296), Shaw's concise popular account (272), and Martin Russ's impressionistic *Line of Departure* (260) recreate the hard-fought and controversial battle for the Japanese stronghold in the Gilberts. Robert D. Heinl, in *The Marshalls* (117), describes the capture of Majuro, Roi-Namur, Kwajalein, and Eniwetok. The Marianas campaign can be followed in Hoffman's monographs on Saipan (129) and Tinian (130), and Lodge's on the recapture of Guam (163). Philip A. Crowl (63) covers the Marianas operations from the United States Army side.

Operations in the Western Pacific, culminating in the stubborn battle for Iwo Jima, receive coverage in the official *Western Pacific Operations,* by Garand and Strobridge (325d). Hough in *Assault on Peleliu* (132) analyzes the principal action in the Palau Islands. For Iwo Jima, the official monograph by Bartley (9) may be supplemented by Nalty's account of the famous flag raising on Mount Suribachi (216) and Newcomb's thorough *Iwo Jima* (222). Heinl deals with controversies over naval gunfire support in "Target: Iwo" (120).

Okinawa, the last and largest Marine amphibious assault of the war, occupies much of the final official Marine volume by Frank and Shaw (325e). Nichols and Shaw describe this long costly struggle in a marine monograph (224), while the Belotes, in *Typhoon of Steel* (14), provide the most complete unofficial history. Benis M. Frank has contributed two concise popular studies: *Okinawa: Touchstone to Victory* (98) and *Okinawa: The Great Island Battle* (97). The latter book draws heavily on reminiscences of Japanese survivors. Bauer and Coox, in "Olympic vs. Ketsu-Go" (13), analyze American and Japanese plans for the unfought climactic battle for the home islands. The post-VJ-Day marine role in the occupations of Japan and North China is described in two studies by Shaw (273, 274) and in the final Marine Corps World War II volume (325e). Churley (44) presents a contemporaneous account of activities in North China.

Histories are available of each of the six Marine divisions mobilized during World War II (6, 36, 41, 42, 143, 185, 242). Charles Updegraph's official monograph (339) tells the story of such special units as defense battalions, parachute battalions, glider and barrage balloon units, and the heroic but controversial Raider battalions. Still another official Marine Corps study by Johnstone (147) deals with parachute units.

Robert Sherrod's *Marine Aviation in World War II* (277) is a detailed overall account of Marine air operations. It may be supplemented by De Chant's *Devilbirds* (72). Thomas G. Miller, in *Cactus Air Force* (191), describes Marine and Navy aviation on Guadalcanal, while Charles W. Boggs, Jr., in an official monograph, discusses Marine air support for the Allied invasion of the Philippines (21). Details of fighter combat can be found in the memoirs of marine aces Gregory ("Pappy") Boyington (24) and Joe Foss (92), and in Sims's chronicle of Navy and Marine aces (285).

In World War II, the Marine Corps for the first time enlisted a substantial number of blacks. Their story is told in the official study by Henry I. Shaw, Jr., and Ralph Donnelly, *Blacks in the Marine Corps* (275). Women also served, as recounted in Meid's *Marine Corps Women's Reserve in World War II* (187). An unusual but important ethnic Marine unit is described by Doris A. Paul in *Navaho Code Talkers* (239).

Other special topics have received attention in articles and monographs. Heinl (118) traces the wartime development of naval gunfire support for amphibious landings. Condit, Diamond, and Turnbladh (51) describe Marine Corps World War II ground training. Martin Boyle (25) and John White (349) recount the experiences of Marines captured by the Japanese early in the war, as does the final official Marine Corps history volume (325e). Hawkins (112) tells the story of his years as a guerrilla in the Philippines.

Personal accounts of combat by Marines and war correspondents are legion. Among the most memorable are Lucas's *Combat Correspondent* (165), Hersey's *Into the Valley* (123), Hunt's *Coral Comes High* (137), and Leckie's *Helmet for My Pillow* (156). Smith (291) has assembled an anthology of pieces by marines and correspondents covering all the Pacific campaigns. Leon Uris's *Battle Cry* (340) is typical of a genre of semiautobiographical Marine World War II novels. Others of this variety are listed in the bibliography on marines in fiction by Stobridge (298). A sampling of Marine Corps combat art may be found in Aimee Crane's *Marines at War* (61).

THE COLD WAR ERA, 1945-75. During the post-World War II decades, the Marine Corps struggled for survival in legislative battles over military unification and tried to maintain its ability to conduct amphibious assaults in the face of nuclear weapons. Aside from a master's thesis by Gordon W. Keiser (150), no detailed account of the Marine role in the 1944-1947 unification debates has been produced, but the Marine Corps oral history collection (96) is rich in reminiscences of marine participants. Marine efforts to adapt amphibious assault tactics to the atomic era can be followed in Clifford's *Progress and Purpose* (45), and in the studies of Marine employment of the helicopter by Montross (195), Rawlins (246), and Fails (88).

In a long series of cold war confrontations, Marines constituted a force in readiness which the United States used to exert influence, sometimes by actual commitment, more often by mere offshore presence. Blechman and Kaplan, in their study of armed forces as a political instrument (20), give due attention to the employment of Marines in such actions. Shulimson, in *Marines in Lebanon* (281), describes Marine operations during the 1958 Middle East crisis. This official Marine Corps account may be supplemented by McClintock's "American Landing in Lebanon" (180), an eyewitness report by the United States ambassador. Ringler and Shaw, in another official study (252), survey Marine participation in the 1965 intervention in the Dominican Republic, while James A. Dare (66) provides a firsthand account of the same operation.

As cold war changed to detente in the 1970s, the military effectiveness and political usefulness of an amphibious Marine Corps again came into question. The Brookings Institution study by Binkin and Record (16) examines the basic problems and alternatives from a viewpoint critical of the Marine Corps as presently organized. The Marine Corps side of this debate, and current Marine developments and problems in general, can be followed in the *Marine Corps Gazette* (170) and the *U. S. Naval Institute Proceedings* (329).

THE KOREAN CONFLICT, 1950-53. In Korea, Marines were committed to fight a large-scale Asian land war. The official five-volume work *U. S. Marine Operations in Korea* (327) is the most comprehensive account of Marine participation, which may be supplemented by O'Quinlivan and Santelli's official annotated bibliography (234). For the course of the war as a whole, David Rees's *Korea* (248) is a convenient and judicious summary. Spanier, in *The Truman-MacArthur Controversy* (293), traces the strategy debates. Andrew Geer, in *The New Breed* (101), recounts Marine operations during the first year of the war.

Marine actions in defense of the Pusan Perimeter and in MacArthur's brilliant amphibious "end-run" to Inchon are described by Montross and Canzona in the first two volumes (327a, 327b) of the Marine Corps official history. Robert D. Heinl, Jr., in *Victory at High Tide* (121), tells the story of the Inchon-Seoul campaign in lively detail and places this amphibious triumph in the context of the earlier unification controversy and the debates over atomic-age marine roles and missions. Heinl's study may be supplemented by

Sheldon's *Hell or High water* (276). Willoughby (355) and Whitney (351) present MacArthur's view of the operation.

Chinese intervention and the fighting withdrawal of the 1st Marine Division from Chosin Reservoir are recounted in the thrid marine official volume (327c) and in Robert Leckie's *March to Glory* (157). The last two Marine Corps volumes (327c, 327d) cover operations as the front stabilized and truce talks began. Tactical problems in the static phase of the conflict are analyzed in Norman W. Hicks's master's thesis (125) on outpost warfare.

Montross (195) and Rawlins (246) describe Marine experiments and advances in the tactical and logistic use of the helicopter in Korea. Giusti (102) discusses mobilization of the Marine Reserve for the conflict. A master's thesis by James A. MacDonald, Jr. (168), and the fifth volume of the Marine Corps official series (327e) deal with the ordeal of Marine prisoners of war. The Navy Department history of the Chaplain Corps includes a volume (331) on chaplains serving with Marine units in Korea.

An enlisted Marine's view of the later stages of the war can be found in *The Last Parallel,* by Martin Russ (259). War correspondent Marguerite Higgins, in *War in Korea* (126), reports front-line action from Inchon through the Chosin breakout. The classic photographic study of combat marines in Korea, from Pusan to Chosin, is David Douglas Duncan's *This Is War!* (81).

VIETNAM AND SOUTHEAST ASIA, 1954–75. In Southeast Asia, Marines waged essentially a nonamphibious land war, one that in some respects resembled their earlier campaigns in the Caribbean and Central America. The Marine Corps History and Museums Division is now (1978) preparing a multivolume history of the Marine involvement in Southeast Asia from the advisory beginnings in 1954 through the final evacuation in 1975. The series will include both chronological and topical volumes. As an interim reference, the division has published *The Marines in Vietnam* (326), a collection of articles from the *Marine Corps Gazette* and the *U. S. Naval Institute Proceedings* on various aspects of the conflict. During the period of major Marine troop commitments, Fleet Marine Force Pacific issued monthly reports (328) on Vietnam operations. Now declassified, these documents contain much useful detail, especially on tactics and logistics, but are propagandistic in their overall interpretation of events and must be used with caution.

General sources on the war, including the Pacific Command *Report on the War* (337), the "Pentagon Papers" (314), and Gen. William C. Westmoreland's *A Soldier Reports* (348), besides establishing the context of events, include much detail on Marine activities. Westmoreland's memoirs are especially informative, and sometimes unintentionally revealing, on his strategic disagreements with Marine commanders.

Two of the official Marine Corps operational histories have been published: Whitlow's (350) on pre-1965 advisory and helicopter operations, and Shulimson and Johnson's (282) on the 1965 landing at Da Nang and buildup of Marine forces in northern South Vietnam. Moyers S. Shore, in an earlier Marine Corps study (279), describes the 1968 siege of Khe Sanh. Bernard C. Nalty (209) covers United States Air Force operations in the same campaign. The marines' stubborn house-to-house battle for Hue, as well as the 1968 Tet Offensive as a whole, are described in Don Oberdorfer's *Tet!* (226). Francis J.

West, Jr. analyzes a variety of squad, platoon, and company size Marine actions in *Small Unit Action in Vietnam* (345). Keith B. McCutcheon (183) summarizes air operations. Marine activity during the American evacuations from Cambodia and South Vietnam and the retaking of the *Mayaguez* is recounted by the commanders involved in a series of *Marine Corps Gazette* articles (10, 33, 34, 35, 141). Roy Rowan's jounalistic *Four Days of Mayaguez* (256) and the congressional hearings and report (312) on the *Mayaguez* incident contain much information on the Marines' role.

Marine efforts to "win the hearts and minds" of the Vietnamese are described in official pamphlets by Parker (237) and Stolfi (297). West, in *The Village* (346), vividly narrates the story of a successful Marine effort to pacify one village. William R. Corson, in *The Betrayal* (57), at once applauds Marine contributions to pacification and denounces what Corson considers a generally incorrect American war strategy. Gen. Lewis W. Walt, USMC, who commanded Marine forces in Vietnam during 1965–67, emphasizes pacification in his memoir, *Strange War, Strange Strategy* (343), while vigorously asserting the justice of the American and South Vietnamese cause. The official Navy study by Hooper (131); articles by Soper (292), Collins (49), and Huff (135); and the report of the United States Joint Logistic Review Board (315) contain much detail on supply and other support of the Marines in Vietnam.

Among accounts of the war by military participants and jounalists now making their appearance, a number deal with Marine operations. *The Letters of PFC Richard E. Marks* (171) contain observations of an enlisted man later killed in action. Martin Russ's *Happy Hunting Ground* (258) and Michael Herr's *Dispatches* (122) present journalistic impressions. Ron Kovic (152), Philip D. Caputo (32), and Charles R. Anderson (3) are among the former marines who have written testaments of their service. The novels *Body Count* (136), *Sand in the Wind* (255), and *Fields of Fire* (344) present varying viewpoints on the marines' Vietnam experience. All of these works reflect, in varying degrees, disillusionment with a confusing, dirty war. David Douglas Duncan, in *War without Heroes* (82), again captures episodes of the Marines' war in photographs.

MARINE AVIATION, 1912–75. The development of Marine Corps aviation from its beginnings in 1912 to its emergence as an arm of the Fleet Marine Force in the 1930s is described in Johnson's *Marine Aviation: the Early Years* (140). The histories of naval avaiation by Caidin (29), Turnbull and Lord (307), and Van Deurs (341) provide the context for marine air activities, as well as much detail on the earliest Marine fliers.

Marine aviation in World War II is covered comprehensively by Sherrod (277). Postwar Marine fixed-wing aviation has not yet received book-length official or unofficial treatment and must be traced through the Marine Corps Korean War histories (327), McCutcheon's Vietnam article (183), and the projected Marine Corps Vietnam series. Helicopters in the Marine Corps, in contrast, are the subject of three thorough studies by Montross (195), Rawlins (246), and Fails (88).

Marine Corps aircraft from 1913 to 1965 are listed with specifications in an official pamphlet (319), a portion of which is reprinted in Johnson's history. Aviation historian William T. Larkins (153) lists and illustrates most pre-1959 Marine aircraft, while Paul R. Matt (175) traces the development of navy and

Marine fighter planes. James S. Santelli, in his annotated bibliography of Marine close air support (262), includes writings on this mission, the principal reason for existence of Marine aviation, from Nicaragua in 1927 through the Vietnam Conflict.

INSTITUTIONAL ASPECTS OF THE MARINE CORPS. Official monographs cover a number of nonoperational aspects of Marine Corps development, including staff organization (52); officer procurement (215); ranks and grades (219); inspection (214); orderlies, servants, and security guards (208); and engineers (76). These publications are generally brief and factual. In addition, the Marine Corps has published an annotated bibliography on Marine artillery (77).

Marine Corps enlistment of blacks and the experience of blacks in the Corps from World War II to the 1970s are dealt with in the official study by Shaw and Donnelly (275). Hewitt (124) and Meid (187) recount the enlistment and employment of women Marine reserves in World Wars I and II. The Marine Corps Reserve has published a useful, but far from definitive, history (318) of its own.

Robert Barde (7) and O'Quinlivan and Frank (231) trace the history of Marine Corps competitive marksmanship. Two Marine Corps pamphlets by Elmore A. Champie recount the histories of the recruit depots at Parris Island, South Carolina (40), and San Diego, California (39). Robert M. Witty, in *Marines of the Margarita* (358), outlines the development of Camp Pendleton from a Spanish *rancho* to a gigantic Marine base.

The rigors of "Boot Camp" have become part of Marine Corps legend and occasionally have given rise to tragic excesses. William B. McKean, in *Ribbon Creek* (184), tells one version of the story of a widely publicized 1956 drowning of a recruit and the subsequent investigation. Jeffers and Levitan in *See Parris and Die* (139) make allegations of brutality during the 1960s.

In the early twentieth century, the Marine Corps led the way among the armed services in developing an aggressive public-relations program. Robert G. Lindsay, in *This High Name* ((161), examines Marine Corps publicity efforts, while Benis M. Frank (95) tells the story of Marine Corps combat correspondents in World War II, Korea, and Vietnam. The Marine band, itself a major publicity asset of the corps, and it most famous director, John Philip Sousa, are described in Kenneth Berger's *The March King and His Band* (15).

BIOGRAPHY AND AUTOBIOGRAPHY. The biographical dictionaries by Karl Schuon (270), Charles L. Lewis (160), and Jane Blakeney (18) contain basic information about many prominent and heroic marines. The Blakeney volume also includes unit decorations and honors. Hamersly's *Records* (110) of Marine Corps and Navy officers is valuable for the bare facts on otherwise obscure individuals of the late nineteenth and early twentieth centuries, while Callahan's list (31) of Navy and Marine officers, the annual Navy registers (333), and the Marine Corps lineal lists (316) indicate at least who served, when, where, and at what rank.

Book-length biographies of Marine Corps leaders are few. Those available include lives of Edward F. Carlson of the Raiders (19), Holland M. Smith (56), "Chesty" Puller (67), and Roy S. Gieger (354). Hans Schmidt's biography of Smedley D. Butler (266) at least partially fills a large gap in Marine biographical literature. Two studies have been done of the marine artist-writer, John W. Thomason (353, 225).

Memoirs and autobiographies of Marines include those of John A. Lejeune (159), George Barnett (8), Smedley Butler (303), and Alexander A. Vandegrift (342). The writings of such lower-ranking Marines as Frederic M. Wise (357), Albertus W. Catlin (37), Mitchell Paige (235), Fred S. Robillard (253), and "Pappy" Boyington (24) are of varying accuracy and interest.

UNIFORMS, WEAPONS, AND TRADITIONS. Descriptions and illustrations of Marine uniforms of various periods can be found in McClellan's *Uniforms of the American Marines* (177), Rankin's *Uniforms of the Sea Services* (245), and Magruder's "A Touch of Tradition" (169). Rankin's *Small Arms of the Sea Services* (244) is a basic guide to Marine as well as Navy individual weapons.

The Marine Corps is rich in lore and tradition. Karl Schuon, in *Home of the Commandants* (269), tells the story of the historic Washington, D.C., Marine Barracks, as well as of the commandant's residence located there. Driscoll recounts the evolution of the Marine emblem in *Eagle, Globe, and Anchor* (80). The Marine Corps Historical Division has published a short pamphlet (320) on Marine Corps lore. The semiofficial *Marine Officer's Guide* (302) also contains much information on Marine custom and tradition.

MUSEUM RESOURCES. The Marine Corps Museum, a component of the Marine Corps Historical Center (366), contains a rich collection of Marine artifacts. The main museum, located in the historical center building in the Washington Navy Yard, includes a "Time Tunnel" of permanent exhibits of weapons, uniforms, equipment, documents, and memorabilia representing all periods of Marine Corps history, as well as a gallery of frequently changed special exhibits.

At the Marine base at Quantico, Virginia, the aviation branch of the Marine Corps Museum, still under development, which will be housed in historic aircraft hangars, eventually will display airplanes and artifacts portraying Marine aviation history from 1912 to the present. Portions of this museum are now open to the public. Also at Quantico, but not regularly open to the public, is the Marine Corps' comprehensive collection of small arms and automatic weapons. Qualified scholars may apply for permission to examine this collection or items from it. The Marine Corps still photograph and motion picture archives, located at Quantico under the administrative cognizance of the Marine Corps Historical Center, contains millions of feet of Marine-related newsreel, training, and documentary film, some of which dates back to World War I.

RESEARCH OPPORTUNITIES. In spite of the public visibility and heroic military record of the Marine Corps, scholarly exploration of its history is only just beginning. Most Marine Corps history thus far has been "autobiographical" in nature, produced either by serving or retired Marines or by official Marine Corps historians. While many of these works are of high quality, they inevitably reflect a particular point of view and ask a limited range of questions. The field is wide open for "biographical" treatment of Marine Corps development by historians not emotionally or officially tied to the corps. Opportunities are especially extensive in institutional, political, and social areas of Marine history.

Space does not permit a comprehensive listing of untouched Marine Corps topics. Most prominent Marines still lack adequate biographies, and collective social histories of the officer corps and enlisted force are badly needed. The long commandancy of Archibald Henderson (1820–59), who did much to shape the foundations of the Marine Corps as a distinct service, requires thorough examination. Studies are needed of the development of the Marine Corps' relationship to the navy. Even more enlightening would be a thorough examination of the Corps' long-standing support in Congress, which has helped the Marines overcome repeated executive branch threats to their organizational survival.

Marine officer professionalization, as well as the development of the Marine Corps Schools, still await detailed study. A comprehensive history of marine aviation, emphasizing organization, manpower, equipment, and mission, from 1912 to the present, has yet to be written. Marine Corps recruiting and recruit training are yet another open field for research. While Isley and Crowl (138) deal adequately with the development of marine amphibious doctrine and tactics in the 1930s and 1940s, much more work is required on the period 1900–1929, particularly on the process by which the marines moved from a defensively oriented advance-base force to the offensively directed Fleet Marine Force. The organizational response of the Marine Corps to the manpower and logistic requirements of the Caribbean and Central American interventions awaits unified treatment, as do the command relations between the Marines, the Navy, and the State Department in these campaigns. Many aspects of post-1945 Marine Corps history are an unploughed field.

BIBLIOGRAPHY

1. Abbot, Willis J. *Soldiers of the Sea: the Story of the United States Marine Corps.* New York: Dodd, Mead, 1919.
2. Allard, Dean C., and Betty Bern. *U. S. Naval History Sources in the Washington Area and Selected Research Subjects.* Washington, D.C.: Naval History Division, 1970.
3. Anderson, Charles R. *The Grunts.* San Rafael, Calif.: Presidio Press, 1976.
4. *Army and Navy Journal.* New York, 1863–1950.
5. Asprey, Robert B. *At Belleau Wood.* New York: G. P. Putnam's Sons, 1965.
6. Arthur, Robert A., and Kenneth Cohlmia. *The Third Marine Division.* Washington, D.C.: Infantry Journal Press, 1948.
7. Barde, Robert E. *The History of Marine Corps Competitive Marksmanship.* Washington, D.C.: Marksmanship Branch, G-3 Division, Headquarters U.S. Marine Corps, 1961.
8. Barnett, George. "Soldier and Sailor, Too." Unpublished manuscript. Washington, D.C.: History and Museums Division, Headquarters U.S. Marine Corps, n.d.
9. Bartley, Whitman S. *Iwo Jima: Amphibious Epic.* Washington, D.C.:

Historical Branch, G-3 Division, Headquarters U.S. Marine Corps, 1954.

10. Batchelder, Sydney H., and David A. Quinlan. "Operation Eagle Pull." *Marine Corps Gazette,* May 1976, 47-60.

11. Bauer, K. Jack. "The Korean Expedition of 1871." *U.S. Naval Institute Proceedings,* February 1948, 197-203.

12. Bauer, K. Jack. *Surfboats and Horse Marines: U. S. Naval Operations in the Mexican War, 1846-1848.* Annapolis: U.S. Naval Institute, 1969.

13. Bauer, K. Jack, and Alvin C. Coox. "Olympic vs Ketsu-Go." *Marine Corps Gazette,* August 1965, 32-44.

14. Belote, James H. and William M. *Typhoon of Steel: the Battle of Okinawa.* New York: Harper and Row, 1970.

15. Berger, Kenneth. *The March King and His Band: the Story of John Philip Sousa.* New York: Exposition Press, 1957.

16. Binkin, Martin, and Jeffrey Record. *Where Does the Marine Corps Go from Here?* Washington, D.C. Brookings Institution, 1976.

17. Bivins, Harold A. *An Annotated Bibliography of Naval Gunfire Support.* Washington, D.C.: Historical Division, Headquarters U.S. Marine Corps, 1971.

18. Blakeney, Jane. *Heroes, U. S. Marine Corps, 1861-1955.* Washington, D.C.: Blakeney Publishers, 1957.

19. Blankfort, Michael. *The Big Yankee: the Life of Carlson of the Raiders.* Boston: Little, Brown, 1947.

20. Blechman, Barry M., and Stephen S. Kaplan. *The Use of Armed Forces as a Political Instrument.* Washington, D.C.: The Brookings Institution, 1976.

21. Boggs, Charles W., Jr. *Marine Aviation in the Philippines.* Washington, D.C.: Historical Division, Headquarters U.S. Marine Corps, 1951.

22. Boyd, Thomas. *Points of Honor.* New York: Charles Scribner's Sons, 1925.

23. Boyd, Thomas. *Through the Wheat.* New York: Charles Scribner's Sons, 1927.

24. Boyington, Gregory. *Baa, Baa Black Sheep.* New York: Putnam, 1958.

25. Boyle, Martin. *Yanks Don't Cry.* New York: Random House, 1963.

26. Brown, Wilburt S. *The Amphibious Campaign for West Florida and Louisiana, 1814-1815: A Critical Review of Strategy and Tactics at New Orleans.* University, Ala.: University of Alabama Press, 1969.

27. Buker, George E. *Swamp Sailors: Riverine Warfare in the Everglades, 1835-1842.* Gainesville, Fla.: The University Presses of Florida, 1975.

28. Burrus, L. D. *The Ninth Marines: A Brief History of the Ninth Marine Regiment.* Washington, D.C.: Infantry Journal Press, 1946.

29. Caidin, Martin. *Golden Wings: A Pictorial History of the United States Navy and Marine Corps in the Air.* New York: Random House, 1960.

30. Calder, Bruce J. "*Caudillos* and *Gavilleros* versus the U. S. Marines in the Dominican Intervention, 1916-1924." *Hispanic-American Historical Review* 58 (November, 1978): 649-75.

31. Callahan, Edward W., ed. *List of Officers of the Navy of the United*

States and of the Marine Corps from 1775 to 1900. New York: L. R. Hamersly Co., 1901.

32. Caputo, Philip D. *A Rumor of War.* New York: Holt, Rinehart and Winston, 1977.

33. Carey, Richard E., and David A. Quinlan. "Frequent Wind: Planning." *Marine Corps Gazette,* March 1976, pp. 35–45.

34. Carey, Richard E., and David A. Quinlan. "Frequent Wind: Organization and Assembly." *Marine Corps Gazette,* February 1976, pp. 16–24.

35. Carey, Richard E., and David A. Quinlan. "Frequent Wind: Execution." *Marine Corps Gazette,* April 1976, pp. 35–45.

36. Cass, Bevan C. *History of the Sixth Marine Division.* Washington, D.C.: Infantry Journal Press, 1948.

37. Catlin, Albertus W. *"With the Help of God and a Few Marines."* Garden City: Doubleday, Page, 1919.

38. Chadwick, French Ensor. *The Relations of the United States and Spain: The Spanish-American War.* 2 vols. New York: Charles Scribner's, 1911.

39. Champie, Elmore A. *Brief History of the Marine Corps Base and Recruit Depot, San Diego, California.* Washington, D.C.: Historical Branch, G-3 Division, Headquarters U.S. Marine Corps, 1959.

40. Champie, Elmore. *A Brief History of the Marine Corps Recruit Depot, Parris Island, South Carolina, 1891–1962.* Washington, D.C.: Historical Branch, G-3 Division, Headquarters U.S. Marine Corps, 1962.

41. Chapin, John C. *The Fifth Marine Division in World War II.* Washington, D.C.: Historical Division, Headquarters, U.S. Marine Corps, 1945.

42. Chapin, John C. *The Fourth Marine Division in World War II.* Washington, D.C.: Historical Division, Headquarters, U.S. Marine Corps, 1945.

43. Church, Frank L. *Civil War Marine: A Diary of the Red River Expedition, 1864.* Edited and annotated by James P. Jones and Edward F. Keuchel. Washington, D.C.: History and Museums Division, Headquarters U.S. Marine Corps, 1975.

44. Churley, Robert A. "The North China Operation." *Marine Corps Gazette,* October 1947, pp. 10–16; November 1947, pp. 17–22.

45. Clifford, Kenneth J. *Progress and Purpose: A Developmental History of the United States Marine Corps, 1900–1970.*

46. Clifford, Kenneth J. *The United States Marines in Iceland, 1941–1942.* Rev. ed. Washington, D.C.: Historical Division, U.S. Marine Corps, 1970.

47. Coker, Charles F. *Register of the Henry Clay Cochrane Papers, 1809–1957.* Quantico, Va.: U.S. Marine Corps Museum, 1968.

48. Colby, Chester M. "The United States Marines in the Penobscot Bay Expedition, 1779." *Marine Corps Gazette,* December 1918, pp. 281–92.

49. Collins, Frank C., Jr. "Maritime Support of the Campaign in I Corps." *Naval Review 1971* (Annapolis: U.S. Naval Institute, 1971), pp. 156–79.

50. Collum, Richard S. *History of the United States Marine Corps.* 2d ed. New York: Hamersly, 1903.

51. Condit, Kenneth W., Gerald Diamond, and Edwin T. Turnbladh. *Marine Corps Ground Training in World War II.* Washington, D.C.: Historical Branch, G-3 Division, Headquarters U.S. Marine Corps, 1956.

52. Condit, Kenneth W., and John H. Johnstone. *A Brief History of Marine Corps Staff Organization.* Washington, D.C. Historical Branch, G-3 Division Headquarters U.S. Marine Corps, 1963.

53. Condit, Kenneth W., and Edwin T. Turnbladh. *Hold High the Torch: A History of the 4th Marines.* Washington, D.C.: Historical Branch, G-3 Division, Headquarters U.S. Marine Corps, 1960.

54. Conn, Stetson, Rose C. Engleman, and Byron Fairchild. *Guarding the United States and Its Outposts. United States Army in World War II—The Western Hemisphere.* Washington, D.C.: Office of the Chief of Military History, U.S. Army, 1964.

55. Connor, Howard M. *The Spearhead: the World War II History of the 5th Marine Division.* Washington, D.C.: Infantry Journal Press, 1950.

56. Cooper, Norman M. "The Military Career of General Holland M. Smith, USMC." Ph.D. dissertation, The University of Alabama, 1974.

57. Corson, William R. *The Betrayal.* New York: W. W. Norton and Co., Inc., 1968.

58. Cosmas, Graham A., ed. *Marine Flyer in France: The Diary of Captain Alfred A. Cunningham, November 1917–January 1918.* Washington, D.C.: History and Museums Division, Headquarters U.S. Marine Corps, 1974.

59. Craige, John H. *Black Baghdad.* New York: Minton, Balch, and Company, 1928.

60. Craige, John H. *Cannibal Cousins.* New York: Minton, Balch, and Company, 1934.

61. Crane, Aimee. *Marines at War.* New York: Hyperion Press, 1943.

62. Creswell, John. *Generals and Admirals: the Story of Amphibious Command.* London: Longmans, Green, 1952.

63. Crowl, Philip A. *Campaign in the Marianas. United States Army in World War II—the War in the Pacific.* Washington, D.C.: Office of the Chief of Military History, U.S. Army, 1960.

64. Cummins, Lejeune. *Quijote on a Burro: Sandino and the Marines, a Study of the Formulation of Foreign Policy.* Berkeley: the author, 1958.

65. Cunningham, Winfield S. *Wake Island Command.* Boston: Little, Brown, 1961.

66. Dare, James A. "Dominican Diary." *U. S. Naval Institute Proceedings,* December 1965, pp. 36–54.

67. Davis, Burke. *Marine! The Life of Lieutenant General Lewis B. (Chesty) Puller, USMC (ret).* Boston: Little, Brown, 1962.

68. Davis, Doris S., comp. *Register of the John Lloyd Broome Papers, 1849–1898.* Quantico, Va.: U.S. Marine Corps Museum, 1972.

69. Davis, Doris S., comp. *Register of the Levi Twiggs Papers, 1834–1850.* Quantico, Va.: U.S. Marine Corps Museum, n.d.

70. Davis, Doris S., comp. *Register of the George C. Reid Papers, 1898–1960.* Quantico, Va.: U.S. Marine Corps Museum, n.d.

71. Davis, Doris S., and Jack B. Hilliard, comps. *Register of the Samuel Miller Papers, 1814–1856.* Quantico, Va.: U.S. Marine Corps Museum, n.d.

72. DeChant, John A. *Devilbirds: The Story of United States Marine Corps Aviation in World War II.* New York: Harper and Brothers Publishers, 1947.

73. Devereux, James P.S. *The Story of Wake Island.* Philadelphia: Lippincott, 1947.

74. Devlin, John S., ed. *The Marine Corps in Mexico; Setting forth It's Conduct as Established by Testimony before a General Court Martial. . . .* Washington, D.C.: L. Towers, 1852.

75. Dollen, Charles, and the Library Staff of the University of San Diego. *Bibliography of the United States Marine Corps.* New York: The Scarecrow Press, Inc., 1963.

76. Donnelly, Ralph W. *A Brief History of U. S. Marine Engineers.* Washington: Historical Branch, G-3 Division, Headquarters U.S. Marine Corps, 1968.

77. Donnelly, Ralph W. *An Annotated Bibliography of United States Marine Corps Artillery.* Washington: Historical Division, Headquarters U.S. Marine Corps, 1970.

78. Donnelly, Ralph W. *The History of the Confederate States Marine Corps.* Washington: the author, 1976.

79. Donovan, James A., Jr. *The United States Marine Corps.* New York: Frederick A. Praeger, 1967.

80. Driscoll, John A. *The Eagle, Globe and Anchor, 1868–1968.* Quantico, Va.: Marine Corps Museum, 1971.

81. Duncan, David Douglas. *This is War! A Photo-Narrative in Three Parts.* New York: Harper and Brothers, 1951.

82. Duncan, David Douglas. *War without Heroes.* New York: Harper and Row, 1970.

83. Dyer, George C. *The Amphibians Came to Conquer: the Story of Richmond Kelly Turner.* 2 vols. Washington, D.C.: GPO, 1971.

84. Ellsworth, Harry A. *One Hundred Eighty Landings of United States Marines, 1800–1934.* [1934?] Reprint. Washington, D.C.: History and Museums Division, Headquarters U.S. Marine Corps, 1974.

85. Emmet, Robert. *A Brief History of the 11th Marines.* Washington, D.C.: Historical Branch, G-3 Division, Headquarters U.S. Marine Corps, 1968.

86. Emmons, Roger M. "The First Marine Aviation Force, 1917–1918: Development and Deployment." *Cross and Cockade: the Journal of the Society of World War I Aero Historians,* summer 1965, pp. 173–86; autumn 1965, pp. 272–92.

87. Esposito, Vincent J. *The West Point Atlas of American Wars.* 2 vols. New York: Praeger, 1959.

88. Fails, William R. *Marines and Heliocopters, 1962–1973.* Washington, D.C.: History and Museums Division, Headquarters U.S. Marine Corps, 1978.

89. Fairchild, Byron. "Decision to Land United States Forces in Iceland."

In *Command Decisions,* edited by Kent Roberts Greenfield, pp. 73–97. Washington, D.C.: Office of the Chief of Military History, U.S. Army, 1960.

90. Field, Cyril. *Britain's Sea-Soldiers: A History of the Royal Marines.* 2 vols. Liverpool: The Lyceum Press, 1924.

91. Fleming, Peter. *The Siege at Peking.* New York: Harper and Brothers, 1959.

92. Foss, Joe, and Walter Simmons. *Joe Foss, Flying Marine: The Story of His Flying Circus.* New York: Books, Inc., 1943.

93. Frances, Anthony A. *History of the Marine Corps Schools.* Quantico, Va.: USMC, 1945.

94. Frank, Benis M. *A Brief History of the 3d Marines.* Washington, D.C.: Historical Branch, G-3 Division, Headquarters U.S. Marine Corps, 1961.

95. Frank, Benis M. *Denig's Demons and How They Grew: The Story of Marine Corps Combat Correspondents, Photographers and Artists.* Washington, D.C.: Marine Corps Combat Correspondents and Photographers' Association, Inc., 1967.

96. Frank, Benis M. *Marine Corps Oral History Collection Catalog.* Washington, D.C.: History and Museums Division, Headquarters U.S. Marine Corps, 1973.

97. Frank, Benis M. *Okinawa: The Great Island Battle.* New York: E. P. Dutton and Company. 1978.

98. Frank, Benis M. *Okinawa: Touchstone to Victory.* New York: Ballantine Books, 1970.

99. Fuller, Stephen M., and Graham A. Cosmas. *Marines in the Dominican Republic, 1916-1924.* Washington, D.C.: History and Museums Division, Headquarters U.S. Marine Corps, 1974.

100. Furer, Julius A. *Administration of the Navy Department in World War II.* Washington, D.C.: GPO, 1959.

101. Geer, Andrew. *The New Breed: The Story of the U. S. Marines in Korea.* New York: Harper and Brothers, 1952.

102. Giusti, Ernest H. *The Mobilization of the Marine Corps Reserve in the Korean Conflict.* Washington, D.C.: Historical Branch, G-3 Division, Headquarters U.S. Marine Corps, 1967.

103. Glickert, Robert W. "The Role of the United States Marine Corps in the Boxer Rebellion." Master's thesis, American University, 1962.

104. Gordon, Martin K., comp. *Joseph Henry Pendleton, 1860-1942: Register of His Personal Papers.* Washington, D.C.: History and Museums Division, Headquarters U.S. Marine Corps, 1975.

105. Gordon, Martin K., comp. *Register of the Louis McCarty Little Papers, 1878-1960, and Undated.* Quantico, Va.: U.S. Marine Corps Museum, 1971.

106. Gordon, Martin K., comp. *Register of the Wilburt Scott Brown Papers, 1900-1968.* Quantico, Va.: U.S. Marine Corps Museum, 1973.

107. Graves, Charles. "'And Saint David'—Comrades in Arms." *Marine Corps Gazette,* March 1951, pp. 58–59.

108. Griffith, Samuel B. *The Battle for Guadalcanal.* New York: Lippincott, 1963.

109. Halsey, William F. *Admiral Halsey's Story*. New York: McGraw-Hill, 1947.

110. Hamersly, Lewis R. *The Records of Living Officers of the U. S. Navy and Marine Corps*. 6 vols. Philadelphia: L. R. Hamersly, 1870, 1878, 1890, 1894, 1898, 1902.

111. Hanks, C. C. "A Cruise for Gunpowder," *United States Naval Institute Proceedings,* March 1939, pp. 324–27.

112. Hawkins, Jack. *Never Say Die*. Philadelphia: Dorrance and Company, 1961.

113. Hayashi, Saburo and Alvin C. Coox. *Kogun: The Japanese Army in the Pacific War*. Quantico, Va.: Marine Corps Association, 1959.

114. Healy, David F. *Gunboat Diplomacy in the Wilson Era: the U. S. Navy in Haiti, 1915-1916*. Madison: The University of Wisconsin Press, 1976.

115. Heinl, Robert D., Jr. *The Defense of Wake*. Washington, D.C.: Historical Section, Division of Public Information, Headquarters U.S. Marine Corps, 1947.

116. Heinl, Robert D., Jr. *Marines at Midway*. Washington, D.C.: Historical Section, Division of Public Information, Headquarters U.S. Marine Corps, 1948.

117. Heinl, Robert D., Jr., and John A. Crown. *The Marshalls: Increasing the Tempo*. Washington, D.C.: Historical Branch, G-3 Division, Headquarters U.S. Marine Corps, 1954.

118. Heinl, Robert D., Jr."Naval Gunfire Support in Landings." *Marine Corps Gazette,* September 1945, pp. 40–43.

119. Heinl, Robert D., Jr. *Soldiers of the Sea: The United States Marine Corps, 1775-1962*. Annapolis: U. S. Naval Institute, 1962.

120. Heinl, Robert D., Jr. "Target: Iwo." *U. S. Naval Institute Proceedings,* July 1963, pp. 70–82.

121. Heinl, Robert D., Jr. *Victory at High Tide: The Inchon-Seoul Campaign*. Philadelphia: Lippincott, 1968.

122. Herr, Michael. *Dispatches*. New York: Alfred A. Knopf, 1977.

123. Hersey, John. *Into the Valley: A Skirmish of the Marines*. New York: Alfred A. Knopf, 1943.

124. Hewitt, Linda L. *Women Marines in World War I*. Washington, D.C.: History and Museums Division, Headquarters U.S. Marine Corps, 1974.

125. Hicks, Norman W. "U. S. Marine Operations in Korea, 1950-1953, with Special Emphasis on Outpost Warfare." Master's thesis, University of Maryland, 1962.

126. Higgins, Marguerite. *War in Korea: The Report of a Woman Combat Correspondent*. Garden City, N.Y.: Doubleday and Company, Inc., 1951.

127. Hilliard, Jack B., comp. *An Annotated Bibliography of the United States Marine Corps in the First World War*. Washington, D.C.: Historical Branch, G-3 Division, Headquarters U.S. Marine Corps, 1967.

128. Hilliard, Jack B., and Harold A. Bivins. *An Annotated Reading List of United States Marine Corps History*. Washington, D.C.: History and Museums Division, Headquarters U.S. Marine Corps. 1971.

129. Hoffman, Carl W. *Saipan: The Beginning of the End.* Washington, D.C.: Historical Division, Headquarters U.S. Marine Corps, 1950.

130. Hoffman, Carl W. *The Seizure of Tinian.* Washington, D.C.: Historical Division, Headquarters U.S. Marine Corps, 1951.

131. Hooper, Edwin B. *Mobility, Support, Endurance: A Story of Naval Operational Logistics in the Vietnam War, 1965-1968.* Washington, D.C.: G.P.O., 1972.

132. Hough, Frank O. *The Assault on Peleliu.* Washington, D.C.: Historical Division, Headquarters U.S. Marine Corps, 1950.

133. Hough, Frank O. *The Island War: The United States Marine Corps in the Pacific.* Philadelphia: Lippincott, 1947.

134. Hough, Frank O., and John A. Crown. *The Campaign on New Britain.* Washington, D.C.: Historical Branch, G-3 Division, Headquarters U.S. Marine Corps, 1952.

135. Huff, K. P. "Building the Advanced Base at Da Nang." *Naval Review, 1968* (Annapolis: U.S. Naval Institute, 1968), pp. 88-113.

136. Huggett, William T. *Body Count.* New York: Putnam, 1973.

137. Hunt, George P. *Coral Comes High.* New York: Harper and Brothers, 1946.

138. Isely, Jeter A., and Philip A. Crowl. *The U. S. Marines and Amphibious War: Its Theory and Its Practice in the Pacific.* Princeton: Princeton University Press, 1951.

139. Jeffers, Harry P., and Dick Levitan. *See Parris and Die: Brutality in the U. S. Marines.* New York: Hawthorne Books, 1971.

140. Johnson, Edward C. *Marine Corps Aviation: The Early Years, 1912-1940.* Washington, D.C.: History and Museums Division, Headquarters U.S. Marine Corps, 1977.

141. Johnson, J. M., R. W. Austin, and D. A. Quinlan. "Individual Heroism Overcame Awkward Command Relationships, Confusion and Bad Information off the Cambodian Coast." *Marine Corps Gazette,* October 1977, pp. 24-34.

142. Johnson, Maizie, comp. *Records of the United States Marine Corps: National Archives Inventory, Record Group 127.* Washington, D.C.: National Archives and Records Service, 1970.

143. Johnston, Richard W. *Follow Me: The Story of the Second Marine Division in World War II.* New York: Random House, 1948.

144. Johnstone, John H. *A Brief History of the 1st Marines.* Rev. ed. Washington, D.C.: Historical Branch, G-3 Division, Headquarters U.S. Marine Corps, 1960.

145. Johnstone, John H. *A Brief History of the 2d Marines.* Washington, D.C.: Historical Branch, G-3 Division, Headquarters U.S. Marine Corps, 1961.

146. Johnstone, John H. *An Annotated Bibliography of the United States Marines in Guerrilla-Type Actions.* Washington, D.C.: Historical Branch, G-3 Division, Headquarters U.S. Marine Corps, 1961.

147. Johnstone, John H. *United States Marine Corps Parachute Units.* Washington, D.C.: Historical Branch, G-3 Division, Headquarters U.S. Marine Corps, 1961.

148. Jones, E. Alfred. "The American Regiment in the Carthagena Expedition." *Virginia Magazine of History,* January 1922, pp. 1-20.

149. Karsten, Peter. *The Naval Aristocracy: The Golden Age of Annapolis and the Emergence of Modern American Navalism.* New York: Free Press, 1972.

150. Keiser, Gordon W. "The U. S. Marine Corps and Unification, 1944-1947: "The Politics of Survival." Master's thesis, Tufts University, 1971.

151. King, Joseph E. "The Fort Fisher Campaigns, 1864-1865." *U. S. Naval Institute Proceedings,* August 1951, pp. 842-55.

152. Kovic, Ron. *Born on the Fourth of July.* New York: McGraw-Hill, 1976.

153. Larkins, William T. *U. S. Marine Aircraft, 1914-1959.* Concord, Calif.: Aviation History Publications, 1959.

154. *Leatherneck.* Quantico, Va., and Washington, D.C.: 1917-   .

155. Leckie, Robert. *Challenge for the Pacific: Guadalcanal, the Turning Point of the War.* Garden City, N.Y.: Doubleday, 1965.

156. Leckie, Robert. *Helmet for My Pillow.* New York: Random House, 1957.

157. Leckie, Robert. *The March to Glory.* New York: World, 1960.

158. Leckie, Robert. *Strong Men Armed: The United States Marines against Japan.* New York: Random House, 1962.

159. Lejeune, John A. *The Reminiscences of a Marine.* Philadelphia: Dorrance, 1930.

160. Lewis, Charles L. *Famous American Marines.* Boston: D.C. Page and Company, 1950.

161. Lindsay, Robert G. *This High Name: Public Relations and the U. S. Marine Corps.* Madison, Wis.: University of Wisconsin Press, 1956.

162. Lloyd, Malcolm, Jr. "The Taking of the Bahamas by the Continental Navy in 1776." *Pennsylvania Magazine of History and Biography,* July 1925, pp. 349-66.

163 Lodge, O. R. *The Recapture of Guam.* Washington, D.C.: Historical Branch, G-3 Division, Headquarters U.S. Marine Corps, 1954.

164. Lonn, Ella. "The Extent and Importance of Federal Naval Raids on Salt-Making in Florida, 1862-1865," *Florida Historical Society Quarterly,* July 1932, pp. 167-84.

165. Lucas, Jim G. *Combat Correspondent.* New York: Reynal and Hitchcock, 1944.

166. Lyon, Eunice M. "The Unpublished Papers of Major General Smedley Darlington Butler, USMC: A Calendar." Master's thesis, Catholic University of America, 1962.

167. Macaulay, Neill. *The Sandino Affair.* Chicago: Quadrangle Books, 1967.

168. MacDonald, James A., Jr. "The Problems of U. S. Marine Corps Prisoners of War in Korea." Master's thesis, University of Maryland, 1961.

169. Magruder, John H., III. "A Touch of Tradition: Full Color Prints of the Uniforms of the U. S. Marine Corps." *Marine Corps Gazette,* 1954.

170. *Marine Corps Gazette.* Quantico, Va., 1916-   .

171. Marks, Richard E. *The Letters of Pfc. Richard E. Marks, USMC.* Philadelphia: Lippincott, 1967.

172. Marti, Werner H. *Messenger of Destiny: The California Adventures,*

1846-1848, of Archibald H. Gillespie, U. S. Marine Corps. San Francisco: John Howell Books, 1960.

173. Matloff, Maurice. *Strategic Planning for Coalition Warfare, 1943-1944. United States Army in World War II—The War Department.* Washington, D.C.: Office of the Chief of Military History, U.S. Army, 1959.

174. Matloff, Maurice, and Edwin M. Snell. *Strategic Planning for Coalition Warfare, 1941-1942. United States Army in World War II—The War Department.* Washington, D.C.: Office of the Chief of Military History, U.S. Army, 1953.

175. Matt, Paul R., comp. *United States Navy and Marine Corps Fighters, 1918-1962.* Edited by Bruce Robertson. Los Angeles: Aero Publishers, Inc., 1962.

176. McClellan, Edwin N. "History of the United States Marine Corps." 2 vols. Unpublished manuscript. Washington, D.C.: Historical Section, Headquarters U.S. Marine Corps, 1925-1932.

177. McClellan, Edwin N. *Uniforms of the American Marines, 1775-1829.* Reprint. Washington, D.C.: History and Museums Division, Headquarters U.S. Marine Corps, 1974.

178. McClellan, Edwin N. *The United States Marine Corps in the World War.* Washington, D.C.: GPO, 1920.

179. McClellan, Edwin N., and John H. Craige, "American Marines in the Battles of Trenton and Princeton." *Marine Corps Gazette,* September 1921, pp. 279-88.

180. McClintock, Robert. "The American Landing In Lebanon." *U. S. Naval Institute Proceedings,* October 1962, pp. 65-79.

181. McClusker, John J., Jr. "The American Invasion of Nassau in the Bahamas." *American Neptune,* July 1965, pp. 189-217.

182. McCrocklin, James H., comp. *Garde d' Haiti: Twenty Years of Organization and Training by the U. S. Marine Corps.* Annapolis: U.S. Naval Institute, 1956.

183. McCutcheon, Keith B. "Marine Aviation in Vietnam, 1962-1970." *Naval Review, 1971* (Annapolis: U.S. Naval Institute, 1971), pp. 122-55.

184. McKean, William B. *Ribbon Creek.* New York: Dial Press, 1958.

185. McMillan, George. *The Old Breed: A History of the First Marine Division in World War II.* Washington, D.C.: Infantry Journal Press, 1949.

186. Megee, Vernon E. "United States Military Intervention in Nicaragua, 1909-1932." Master's thesis, University of Texas at Austin, 1963.

187. Meid, Pat. *Marine Corps Women's Reserve in World War II.* Washington, D.C.: Historical Branch, G-3 Division, Headquarters U.S. Marine Corps, 1964.

188. Metcalfe, Clyde H. *A History of the United States Marine Corps.* New York: G. P. Putnam's Sons, 1939.

189. *Military Affairs.* Various places, now Manhattan, Kans., 1937– . Cumulative index, 1937-68, and annually thereafter.

190. Miller, John G. "William Freeland Fullam's War with the Corps." *U. S. Naval Institute Proceedings,* November 1975, pp. 37-45.

191. Miller, Thomas G. *The Cactus Air Force.* New York: Harper and Row, 1969.

192. Millett, Allan R. *The United States Marine Corps.* New York: The Free Press, 1980.

193. Millett, Allan R., and B. Franklin Cooling, III. *Doctoral Dissertations in Military Affairs.* Manhattan, Kans.: Kansas State University Library, 1972. Annually thereafter in *Military Affairs.*

194. Millett, Richard. *Guardians of the Dynasty.* Maryknoll, N.Y.: Orbis Books, 1977.

195. Montross, Lynn. *Cavalry of the Sky: The Story of U. S. Marine Combat Helicopters.* New York: Harper and Brothers, 1954.

196. Montross, Lynn. "Money by the Cartload." *Leatherneck,* August 1956, pp. 48–51.

197. Montross, Lynn. *The United States Marines: A Pictorial History.* New York: Rinehart, 1959.

198. Moran, J. B. *Creating a Legend: The Descriptive Catalog of Writing about the U. S. Marine Corps.* Chicago: Moran Andrews, 1973.

197. Morison, Samuel Eliot. *History of United States Naval Operations in World War II.* 15 vols. Boston: Little, Brown, 1948–62.

200. Morison, Samuel Eliot. *Old Bruin: Commodore Matthew C. Perry, 1794–1858.* Boston: Little, Brown, 1967.

201. Morison, Samuel Eliot. *The Two Ocean War: A Short History of the United States Navy in the Second World War.* Boston: Little, Brown, 1963.

202. Morton, Louis, "Army and Marines on the China Station: A Study of Military and Political Rivalry." *Pacific Historical Review,* February 1960, pp. 51–73.

203. Morton, Louis. *Strategy and Command: the First Two Years. United States Army in World War II—The War in the Pacific.* Washington, D.C.: Office of the Chief of Military History, U.S. Army, 1962.

204. Moskin, J. Robert. *The U. S. Marine Corps Story.* New York: McGraw-Hill, 1977.

205. Munro, Dana G. *Intervention and Dollar Diplomacy in the Caribbean, 1900–1921.* Princeton, N.J.: Princeton University Press, 1964.

206. Munro, Dana G. *The United States and the Caribbean Republics, 1921–1933.* Princeton, N.J.: Princeton University Press, 1974.

207. Myers, John T. "Military Operations and Defenses of the Siege of Peking." *U. S. Naval Institute Proceedings,* September 1902, pp. 541–51.

208. Nalty, Bernard C. *A Brief History of Certain Aspects of Manpower Utilization in the Marine Corps.* Washington, D.C.: Historical Branch, G-3 Division, Headquarters U.S. Marine Corps, 1959.

209. Nalty, Bernard C. *Air Power and the Fight for Khe Sanh.* Washington, D.C.: Office of Air Force History, 1973.

210. Nalty, Bernard C. *"At All Times Ready. . . :" The United States Marines at Harper's Ferry and in the Civil War.* Washington, D.C.: Historical Branch, G-3 Division, Headquarters U.S. Marine Corps, 1966.

211. Nalty, Bernard C. *The Barrier Forts: a Battle, a Monument, and a*

Mythical Marine. Washington, D.C.: Historical Branch, G-3 Division, Headquarters U.S. Marine Corps, 1958.

212. Nalty, Bernard C. "Blue and Gray." *Leatherneck,* November 1960, pp. 54–57.

213. Nalty, Bernard C. *Guests of the Conquering Lion: the Diplomatic Mission to Abyssinia, 1903*. Washington, D.C.: Historical Branch, G-3 Division, Headquarters U.S. Marine Corps, 1959.

214. Nalty, Bernard C. *Inspection in the U. S. Marine Corps, 1775–1957*. Washington, D.C.: Historical Branch, G-3 Division, Headquarters U.S. Marine Corps, 1960.

215. Nalty, Bernard C. *Marine Corps Officer Procurement: A Brief History*. Washington: Historical Branch, G-3 Division, Headquarters U.S. Marine Corps, 1958.

216. Nalty, Bernard C. *The United States Marines on Iwo Jima: The Battle and the Flag Raising*. Washington; Historical Branch, G-3 Division, Headquarters U.S. Marine Corps, 1967.

217. Nalty, Bernard C. *The United States Marines in Nicaragua*. Rev. ed. Washington: Historical Branch, G-3 Division, Headquarters U.S. Marine Corps, 1968.

218. Nalty, Bernard C. *The United States Marines in the War with Spain*. Rev. ed. Washington: Historical Branch, G-3 Division, Headquarters U.S. Marine Corps, 1967.

219. Nalty, Bernard C., Truman R. Strobridge, and Edwin T. Turnbladh. *United States Marine Corps Ranks and Grades, 1775–1962*. Washington: Historical Branch, G-3 Division, Headquarters U.S. Marine Corps, 1962.

220. Neufeld, Gabrielle M. *Marines in the Mexican War, 1846–1848*. Washington: History and Museums Division, Headquarters U.S. Marine Corps, forthcoming.

221. Neumann, William L. *America Encounters Japan: From Perry to MacArthur*. Baltimore: Johns Hopkins Press, 1963.

222. Newcomb, Richard F. *Iwo Jima*. New York: Holt, Rinehart and Winston, 1965.

223. Niblack, Albert P. "Operations of the Navy and the Marine Corps in the Philippine Archipelago, 1898–1902." *U. S. Naval Institute Proceedings,* December 1904, pp. 745–53; June 1905, pp. 463–64; September 1905, p. 698.

224. Nichols, Charles S., Jr., and Henry I. Shaw, Jr. *Okinawa: Victory in the Pacific*. Washington, D.C.: Historical Branch, G-3 Division, Headquarters U.S. Marine Corps, 1955.

225. Norwood, W. D., Jr. *John W. Thomason, Jr*. Austin, Tex.: Steck-Vaughn Company, 1969.

226. Oberdorfer, Don. *Tet!* Garden City, N.Y.: Doubleday, 1971.

227. O'Connor, Raymond G. "The U. S. Marines in the 20th Century: Amphibious Warfare and Doctrinal Debates." *Military Affairs,* October 1974, pp. 97–103.

228. O'Connor, Richard. *The Spirit Soldiers: A Historical Narrative of the Boxer Rebellion*. New York: G. P. Putnam's Sons, 1973.

229. O'Quinlivan, Michael. *An Annotated Bibliography of Marines in the*

Civil War. Washington, D.C.: Historical Branch, G-3 Division, Headquarters U.S. Marine Corps, 1961.

230. O'Quinlivan, Michael. *An Annotated Bibliography of the United States Marines in the Boxer Rebellion.* Washington, D.C.: Historical Branch, G-3 Division, Headquarters U.S. Marine Corps, 1961.

231. O'Quinlivan, Michael, and Benis M. Frank. *The Lauchheimer Trophy.* Rev. ed. Washington, D.C.: Historical Branch, G-3 Division, Headquarters U.S. Marine Corps, 1962.

232. O'Quinlivan, Michael, and Jack B. Hilliard. *An Annotated Bibliography of the United States Marine Corps in the Second World War.* Washington, D.C.: Historical Branch, G-3 Division, Headquarters U.S. Marine Corps, 1965.

233. O'Quinlivan, Michael, and Bernard C. Nalty, "Ambush in Samoa." *Leatherneck,* November 1959, pp. 30–31.

234. O'Quinlivan, Michael, and James S. Santelli. *An Annotated Bibliography of the United States Marine Corps in the Korean War.* Rev. ed. Washington: Historical Division, Headquarters U.S. Marine Corps, 1970.

235. Paige, Mitchell. *A Marine Named Mitch: An Autobiography of Mitchell Paige, Colonel, U. S. Marine Corps, Retired.* New York: Vantage Press, 1975.

236. Parker, William D. *A Concise History of the United States Marine Corps, 1775–1969.* Washington, D.C.: Historical Division, Headquarters U.S. Marine Corps, 1970.

237. Parker, William D. *U. S. Marine Corps Civil Affairs in I Corps, Republic of South Vietnam, April 1966 to April 1967.* Washington, D.C.: Historical Division, Headquarters U.S. Marine Corps, 1970.

238. Parrish, Thomas, ed. *Encyclopedia of World War II.* New York: World Publishing Company, 1978.

239. Paul, Doris A. *Navaho Code Talkers.* Philadelphia: The Dorrance Company, 1973.

240. Pierce, Philip N., and Lewis Myers. "The Seven Years' War." *Marine Corps Gazette,* September 1948, pp. 32–38.

241. Pratt, Fletcher. *The Marines' War: An Account of the Struggle for the Pacific from Both American and Japanese Sources.* New York: Sloane, 1948.

242. Proehl, Carl W. *The Fourth Marine Division in World War II.* Washington, D.C.: Infantry Journal Press, 1946.

243. Quirk, Robert E. *An Affair of Honor: Woodrow Wilson and the Occupation of Vera Cruz.* Lexington: University of Kentucky Press, 1962.

244. Rankin, Robert H. *Small Arms of the Sea Services.* New Milford, Conn.: N. Flayderman, 1972.

245. Rankin, Robert H. *Uniforms of the Sea Services: A Pictorial History.* Annapolis: U.S. Naval Institute, 1962.

246. Rawlins, Eugene W. *Marines and Helicopters, 1946–1962.* Washington, D.C.: History and Museums Division, Headquarters U.S. Marine Corps, 1976.

247. Reber, John J. "Pete Ellis: Amphibious Warfare Prophet." *U. S. Naval Institute Proceedings,* November 1977, pp. 53–64.

248. Rees, David. *Korea: The Limited War.* New York: St. Martin's Press, 1964.

249. Rentz, John N. *Bougainville and the Northern Solomons.* Washington, D.C.: Historical Section, Division of Public Information, Headquarters U.S. Marine Corps, 1948.

250. Rentz, John N. *Marines in the Central Solomons.* Washington, D.C.: Historical Branch, G-3 Division, Headquarters U.S. Marine Corps, 1952.

251. Reynolds, John G. *Conclusive Exculpation of the Marine Corps in Mexico . . . and Collateral Documents.* New York: Stringer and Townsend, 1853.

252. Ringler, Jack K., and Henry I. Shaw, Jr. *U. S. Marine Corps Operations in the Dominican Republic, April-June 1965.* Washington, D.C.: Historical Division, Headquarters U.S. Marine Corps, 1970.

253. Robillard, Fred S. *As Robie Remembers.* Bridgeport, Conn.: Wright Investors' Service, 1969.

254. Roe, Thomas G., et al. *A History of Marine Corps Roles and Missions, 1775-1962.* Washington, D.C.: Historical Branch, G-3 Division, Headquarters U.S. Marine Corps, 1962.

255. Roth, Robert. *Sand in the Wind.* Boston: Little, Brown, 1973.

256. Rowan, Ray. *The Four Days of Mayaguez.* New York: W. W. Norton and Company, Inc., 1975.

257. Rowell, Ross E. "Aircraft in Bush Warfare." *Marine Corps Gazette,* September 1929, pp. 180-203.

258. Russ, Martin. *Happy Hunting Ground.* New York: Atheneum, 1968.

259. Russ, Martin. *The Last Parallel: A Marine's War Journal.* New York: Rinehart and Company, 1957.

260. Russ, Martin. *Line of Departure: Tarawa.* Garden City, N.Y.: Doubleday and Company, Inc., 1975.

261. Russell, William H. "The Genesis of Fleet Marine Force Doctrine." *Marine Corps Gazette,* April-July 1951, November 1955.

262. Santelli, James S. *An Annotated Bibliography of the United States Marine Corps' Concept of Close Air Support.* Washington, D.C.: Historical Branch, G-3 Division, Headquarters U.S. Marine Corps, 1968.

263. Santelli, James S. *A Brief History of the 4th Marines.* Washington, D.C.: History and Museums Division, Headquarters U.S. Marine Corps, 1970.

264. Santelli, James S. *A Brief History of the 8th Marines.* Washington, D.C.: History and Museums Division, Headquarters U.S. Marine Corps, 1976.

265. Schaffer, Ronald. "The 1940 Small Wars Manual and the 'Lessons of History.'" *Military Affairs,* April 1972, pp. 46-51.

266. Schmidt, Hans R. *A Biography of Smedley D. Butler.* Bloomington, Ind.: Indiana University Press, forthcoming.

267. Schmidt, Hans R. *The United States Occupation of Haiti, 1915-1934.* New Brunswick, N.J.: Rutgers University Press, 1971.

268. Schott, Joseph L. *The Ordeal of Samar.* Indianapolis, Ind.: Bobbs-Merrill, 1964.

269. Schuon, Karl. *Home of the Commandants.* Rev. ed. Washington, D.C.: Leatherneck Association, 1974.
270. Schuon, Karl, ed. *U. S. Marine Corps Biographical Dictionary.* New York: Watts, 1963.
271. Shaw, Henry I., Jr. "Penobscot Assault—1779." *Military Affairs,* summer, 1953, pp. 83–94.
272. Shaw, Henry I., Jr. *Tarawa: A Legend Is Born.* New York: Ballantine Books, 1969.
273. Shaw, Henry I., Jr. *The United States Marines in North China, 1945–1949.* Washington, D.C.: Historical Branch, G-3 Division, Headquarters U.S. Marine Corps, 1960.
274. Shaw, Henry I., Jr. *The United States Marines in the Occupation of Japan.* Washington, D.C.: Historical Branch, G-3 Division, Headquarters U.S. Marine Corps, 1961.
275. Shaw, Henry I., Jr., and Ralph W. Donnelly. *Blacks in the Marine Corps.* Washington, D.C.: History and Museums Division, Headquarters U.S. Marine Corps, 1975.
276. Sheldon, Walter J. *Hell or High Water: MacArthur's Landing at Inchon.* New York: Macmillan, 1968.
277. Sherrod, Robert L. *History of Marine Corps Aviation in World War II.* Washington, D.C.: Combat Forces Press, 1952.
278. Sherrod, Robert L. *Tarawa: The Story of a Battle.* New York: Duell, Sloan, and Pearce, 1954.
279. Shore, Moyers S. *The Battle for Khe Sanh.* Washington, D.C.: GPO, 1969.
280. Shulimson, Jack. "First to Fight: Marine Corps Expansion, 1914–1918." *Prologue,* spring 1976, pp. 5–16.
281. Shulimson, Jack. *Marines in Lebanon.* Washington, D.C.: Historical Branch, G-3 Division, Headquarters U.S. Marine Corps, 1968.
282. Shulimson, Jack, and Charles M. Johnson. *U. S. Marines in Vietnam, 1965: The Landing and the Buildup.* Washington, D.C: History and Museums Division, Headquarters U.S. Marine Corps, 1978.
283. Simmons, Edwin H. "The Federals and Fort Fisher." *Marine Corps Gazette,* January 1951, pp. 52–59; February 1951, pp. 46–53.
284. Simmons, Edwin H. *The United States Marines, 1775–1975.* New York: The Viking Press, 1976.
285. Sims, Edward H. *Greatest Fighter Missions of the Top Navy and Marine Aces of World War II.* New York: Harper, 1962.
286. Smelser, Marshall. *The Congress Founds the Navy, 1787–1789.* South Bend: University of Notre Dame Press, 1959.
287. Smith, Charles R. *A Brief History of the 12th Marines.* Washington, D.C.: Historical Division, Headquarters U.S. Marine Corps, 1972.
288. Smith, Charles R. *Marines in the Revolution: A History of the Continental Marines in the American Revolution, 1775–1783.* Washington, D.C.: History and Museums Division, Headquarters U.S. Marine Corps, 1975.
287. Smith, Holland M., and Percy Finch. *Coral and Brass.* New York: Scribner, 1949.
290. Smith, Julian C., et al. *A Review of the Organization and Operations*

of the Guardia Nacional de Nicaragua. Quantico, Va.: Marine Corps Schools, 1937.

291. Smith, Stanley E. *The United States Marine Corps in World War II: The One-Volume History, from Wake to Tsingtao, by the Men Who Fought in the Pacific and by Distinguished Marine Experts, Authors, and Newspapermen.* New York: Random House, 1969.

292. Soper, James B. "A View from FMFPac of Logistics in the Western Pacific, 1965-1971." *Naval Review, 1972* (Annapolis: U.S. Naval Institute, 1972), pp. 222-39.

293. Spanier, John W. *The Truman-MacArthur Controversy and the Korean War.* New York: Norton, 1965.

294. Sprout, Harold and Margaret. *The Rise of American Naval Power, 1776-1918.* Princeton: Princeton University Press, 1946.

295. Sprout, Harold and Margaret. *Toward a New Order of Sea Power.* Princeton: Princeton University Press, 1946.

296. Stockman, James B. *The Battle for Tarawa.* Washington, D.C.: Historical Section, Division of Public Information, Headquarters U.S. Marine Corps, 1947.

297. Stolfi, Russell H. *U. S. Marine Corps Civic Action Efforts in Vietnam, March 1965-March 1966.* Washington, D.C.: Historical Branch, G-3 Division, Headquarters U.S. Marine Corps, 1968.

298. Strobridge, Truman R. *An Annotated Bibliography of the United States Marines in American Fiction.* Washington, D.C.: Historical Branch, G-3 Division, Headquarters U.S. Marine Corps, 1963.

299. Strobridge, Truman R. *A Brief History of the 9th Marines.* Washington, D.C.: Historical Branch, G-3 Division, Headquarters U.S. Marine Corps, 1961.

300. Sweetman, Jack. *The Landing at Vera Cruz, 1914: The First Complete Chronicle of a Strange Encounter in April 1914, when the United States Navy Captured and Occupied the City of Vera Cruz, Mexico.* Annapolis: U.S. Naval Institute, 1968.

301. Tan, Chester C. *The Boxer Catastrophe.* New York: Columbia University Press, 1955.

302. Thomas, Gerald C., Robert D. Heinl, Jr., and Arthur A. Ageton. *The Marine Officer's Guide.* 3rd ed., rev. Annapolis: U.S. Naval Institute, 1967.

303. Thomas, Lowell. *Old Gimlet Eye: The Adventures of Smedley D. Butler.* New York: Farrar and Rhinehart, 1933.

304. Thomason, John W., Jr. *—And a Few Marines.* New York: Charles Scribner's Sons, 1943.

305. Thomason, John W., Jr. *Fix Bayonets!* New York: Charles Scribner's Sons, 1925.

306. Tregaskis, Richard. *Guadalcanal Diary.* New York: Blue Ribbon Books, 1943.

307. Turnbull, Archibald D., and Clifford L. Lord. *History of United States Naval Aviation.* New Haven: Yale University Press, 1949.

308. Tyson, Carolyn A., ed. *The Journal of Frank Keeler, Guantanamo Bay, Cuba, 1898.* Quantico, Va.: Marine Corps Museum, 1968.

309. Tyson, Carolyn A., comp. *Marine Amphibious Landing in Korea, 1871.* Washington, D.C.: Naval Historical Foundation, 1966.

310. Tyson, Carolyn A., and Rowland P. Gill, comps. *An Annotated Bibliography of Marines in the American Revolution.* Washington, D.C.: Historical Division, Headquarters U.S. Marine Corps, 1972.

311. U.S. Congress. *American State Papers: Documents, Legislative and Executive, of the Congress of the United States.* 38 vols. Washington, D.C.: Gales and Seaton, 1832-61.

312. U.S. Congress. House. *Seizure of the Mayaguez. Hearings before the Committee on International Relations and Its Subcommittee on International Political and Military Affairs.* 4 parts. 94th Cong., 1st sess., 1975.

313. U.S. Congress. Senate *Inquiry into the Occupation and Administration of Haiti and Santo Domingo.* 2 vols. Washington, D.C.: GPO, 1921-22.

314. U.S. Department of Defense. *United States-Vietnam Relations, 1945-1967.* 12 vols. Washington, D.C.: GPO, 1971.

315. U.S. Joint Logistics Review Board. *Logistic Support in the Vietnam Era: A Report.* Washington, D.C.: The Board, 1970.

316. U.S. Marine Corps. *Combined Lineal List of Officers on Active Duty in the Marine Corps.* Washington, D.C.: GPO, 1943-   .

317. U.S. Marine Corps. *Small Wars Manual: United States Marine Corps, 1940.* 1940. Reprint with an introduction by Ronald Schaffer. Manhattan, Kans.: MA/AH, 1977.

318. U.S. Marine Corps. Division of Reserve. *The Marine Corps Reserve: A History.* Washington, D.C.: U.S. Marine Corps, Division of Reserve, 1966.

319. U.S. Marine Corps. Historical Branch, G-3 Division, Headquarters U.S. Marine Corps. *Marine Corps Aircraft, 1913-1965.* Rev. ed. Washington, D.C.: The Branch, 1967.

320. U.S. Marine Corps. Historical Branch, G-3 Division, Headquarters U.S. Marine Corps. *Marine Corps Lore.* Washington, D.C.: The Branch, 1960.

321. U.S. Marine Corps. Historical Branch, G-3 Division, Headquarters U.S. Marine Corps. *The United States Marines in the Dominican Republic, Haiti, and Nicaragua: A Bibliography of Published Works and Magazine Articles.* Washington, D.C.: The Branch, 1958.

322. U.S. Marine Corps. Historical Division, Headquarters U.S. Marine Corps. *Marine Corps Historical Bibliographies.* Washington, D.C.: The Division, 1961-   .

323. U.S. Marine Corps. Historical Section, Headquarters U.S. Marine Corps. "Samuel Nicolas, the First Marine Officer." *Marine Corps Gazette,* December 1925, pp. 194-96.

324. U.S. Marine Corps. History and Museums Division, Headquarters U.S. Marine Corps. *A Chronology of the United States Marine Corps.* 4 vols. Washington: History and Museums Division, Headquarters U.S. Marine Corps, 1965-   .

325. U.S. Marine Corps. History and Museums Division, Headquarters U.S. Marine Corps. *History of U. S. Marine Corps Operations in World War II.* 5 vols. Washington: 1958-1971.

    325a.   Vol. 1. Hough, Frank O., Verle E. Ludwig, and Henry I. Shaw, Jr. *Pearl Harbor to Guadalcanal.* Washington:

Historical Branch, G-3 Division, Headquarters U.S. Marine Corps, 1958.

325b.   Vol. 2. Shaw, Henry I., Jr., and Douglas T. Kane. *Isolation of Rabaul.* Washington: Historical Branch, G-3 Division, Headquarters U.S. Marine Corps, 1963.

325c   Vol. 3. Shaw, Henry I., Jr., Bernard C. Nalty, and Edwin T. Turnbladh. *Central Pacific Drive.* Washington: Historical Branch, G-3 Division, Headquarters U.S. Marine Corps, 1966.

325d.   Vol. 4. Garand, George W., and Truman R. Strobridge. *Western Pacific Operations.* Washington: Historical Division, Headquarters U.S. Marine Corps, 1971.

325e.   Vol. 5. Frank, Benis M., and Henry I. Shaw, Jr. *Victory and Occupation.* Washington: Historical Branch, G-3 Division, Headquarters U.S. Marine Corps, 1968.

326.   U.S. Marine Corps. History and Museums Division, Headquarters U.S. Marine Corps. *The Marines in Vietnam, 1954-1973: An Anthology and Annotated Bibliography.* Washington, D.C.: The Division, 1974.

327.   U.S. Marine Corps. History and Museums Division, Headquarters U.S. Marine Corps. *U.S. Marine Operations in Korea, 1950-1953.* 5 vols. Washington: 1954-1972.

327a.   Vol. 1. Montross, Lynn, and Nicholas A. Canzona. *The Pusan Perimeter.* Washington: Historical Branch, G-3 Division, Headquarters U.S. Marine Corps, 1954.

327b.   Vol. 2. Montross, Lynn, and Nicholas A. Canzona. *The Inchon-Seoul Operation.* Washington: Historical Branch, G-3 Division, Headquarters U.S. Marine Corps, 1955.

327c.   Vol. 3. Montross, Lynn, and Nicholas A. Canzona. *The Chosin Reservoir Campaign.* Washington: Historical Branch, G-3 Division, Headquarters U.S. Marine Corps, 1957.

327d.   Vol. 4. Montross, Lynn, Hubard D. Kuokka, and Norman W. Hicks. *The East-Central Front.* Washington: Historical Branch, G-3 Division, Headquarters U.S. Marine Corps, 1962.

327e.   Vol. 5. Meid, Pat, and James M. Yingling. *Operations in West Korea.* Washington: Historical Branch, G-3 Division, Headquarters U.S. Marine Corps, 1972.

328.   U.S. Marine Corps. Fleet Marine Force Pacific. *Operations of U.S. Marine Forces, Vietnam, 1965-1971.* Camp Smith, Hawaii: Fleet Marine Force Pacific, 1965-71.

329.   *U.S. Naval Institute Proceedings.* Annapolis, 1874–   .

330.   U.S. Navy Department. *Annual Report of the Secretary of the Navy.* Washington, D.C.: Various publishers, 1821-1948.

331.   U.S. Navy Department. Bureau of Naval Personnel. *The History of the Chaplain Corps, United States Navy.* Vol. 6, *During the Korean War, 27 June 1950-27 June 1954.* Washington, D.C.: GPO, 1960.

332.   U.S. Navy Department. *Official Records of the Union and Confeder-*

ate Navies in the War of the Rebellion. 30 vols. Washington, D.C.: GPO, 1894–1921.

333. U.S. Navy. Bureau of Navigation. *Register of Commissioned and Warrant Officers of the United States Navy and Marine Corps and Reserve Officers on Active Duty.* Washington, D.C.: GPO and various publishers, 1798– .

334. U.S. Navy Department. Office of Naval Records and Library. *Naval Documents Related to the Quasi-War between the United States and France.* 7 vols. Washington, D.C.: GPO, 1935–38.

335. U.S. Navy Department. Office of Naval Records and Library. *Naval Documents Related to the United States Wars with the Barbary Powers.* 6 vols. Washington, D.C.: GPO, 1939–44.

336. U.S. Navy Department. Office of Naval Records and Library. *Register of Officer Personnel, United States Navy and Marine Corps, and Ships' Data, 1801–1807.* Washington, D.C.: GPO, 1945.

337. U.S. Pacific Command. *Report on the War in Vietnam as of 30 June 1968.* Washington, D.C.: GPO, 1969.

338. U.S. State Department. *Papers Relating to the Foreign Relations of the United States.* Washington, D.C.: GPO, 1861– .

339. Updegraph, Charles L. *U. S. Marine Corps Special Units of World War II.* Washington, D.C.: Historical Division, Headquarters U.S. Marine Corps, 1972.

340. Uris, Leon. *Battle Cry.* New York: G. P. Putnam's Sons, 1953.

341. Van Deurs, George. *Wings for the Fleet.* Annapolis: U.S. Naval Institute, 1961.

342. Vandegrift, Alexander A., and Robert B. Asprey. *Once a Marine: The Memoirs of General A. A. Vandegrift, U. S. Marine Corps.* New York: Norton, 1964.

343. Walt, Lewis W. *Strange War, Strange Strategy: A General's Report on Vietnam.* New York: Funk and Wagnalls, 1970.

344. Webb, James. *Fields of Fire.* Englewood Cliffs, N.J.: Prentice-Hall, 1978.

345. West, Francis J. *Small Unit Action in Vietnam, Summer 1966.* Washington, D.C.: History and Museums Division, Headquarters U.S. Marine Corps, 1967.

346. West, Francis J. *The Village.* New York: Harper and Row, 1972.

347. West, Lucy (Brewer). *The Female Marine, or Adventures of Miss Lucy Brewer. . . .* 5th ed. 1817. Reprint (with an introduction by Alexander Medlicott, Jr.). New York: Da Capo Press, 1966.

348. Westmoreland, William C. *A Soldier Reports.* Garden City, N.Y.: Doubleday and Company, Inc., 1976.

349. White, John A. *The United States Marines in North China.* Millbrae, Calif.: John A. White, 1974.

350. Whitlow, Robert H. *U. S. Marines in Vietnam: The Advisory and Combat Assistance Era, 1954–1964.* Washington, D.C.: GPO, 1977.

351. Whitney, Courtney. *MacArthur: His Rendezvous with Destiny.* New York: Alfred A. Knopf, 1956.

352. Wiegand, Wayne A. "The Lauchheimer Controversy: A Case of Group Political Pressure during the Taft Administration." *Military Affairs,* April 1976, pp. 54–59.

353. Willock, Roger. *Lone Star Marine: A Biography of the Late Colonel John W. Thomason, Jr., USMC.* Princeton: the author, 1961.
354. Willock, Roger. *Unaccustomed to Fear: A Biography of the Late General Roy S. Geiger, USMC.* Princeton: the author, 1968.
355. Willoughby, Charles A., and John Chamberlain. *MacArthur, 1941–1951.* New York: McGraw-Hill, 1954.
356. Wirkus, Faustin, and Taney Dudley. *The White King of La Gonaive.* Garden City, N.Y.: Garden City Publishing Company, 1931.
357. Wise, Frederic M., and Meigs O. Frost. *A Marine Tells It to You.* New York: J. H. Sears and Company, Inc., 1929.
358. Witty, Robert M. *The Story of Camp Pendleton and the Leathernecks Who Train on a Famous California Ranch: Marines of the Margarita.* San Diego, Calif.: Frye and Smith, Ltd., 1970.
359. Wood, Charles Anthony. *Marine Corps Personal Papers Collection Catalog.* Washington, D.C.: History and Museums Division, Headquarters U.S. Marine Corps, 1974.
360. Wood, Charles A., and Jack B. Hilliard, comps. *Register of the McLane Tilton Papers, 1861–1914.* Quantico, Va.: U.S. Marine Corps Museum, n.d.
361. Yingling, James M. *A Brief History of the 5th Marines.* Washington, D.C.: Historical Branch, G-3 Division, Headquarters U.S. Marine Corps, 1963.
362. Zimmerman, John L. *The Guadalcanal Campaign.* Washington, D.C.: Historical Section, Division of Public Information, Headquarters U.S. Marine Corps, 1949.

ARCHIVES AND MANUSCRIPT REPOSITORIES

363. Hoover Institution of War, Revolution, and Peace, Palo Alto, California 92605.
364. James C. Breckinridge Library, Marine Corps Development and Education Command, Quantico, Virginia 22134.
365. Library of Congress, Manuscript Division, Washington, D.C. 20540.
366. U.S. Marine Corps Historical Center, Building 58, Washington Navy Yard. Mailing address: Code HD, Headquarters U.S. Marine Corps, Washington, D.C. 20380.
367. U.S. National Archives, 8th St. and Pennsylvania Ave., NW, Washington, D.C. 20408.
368. Operational Archives, U.S. Naval History Division, Bldg. 210, Washington Navy Yard, Washington, D.C. 20374.

XXI

NUCLEAR WAR AND ARMS CONTROL

Calvin L. Christman

When the first atomic bomb lit the sky on 16 July 1945 near Alamogordo, New Mexico, the world faced a weapon of almost limitless force. As some scientists at the site hugged and danced in their spontaneous celebration of a successful test, others were more thoughtful about the power they had unleashed. Physicist J. Robert Oppenheimer, as he watched the glowing cloud climb into the early morning air, thought of the sacred Hindu meditation from the *Bhagavad-Gita:*

> If the radiance of a thousand suns
> Were to burst at once into the sky,
> That would be like the splendor
>   of the Mighty One . . .
> I am become Death
> The shatterer of worlds.

Though often repeated, the quotation has lost none of its meaning in the years since that first test, and much of the world's effort since that day has been toward understanding the implications of nuclear weapons and finding the means to negate that Hindu prophecy.

In studying the literature in this field, the reader should be aware of chapters X, XVI, and XVII in the 1975 edition of this *Guide* and chapters X, XV, XVI, and XVIII of the present volume. For reasons of unity some of the more important works from these chapters have been repeated in this essay. Others, however, have not been; nor, because of the overlap, have lists of indexes, congressional hearings, and manuscript collections been repeated. Thus, the reader should not neglect these other chapters. Research for this essay ended in the fall of 1978.

REFERENCE WORKS AND PERIODICALS. Neville Brown's *Nuclear War* (41) and Albert Legault and George Lindsey's more recent *The Dynamics of the Nuclear Balance* (143) provide helpful introductions to the subject of East-West nuclear balance. The International Institute for Strategic Studies in London compiles two authoritative annuals, *The Military Balance* (326), particularly emphasizing the armed forces of NATO and Warsaw Pact nations, and *Strategic Survey* (327), with special stress on strategic developments. The Stockholm International Peace Research Institute (SIPRI) also produces *World Armaments and Disarmament* (328), an important annual that includes tables, charts, and a select bibliography. In addition, SIPRI publishes other works on specific armament topics which will be discussed elsewhere in this essay. Lastly, the recently initiated *Strategic Studies Reference Guide* (329) furnishes a comprehensive abstracting of articles in the field.

Since 1945, a number of publications have given important consideration to nuclear weaponry, strategy, and arms control. Foremost among these have been the *Adelphi Papers* (330), *Bulletin of the Atomic* Scientists (338), *Foreign Affairs* (345), *Foreign Policy* (346), *Journal of Conflict Resolution* (352), *Orbis* (357) and *Survival* (363); and all of the aforementioned have had a considerable role in exploring and shaping postwar nuclear thought. Though discussion of strategic issues seemed to wane in the late 1960s during the Vietnam Conflict, the mid-1970s marked a renewal of interest, with the appearance of a number of new publications devoting major portions to these issues: *AEI Defense Review* (331), *Comparative Strategy* (342), *International Security* (350), *Strategic Review* (362), and *Washington Review of Strategic and International Studies* (366). Additionally, some coverage can be found in various military journals, including *Air Force Magazine* (333), *Air University Review* (334), *Military Review* (355), *Naval War College Review* (356), *Parameters* (358), and *United States Naval Institute Proceedings* (364), as well as in such civilian academic journals as *Aerospace Historian* (332), *Military Affairs* (354), and *World Politics* (367). *Scientific American* (361) sometimes includes important articles on technical aspects of nuclear war and weaponry, as do the trade journals *Aviation Week and Space Technology* (337), *Flight International* (344), and *Interavia* (348). Valuable material on arms control and disarmament can be found in *Arms Control Today* (366), *Bulletin of Peace Proposals* (339), *Disarmament News & Views* (343), *Instant Research on Peace and Violence* (347), *Journal of Peace Research* (353), *Peace and Change: A Journal of Peace Research* (359), *Peace Research Abstracts Journal* (360), and *War/Peace Report* (365). Though the Library of Congress no longer publishes *Arms Control and Disarmament* (335), it is still valuable for understanding arms control thought and trends in the 1960s and early 1970s.

Publications giving attention to civil defense concerns include *Civil Defense Technical Reports* (340), *Civil Preparedness Today: Foresight* (341), *International Civil Defense* (349), and *Journal of Civil Defense* (351).

NUCLEAR DEVELOPMENT. Essential for an understanding of the development of the atomic bomb is volume one of Hewlett and Anderson's *A History of the United States Atomic Energy Commission* (111). This detailed official history is buttressed by extensive notes and a full bibliography. Though completed in 1945, Smyth's official report (228) on the Manhattan District is still helpful. More extensive material on the fission bomb's development can be found in *Manhattan Project: Official History and Documents* (154), which makes available some ten thousand pages of documents declassified in 1976, and in a shorter edited collection of primarily technical information, *The Secret History of the Atomic Bomb* (40). Congress (295) has compiled the public laws, legislative histories, international agreements, and other materials dealing with atomic energy. Groves (106), Compton (379), and Lilienthal (148) supply memoirs of the atomic bomb's development and the early days of nuclear power.

The use of the bomb on Hiroshima and Nagasaki has generated intense debate among historians. Though some have argued that the bomb understandably was seen by policymakers as a legitimate weapon to end the war quickly and without a sanguinary invasion of Japan, others have perceived the bomb as a diplomatic weapon used for its possible impression not on Japan, but on the Soviet Union. As a result, the latter conclude that the bomb did not echo the last shot of World War II, but sounded the first shot of the cold war. Though a detailed discussion of this controversy is outside the constraints of this chapter, various elements of this debate can be found in works by Amrine (3), Bernstein (22,23), Alperovitz (2), Giovannitti and Freed (87), Blackett (26), Stimson and Bundy (234), Baldwin (6), Feis (76), Kolko (138), Schoenberger (216), and Sherwin (220), the last including an excellent essay on primary sources that will benefit anyone initiating research on the early history of atomic policy. Fogelman (78), Bernstein (21), and Baker (5) have edited collections of essays on the decision to use the bomb; the last two authors include excellent bibliographical essays of secondary literature. Bernstein also explores this historiographical controversy in an article in *Peace and Change* (20).

Warner Schilling's classic article "The H-Bomb Decision: How to Decide without Actually Choosing" (215) and the authoritative second volume of Hewlett and Duncan's *History of the United States Atomic Energy Commission* (112) furnish the best treatment of the decision to develop the hydrogen bomb. Conflicting views on the wisdom of building this weapon came from two giants within the world of nuclear scientists, Edward Teller and J. Robert Oppenheimer. Herbert York, a noted scientist himself and past scientific advisor to the White House, explores this intense debate in *The Advisors* (277) and concludes that Oppenheimer, who counseled against the bomb's development, was correct. Within his discussion, York also provides insights into the rivalry between the Lawrence Livermore Laboratory and Los Alamos Scientific Laboratory. Other works relating to the sharp controversy that swirled around the bomb, these men, and the internal and external security of the nation can be found in works by Strauss (242), Davis (66), Michelmore (157), Wilson (268), Moss (161), and Blumberg and Owens (28). Basic to one's understanding of the entire subject of the bomb are the security hearings published by the Atomic Energy Commission, *In the Matter of J. Robert Oppenheimer* (284).

NUCLEAR THOUGHT. One of the phenomena occurring in the postwar era was that most of the serious strategic thinking about the implications of nuclear weapons came from civilians, not the military. These strategists, often trained in political science or mathematics and based within universities or private "think tanks" such as the RAND Corporation, led the way toward a theory and science of nuclear strategy. Reaching their height of impact in the late 1950s and early 1960s, the writings of these civilians seemed to subside as the United States involvement in Vietnam deepened. By that time, some of the theorists held positions within the government which reduced their freedom of expression and linked them with establishment policies. Others came under attack for fostering a callous theory of pseudo-mathematics and science that left no place for humanity's emotion, morality, or history. In addition, American nuclear strength seemed unrivaled and secure, and Southeast Asia rather than strategic problems held the attention of the country. With the end of the United States entanglement in Vietnam, the loss of its strategic superiority over the Soviet Union, and the search for substantial arms control, strategists again surfaced, but with more caution and humility than before, for the answers to controlling weapons and preventing war no longer seemed so facile and sure.

Harry Coles's "Strategic Studies since 1945: The Era of Overthink" (59) presents a concise survey and discussion of major strategic thinkers, a subject also covered in articles by Bull (46), Gray (96), and Quester (195). Roy Licklider's *The Private Nuclear Strategists* (146) is the best book on the subject. Supported by an excellent bibliography, Licklider analyzes the characteristics of this movement. Colin Gray's "Across the Nuclear Divide—Strategic Studies, Past and Present" (92) stresses that theorists need to explore the continuity rather than discontinuity of the pre- and postnuclear world. Thus, a study of security problems before 1945 may help in understanding and anticipating the problems of today. Quester lends support to this advice in his important *Deterrence before Hiroshima* (197), arguing that inchoate deterrent theory existed before 1945 and, under the pressures of war, mutual restraints broke down. Thus, rationality may not necessarily be able to control events, a point also argued by Sallager's *The Road to Total War* (211). Similar to Quester's work, this book studies German-British bombing during World War II and its escalation from counterforce (military forces) to countervalue (cities) targeting; it speculates that a similar irrational escalation would occur in a general war today.

The best discussions of past and present strategic thought and issues are found in John Baylis' *Contemporary Strategy* (12) and Jerome Kahan's *Security in the Nuclear Age* (122). Pfaltzgraff in "The Evolution of American Nuclear Thought" (185) and Brodie in "The Development of Nuclear Strategy" (34) give more concise treatments. Coverage of nuclear thought as it had evolved by the mid-1960s can be found in works by Howard (115), Kissinger (133), Aron (4), and Schwarz (217). Moulton's *From Superiority to Parity* (162) and Quester's *Nuclear Diplomacy* (198) survey the overall nuclear environment in which this thought took place, while Gowing (90), Pierre (188), Rosecrance (206), Snyder (231), and Kelleher (128) discuss nuclear thought and policies among American allies.

From its inception, nuclear theory rested on the foundation of deterrence: a potential enemy is deterred from attacking because of the fear or threat of the damage that could be inflicted by a retaliatory nuclear strike. Bernard Brodie was the first to discuss these implications. In an edited group of essays published in 1946 entitled *The Absolute Weapon* (33), Brodie argued that the United States must preserve its ability to retaliate after an attack. Unlike the past, such military capacity would not exist for the purpose of winning a war, but of preventing one. With the overwhelming United States nuclear superiority during the first decade of the nuclear age, few questioned its ability to deter Soviet nuclear aggression. The Korean War and the growing instability within the Third World, however, demonstrated that all conflicts would not be nuclear in nature, and some in the United States, such as Kaufmann (127), Osgood (178), Taylor (245), and Kissinger (135), began to discuss the use of nuclear weapons on a tactical level or the need for a more flexible military force which could check nonnuclear conflicts. Nor was this the only concern of strategic thinkers. The Soviets had developed a nuclear strike force of their own, and the launching of Sputnik in 1957 had underscored that fact. In his influential article of 1959 entitled "The "Delicate Balance of Terror" (270), Albert Wohlstetter argued that deterrence must take this Soviet capacity into account. The United States retaliatory force relied on strategic bombers, Wohlstetter pointed out, yet these unprotected bombers could not survive a surprise Soviet attack, since they could be destroyed on their runways. Thus, the bomber force in reality possessed an ability only to initiate a war (first-strike), rather than to retaliate after an attack (second-strike). The insecurity of the bombers made deterrence disturbingly imbalanced by rewarding a nation that could strike first. Rather than deterring war, the very vulnerability of the bomber force could evoke one. Bernard Brodie, who had worked with Wohlstetter in the RAND Corporation, presented some of these same points in *Strategy in the Missile Age* (37). If deterrence were to succeed, Brodie argued, the United States must have a secure second-strike force, adequate civil defense preparation, and an ability to manage nonnuclear threats. Oskar Morgenstern, a Princeton economist, also discussed the need for an invulnerable deterrent in *The Question of National Defense* (160), and pushed for an "Oceanic System" of submarines and seaplanes as the answer.

The early 1960s saw the continuation of the debate. Thomas Schelling's *The Strategy of Conflict* (213) explored the theory of threats as it related to international relations. He analyzed bargaining and the inherent logic involved in the threat of nuclear violence in *Arms and Influence* (212). Snyder's *Deterrence and Defense* (229) noted the often-ignored relationship between the two ideas, pointing out that a military strategy designed to deter war might not be the best for defense if a war did occur. And nuclear war was not impossible, as Herman Kahn pointed out in his controversial studies, *On Thermonuclear War* (123) and *Thinking about the Unthinkable* (124). Only by serious thinking about nuclear war, Kahn argued, could it be prevented. And, if prevention proved impossible, the United States must know what options to follow in fighting and surviving such a conflict.

This period also saw exploration of arms control and disarmament, a subject largely ignored previously by strategic thinkers. In 1961, Schelling and Halperin published *Strategy and Arms Control* (214), arguing that arms control must be seen as part of national strategy, not something outside and separate. In addition, they pointed out that disarmament would not necessarily be a panacea, but might increase instability within international relations rather than decrease it. J. David Singer also studied the link between strategy and arms control in his *Deterrence, Arms Control, and Disarmament* (222), concluding that the United States deterrent force must be finite in size, invulnerable to attack, and controlled in its reaction. Once these conditions were established, the United States could move toward arms control, which would provide the bridge to the ultimate goal of disarmament.

These authors were not without their critics. Robert Strausz-Hupé's *A Forward Strategy for America* (243) called for a policy that would assure military, political, and psychological superiority over Russia, or the United States would not survive. P. M. S. Blackett, a British physicist who was one of the first to question the motives behind the bombing of Hiroshima and Nagasaki, cast doubts on the validity of much of the Western strategic output in his collection of essays, *Studies of War* (27). And Philip Green's *Deadly*

Logic (101), published in 1966, questioned the basic assumptions upon which strategic thinkers had based their analysis.

Current nuclear thought in the 1970s has seemed less theoretical, reflective, and self-assured; instead, it has generally concentrated on technical issues of targeting, weaponry, composition of nuclear forces, arms control, and the specific implications that these issues have on deterrent stability. The clear nuclear lead that the United States held in the early 1960s has been overtaken by the impressive strides made by the Soviet Union, and the two nations find themselves in a rough position of parity, though each holds advantages over the other in certain nuclear capabilities.

Some of these issues receive treatment in Albert Wohlstetter's provocative *Legends of the Strategic Arms Race* (272). Expressing his ideas first in a series of articles in *Foreign Policy* (271, 275), Wohlstetter argues that the United States has consistently underestimated, not overestimated, Soviet developments of nuclear weapons; that major technological improvements of weaponry have increased stability rather than decreased it; and that both the United States budget for strategic weapons and the destructive power of these weapons have declined since the early 1960s, not increased. Nacht's "The Delicate Balance of Error" (164) questions Wohlstetter's conclusions. Paul Nitze (170) disputes the stability of deterrence, believing that the Soviets are aiming for superiority. With the Soviet advantage in missile throw-weight (the size of warheads that can be delivered on a target), Nitze reasons that the United States ability to deter an attack has lessened. Thus, to increase stability, the United States needs to decrease its vulnerability through a mobile retaliatory missile system (MX Missile) and an expanded civil defense program. Lodal (149) answers Nitze's concerns, stating that the importance of throw-weight has been overestimated and that the best solution rests with the Strategic Arms Limitation Talks (SALT). Two RAND studies by Lambeth (140) and Conover (61) cover some of these same issues as they relate to deterrence.

Since the development and deployment of Soviet intercontinental ballistic missiles (ICBMs), the United States has concluded that stable deterrence rests on the concept of mutual assured destruction (MAD), when both sides have the assured ability to inflict unacceptable damage upon the other, even after absorbing a surprise first-strike. As a result, the threat of assured destruction prevents war and maintains deterrent stability. Basic to this idea is the concept that for deterrence to work a nation's retaliatory force must be invulnerable from a first-strike, else it would lose this assured destructive ability. Because of this, deterrence is strengthened if both nations follow a countervalue (cities) rather than counterforce (military forces) strategy. In effect, the cities and people of each country are held hostage by the retaliatory force of the other. Any effort to target a nation's retaliatory force of bombers and missiles rather than the cities is seen as destabilizing; it would imply that an opponent was trying to gain a first-strike advantage over the other by eliminating its ability to strike back and that a war-winning rather than war-deterring policy was being followed.

Some have questioned whether this concept of the 1960s and 1970s can survive the coming decades. Fred Iklé (116) believes that many of the pieces upon which MAD was built have lost their validity and that MAD depends too much on the Soviet perception being identical to that of the United States. As a result, Iklé concludes, the United States should consider counterforce targeting. Van Cleave and Barnett (254) discuss the same point, arguing that a flexible counterforce doctrine is needed if deterrence should collapse, a point made also by then Secretary of Defense Schlesinger (304). Panofsky (180), Scoville (218), and Carter (52) question the wisdom of this reasoning, pointing out that counterforce strategy cannot be distinguished from a first-strike capability that could undermine deterrence. Greenwood and Nacht (104) summarize this debate, and additional comments on the plus and minus points of counterforce strategy come from Hoeber and Hoeber (113), Davis (64), Porro (191), Ball (7), and Snyder (230). Earlier opinions of counterforce strategy, published in the 1960s at a time when Secretary of Defense McNamara expressed some interest in the idea, come from Waskow (263) and Fryklund (82). Kincade (131) and Albert (1), searching for a doctrine that avoids the destabilizing effects of counterforce or the potentially massive civilian casualities of countervalue, propose maintaining deterrence by a minimum nuclear force capable of destroying an opponent's economic infrastructure. Further discussion of targeting, weaponry, and their implications in the future will be covered later in the chapter.

Alexander George and Richard Smoke in *Deterrence in American Foreign Policy* (86) place deterrent theory within an historical context. In their examination of eleven deterrent case studies from the Berlin blockade through the Cuban missile crisis, the authors analyze the basis of deterrent theory, reappraise it, and suggest areas that need modification. Excellent chapter bibliographies support their discussion of both deterrence and the various case studies. Smoke's *War: Controlling Escalation* (227) also rests on an historical foundation, for it looks at five previous wars to determine why some conflicts escalated while others did not. Other examinations of war and deterrence come from Naroll (167) and Morgan (159).

The shape of the nuclear future is explored by Gompert's *Nuclear Weapons and World Politics* (88), which speculates on four different nuclear worlds ranging from nuclear proliferation to a denuclearized world and on the implications they would bring to international relations. Other discussions of nuclear weapons and world affairs come from Williams (264), Nash (168), Rosecrance (207), Erickson (381), Quester (199), and Overholt (179), while Walters (260) and Gray (95) explore geopolitical factors and nuclear strategy.

Within the consideration of nuclear thought, some have questioned the morality both of nuclear strategists and nuclear war. Morton Kaplan's *Strategic Thinking and Its Moral Implications* (126) explores the validity and morality of nuclear analysis in a collection of essays and debates. Anatol Rapoport discusses the same concerns in his *Strategy and Conscience* (202). Nuclear ethics and morality are the subject for Robert Batchelder's *The Irreversible Decision, 1939–1950* (11), with other treatments of war and morality coming from Walzer (261), Cohen (56), Nagle (166), and O'Brien (176), who contributes an extensive bibliography, as does Brown (321).

In viewing the entire question of nuclear war and thought, one should not forget the excellent collection of readings available. Those of Endicott and Stafford (73) and Pranger and Labrie (192) are especially good, while Rosi's (209) and Johnson and Schneider's (120) are also helpful. Knorr looks at the historical dimensions of national security problems in his collection of essays (137), and Brody (38) and the army (315) provide bibliographies on deterrence.

In addition, there are the various materials released by Congress (286, 292, 309, 310).

NUCLEAR WEAPONS. Norman Polmar's *Strategic Weapons* (189) furnishes a concise introduction to the development and deployment of strategic weapons since 1945. Its emphasis is on the weapons themselves rather than on the impact of technological developments upon strategy. More detailed coverage of strategic forces can be found in the chapters on strategic nuclear trends in the volumes by Collins (60, 378) and in the previously mentioned annuals by the International Institute for Strategic Studies (326, 327). Quanbeck and Blechman (194) examine budget implications of strategic forces, while Garwin (83) and Congress (297) provide material on technology. In addition, one should remember the various annual statements published by the Department of Defense (395, 396, 397).

Except for Edmund Beard's *Developing the ICBM* (13, see Chapter XVI) and the release of the full text of the Gaither Report of 1957 (301), little has appeared on ICBM development since the first edition of this *Guide,* though there have been studies of ICBM-related weapons. A possible way to defeat incoming ICBM warheads is the antiballistic missile (ABM), and it generally has been assumed that it was conceived and developed specifically for this purpose. In turn, whereas the ABM was viewed as a way to defeat the ICBM, multiple independently targetable reentry vehicles (MIRVs) were perceived as a way not only to increase the efficacy of a single missile but also to defeat an ABM system. The defense would be swamped by the large numbers of MIRVs entering the atmosphere, thus being unable to intercept them all. That, at least, is the action-reaction explanation of weapons development—the action of building one weapon triggers the reaction of deploying a weapon to defeat it, and so on. Recent work, however, casts doubt on the validity of this view. Ernest Yanarella, *The Missile Defense Controversy* (276), traces the history of the ABM system from Eisenhower to Nixon and argues that technology drove strategy, not the other way around. Ronald Tammen, *MIRV and the Arms Race* (244), concludes that MIRV development flowed from domestic pressures rather than from a response to Soviet ABM development. Greenwood's *Making the MIRV* (102) sheds additional light on the complexities and multiple forces involved in the decision-making process. A scientist's view comes from Herbert York's "The Origins of MIRV" (279).

While previous strategic debates have revolved around "missile gaps" and the development of the ABM, the question of ICBM vulnerability may well be the major issue of the early 1980s. Previously, the inaccuracy of Soviet missiles limited them to a countervalue capacity. Technical improvements, however, have provided them with the accuracy to target individual Minuteman ICBM silos, thus threatening this retaliatory force and furnishing the Soviet ICBMs with a counterforce ability. With the previous larger Soviet warheads coupled to this newfound accuracy, there is a fear that the United States land-based Minuteman ICBM force is no longer invulnerable to a Soviet first-strike. This development erodes the United States ability to retaliate and hence the stability of deterrence. Tsipis (247) and Brown (42) discuss missile accuracy, while Nitze (170), Gray (94, 99), Conover (61), Davis and Schilling (65), Steinbruner and Garwin (233), Ulsamer (252), and McGlinchey and Seelig (156) explore various aspects of the debate, though most articles on strategic issues published in the late 1970s make at least passing reference to the question. Much of the debate centers on whether a theoretical ability of the Soviet Union is, in actuality, either technically possible or strategically rational. Freeman's *U.S. Intelligence and the Soviet Strategic Threat* (80) provides an excellent examination of how the vulnerability issue affects United States intelligence estimates of the Soviet strategic threat.

A possible solution to the problem of Minuteman vulnerability is the deployment of the new MX ICBM. Along with a greater throw-weight and increased accuracy, the MX would be deployed in a mobile configuration (some of the possibilities considered are for the MX to be launched from an airplane, from a rail within a buried trench, or from one of a number of available underground silos or ground-level shelters). Ball and Coleman's "The Land-Mobile ICBM System" (8) surveys some of the possibilities of a mobile system, while Slay (224) and Ulsamer (251) look at the MX itself. Though the MX may lessen the vulnerability anxiety, it creates problems of its own. While its capacity to be hidden and moved increases its ability to survive an attack, this very characteristic increases the problems of arms control, since it is difficult to verify the number of missiles deployed if one cannot find them; it may be difficult to have both secure arms control and land-based invulnerability. Additionally the increased accuracy of the MX provides it with a clear counterforce ability against Soviet missiles, something that Soviet strategists cannot ignore, since a greater proportion of their nuclear force is comprised of land-based missiles than that of the United States. Clearly the resolution of the vulnerability issue has wide ramifications.

Land-based ICBMs have provided only one part of the United States retaliatory force. Another portion has been the B-52 strategic bomber, first deployed in the 1950s. Because of the B-52's advancing age and the increased sophistication of Soviet air defenses, the Air Force pushed the development of the B-1 bomber as a replacement that would keep the manned bomber a viable deterrent force into the next century. Berman (19) looks at the issues in the debate over the bomber, while McCarthy (155) presents the case for its deployment. Quanbeck and Wood argue against the B-1 in *Modernizing the Strategic Bomber* (193), concluding that the B-52 armed with air-launched cruise missiles (ALCMs) and later replaced by a stand-off bomber equipped with ALCMs would be the most effective in terms of cost and performance, a conclusion also reached by President Carter when he cancelled the B-1. With his decision, the cruise missile (a small pilotless air-breathing missile that would approach its target at subsonic speed and very low altitude) assumed increased importance for the United States nuclear force. The implications this weapon holds for both deterrence and arms control are covered by Tsipis (248, 249), Cameron (376), Kennedy (129), Ohlert (177), Vershbow (257) and Burt (47), while Pfaltzgraff and Davis's *The Cruise Missile* (186) argues for its rapid development and deployment free of arms control restrictions. The army provides a short bibliography on this missile (314).

While manned bombers and land-based missiles have comprised two components of the United States retaliatory force, the third part of this traid has been its submarine-launched ballistic missiles (SLBMs). Because the SLBM system can hide beneath the oceans of the world, it possesses near invulnerability from attack, making it an especially effective deterrent. This characteristic would be lost, however, if substantial improvements were made in the field of antisubmarine warfare (ASW) *The Future of the Sea-Based Deterrent* (250) and *Tactical and Strategic Antisubmarine Warfare* (238) conclude that, for the foreseeable future, ASW developments will not threaten the SLBM, thus continuing to make this system the most stable deterrent available. Polmar and Paolucci (190) have also explored the future of the sea-based deterrent. With the cancellation of the B-1 and the increased susceptibility of land-based missiles, Davis (63) and Gray (99) have questioned whether the United States will continue the triad (ICBMs, SLBMs, and bombers) that it has had since the early 1960s or, instead, largely depend on a sea-based retaliatory force. Beyond this current debate over the composition of nuclear forces still lies the uncertain factor of technology, as exemplified by recent talk of laser or particle-beam weapons (181, 182, 205, 226) which could destroy ICBM and SLBM warheads, reopen the ABM controversy, and force a complete reevaluation of deterrent forces and strategy.

The Department of Defense and the Stockholm International Peace Research Institute (SIPRI) furnish the most complete discussion of the possible consequences of nuclear warheads in *The Effects of Nuclear Weapons* (318) and *Weapons of Mass Destruction and the Environment* (239), respectively, with the latter including a valuable bibliography. Other explorations of the topic come from Iklé (117), Winter (269), and Drell (380), while Congress (303, 305) has investigated the possible results of a limited counterforce strike on the United States.

Since the early 1960s, the United States has spent little time or money on considerations of civil defense. To many thinkers, civil defense was not only hopeless in a general nuclear exchange, but also unsettling to deterrence, since a large civil defense program implied that a country believed that a nuclear war was survivable, thus undermining the mutual suicide underpinnings of MAD. By the mid-1970s, however, the Soviets were showing considerable effort in this area, causing speculation that they either no longer believed in the American concept of MAD or never had; instead of working to deter a war, they seemed to be preparing to win one if it should occur. As a result, a considerable debate over civil defense has reopened, as writings by Kincade (130), Kaplan (125, 388), Gouré (89), Broyles (43), Kozicharow (139), and material from Congress (287, 298, 299, 300, 311) and the Department of State (319) indicate.

Not all nuclear warheads are deployed for strategic use. Since the Eisenhower administration, the United States has placed tactical nuclear weapons in Europe for the support of NATO. By the mid-1970s, the number of United States tactical warheads in Europe had reached approximately seven thousand, and NATO had over three thousand tactical delivery vehicles available to use them. The efficacy of such a force for purposes of deterrence, however, has been questioned, for in a NATO-Warsaw Pact conflict the warheads would destroy much of the territory NATO was striving to defend and might cause a rapid escalation of the conflict into a general war. Jeffrey Record, *U.S. Nuclear Weapons in Europe* (203), and William R. Van Cleave and S.T. Cohen, *Tactical Nuclear Weapons* (255), examine these issues and, while not coming to a consensus on all points, call for a reevaluation of United States policy. Joshua and Hahn (121), Holst and Nerlich (114), Dyer (71, 72), Wörner (399), Gray (93), Cohen and Lyons (58), Nitze (389), Brenner (31), Bennett (17), Sinnreich (223), and Congress (285) furnish recent discussions of

NATO and nuclear weapons. The army also has compiled a massive bibliography (313).

Some analysts view the enhanced radiation warhead as a possible way to avoid large-scale collateral damage if nuclear weapons have to be used to defend NATO countries. Popularly called the neutron bomb, this tactical warhead produces relatively little blast or heat damage, but its high-energy radiation can be lethal even through armor. As a result, it might neutralize large Warsaw Pact armor formations without destroying surrounding cities or countryside. Miettinen (158), Vardamis (256), Frye (81), Cohen (57), Shreffler (221), and Kistiakowsky (136) discuss the strong and weak points of this weapon. So far, little attention has been given to the possible use of the neutron warhead as a strategic weapon to neutralize the effectiveness of hardened Soviet civil-defense shelters.

ARMS CONTROL AND SALT. Hedley Bull's *The Control of the Arms Race* (45), originally published in 1961, still provides perhaps the best introduction to the subject of controlling the arms race. Written in terms readily understood by a layman, its analysis stresses the problems of control, rather than solutions. Bechhoefer in *Postwar Negotiations for Arms Control* (15) details arms control efforts from World War II until 1960 and effectively summarizes the views of the major powers; and Noel-Baker covers much of the same time span in *The Arms Race* (173). The fall 1960 issue of *Daedalus,* published in book form as *Arms Control, Disarmament, and National Security* (30), investigates a wide variety of important concerns related to arms control and demonstrates early academic thought on the subject. Chalmers Roberts's *The Nuclear Years* (204) supplies a concise history of the environment in which the first fifteen years of postwar arms discussion took place.

In the summer of 1975, *Daedalus* issued another significant essay collection, published as *Arms, Defense Policy, and Arms Control* (151). Within its study of specific arms control topics, it stresses that inter- and intranational politics have proven far more complex than originally expected, a conclusion supported by other recent studies. Additional collections of essays include those by Carlton and Schaerf (50, 51), Bertram (369), Barton and Weiler (10), Kincade and Porro (132), York (278), Pfaltzgraff (184), Alford (368), Sharp (219), and Benoit and Boulding (18), the last set discussing economic problems that may stem from disarmament.

James Dougherty's *How to Think about Arms Control and Disarmament* (70) is a helpful recent introduction to the subject, while Walter C. Clemens's *The Superpowers and Arms Control* (53) analyzes the perceptions, domestic pressures, motivations, and concerns behind the United States and Soviet positions. Gray covers some of the same material in *The Soviet-American Arms Race* (98), challenges the assumptions of the simple action-reaction causation of the arms race, and points out the major factors that propel an arms race. He concludes with a negative assessment of SALT, believing that it does not reduce the possibility of war and that the United States, instead, must endeavor to regain genuine strategic equivalency with the Soviet Union. An opposite view can be found in works by Cox (62) and Lens (144), who perceive the arms race as caused by the Soviets reacting to the excessive defense spending of the United States. The arms race, therefore, would end if only the United States unilaterally reduced its strategic programs; the Soviets, Cox and

Lens predict, would then follow suit. Becker (16) looks at military spending and arms control, Levine (145) analyzes the various schools of thought regarding arms control, and Spanier and Nogee (232) and Myrdal (163) discuss the politics and gamesmanship of disarmament. Additional thoughts come ·from Gray (100), Bertram (370), Warnke (262), Stone (240, 241), Brodie (373), and Bull (44), while Dupuy and Hammerman, *A Documentary History of Arms Control and Disarmament* (325), and the Arms Control and Disarmament Agency (ACDA) provide collections of documents (282, 283). Burns, *Arms Control and Disarmament* (322), is a major addition to earlier bibliographical listings (324, 312, 320). Added information comes in the annual report of the ACDA (281) and hearings (291) by Congress.

The role played by technology within arms control is examined in Biddle's *Weapons Technology and Arms Control* (24), with particular emphasis placed on the role of warheads and delivery systems. Technology is generally seen as a negative force in limiting arms: Gelber (85) stresses the need for political leaders to gain additional control over the development process; Doty (69) Verification can build controls and concludes that the effort to halt the arms race is being lost; and Brooks (39) believes the limitations on technology would benefit arms control and international security. Wohlstetter (273) questions some of these views in his previously mentioned article "Legends of the Strategic Arms Race" (272).

A key element in any politically acceptable arms control agreement is verification, an ingredient that may be at variance with the need to increase deterrent stability by hiding the retaliatory force, as mentioned before with the MX missile. Barnet and Falk (9) and Wainhouse (259) provided early explorations of verification factors and problems. More recently, Robert Perry in *The Faces of Verification* (183) and SIPRI in *Strategic Disarmament, Verification and National Security* (237) study the subject, while Greenwood (103) comments on a major means of verification, that of space satellites.

In 1963, after an earlier abortive effort to limit atmospheric nuclear testing, the United States, Great Britain, and the Soviet Union agreed to halt all nuclear testing above ground, under water, and in outer space. Robert Divine's *Blowing on the Wind* (68) recreates the intense debate within the United States that preceeded the Test Ban Treaty, while Jacobson and Stein (118), Terchek (246) and Dean (67) discuss the treaty negotiations. Since the 1963 treaty, Congress (308) has pondered the implications of a treaty that would prohibit the below-ground testing allowed under the original agreement, a proposal examined by Westervelt (398), Helm (386), and Brennan (372). The United States and Soviets have decided to ban underground tests of warheads exceeding 150 kilotons (equivalent of 150,000 tons of TNT).

Along with limiting nuclear testing, the United States, Britain, and the Soviet Union in 1968 signed the Non-Proliferation Treaty, an effort to halt the spread of nuclear weapons to nonnuclear powers. The problem of an increasing number of nuclear nations, termed "horizontal proliferation," is covered in a recent issue of the *Annals of the American Academy of Political and Social Science* (174) and in a comprehensive treatment by the SIPRI, *Nuclear Proliferation Problems* (235). An earlier exploration of the situation, published prior to the Non-Proliferation Treaty, can be found in Beaton and Maddox's *The Spread of Nuclear Weapons* (14). Jensen's *Return from the Nuclear Brink* (119) covers all aspects of the treaty; Quester's *The Politics of*

Nuclear Proliferation (200) emphasizes the importance of domestic politics affecting nuclear and near-nuclear nations, while the same author (196) also explores the implications of India's detonation of an atomic bomb in 1974. Epstein (74), Greenwood (105, 385), Hamilton (109), Lawrence and Larus (142), Burt (48), Nye (175), Maddox (153), and Schelling (391) provide additional comments on proliferation.

Part of the Non-Proliferation Treaty concerned the need to see that the peaceful development of nuclear energy in nonnuclear nations did not lead to the acquisition of nuclear weapons. Michael Guhin's *Nuclear Paradox* (107) points out the difficulty of this task, since the same technology serves nuclear-generated electric power and nuclear warheads. Willrich (265) and SIPRI (236) examine the complexities of attempting to construct effective international safeguards; and Willrich and Taylor (266) discuss the increasing risks that, as the number of nuclear power plants increase, terrorist groups might obtain weapons-grade nuclear material; Willrich and Taylor also propose specific guidelines for a safeguard system. In addition to the above, the army (316) has compiled a recent bibliography on the issue of proliferation and there are the usual hearings by Congress (288, 289, 290, 293, 302, 306, 307).

John Newhouse's *Cold Dawn* (169) remains the major study of the negotiations leading to SALT I, signed May 1972 in Moscow, and Willrich and Rhinelander (267) have edited a collection of essays assessing this first agreement. Lewis Frank (79) speculates on the Soviet perspective toward the United States and SALT, and Pfaltzgraff and Davis (187) cast a skeptical look at the effort toward a follow-up agreement (SALT II), fearing that too many advantages will accrue to the Soviet Union. This effort at a second strategic arms pact has generated much debate concerning the potential positive and negative implications of SALT, with articles by Rostow (210), Nitze (171, 172), Gray (97), Hamlett (110), Gelber (84), Burt (49), Bresler and Gray (32), and Nacht (165) indicating the issues and opinions that have been aired. Lord (152), Lodal (150), Slocombe (394), and Rathjens (390) show the key linkage between verification problems and SALT; Coffey in *Arms Control and European Security* (54), Birrenbach (25), and Iklé (387) relate SALT to the security concerns of NATO, with Coffey furnishing an especially comprehensive effort in his treatment of negotiations as they relate to strategic nuclear, theater nuclear, and nonnuclear levels. Burns and Hoffman in *The SALT Era* (323) supply a bibliography, as does the Army (317), and there are hearings by Congress (294).

RESEARCH NEEDED. There exist no full scholarly biographies of such important figures in nuclear development as Gen. Leslie Groves and Edward Teller. There is also a need for a comprehensive history of postwar strategic thought and thinkers. Little work has been done on the oscillations of civil defense discussion or on how films and novels (374, 375, 383, 384, 392, 393, 400, 401) dealing with nuclear catastrophe have affected popular perceptions of nuclear thought and weapons. Though important bits and pieces exist on the interrelationship of technology and strategy, no one has undertaken a full treatment that ties together the development of postwar strategic weaponry, policy, and technology. Additionally, important study remains to be done on the problems of achieving invulnerability of strategic forces, stable deterrence, and verifiable arms control simultaneously.

BIBLIOGRAPHY

ARTICLES AND BOOKS

1. Albert, Bernard. "Constructive Counterpower." *Orbis,* summer 1976.
2. Alperovitz, Gar. *Atomic Diplomacy: Hiroshima and Potsdam.* New York: Simon and Schuster, 1965.
3. Amrine, Michael. *The Great Decision: The Secret History of the Atomic Bomb.* New York: Putnam's, 1959.
4. Aron, Raymond. *The Great Debate: Theories of Nuclear Strategy.* Garden City, N.Y.: Doubleday, 1965.
5. Baker, Paul R., ed. *The Atomic Bomb: The Great Decision.* 2d ed. Hinsdale, Ill.: Dryden, 1976.
6. Baldwin, Hanson W. *Great Mistakes of the War.* New York: Harper & Brothers, 1950.
7. Ball, Desmond J. "The Counterforce Potential of American SLBM Systems." *Journal of Peace Research* 14, no. 1 (1977).
8. Ball, Desmond J., and Edwin Coleman. "The Land-Mobile ICBM System: A Proposal." *Survival,* July/August 1977.
9. Barnet, Richard J., and Richard A. Falk, eds. *Security in Disarmament.* Princeton, N.J.: Princeton University, 1965.
10. Barton, John H., and Lawrence D. Weiler, eds. *International Arms Control: Issues and Agreements.* Stanford, Calif.: Stanford University, 1977.
11. Batchelder, Robert C. *The Irreversible Decision, 1939–1950.* New York: Macmillan, 1961.
12. Baylis, John et al. *Contemporary Strategy: Theories and Policies.* New York: Holmes & Meier, 1975.
13. Beard, Edmund. *Developing the ICBM: A Study in Bureaucratic Politics.* New York: Columbia University, 1976.
14. Beaton, Leonard, and John Royden Maddox. *The Spread of Nuclear Weapons.* New York: Praeger, 1962.
15. Bechhoefer, Bernhard G. *Postwar Negotiations for Arms Control.* Washington, D.C.: Brookings Institution, 1961.
16 Becker, Abraham S. *Military Expenditure Limitation for Arms Control.* Cambridge, Mass.: Ballinger, 1977.
17. Bennett, W. S., R. R. Sandoval, and R. G. Shreffler. "A Credible Nuclear-Emphasis Defense for NATO." *Orbis,* summer 1973.
18. Benoit, Emile, and Kenneth E. Boulding, eds. *Disarmament and the Economy.* New York: Harper and Row, 1963.
19. Berman, Robert. "The B-1 Bomber." In *Current Issues in U.S. Defense Policy,* edited by David T. Johnson and Barry R. Schneider. New York: Praeger, 1976.
20. Bernstein, Barton J. "The Atomic Bomb and American Foreign Policy, 1941–1945: An Historiographical Controversy." *Peace and Change,* spring 1974.
21. Bernstein, Barton J., ed. *The Atomic Bomb: The Critical Issues.* Boston: Little, Brown, 1976.
22. Bernstein, Barton J. "The Quest for Security: American Foreign Policy and International Control of Atomic Energy, 1942–1946." *Journal of American History,* March 1974.

23. Bernstein, Barton J. "Roosevelt, Truman and the Atomic Bomb, 1941–1945: A Reinterpretation." *Political Science Quarterly,* spring 1975.

24. Biddle, W. F. *Weapons Technology and Arms Control.* New York: Praeger, 1972.

25. Birrenbach, Kurt. "European Security: NATO, SALT and Equilibrium." *Orbis,* summer 1978.

26. Blackett, P. M. S. *Fear, War, and the Bomb: Military and Political Consequences of Atomic Energy.* New York: McGraw-Hill, 1948.

27. Blackett, P. M. S. *Studies of War: Nuclear and Conventional.* New York: Hill and Wang, 1962.

28. Blumberg, Stanley A., and Gwinn Owens. *Energy and Conflict: The Life and Times of Edward Teller.* New York: Putnam's, 1976.

29. Bottome, Edgar M. *The Balance of Terror: A Guide to the Arms Race.* Boston: Beacon, 1971.

30. Brennan, Donald G., ed. *Arms Control, Disarmament, and National Security.* New York: George Braziller, 1961.

31. Brenner, Michael. "Tactical Nuclear Stategy and European Defense: A Critical Reappraisal." *International Affairs,* January 1975.

32. Bresler, Robert J., and Robert C. Gray. "The Bargaining Chip and SALT." *Political Science Quarterly,* spring 1977.

33. Brodie, Bernard, ed. *The Absolute Weapon: Atomic Power and World Order.* Harcourt, Brace, 1946.

34. Brodie, Bernard. "The Development of Nuclear Strategy." *International Security,* spring 1978.

35. Brodie, Bernard. *Escalation and the Nuclear Option.* Princeton, N.J.: Princeton University, 1966.

36. Brodie, Bernard. "Strategic Thinkers, Planners, Decison-Makers." In *War and Politics,* edited by Bernard Brodie. New York: Macmillan, 1973.

37. Brodie, Bernard. *Strategy in the Missile Age.* Princeton, N.J.: Princeton University, 1959.

38. Brody, Richard A. "Deterrence Strategies: An Annotated Bibliography." *Journal of Conflict Resolution,* December 1960.

39. Brooks, Harvey. "The Military Innovation System and the Qualitative Arms Race." *Daedalus,* 104, no. 3 (1975).

40. Brown, Anthony Cave, and Charles B. MacDonald, eds. *The Secret History of the Atomic Bomb.* New York: Dial, 1977.

41. Brown, Neville. *Nuclear War: The Impending Strategic Deadlock.* New York: Praeger, 1965.

42. Brown, Thomas A. "Missile Accuracy and Strategic Lethality." *Survival,* March-April 1976.

43. Broyles, Arthur A., Eugen P. Wigner, and Sidney D. Drell. "Civil Defense in Limited War—A Debate." *Physics Today,* April 1976.

44. Bull, Hedley. "Arms Control and World Order." *International Security,* summmer 1976.

45 Bull, Hedley. *The Control of the Arms Race.* 2d ed. New York: Praeger, 1965.

46. Bull, Hedley. "Strategic Studies and Its Critics." *World Politics,* July 1968.

47. Burt, Richard. "The Cruise Missile and Arms Control." *Survival,* January/February 1976.
48. Burt, Richard. "Nuclear Proliferation and the Spread of New Conventional Weapons Technology." *International Security,* winter 1977.
49. Burt, Richard. "The Scope and Limits of SALT." *Foreign Affairs,* July 1978.
50 Carlton, David, and Carlo Schaerf, eds. *Arms Control and Technological Innovation.* New York: John Wiley, 1977.
51. Carlton, David, and Carlo Schaerf, eds. *The Dynamics of the Arms Race.* New York: John Wiley, 1975.
52 Carter, Barry. "Nuclear Strategy and Nuclear Weapons." *Scientific American,* May 1974.
53. Clemens, Walter C., Jr. *The Superpowers and Arms Control: From Cold War to Interdependence.* Lexington, Mass.: Lexington Books, 1973.
54. Coffey, Joseph I. *Arms Control and European Security: A Guide to East-West Negotiations.* New York: Praeger, 1977.
55. Coffey, Joseph I. *Strategic Power and National Security.* Pittsburgh: University of Pittsburgh, 1971.
56. Cohen, Marshall, Thomas Nagel, and Thomas Scanlon, eds. *War and Moral Responsibility.* Princeton, N.J.: Princeton University, 1974.
57. Cohen, S. T. "Enhanced Radiation Warheads: Setting the Record Straight." *Strategic Review,* winter 1978.
58 Cohen, S.T., and W. C. Lyons. "A Comparison: U.S.-Allied and Soviet Nuclear Force Capabilities and Policies." *Orbis,* spring 1975.
59. Coles, Harry L. "Strategic Studies since 1945: The Era of Overthink." *Military Review,* April 1973.
60. Collins, John M. *American and Soviet Military Trends since the Cuban Missile Crisis.* Washington, D.C.: Georgetown University, 1978.
61. Conover, C. Johnston. *U.S. Stategic Nuclear Weapons and Deterrence.* Santa Monica, Calif.: RAND, 1977.
62. Cox, Arthur Macy. *The Dynamics of Detente: How to End the Arms Race.* New York: W. W. Norton, 1976.
63. Davis, Jacquelyn K. "End of the Strategic Triad?" *Strategic Review,* winter 1978.
64. Davis, Lynn Etheridge. "Limited Nuclear Options: Deterrence and the New American Doctrine." *Adelphi Papers,* no. 121, winter 1975/76.
65. Davis, Lynn Etheridge, and Warner R. Schilling. "All You Ever Wanted to Know about MIRV and ICBM Calculations But Were Not Cleared to Ask." *Journal of Conflict Resolution,* June 1973.
66. Davis, Nuel Pharr. *Lawrence and Oppenheimer.* New York: Simon and Schuster, 1968.
67. Dean, Arthur H. *Test Ban and Disarmament: The Path of Negotiation.* New York: Harper & Row, 1966.
68. Divine, Robert A. *Blowing on the Wind: The Nuclear Test Ban Debate, 1954–1960.* New York: Oxford University, 1978.
69. Doty, Paul, Albert Carnesale, and Michael Nacht. "The Race to Control Nuclear Arms." *Foreign Affairs,* October 1976.

70. Dougherty, James E. *How to Think about Arms Control and Disarmament.* New York: Crane, Russak, 1973.
71. Dyer, Philip W. "Tactical Nuclear Weapons and Deterrence in Europe." *Political Science Quarterly,* summer 1977.
72. Dyer, Philip W. "Will Tactical Nuclear Weapons Ever Be Used?" *Political Science Quarterly,* June 1973.
73. Endicott, Lt. Col. John E., and Maj. Roy W. Stafford, Jr., eds. *American Defense Policy.* 4th ed. Baltimore: Johns Hopkins, 1977.
74. Epstein, William. *The Last Chance: Nuclear Proliferation and Arms Control.* New York: Free Press, 1976.
75. Ermarth, Fritz W. "Contrasts in American and Soviet Strategic Thought." *International Security,* fall 1978.
76. Feis, Herbert. *The Atomic Bomb and the End of World War II.* Princeton, N.J.: Princeton University, 1966.
77. Feld, Bernard T., et al. *Impact of New Technologies on the Arms Race.* Cambridge, Mass.: M.I.T. Press, 1971.
78. Fogelman, Edwin, ed. *Hiroshima: The Decision to Use the A-Bomb.* New York: Scribner's, 1964.
79. Frank, Lewis Allen. *Soviet Nuclear Planning: A Point of View on SALT.* Washington, D.C.: American Enterprise Institute, 1977.
80. Freedman, Lawrence. *U.S. Intelligence and the Soviet Strategic Threat.* Boulder, Colo.: Westview, 1977.
81. Frye, Alton. "Slow Fuse on the Neutron Bomb." *Foreign Policy,* summer 1978.
82. Fryklund, Richard. *100 Million Lives: Maximum Survival in a Nuclear War.* New York: Macmillan, 1962.
83. Garwin, Richard L. "Effective Military Technology for the 1980's." *International Security,* fall 1976.
84. Gelber, Harry G. "SALT and the Strategic Future." *Orbis,* summer 1978.
85. Gelber, Harry G. "Technical Innovations and Arms Control." *World Politics,* July 1974.
86. George, Alexander L., and Richard Smoke. *Deterrence in American Foreign Policy: Theory and Practice.* New York: Columbia University, 1974.
87. Giovannitti, Leon, and Fred Freed. *The Decision to Drop the Bomb.* New York: Coward-McCann, 1965.
88. Gompert, David C., et al. *Nuclear Weapons and World Politics: Alternatives for the Future.* New York: McGraw-Hill, 1977.
89. Gouré, Leon. *War Survival in Soviet Strategy.* Miami: University of Miami, 1976.
90. Gowing, Margaret. *Independence and Deterrence: Britain and Atomic Energy, 1945-1952.* 2 vols. New York: St. Martin's, 1975.
91. Graham, Daniel. "The Intelligence Mythology of Washington." *Strategic Review,* summer 1976.
92. Gray, Colin S. "Across the Nuclear Divide—Strategic Studies, Past and Present." *International Security,* summer 1977.
93. Gray, Colin S. "Deterrence and Defense in Europe: Revising NATO's Theatre Nuclear Posture." *Strategic Review,* spring 1975.

94. Gray, Colin S. "The Future of Land-Based Missile Forces." *Adelphi Papers*, no. 140, winter 1977.

95. Gray, Colin S. *The Geopolitics of the Nuclear Era: Heartland, Rimlands, and the Technological Revolution.* New York: Crane, Russak, 1977.

96. Gray, Colin S. "The Rise and Fall of Academic Strategy." *Journal of the Royal United Services Institute for Defense Studies* 116 (1971).

97. Gray, Colin S. "SALT and the American Mood." *Strategic Review,* summer 1975.

98. Gray, Colin S. *The Soviet-American Arms Race.* Lexington, Mass.: Lexington Books, 1976.

99. Gray, Colin S. "The Strategic Forces Triad: End of the Road?" *Foreign Affairs,* July 1978.

100. Gray, Colin S. "Urge to Compete: Rationales for Arms Racing." *World Politics,* January 1974.

101. Green, Philip. *Deadly Logic: The Theory of Nuclear Deterrence.* Columbus: Ohio State University, 1966.

102. Greenwood, Ted. *Making the MIRV: A Study of Defense Decision Making.* Cambridge, Mass.: Ballinger, 1975.

103. Greenwood, Ted. "Reconnaissance and Arms Control." *Scientific American,* February 1973.

104. Greenwood, Ted, and Michael L. Nacht. "The New Nuclear Debate: Sense or Nonsense?" *Foreign Affairs,* July 1974.

105. Greenwood, Ted, Harold A. Feiveson, and Theodore B. Taylor. *Nuclear Proliferation: Motivations, Capabilities, and Strategies for Control.* New York: McGraw-Hill, 1977.

106. Groves, Leslie R. *Now It Can Be Told: The Story of the Manhattan Project.* New York: Harper, 1962.

107. Guhin, Michael. *Nuclear Paradox: Security Risks of the Peaceful Atom.* Washington, D.C.: American Enterprise Institute, 1976.

108. Hadley, Arthur T. *The Nation's Safety and Arms Control.* New York: Viking, 1961.

109. Hamilton, Michael P., ed. *To Avoid Catastrophe: A Study in Future Nuclear Weapons Policy.* New York: Erdmans, 1977.

110. Hamlett, Bruce D. "SALT: The Illusion and the Reality." *Strategic Review,* summer 1975.

111. Hewlett, Richard G., and Oscar E. Anderson, Jr. *A History of the United States Atomic Energy Commisssion.* Vol. 1, *The New World, 1939–1946.* University Park: Pennslyvania State University, 1962.

112. Hewlett, Richard G., and Francis Duncan. *A History of the United States Atomic Energy Commission.* Vol. 2, *Atomic Shield, 1947–1952.* University Park: Pennslyvania State University, 1969.

113. Hoeber, Amoretta M., and Francis P. Hoeber. "The Case against the Case against Counterforce." *Strategic Review,* fall 1975.

114. Holst, Johan J., and Uwe Nerlich, eds. *Beyond Nuclear Deterrence: New Aims, New Arms.* New York: Crane, Russak, 1977.

115. Howard, Michael. "The Classical Strategists." In *Studies in War and Peace,* edited by Michael Howard. New York: Viking, 1972.

116. Iklé, Fred C. "Can Nuclear Deterrence Last Out the Century?" *Foreign Affairs,* January 1973.

117. Iklé, Fred C. *The Social Impact of Bomb Destruction.* Norman: University of Oklahoma, 1958.
118. Jacobson, Harold Karan, and Eric Stein. *Diplomats, Scientists, and Politicians: The United States and the Nuclear Test Ban Negotiations.* Ann Arbor: University of Michigan, 1966.
119. Jensen, Lloyd. *Return from the Nuclear Brink: National Interest and the Nuclear Nonproliferation Treaty.* Lexington, Mass.: Lexington Books, 1974.
120. Johnson, David T., and Barry R. Schneider, eds. *Current Issues in U.S. Defense Policy.* New York: Praeger, 1976.
121. Joshua, Wynfred, and Walter Hahn. *Nuclear Politics: America, France, and Britain.* Beverly Hills, Calif.: Sage Publications, 1973.
122. Kahan, Jerome H. *Security in the Nuclear Age: Developing U.S. Strategic Arms Policy.* Washington, D.C.: Brookings Institution, 1975.
123. Kahn, Herman. *On Thermonuclear War.* 2d ed. Princeton, N.J.: Princeton University, 1961.
124. Kahn, Herman. *Thinking about the Unthinkable.* New York: Horizon, 1962.
125. Kaplan, Fred M. "Soviet Civil Defense: Some Myths in the Western Debate." *Military Review,* March 1979.
126. Kaplan, Morton A., ed. *Strategic Thinking and Its Moral Implications.* Chicago: University of Chicago, 1973.
127. Kaufmann, William W. ed. *Military Policy and National Security.* Princeton, N.J.: Princeton University, 1956.
128. Kelleher, Catherine McArdle. *Germany and the Politics of Nuclear Weapons.* New York: Columbia University, 1975.
129. Kennedy, Robert. "The Cruise Missile and the Strategic Balance." *Parameters,* March 1978.
130. Kincade, William H. "Repeating History: The Civil Defense Debate Renewed." *International Security,* winter 1978.
131. Kincade, William H. "A Strategy for All Seasons: Targeting Doctrine and Strategic Arms Control." *Bulletin of the Atomic Scientists,* May 1978.
132. Kincade, William H., and Jeffrey D. Porro. *Negotiating Security: An Arms Control Reader.* Washington, D.C.: Carnegie Endowment for International Peace, 1979.
133. Kissinger, Henry A. "American Strategic Doctrine and Diplomacy." In *The Theory and Practice of War,* edited by Michael Howard. Bloomington: Indiana University, 1965.
134. Kissinger, Henry A. *The Necessity for Choice: Prospects of American Foreign Policy.* New York: Harper & Brothers, 1961.
135. Kissinger, Henry A. *Nuclear Weapons and Foreign Policy.* New York: Harper & Brothers, 1957.
136. Kistiakowsky, George B. "Weaponry: The Folly of the Neutron Bomb." *Atlantic Monthly,* June 1978.
137. Knorr, Klaus, ed. *Historical Dimensions of National Security Problems.* Lawrence: University Press of Kansas, 1976.
138. Kolko, Gabriel. *The Politics of War: The World and United States Foreign Policy, 1943-1945.* New York: Random House, 1968.

139. Kozicharow, Eugene. "Nuclear Attack Survival Aspects Studied." *Aviation Week and Space Technology,* 14 November 1977.

140. Lambeth, Benjamin S. *Selective Nuclear Options in American and Soviet Strategic Policy.* Santa Monica, Calif.: RAND, 1976.

141. Larus, Joel. *Nuclear Weapons Safety and the Common Defense.* Columbus: Ohio State University, 1967.

142. Lawrence, Robert M., and Joel Larus, eds. *Nuclear Proliferation: Phase II.* Lawrence: University Press of Kansas, 1974.

143. Legault, Albert, and George Lindsey. *The Dynamics of the Nuclear Balance.* Rev. ed. Ithaca, N.Y.: Cornell University, 1976.

144. Lens, Sidney. *The Day before Doomesday: An Anatomy of the Nuclear Arms Race.* Garden City, N.Y.: Doubleday, 1977.

145. Levine, Robert A. *The Arms Debate.* Cambridge: Harvard University, 1963.

146. Licklider, Roy E. *The Private Nuclear Strategies.* Columbus: Ohio State University, 1971.

147. Liddell Hart B.H. *The Revolution in Warfare.* London: Faber, 1946.

148. Lilienthal, David E. *The Journals of David E. Lilienthal.* Vol. 2, *The Atomic Energy Years, 1945–1950.* New York: Harper & Row, 1964.

149. Lodal, Jan M. "Assuring Strategic Stability: An Alternative View." *Foreign Affairs,* April 1976.

150. Lodal, Jan M. "Verifying SALT." *Foreign Policy,* fall 1976.

151. Long, Franklin A., and George W. Rathjens, eds. *Arms, Defense Policy, and Arms Control.* New York: Norton, 1976.

152. Lord, Carnes. "Verification and the Future of Arms Control." *Strategic Review,* spring 1978.

153. Maddox, John. "Prospects for Nuclear Proliferation." *Adelphi Papers,* no. 113, spring 1975.

154. *Manhattan Project: Official History and Documents.* Washington, D.C.: University Publications of America, 1978. Microfilm.

155. McCarthy, John F., Jr. "The Case for the B-1 Bomber." *International Security,* fall 1976.

156. McGlinchey, Lt. Col. Joseph, and Jacob Seelig. "Why ICBM's Can Survive a Nuclear Attack." *Air Force Magazine,* September 1974.

157. Michelmore, Peter. *The Swift Years: The Robert Oppenheimer Story.* New York: Dodd, Mead, 1969.

158. Miettinen, Jorma K. "Enhanced Radiation Warfare." *Bulletin of the Atomic Scientists,* September 1977.

159. Morgan, Patrick M. *Deterrence: A Conceptual Analysis.* Beverly Hills, Calif.: Sage, 1977.

160. Morgenstern, Oskar. *The Question of National Defense.* New York: Random House, 1959.

161. Moss, Norman. *Men Who Play God: The Story of the Hydrogen Bomb.* Rev. ed. Baltimore: Penguin, 1972.

162. Moulton, Harland B. *From Superiority to Parity: The United States and the Strategic Arms Race, 1961–1971.* Westport, Conn.: Greenwood, 1973.

163. Myrdal, Alva. *The Game of Disarmament: How the United States and Russia Run the Arms Race.* New York: Pantheon, 1977.

164. Nacht, Michael. "The Delicate Balance of Error." *Foreign Policy,* summer 1975.
165. Nacht, Michael L. "The Vladivostok Accord and American Technological Options." *Survival,* May/June 1975.
166. Nagle, William J., ed. *Morality and Modern Warfare: The State of The Question.* Baltimore: Helicon, 1960.
167. Naroll, Raoul, Vern L. Bullough, and Frada Naroll. *Military Deterrence in History: A Pilot Cross-Historical Survey.* New York: State University of New York, 1974.
168. Nash, Henry T. *Nuclear Weapons and International Behavior.* Leyden, The Netherlands: A. W. Sijthoff, 1975.
169. Newhouse, John. *Cold Dawn: The Story of SALT.* New York: Holt, Rinehart and Winston., 1973.
170. Nitze, Paul H. "Assuring Strategic Stability in an Era of Detente." *Foreign Affairs,* January 1976.
171. Nitze, Paul H. "Soviet's Negotiating Style Assayed" and "Nitze Delineates U.S.-Soviet Differences." *Aviation Week and Space Technology,* 17 and 24 February 1975.
172. Nitze, Paul H. "The Vladivostok Accord and SALT." *Review of Politics,* April 1975.
173. Noel-Baker, Philip J. *The Arms Race.* New York: Oceana Publications, 1958.
174. "Nuclear Proliferation: Prospects, Problems, and Proposals." *Annals of the American Academy of Political and Social Science,* March 1977.
175. Nye, Joseph S. "Nonproliferation: A Long-Term Strategy." *Foreign Policy,* April 1978.
176. O'Brien, William V. *Nuclear War, Deterrence, and Morality.* New York: Newman, 1967.
177. Ohlert, Edward J. "Strategic Deterrence and the Cruise Missile." *Naval War College Review,* winter 1978.
178. Osgood, Robert E. *Limited War: The Challenge to American Strategy.* Chicago: University of Chicago, 1957.
179. Overholt, William H., ed. *Asia's Nuclear Future.* Boulder, Colo.: Westview, 1977.
180. Panofsky, Wolfgang K. H. "The Mutual-Hostage Relationship between America and Russia." *Foreign Affairs,* October 1973.
181. Parmentola, John, and Kosta Tsipis. "Particle-Beam Weapons." *Scientific American,* April 1979.
182. *Particle-Beam Weapon Development.* New York: Aviation Week & Space Technology Reprint Department, 1978.
183. Perry, Robert. *The Faces of Verification: Strategic Arms Control for the 1980s.* Santa Monica, Calif.: RAND, 1977.
184. Pfaltzgraff, Robert L., Jr., ed. *Contrasting Approaches to Strategic Arms Control.* Lexington, Mass.: Lexington Books, 1974.
185. Pfaltzgraff, Robert L., Jr. "The Evolution of American Nuclear Thought." *War, Strategy, and Maritime Power.* Edited by B. Mitchell Simpson III. New Brunswick, N.J.: Rutgers University, 1977.
186. Pfaltzgraff, Robert L., Jr., and Jacquelyn K. Davis. *The Cruise*

Missile: Bargaining Chip or Defense Bargain? Cambridge, Mass.: Institute for Foreign Policy Analysis, 1977.

187. Pfaltzgraff, Robert L., Jr., and Jacquelyn K. Davis. *SALT II: Promise or Precipice?* Miami: Center for Advanced International Studies, 1976.

188. Pierre, Andrew J. *Nuclear Politics: The British Experience with an Independent Strategic Force, 1939–1970.* New York: Oxford University, 1972.

189. Polmar, Norman. *Strategic Weapons: An Introduction.* New York: Crane, Russak, 1975.

190. Polmar, Norman, and D. A. Paolucci. "Sea-Based 'Strategic' Weapons for the 1980s and Beyond." *Naval Review 1978* (Annapolis: United States Naval Institute, 1978).

191. Porro, Jeffrey D. "Counterforce and the Defense Budget." *Arms Control Today,* February 1978.

192. Pranger, Robert J., and Roger P. Labrie, eds. *Nuclear Strategy and National Security: Points of View.* Washington, D.C.: American Enterprise Institute, 1977.

193. Quanbeck, Alton H., and Archie L. Wood. *Modernizing the Strategic Bomber Force: Why and How.* Washington, D.C.: Brookings Institution, 1976.

194. Quanbeck, Alton H., and Barry M. Blechman. *Strategic Forces, Issues for the Mid-Seventies.* Washington, D.C.: Brookings Institution, 1973.

195. Quester, George H. "Can Deterrence Be Left to the Deterrent?" *Policy* 7, no. 4 (1975).

196. Quester, George H. "Can Proliferation Now Be Stopped." *Foreign Affairs,* October 1974.

197. Quester, George H. *Deterrence before Hiroshima: The Airpower Background of Modern Strategy.* New York: Wiley, 1966.

198. Quester, George H. *Nuclear Diplomacy: The First Twenty-Five Years.* New York: Dunellen, 1970.

199. Quester, George H. *Offense and Defense in the International System.* New York: Wiley, 1977.

200. Quester, George. *The Politics of Nuclear Proliferation.* Baltimore: Johns Hopkins, 1973.

201. Ramsey, Paul. *The Limits of Nuclear War: Thinking about the Do-Able and the Un-Do-Able.* New York: Council on Religion and International Affairs, 1963.

202. Rapoport, Anatol. *Strategy and Conscience.* New York: Harper & Row, 1964.

203. Record, Jeffrey. *U.S. Nuclear Weapons in Europe: Issues and Alternatives.* Washington, D.C.: Brookings Institute, 1974.

204. Roberts, Chalmers M. *The Nuclear Years: The Arms Race and Arms Control, 1945–1970.* New York: Praeger, 1970.

205. Robinson, Clarence A., Jr. "Soviets Push for Beam Weapon." *Aviation Week and Space Technology,* 2 May 1977.

206. Rosecrance, R. N. *Defense of the Realm: British Strategy in the Nuclear Epoch.* New York: Columbia University, 1968.

207. Rosecrance, Richard, ed. *The Future of the International Strategic System.* San Francisco: Chandler, 1972.
208. Rosecrance, Richard. "Strategic Deterrence Reconsidered." *Adelphi Papers,* no. 116, Spring 1975.
209. Rosi, Eugene J., ed. *American Defense and Détente: Readings in National Security Policy.* New York: Dodd, Mead, 1973.
210. Rostow, Eugene V. "The Case against SALT II." *Commentary,* February 1979.
211. Sallager, Frederick M. *The Road to Total War.* New York: Van Nostrand Reinhold, 1975.
212. Schelling, Thomas C. *Arms and Influence.* New Haven, Conn.: Yale University, 1966.
213. Schelling, Thomas C. *The Strategy of Conflict.* Cambridge: Harvard University, 1960.
214. Schelling, Thomas C., and Morton H. Halperin. *Strategy and Arms Control* New York: Twentieth Century Fund, 1961.
215. Schilling, Warner R. "The H-Bomb Decision: How to Decide without Actually Choosing." *Political Science Quarterly,* March 1961.
216. Schoenberger, Walter Smith. *Decision of Destiny.* Athens: Ohio University, 1969.
217. Schwarz, Urs. *American Strategy: A New Perspective: The Growth of Politico-Military Thinking in the United States.* Garden City, N.Y.: Doubleday, 1966.
218. Scoville, Herbert, Jr.. "Flexible MADness?" *Foreign Policy,* spring 1974.
219. Sharp, Jane M. O., ed. *Opportunities for Disarmament.* Washington, D.C.: Carnegie Endowment for International Peace, 1978.
220. Sherwin, Martin J. *A World Destroyed: The Atomic Bomb and the Grand Alliance.* New York: Knopf, 1975.
221. Shreffler, R. G. "The Neutron Bomb for NATO Defense: An Alternative." *Orbis,* winter 1978.
222. Singer, J. David. *Deterrence, Arms Control, and Disarmament: Toward a Synthesis in National Security Policy.* Columbus: Ohio State University, 1962.
223. Sinnreich, Richard H. "NATO's Doctrinal Dilemma." *Orbis,* summer 1975.
224. Slay, Alton D. "MX: A New Dimension in Strategic Deterrence." *Air Force Magazine,* September 1976.
225. Slessor, Sir John. *The Great Deterrent.* New York: Praeger, 1957.
226. Smernoff, Barry J. "Strategic and Arms Control Implications of Laser Weapons: A Preliminary Assessment." *Air University Review,* January/February 1978.
227. Smoke, Richard. *War: Controlling Escalation.* Cambridge: Harvard University, 1978.
228. Smyth, Henry DeWolf. *Atomic Energy for Military Purposes: The Official Report on the Development of the Atomic Bomb under the Auspices of the United States Government, 1940–45.* Princeton, N.J.: Princeton University, 1945.
229. Snyder, Glen H. *Deterrence and Defense: Toward a Theory of National Security.* Princeton, N.J.: Princeton University, 1961.

230. Snyder, Jack L. *The Soviet Strategic Culture: Implications for Limited Nuclear Operations.* Santa Monica, Calif.: RAND, 1977.
231. Snyder, William P. *The Politics of British Defense Policy, 1945-1962.* Columbus: Ohio State University, 1964.
232. Spanier, John W., and Joseph L. Nogee. *The Politics of Disarmament: A Study in Soviet-American Gamesmanship.* New York: Praeger, 1962.
233. Steinbruner, John D., and Thomas M. Garwin. "Strategic Vulnerability: The Balance between Prudence and Paranoia." *International Security,* summer 1976.
234. Stimson, Henry L., and McGeorge Bundy. *On Active Service in Peace and War.* New York: Harper & Brothers, 1948.
235. Stockholm International Peace Research Institute. *Nuclear Proliferation Problems.* Cambridge, Mass.: M.I.T., 1974.
236. Stockholm International Peace Research Institute. *Safeguards against Nuclear Proliferation.* Cambridge, Mass.: M.I.T., 1975.
237. Stockholm International Peace Research Institute. *Strategic Disarmament, Verification and National Security.* New York: Crane, Russak, 1978.
238. Stockholm International Peace Research Institute. *Tactical and Strategic Antisubmarine Warfare.* Cambridge, Mass.: M.I.T., 1974.
239. Stockholm International Peace Research Institute. *Weapons of Mass Destruction and the Environment.* New York: Crane, Russak, 1977.
240. Stone, Jeremy J. *Containing the Arms Race.* Cambridge, Mass.: M.I.T., 1966.
241. Stone, Jeremy J. *Strategic Persuasion: Arms Limitations through Dialogue.* New York: Columbia University, 1967.
242. Strauss, Lewis L. *Men and Decisions.* Garden City, N. Y.; Doubleday, 1962.
243. Strausz-Hupé, Robert, William R. Kintner, and Stefan T. Possony. *A Forward Strategy for America.* New York: Harper & Brothers, 1961.
244. Tammen, Ronald L. *MIRV and the Arms Race: An Interpretation of Defense Strategy.* New York: Praeger, 1973.
245. Taylor, Gen. Maxwell D. *The Uncertain Trumpet.* New York: Harper & Brothers, 1960.
246. Terchek, Ronald J. *The Making of the Test Ban Treaty.* The Hague: Martinus Nijhof, 1970.
247. Tsipis, Kosta. "The Accuracy of Strategic Missiles." *Scientific American,* July 1975.
248. Tsipis, Kosta. "Cruise Missiles." *Scientific American,* February 1977.
249. Tsipis, Kosta. "The Long-Range Cruise Missile." *The Bulletin of Atomic Scientists,* April 1975.
250. Tsipis, Kosta, Anne H. Cahn, and Bernard T. Feld, eds. *The Future of the Sea-Based Deterrent.* Cambridge, Mass.: M.I.T., 1973.
251. Ulsamer, Edgar. "M-X: The Missile System for the Year 2000." *Air Force Magazine,* March 1973.
252. Ulsamer, Edgar. "Our ICBM Force: The Vulnerability Myth." *Air Force Magazine,* August 1974.
253. Ulsamer, Edgar. "Warhead Design and Nuclear Strategy." *Air Force Magazine,* June 1974.

254. Van Cleave, William R., and Roger W. Barnett. "Strategic Adaptability." *Orbis,* Fall 1974.

255. Van Cleave, William R., and S. T. Cohen. *Tactical Nuclear Weapons: An Examination of the Issues.* New York: Crane, Russak, 1978.

256. Vardamis, Lt. Col. Alex A. "The Neutron Warhead: Stormy Past, Uncertain Future." *Parameters,* March 1978.

257. Vershbow, Alexander R. "The Cruise Missile: The End of Arms Control?" *Foreign Affairs,* October 1976.

258. Wadsworth, James J. *The Price of Peace.* New York: Praeger, 1962.

259. Wainhouse, David W. *Arms Control Agreements: Designs for Verification and Organization.* Baltimore: Johns Hopkins, 1968.

260. Walters, Robert E. *Sea Power and the Nuclear Fallacy: A Reevaluation of Global Strategy.* New York: Holmes & Meir, 1975.

261. Walzer, Michael. *Just and Unjust.* New York: Basic Books, 1977.

262. Warnke, Paul C. "Arms Control: A Global Imperative." *Bulletin of the Atomic Scientists,* June 1978.

263. Waskow, Arthur I. *The Limits of Defense.* Garden City, N.Y.: Doubleday, 1962.

264. Williams, Phil. *Crisis Management: Confrontation and Diplomacy in the Nuclear Age.* New York: Halsted, 1976.

265. Willrich, Mason, ed. *International Safeguards and Nuclear Industry.* Baltimore: Johns Hopkins, 1973.

266. Willrich, Mason, and Theodore B. Taylor. *Nuclear Theft: Risks and Safeguards.* Cambridge, Mass.: Ballinger, 1974.

267. Willrich, Mason, and John B. Rhinelander, eds. *SALT: The Moscow Agreements and Beyond.* New York: Free Press, 1974.

268. Wilson, Thomas W., Jr. *The Great Weapons Heresy.* Boston: Houghton Mifflin, 1970.

269. Winter, Sidney G., Jr. *Economic Viability after Thermonuclear War: The Limits of Feasible Production.* Santa Monica, Calif.: RAND, 1963.

270. Wohlstetter, Albert. "The Delicate Balance of Terror." *Foreign Affairs,* January 1959.

271. Wohlstetter, Albert. "Is There a Strategic Arms Race?" *Foreign Policy,* summer 1974.

272. Wohlstetter, Albert. *Legends of the Strategic Arms Race.* Report 75-1. Washington, D.C.: United States Strategic Institute, 1975.

273. Wohlstetter, Albert. "Legends of the Strategic Arms Race." *Strategic Review,* fall 1974.

274. Wohlstetter, Albert. "Optimal Ways to Confuse Ourselves." *Foreign Policy,* fall 1975.

275. Wohlstetter, Albert. "Rivals, But No 'Race.'" *Foreign Policy,* fall 1974.

276. Yanarella, Ernest J. *The Missile Defense Controversy: Strategy, Technology, and Politics, 1955–1972.* Lexington: University Press of Kentucky, 1977.

277. York, Herbert F. *The Advisors: Oppenheimer, Teller, and the Superbomb.* San Francisco: W. H. Freeman, 1976.

278. York, Herbert F., ed. *Arms Control.* San Francisco: W. H. Freeman, 1973.

279. York, Herbert F. "The Origins of MIRV." In *The Dynamics of the Arms Race,* edited by David Carlton and Carlo Schaerf. New York: John Wiley, 1975.
280. Young, Elizabeth. *A Farewell to Arms Control?* Baltimore: Penguin, 1972.

GOVERNMENT MATERIALS

281. U.S. Arms Control and Disarmament Agency. *Annual Report.* Washington, D.C.: G.P.O., 1978. Title varies, 1962–   .
282. U.S. Arms Control and Disarmament Agency. *Arms Control and Disarmament Agreements: Texts and History of Negotiations.* Washington, D.C.: G.P.O., 1977.
283. U.S. Arms Control and Disarmament Agency. *Documents on Disarmament.* Washington, D.C.: G.P.O., 1961–   .
284. U.S. Atomic Energy Commission. *In the Matter of J. Robert Oppenheimer: Transcript of Hearing before Personnel Security Board.* 12 April–6 May 1954. Washington, D.C.: G.P.O., 1954.
285. U.S. Congress. Congressional Budget Office. *Planning U.S. General Purpose Forces: The Theater Nuclear Forces.* Print. 95th Cong., 1st. Sess. January 1977. Y10. 12: N88.
286. U.S. Congress. Congressional Budget Office. *U.S. Strategic Nuclear Forces: Deterrence Policies and Procurement Issues.* Print. 95th Cong., 1st Sess. April 1977. Y10.12: N88/2.
287. U.S. Congress. House. Committee on Armed Services. Subcommittee on Investigation. *Civil Defense Review. Hearings.* 94th Cong., 2nd Sess. 9 February–9 March 1976, Y4.Ar5/2a: 975–76/42.
288. U.S. Congress. House. Committee on International Relations. *Nuclear Antiproliferation Act of 1977. Hearings.* 95th Cong., 1st Sess. 4 April–2 August 1977. Y4. In8/16: N88/5.
289. U.S. Congress. House. Committee on International Relations. *Nuclear Proliferation Factbook. Print.* 95th Cong., 1st Sess. 23 September 1977. Y4. In8/16: N88/6.
290. U.S. Congress. House. Committee on International Relations. *U.S. Foreign Policy and the Export of Nuclear Technology to the Middle East. Hearings.* 93rd Cong., 2nd Sess. 25 June–16 September 1974. Y4 F76/1: N88.
291. U.S. Congress. House. Committee on International Relations. Subcommittee on International Security. . . . *Arms Control and Disarmament Agency Authorization for FY78. Hearings.* 95th Cong., 1st Sess. 4–20 April 1977. Y4. In8/16: Ar5/2/978.
292. U.S. Congress. House. Committee on International Relations. Subcommittee on International Security. . . . *First Use of Nuclear Weapons: Preserving Responsible Control. Hearings.* 94th Cong., 2nd Sess. 16–25 March 1976. Y4. In8/16: N88/3.
293. U.,S. Congress. House. Committee on International Relations. Subcommittee on International Security. . . . *Nuclear Proliferation: Future U.S. Foreign Policy Implications.* 94th Cong., 1st Sess. 21 October–5 November 1975. Y4. In8/16: N88/2.
294. U.S. Congress. House. Committee on International Relations. Subcommittee on. . . . . Scientific Affairs. *Vladivostok Accord: Implica-*

tions to U.S. Security, Arms Control, and World Peace. Hearings. 94th Cong., 1st Sess. 24 June-8 July 1975. Y4. In8/16: V84.

295. U.S. Congress. Joint Committee on Atomic Energy. *Atomic Energy Legislation, through 94th Congress, 2d Session. Print.* 95th Cong., 1st Sess. March 1977. Y4.At7/2: L52/2/977.

296. U.S. Congress. Joint Committee on Atomic Energy. *Development, Use, and Control of Nuclear Energy for the Common Defense and Security and for Peaceful Purposes. Print.* 94th Cong., 2nd Sess. 30 June 1976. Y4.At7/2: D35/976.

297. U.S. Congress. Joint Committee on Atomic Energy. Subcommittee on Military Applications. *Military Applications of Nuclear Technology. Hearings.* 2 Parts. 93rd Cong., 1st Sess. 16 April-29 June 1973. Y4.At7/2: N88/13/pts 1-2.

298. U.S. Congress. Joint Committee on Defense Production. *Civil Preparedness and Limited Nuclear War. Hearings.* 94th Cong., 2nd Sess. 28 April 1976. Y4.D36: C49.

299. U.S. Congress. Joint Committee on Defense Production. *Civil Preparedness Review. Print.* 2 Parts. 95th Cong., 1st Sess. February-April 1977. Y4. D36: C49/2/2pts.

300. U.S. Congress. Joint Committee on Defense Production. *Defense Industrial Base. Hearings.* 3 Parts. 94th Cong., 2nd Sess. 17-24 November 1976. Y4. D36: In2/3pts.

301. U.S. Congress. Joint Committee on Defense Production. *Deterrence and Survival in the Nuclear Age (The "Gaither Report" of 1957).* 94th Cong., 2nd Sess. 1976. Y4. D36: D48.

302. U.S. Congress. Office of Technology Assessment. *Nuclear Proliferation and Safeguards. Print.* 95th Cong., 1st Sess. 30 June 1977. Y3.T22/2: 2N88.

303. U.S. Congress. Senate. Committee on Foreign Relations. Subcommittee on Arms Control, . . . *Analyses of Effects of Limited Nuclear Warfare. Print.* 94th Cong., 1st Sess. September 1975.

304. U.S. Congress. Senate. Committee on Foreign Relations. Subcommittee on Arms Control, . . . *Briefing on Counterforce Attacks. Hearings.* 93rd Cong., 2nd Sess. 11 September 1974. Y4.F76/2: At8.

305. U.S. Congress. Senate. Committee on Foreign Relations. Subcommittee on Arms Control, . . . *Effects of Limited Nuclear Warfare. Hearings.* 94th Cong., 1st Sess. 18 September 1975. Y4.F76/2: N88/9.

306. U.S. Congress. Senate. Committee on Foreign Relations. Subcommittee on Arms Control, . . . *Nonproliferation Issues. Hearings.* 94th Cong., 1st and 2nd Sess. 19 March 1975-8 November 1976. Y4.F76/2: N73/2.

307. U.S. Congress. Senate. Committee on Foreign Relations. Subcommittee on Arms Control, . . . *Nuclear Nonproliferation and Export Controls. Hearings.* 95th Cong., 1st Sess. 23 May-15 June 1977. Y4.F76/2: N88/11.

308. U.S. Congress. Senate. Committee on Foreign Relations. Subcommittee on Arms Control, . . . *To Promote Negotiations for a Comprehensive Test Ban Treaty. Hearings.* 93rd Cong., 1st Sess. 1 May 1973. Y4.F76/2:T28/2.

309. U.S. Congress. Senate. Committee on Foreign Relations. Subcommit-

tee on Arms Control, . . . *U.S.-Soviet Strategic Options. Hearings.* 95th Cong., 1st Sess. 14 January-16 March 1977. Y4.F76/2: Un35/34.

310. U.S. Congress. Senate. Committee on Foreign Relations. Subcommittee on Arms Control, . . . *U.S.-U.S.S.R. Strategic Policies. Hearings.* 93rd Cong., 2nd Sess. 4 May 1974. Y4.F76/2: Un35/22.

311. U.S. Congress. Senate. *U.S. and Soviet City Defense. Document.* 94th Cong., 2nd Sess. 30 September 1976. Senate Document 94-268.

312. U.S. Department of the Army. *Disarmament: A Bibliographic Record, 1916-1960.* Washington, D.C.: G.P.O., 1960.

313. U.S. Department of the Army. *Nuclear Weapons and NATO: Analytical Survey of Literature.* Washington, D.C.: G.P.O., 1975.

314. U.S. Department of the Army. Army Library. *The Cruise Missile: A Selective Bibliography, 1976-1978.* Washington, D.C.: January 1978. Photocopy.

315. U.S. Department of the Army. Army Library. *Deterrence: A Selective Bibliography.* Washington, D.C.: April 1977. Photocopy.

316. U.S. Department of the Army. Army Library. *Nuclear Proliferation: A Selective Bibliography.* Washington, D.C.: September 1977. Photocopy.

317. U.S. Department of the Army. Army Library. *SALT: Strategic Arms Limitation Talks: A Selective Bibliography.* Washington, D.C.: May 1978. Photocopy.

318. U.S. Department of Defense. *The Effects of Nuclear Weapons.* 3rd ed. Washington, D.C.: G.P.O., 1977.

319. U.S. Department of State. *Soviet Civil Defense.* Special Report No. 47. September 1978.

320. U.S. Department of State. Disarmament Administration. *A Basic Bibliography: Disarmament, Arms Control and National Security.* Publication No. 7193. Washington, D.C.: G.P.O., 1961.

BIBLIOGRAPHIES AND REFERENCE WORKS

321. Brown, Noel J. "The Moral Problem of Modern Warfare: A Bibliography." In *Morality and Modern Warfare: The State of the Question,* edited by William J. Nagle. Baltimore: Helicon, 1960.

322. Burns, Richard Dean, ed. *Arms Control and Disarmament: A Bibliography.* Santa Barbara, Calif.: ABC-Clio, 1977.

323. Burns, Richard Dean, and Susan Hoffman. *The SALT Era: A Selected Bibliography.* Los Angeles: California State University, 1977.

324. "Disarmament: A Bibliography." *Survival,* January-February 1960.

325. Dupuy, Trevor N., and Gay M. Hammerman, eds. *A Documentary History of Arms Control and Disarmament.* New York: R. R. Bowker, 1973.

326. International Institute for Strategic Studies. *The Military Balance, 1978-1979.* Boulder, Colo.: Westview, 1978.

327. International Institute for Strategic Studies. *Strategic Survey 1977.* Boulder, Colo.: Westview, 1978.

328. Stockholm International Peace Research Institute. *World Armaments and Disarmament: SIPRI Yearbook 1978.* New York: Crane, Russak, 1978.

329. *Strategic Studies Reference Guide.* Pittsburgh, Pa.: University of Pittsburg, 1975-   .

PERIODICALS
330. *Adelphi Papers.* London, 1963– .
331. *AEI Defense Review.* Washington, D.C.: 1977– .
332. *Aerospace Historian* (formerly *Airpower Historian*). Washington, D.C.: 1954-1969. Manhattan, Kans.: 1970– . Index. Cum. index, *1954-1973.*
333. *Air Force Magazine* (formerly *Air Force and Space Digest).* Washington, D.C.: 1946– . Indexed: Air Un. Lib. Ind.
334. *Air University Review* (formerly *Air University Quarterly Review*). Maxwell Field, Ala.: 1947– . Indexed: Air Un. Lib. Ind.; Eng. Ind.; P.A.I.S.
335. *Arms Control and Disarmament.* Washington, 1964-1973. Index. Indexed: P.A.I.S.
336. *Arms Control Today.* Washington, D.C.: 1971– .
337. *Aviation Week and Space Technology.* New York: 1916– . Indexed: R. G.; B.P.I.
338. *Bulletin of the Atomic Scientists: A Journal of Science and Public Affairs* (formerly *Science and Public Affairs*). Chicago: 1945– . Indexed: Biol. Abstr.; P.A.I.S.; Psychol. Abstr; R.G.
339. *Bulletin of Peace Proposals.* Oslo, Norway: 1970– . Indexed: P.A.I.S.
340. *Civil Defense Technical Reports* (formerly *Civil Defense Technical Bulletin*). Washington, D.C.: 1963– .
341. *Civil Preparedness Today: Foresight.* Washington, D.C.: 1974– .
342. *Comparative Strategy.* Arlington, Va.: 1977– .
343. *Disarmament News & Views.* New York: 1971– . Index.
344. *Flight International.* London: 1909– . Index. Indexed: Br. Tech. Ind.; Eng. Ind.; Air Un Lib Ind.
345. *Foreign Affairs.* New York: 1922– . Index *1922-1972.* Indexed: P.A.I.S.; R.G.; Soc. Sci. Ind.
346. *Foreign Policy.* New York: 1971– .
347. *Instant Research on Peace and Violence.* Tampere, Finland: 1971– .
348. *Interavia.* Geneva, Switzerland: 1946– . Index.
349. *International Civil Defense.* Geneva, Switzerland: 1952– .
350. *International Security.* Cambridge, Mass.: 1976– .
351. *Journal of Civil Defense* (formerly *Survive*). Starke, Fla.: 1968– . Index.
352. *Journal of Conflict Resolution* (formerly *Conflict Resolution*). Beverly Hills, Calif.: 1957– . Index. Indexed: ABC Pol Sci; P.A.I.S.; Soc. Sci. Ind.; Int. Polit. Sci. Abstr.
353. *Journal of Peace Research* (formerly *Journal of Peace*). Oslo, Norway: 1964– . Index. Indexed: Soc. Sci. Ind.
354. *Military Affairs.* Washington, D.C.: 1937-1968. Manhattan, Kans.: 1968– . Index *1937-1968.* Indexed: Air Un. Lib. Ind.; Hist. Abstr.
355. *Military Review.* Fort Leavenworth, Kans.: 1922– . Index *1922-1965.* Indexed: Air Un. Lib. Ind.; P.A.I.S.
356. *Naval War College Review.* Newport, R.I.: 1948– . Cum. index.
357. *Orbis.* Philadelphia: 1957– . Index. Indexed: Amer. Hist. & Life; Curr. Cont.; Hist. Abstr.; Int. Polit Sci. Abstr.; P.A.I.S.: Soc. Sci. Ind.

358. *Parameters: Journal of the U.S. Army War College.* Carlisle Barracks, Pa.: 1971–   .

359. *Peace and Change: A Journal of Peace Research.* Rohnert Park, Calif.: 1972–   .

360. *Peace Research Abstracts Journal.* Oakville, Ontario: 1964–   .

361. *Scientific American.* New York: 1845–   . Index. Indexed: R.G.

362. *Strategic Review.* Cambridge, Mass.: 1973–   .

363. *Survival.* London: 1959–   .

364. *United States Naval Institute Proceedings.* Annapolis, Md.: 1873–   . Index *1874-1956.* Indexed: Air Un. Lib. Ind.; Chem. Abstr.; P.A.I.S.

365. *War/Peace Report.* New York, 1961–   . Index. Indexed: P.A.I.S.

366. *Washington Review of Strategic and International Studies.* New Brunswick, N.J.: 1977–   .

367. *World Politics.* Princeton, N.J.: 1948–   . Index. Indexed: P.A.I.S.

ADDITIONS TO BIBLIOGRAPHY

368. Alford, Jonathan, ed. "The Future of Arms Control: Part III: Confidence-Building Measures." *Adelphi Papers,* no. 149, spring 1979.

369. Bertram, Christoph, ed. "The Future of Arms Control: Part I: Beyond SALT II." *Adelphi Papers,* no. 141, spring 1978.

370. Bertram, Christoph. "The Future of Arms Control: Part II: Arms Control and Technological Change: Elements of a New Approach." *Adelphi Papers,* no. 146, summer 1978.

371. Boulding, Kenneth E. *Conflict and Defense: A General Theory.* New York: Harper, 1962.

372. Brennan, Donald G. "A Comprehensive Test Ban: Everybody or Nobody." *International Security,* summer 1976.

373. Brodie, Bernard. "On the Objectives of Arms Control." *International Security,* summer 1976.

374. Bryant, Peter. *Red Alert.* New York: Ace Books, 1959.

375. Burdick, Eugene, and John H. Wheeler. *Fail-Safe.* New York: McGraw-Hill, 1962.

376. Cameron, Juan. "The Cruise Missile Can Do It All—Almost." *Fortune,* 8 May 1978.

377. Canby, Steven. "Mutual Force Reductions: A Military Perspective." *International Security,* winter 1978.

378. Collins, John M., and Anthony H. Cordesman. *Imbalance of Power: An Analysis of Shifting U.S.-Soviet Military Strengths.* San Rafael, Calif.: Presidio, 1978.

379. Compton, Arthur Holly. *Atomic Quest: A Personal Narrative.* New York: Oxford University Press, 1956.

380. Drell, Sidney D., and Frank von Hippel. "Limited Nuclear War." *Scientific American,* November 1976.

381. Erickson, John. "The Chimera of Mutual Deterrence." *Strategic Review,* spring 1978.

382. Evron, Yair. "The Role of Arms Control in the Middle East." *Adelphi Papers,* no. 138, autumn 1977.

383. Frank, Pat. *Alas, Babylon.* Philadelphia: Lippincott, 1959.

384. Frank, Pat. *Forbidden Area.* Philadelphia: Lippincott, 1956.
385. Greenwood, Ted, George W. Rathjens, and Jack Ruina. "Nuclear Power and Weapons Proliferation." *Adelphi Papers,* no. 130, winter 1976.
386. Helm, Robert W., and Donald R. Westervelt. "The New Test Ban Treaties: What Do They Mean? Where Do They Lead?" *International Security,* winter 1977.
387. Iklé, Fred C. "SALT and Nuclear Balance in Europe." *Strategic Review,* spring 1978.
388. Kaplan, Fred M. "The Soviet Civil Defense Myth." *Bulletin of the Atomic Scientists,* March-April 1978.
389. Nitze, Paul. "The Relationship of Strategic and Theater Nuclear Forces." *International Security,* fall 1977.
390. Rathjens, George. "The Verification of Arms Control Agreements." *Arms Control Today,* July/August 1977.
391. Schelling, Thomas C. "Who Will Have the Bomb?" *International Security,* Summer 1976.
392. Shaheen, Jack G., ed. *Nuclear War Films.* Carbondale: Southern Illinois University, 1978.
393. Shute, Nevil. *On the Beach.* New York: William Morrow, 1957.
394. Slocombe, Walter. "Learning from Experience: Verification Guidelines for SALT II." *Arms Control Today,* February 1976.
395. U.S. Department of Defense. *The FY 19— Department of Defense Program for Research, Development and Acquisition.* Washington, D.C.: 1959–   . Annual.
396. U.S. Department of Defense. *Report of the Secretary of Defense . . . to the Congress on the FY19— Budget, . . .* Washington, D.C.: 1971–   . Title varies. Annual.
397. U.S. Joint Chiefs of Staff. *Statement by Chairman . . . to the Congress on the Defense Posture of the United States for FY19—.* Washington, D.C.: 1971–   . Annual.
398. Westervelt, Donald R. "Candor, Compromise, and the Comprehensive Test Ban." *Strategic Review,* fall 1977.
399. Worner, Manfred. "NATO Defenses and Tactical Nuclear Weapons." *Strategic Review,* fall 1977.
400. Wylie, Philip G. *Tomorrow!* New York: Rinehart, 1954.
401. Wylie, Philip G. *Triumph.* Garden City, N.Y.: Doubleday, 1963.
402. Zumwalt, Adm. Elmo R., Jr. "An Assessment of the Bomber—Cruise Missile Controversy." *International Security,* summer 1977.

XXII

MILITARY LAW, MARTIAL LAW,
AND MILITARY GOVERNMENT

Donald G. Nieman

Since its inception, the American military has dealt routinely with matters of law and government. Under the Articles of War and, more recently, the Uniform Code of Military Justice, military officials have operated a system of military law governing persons in military service. Indeed, they have viewed military law as a tool essential for maintaining discipline. Moreover, military officials' authority has, on occasion, extended to civilians within the United States. Thus in times of rebellion, widespread domestic violence, and threats from abroad, they have enforced martial law, establishing regulations to govern civilians, and arresting and subjecting to military trials civilians who violate those regulations or commit crimes. Finally, in occupying foreign territory, they have established military governments that have exercised vast authority over foreign civilians.

This essay reviews the secondary literature and major primary sources available to students interested in examining these areas of American military history. Although scholars have devoted insufficient attention to the history of military law, martial law, and military government, there is, nevertheless, a small body of literature on these topics. Familiarity with this scholarship— much of it tucked away in law journals and the works of constitutional and legal historians—will enhance military historians' understanding of a vital part of American military institutions. Furthermore, awareness of the gaps in this literature will suggest research that they might profitably undertake.

Unfortunately, the essay focuses almost exclusively on the Army and largely neglects the Navy and the Air Force. Two things account for this. First, the Navy and the Air Force, unlike the Army, have not played significant roles in enforcing martial law and creating military governments. Therefore, the material on these subjects is Army-centered. Second, while the Navy and the Air Force have operated their own systems of law to govern officers and enlisted men, scholars have written little on the history of Navy and Air Force law. As a result, this essay gives these topics little attention. This does not suggest that the topics do not merit investigation but, rather, underscores the need for research on them.

GENERAL STUDIES. Although there is no comprehensive history of American military law, there are several studies which, collectively, serve as an introduction to the subject. Articles by Robert Rollman (167) and Gerald Crump (35) summarize the development of the military justice system from the eighteenth century to the present. Because of the significant role that the Army Judge Advocate General's Corps has played in the development of military law, William Fratcher's "History of the Judge Advocate General's Corps, United States Army" (61) and the official bicentennial history of the corps, *The Army Lawyer* (3) also offer useful overviews of the evolution of military law. While Joseph W. Bishop's thoughtful essay, *Justice Under Fire* (17), deals primarily with contemporary issues, it provides some helpful material on the history of military law.

There are also several general studies which deal with martial law and military government. Robert Rankin, *When Civil Law Fails* (157) and Charles Fairman, *The Law of Martial Rule* (55) survey the development of the theory and practice of martial law. Studies by Bennet Rich (16) and Frederick Wilson (203) are narrative accounts of civil officials' resort to military force to suppress civil disorder, while David Engdahl's essay, "Soldiers, Riots, and Revolutions" (54), is an analysis of the evolution of the Anglo-American law which governs the civil authorities' use of troops to preserve order. Ralph Gabriel's classic article, "American Experience with Military Government" (70), traces the army's military government activities from the Mexican War to the eve of World War II.

JOURNALS. Law journals are among the richest sources of literature on the military and the law. Several journals which focus exclusively on military and martial law—the *Military Law Review* (published by the Army Judge Advocate General's School), the *JAG Journal* (published by the Judge Advocate General of the Navy), and the *Air Force Law Review* (published by the Air Force Judge Advocate General's School)—are of particular value. Also highly useful are the dozens of journals published by university schools of law and professional bar organizations. In addition to these periodicals, of course, journals which specialize in military and legal history (such as *Military Affairs* and the *American Journal of Legal History*) and the standard national, regional, and state historical journals sometimes contain pertinent articles. Such familiar finding aids as *Writings on American History* and *America: History and Life* are helpful in guiding scholars to the most useful periodical literature. Of even greater value, however, are the *Index to Legal Periodicals* and the *Index to Periodical Articles Relating to the Law*. The former provides a subject index to articles published in English-language law journals from the eighteenth century to the present; the latter, which covers the period since 1958, indexes articles published in nonlegal periodicals.

FROM THE REVOLUTION TO THE CIVIL WAR. Very little on the early history of American military law has appeared in print. Fredrick Bernays Wiener's *Civilians Under Military Justice* (198) is an impressively researched scholarly study which examines the authority exercised by British military tribunals in the seventeenth and eighteenth centuries and provides important insights into the origins of American military law. Although they are by no means definitive, Francis Heller's "Military Law in the Continental Army" (88) and Maurer Maurer's "Military Justice Under General Washington" (128) are useful essays which examine American military law during the revolutionary era.

Since historians and lawyers never tire of attempting to read the minds of the framers of the Constitution and Bill of Rights, it is not surprising that there is a sizable body of work on the framers, the Constitution, and the military. In a 1957 article (89), Gordon Henderson argued that the men of the First Congress believed that the provisions of the Bill of Rights (except where they explicitly stated otherwise) would apply to civilians and military personnel alike. Henderson's argument, however, has been effectively challenged in Fredrick Bernays Wiener's essay, "Courts-Martial and the Constitution: The Original Practice" (199). There has also been considerable debate as to whether the framers intended to give the national government authority to raise an army by conscription. Leon Friedman's "Conscription and the Constitution: The Original Understanding" (66) and Charles Lofgren's imaginative and well-argued "Compulsory Military Service and the Constitution: The Original Understanding" (117) contend that the framers did not intend to give Congress authority to compel citizens to serve in the military. Michael Malbin (120), however, argues that, while the framers gave no indication of support for conscription, they intended to give the national government sufficient authority and flexibility to deal with unforeseen problems. Consequently, he suggests that when it resorts to conscription to raise an army, Congress is merely exercising the broad authority with which the framers endowed it. Richard Renner's essay, "Conscientious Objection and the Federal Government, 1787–1792" (160), discusses the way in which the framers of the Bill of Rights dealt with the conscientious objector issue.

For the antebellum period, several contemporary volumes are useful to historians. Treatises by Stephen Benét (15), William De Hart (42), Alexander Macomb (118), Isaac Maltby (121), and John O'Brien (148) are little more than how-to manuals designed to acquaint officers with the court-martial process. Nevertheless, since their publication dates span the period, they serve as a starting point for study of the antebellum system of military justice. Volumes compiled by John Callan (24), Trueman Cross (34), A. R. Hetzel (91), and Alfred Mordecai (137) are helpful statutory compendia which enable scholars to find the statute law which governed the military during the antebellum years.

The secondary literature on the development of military law in the first sixty years of the nineteenth century is virtually nonexistent. Fredrick Bernays Wiener, in his essay on the Bill of Rights and the military (199), provides an excellent introduction to early nineteenth century military criminal procedure. In addition, articles by John McDermott (129) and Richard Knopf (106) provide brief case studies of the harsh realities of enforcement of military criminal law in the antebellum years. Jean Ponton was in 1979 preparing for publication by the Library of Congress a bibliography of published proceedings of antebellum courts-martial that will be of great value to scholars.

There are a number of studies of martial law and military government during the late eighteenth and early nineteenth centuries. Wiener's *Civilians Under Military Justice* (198), cited earlier, includes a discussion of the authority of British military courts over civilians during the seventeenth and eighteenth centuries which is required reading for those who wish to understand early American attitudes toward martial law. George Dennison's important article, "Martial Law: The Development of a Theory of Emergency Powers, 1776-1861" (44), is a perceptive analysis of the transformation of martial law in America during the late eighteenth and early nineteenth centuries. Also valuable on antebellum developments in martial law is Dennison's *The Dorr War* (43), a study of the Rhode Island insurrection of 1842 and its impact on political and legal theory. Justin Smith, "American Rule in Mexico" (181) and George Town Baker III, "Mexico and the War with the United States: A Study in the Politics of Military Occupation" (12) discuss American military government of Mexico in the 1840s and the institutions which the army established in Mexico to try soldiers and civilians. Books by David Y. Thomas (187) and Theodore Grivas (84) examine American military government of the territories during the early nineteenth century.

THE CIVIL WAR AND RECONSTRUCTION. Given historians' fascination with the Civil War era, it is surprising that they have written so little on military law during the 1860s. Wilton B. Moore's "Union Provost Marshals in the Eastern Theater" (136) is a solid study of an important part of the wartime military justice apparatus. Articles by Darrett Rutman (170), John Stibbs (182), and Lewis Laska and James Smith (110) treat the army's "war crimes" trial of Henry Wirz, the Confederate commander of Andersonville prison. William Robinson's monumental *Justice in Grey* (166), a study of the Confederate legal system, contains a brief account of the Confederacy's system of military law.

Scholars have produced a number of works which touch on legal aspects of the Civil War draft. Studies by Jack Leach (111), Joseph Duggan (51), and Eugene Murdock (139,140) examine Union conscription legislation and discuss some of the legal problems that military men encountered in operating the conscription and bounty system. Albert B. Moore's *Conscription and Conflict in the Confederacy* (135) discusses Congress's enactment of conscription legislation, military officials' attempts to enforce it, and the civil courts' rulings in conscription cases. Edward Needles Wright, *Conscientious Objectors in the Civil War* (207) is a scholarly study which discusses some of the legal issues involved in Union and Confederate policy toward conscientious objectors.

There is also a significant body of scholarship dealing with the army's exercise of emergency authority in the wartime North. Harold M. Hyman's *A More Perfect Union* (96), a brilliant recent analysis of American constitutionalism in the Civil War era, offers a significant reexamination of military arrest, detention, and trial of northern civilians during the war, as well as an analysis of wartime developments in the theory of martial law. Still valuable on such matters as suspension of habeas corpus, military arrests, and military censorship of the press is James G. Randall's *Constitutional Problems Under Lincoln* (156). Carl Swisher's *The Taney Court* (184) is a useful recent study which deals with these issues from the vantage point of the Supreme Court. Catherine M. Tarrant, "A Writ of Liberty or A Covenant with Hell?" (185) examines the way in which Congress sought to use the writ of habeas corpus to protect military men who were prosecuted in state courts for official acts, as well as the constitutional issues involved in the debate over wartime habeas corpus suspension. William Whiting's *War Powers Under the Constitution of the United States* (197) is a monumental contemporary analysis of the constitutional bases of the expansion of the army's authority over civilians during the crisis of civil war.

Scholars have also devoted a great deal of attention to *Ex parte Milligan,* the Supreme Court's landmark decision on martial law. Samuel Klaus, *The Milligan Case* (105) is a highly useful documentary history of the case. Interpretations and analyses of the Court's ruling may be found in studies by Harold Hyman (96), Stanley Kutler (107), Charles Fairman (56), and Joseph Gambone (71).

There is also a great deal of scholarship on martial law in the South during and after the war. In addition to the works by Hyman (96), Randall (156), Whiting (197), Kutler (107), and Fairman (56) mentioned earlier, Michael Les Benedict's *A Compromise of Principle* (13) and "Preserving the Constitution" (14) illuminate the constitutional issues involved in military control of the South. Frank Freidel's biography of Francis Lieber (64) and his article, "General Order 100 and American Military Government" (65), discuss the drafting of the Lieber Code, the regulations promulgated by the War Department in 1863 to define the army's authority in occupied territory. James Garner's "General Order 100 Revisited" (72) offers a detailed analysis of the code and its long-term impact on the law of belligerent occupation.

Other studies deal with the activities of the army in the South during the war and its aftermath. Articles by A. H. Carpenter (26) and Robert Futrell (69) provide helpful surveys of wartime occupation. James Sefton's *The United States Army and Reconstruction* (174) is a solid, well-researched account which examines the army's role in preserving order and exercising martial law in the war's immediate aftermath, its relations with the civil governments created by President Andrew Johnson, its role in trying criminals, removing state officials, and conducting elections under the Reconstruction Acts, and its activities in the aftermath of Congress's restoration of the rebel states. Studies by Gerald Capers (25), Elizabeth Doyle (49), George Hendricks (90), Ernest Hooper (92), John Kirkland (104), Peter Maslowski (125), William Richter (162), Kenneth St. Clair (171,172), and Robert Shook (177) deal with occupation policy at the state and local level. Donald Nieman, *To Set the Law in Motion* (142) is an examination of the efforts of the Freedmen's Bureau—a War Department agency staffed largely by army officers—to secure justice for southern blacks.

FROM RECONSTRUCTION TO WORLD WAR I. There are several studies which illuminate developments in military law during the late nineteenth and early twentieth centuries. Jack Foner, *The United States Soldier Between Two Wars* (59) contains an analysis of the operation of the military justice system and the Army's slow and hesitating efforts to reform it during the years 1865–98. David Lockmiller's biography of Enoch Crowder (116), the career military lawyer who entered the Army in 1881 and served as Judge Advocate General from 1912 to 1923, offers important insights into the development of military law during the entire period. So, too, does George Prugh's biographical sketch of William Winthrop (155), the influential writer on military law. Studies by Bruce Dinges (46), Robert Haynes (87), Ann Lane (108), John Marzalek (123), William Robie (165), and John Weaver (194) examine significant courts-martial and courts of inquiry.

Also useful for the study of military law during this period are a number of contemporary works. Treatises by Rollin Ives (98), Edgar Dudley (50), and George Davis (40) are better researched and more thorough than their antebellum counterparts. In a class by itself, however, is William Winthrop's *Military Law and Precedents* (204), originally published in 1886 and issued in a second edition in 1895. Based on exhaustive research in Army regulations, the opinions of the Judge Advocates General, the records of courts-martial, the writings of civilian legal commentators, and the rulings of civilian courts, it became the bible of military lawyers and remains an essential tool for the study of military law. In addition to these treatises, Robert N. Scott's *An Analytical Digest of the Military Laws of the United States* (173), originally published in 1873, and *The Military Laws of the United States* (39), issued periodically by the Judge Advocate General of the Army between 1897 and 1949, provide compilations of statutes governing the military. *A Digest of the Opinions of the Judge Advocate General of the Army* (45), first issued in 1865 and published periodically in revised editions through the 1940s, contains synopses of legal opinions on such diverse matters as court-martial decisions, congressional statutes, claims by private citizens, and contractual matters affecting the War Department.

There is a sizable body of scholarship on late nineteenth and early twentieth century martial law and military government. William J. Birkhimer's *Military Government and Martial Law* (16), originally published in 1892, is an impressive contemporary study. H. W. C. Furman, "Restrictions Upon the Use of the Army Imposed by the Posse Comitatus Act" (68) and G. Norman Lieber, *The Use of the Army in Aid of the Civil Power* (113) deal with the impact of an 1878 statute which prohibited federal officials from using troops to enforce the law except when expressly authorized to do so by the Constitution or by statute. Works by Robert Rankin (157), Bennet Rich (161), and Frederick Wilson (203), mentioned earlier, as well as studies by Robert V. Bruce (21), Almont Lindsey (114), and Jerry M. Cooper (31) treat the army's role in suppressing disturbances connected with late nineteenth and early twentieth century strikes. Doris Appel Graber's *The Development of the Law of Belligerent Occupation, 1863-1914* (81) offers a careful analysis of the evolution of the international law governing armies of occupation from the formulation of the Lieber Code to the adoption of the Hague conventions. Studies by George Coats (28), Graham Cosmas (32), John Gates (73), Howard Gillette (77), and Leonard Wood (206) deal with the American military government of Cuba and the Philippines in the aftermath of the war with Spain, while an essay by Guy Donnell (48) examines the American occupation of Vera Cruz in 1914. Charles Magoon, *Reports on the Law of Civil Government in Territory Subject to Military Government by the Military Forces of the United States* (119), published by the War Department's Bureau of Insular Affairs in 1903, is a useful compilation of reports on legal problems that the army encountered during its turn-of-the-century occupation of Cuba, Puerto Rico, and the Philippines.

WORLD WAR I AND ITS AFTERMATH. There are few secondary works on American military law during World War I. Maurer, "The Court Martialing of Camp Followers During World I" (127) is an important study of the expansion during this period of the army's authority to try civilian employees and civilian dependents of servicemen. Several other works deal with the controversy over reform of the military justice system which raged during and after the war. Terry Brown's article, "The Crowder-Ansell Dispute: The Emergence of General Samuel T. Ansell" (20), discusses Ansell's reform program, War Department officials' hostility to it, and the compromise between reformers and their opponents embodied in the 1920 Articles of War. Two other studies complement Brown's fine essay. Herbert Marguilies, "The Articles of War, 1920: The History of a Forgotten Reform" (122) is a significant analysis of the legislative history of the 1920 articles, while David Lockmiller's biography of Crowder (116), cited above, looks at the controversy from the point of view of an opponent of Ansell's program.

Writers have devoted considerable attention to the American military government of Germany during the years 1918-23. I. L. Hunt, who was in charge of the army's civil affairs section in postwar Germany, wrote the official history (94) of the occupation. It not only served as a textbook in the military government schools established by the army during World War II, but remains useful for scholars. Also helpful is a volume by Gen. Henry T. Allen, commander of the American occupation forces, entitled *The Rhineland Occupation* (1). Among modern studies are Heath Twitchell's biography of Allen (190) and John C. Rasmussen's analysis of American military government policy in postwar Germany (158). In addition, Ernst Fraenkel's *Military Occupation and the Rule of Law: Occupation Government in the Rhineland, 1918-1923* (60) discusses the policies developed and implemented by each of the occupying Allied powers.

WORLD WAR II AND ITS AFTERMATH. There is no secondary literature dealing with military law during the interwar years and little on military law during World War II. William Huie, *The Execution of Private Slovik* (93) is a popular account of one of the most controversial cases in the history of American military law. Alfred Avins's essay, "The Execution of Private Slovik and the Punishment of Short Desertion" (6), is a good scholarly study of the punishment of deserters during World War I and World War II. Avins shows that in both wars, courts-martial generally imposed harsh punishments—including long prison terms and execution—on deserters, but that these sentences were, in most cases, subsequently reduced. He argues that this policy encouraged desertion and suggests that the Army could best deal with the problem of desertion by compelling convicted deserters to serve long terms in prison. Mulford Sibley and Philip Jacob, *Conscription of Conscience* (178) is a thorough analysis of the military and the conscientious objector during World War II which does a good job of treating the legal issues involved.

There are a number of good studies of the army's exercise of martial law during World War II. J. Garner Anthony, *Hawaii Under Army Rule* (2) examines the decision to impose martial law in the islands, the operation of army provost courts and military commissions, army censorship of the press and regulation of labor, the gradual restoration of civilian rule in 1943-44, and the Supreme Court decision ruling the army's actions unconstitutional. Fred Israel's article, "Military Justice in Hawaii, 1941-1944" (97), shows that military courts in Hawaii rode roughshod over the rights of individuals and credits Interior Secretary Harold Ickes with waging a running battle against military rule that ultimately led to the lifting of martial law. Studies by Jacobus ten Broek, Edward Barnhart, and Floyd Mason (186), Roger Daniels (36), Morton Grodzins (85), and Stetson Conn (30) deal with the army's evacuation and incarceration of West Coast Japanese-Americans. Works by Sidney Fine (58), Eugene Rostow (168), and Alpheus T. Mason (126), as well as the study by ten Broek, Barnhart, and Mason (186) cited above, discuss the Supreme Court's cautious refusal to strike down the Army's actions.

Scholars have produced numerous studies of American military government in Europe during and after World War II. Harry Coles and Albert Weinberg, *Civil Affairs: Soldiers Become Governors* (29) is a documentary history of the formulation of military government policy, the training of military government personnel, and wartime military government operations in North Africa, Italy, France, and the Low Countries. C. R. S. Harris, *Allied Military Administration in Italy, 1943-1945* (86) focuses on the British-American military government of Italy, examining the formulation of occupation policy, the operation of military government courts, the regulation of labor, the creation of health and sanitation programs, and the reestablishment of local government. Earl F. Ziemke, *The U.S. Army and the Occupation of Germany, 1944-1946* (209) deals with the army's planning for and establishment of military government in Germany. Works by Eugene Davidson (37), Morris Edwards (53), Oliver Frederiksen (63), John Gimbel (78), Edward Peterson (153), and Harold Zink (210) are general studies of American military government policy in Germany during the late 1940s and the early 1950s. Edward Litchfield, ed., *Governing Post War Germany* (115) and Carl J. Friedrich, ed., *American Experiences in Military Government in World War II* (67) are collections of essays written by scholars who served in military government. Jean Edward Smith, ed., *The Papers of General Lucius Clay: Germany, 1945-1949* (180) is a collection of the correspondence of the head of the American military government in Germany. John Gimbel provides a good case study of American military government at the grass roots in *A German Community Under American Occupation* (79).

Although many of the studies cited in the previous paragraph offer brief treatments of occupation justice, there are several works which deal exclusively with military trial of cases involving civilians in Germany. In a book (146) and a series of articles (143,144,145,147), Eli Nobleman, a lawyer who served as a judge in American military government courts, offers a favorable evaluation of American military justice in Germany from 1944 to 1948. Nobleman's studies describe the establishment of provost courts and military commissions, the jurisdiction which they exercised, and the law and procedure which they applied, and discuss the army's role in reestablishing German courts. In 1948, American officials created a new court system, staffed by American civilians, to adjudicate cases in which both parties were Americans or in which one party was an American and the other a German. An article by William Clark and Thomas Goodman (27), two members of the system's court of appeals, presents a useful account of the operation of these courts. It should, however, be supplemented with Robert Dohini, "Occupation Justice" (47), a harsh critique of the system.

There are fewer studies of the American military government of Japan. Books by Eduard Joost Van Aduard (193) and Harry Emerson Wildes (201) are popular contemporary accounts. Kazuo Kawai's *Japan's American Interlude* (101) and Eric Svenson's "The Military Occupation of Japan: The First Years:

Planning, Policy Formulation and Reforms" (183) are useful scholarly studies. Carl Friedrich's collection of essays (67), mentioned earlier, contains several helpful articles on American military government in Japan. Ralph Braibanti, "Administration of Military Government at the Prefectural Level" (19) examines the operation of American military government at the grass roots.

There is a sizable secondary literature on the trial of World War II era war criminals. James Weingartner, *Crossroads of Death* (195) examines the trial and conviction by an American military court of the German soldiers who perpetrated the Malemedy massacre. A. Frank Reel's *The Case of General Yamashita* (159) is a forceful critique of the trial by an American military commission of the Japanese commander charged with responsibility for atrocities committed by his troops during the Japanese occupation of the Philippines. There are two useful studies of the International Military Tribunal for the Far East and the trial of the major Japanese war criminals. A dissertation by Walter Lee Riley (163) critiques the rational employed by the tribunal to justify conviction of the accused. Richard Minear's *Victors' Justice* (134), a thorough study of the trials based upon impressive archival research, is also highly critical of the tribunal.

Not surprisingly, the bulk of the literature on war crimes deals with the Nuremberg trials. Eugene Davidson, *The Trial of the Germans* (38) provides a good narrative account of the trial of the twenty-two German leaders tried by the International Military Tribunal at Nuremberg. Bradley Smith's *Reaching Judgment at Nuremburg* (179) is a solid scholarly study which examines, from the American perspective, the Allied decision to try German war criminals, the creation of the International Military Tribunal, the strategies pursued by prosecution and defense, and the way in which the tribunal decided the issues which came before it. Also useful are William Bosch, *Judgment on Nuremburg* (18), a study of Americans' responses to the trials; Eugene Gerhart, *America's Advocate: Robert H. Jackson* (76), a biography of the chief prosecutor; and Robert Woetzel, *The Nuremburg Trials in International Law* (205), an analysis of the legal validity and significance of the trials. John Mendelsohn's essay, "Trial by Document" (130), examines the access to documentary evidence given to defendants by both the International Military Tribunal and the American war crimes tribunals. Two published collections of documents—one (188) the complete record of the trials before the International Military Tribunal and the other (189) selected documents from the trials before the American courts—are also of great value to scholars.

THE POST-WORLD WAR II ERA. There are several good general studies of military law in the post-World War II period. William Generous, *Swords and Scales* (75) is a good study of the postwar movement for reform of the military justice system, Congress's adoption of the Uniform Code of Military Justice, and the court decisions, practice, and legislation that shaped the new system during the 1950s and 1960s. Articles by Edmund Morgan (138) and Felix Larkin (109), men who played important roles in drafting the code, are helpful treatments of the creation of the uniform code. William B. Aycock and Seymour Wurfel, *Military Law and the Uniform Code of Military Justice* (11) is a detailed analysis of the code and early rulings on it by the United States Court of Military Appeals. A recent essay by James Jacobs (99) offers a thoughtful interpretation of the transformation of American military law in the thirty years following World War II.

In addition to these general studies, there are a number of works which deal with specific issues in post-World War II military law. Larry Ashlock, "The Military Trial Judge" (4) and Robert Miller, "Who Made the Law Officer a Federal Judge?" (133) trace the expansion of the authority of the trial judge during the 1950s and the 1960s. Sidney Ulmer's *Military Justice and the Right to Counsel* (191) deals with recent developments in an important area of military criminal procedure. Studies by Paul Lermack (112) and Henry Cabell (23) discuss the operation of summary and special courts-martial—tribunals with authority to try minor offenses. Guy Zoghby's "Is There a Military Common Law of Crimes?" (211) is an interesting study of the way in which the Court of Military Appeals has drawn upon military custom and state and federal court decisions to flesh out vague provisions of the uniform code.

There are also several published primary sources which are essential for the study of post-World War II military law. *Decisions of the United States Court of Military Appeals* (41) and *Court Martial Reports* (33) contain the opinions of the Court of Military Appeals. The latter also includes the selected opinions handed down by the Judge Advocates General Board of Review and, after 1969, the Courts of Military Review. For the post-1975 period, decisions of the Court of Military Appeals and selected decisions of the Courts of Review are printed in the *Military Justice Reporter* (131). Statutory provisions affecting the military can be found in Title 10 of the *United States Code*.

The post-World War II changes in military law have spawned a great deal of controversy. Books by Luther West (196) and Robert Sherrill (176) argue that the postwar reforms were illusory and that commanders still have the ability to manipulate trials. Edward Sherman's essay, "The Civilianization of Military Justice" (175), is more restrained and balanced but, nevertheless, argues that serious flaws remain in the military justice system. In *Justice Under Fire (17)*, however, Joseph Bishop contends that the post-World War II reforms were significant and that the military justice system now affords substantial procedural and substantive protection for individual rights.

SPECIAL STUDIES. There are a number of important studies which do not lend themselves to chronological classification. Fredrick Bernays Wiener, "The Militia Clause of the Constitution" (200) traces the steps by which the national government has circumvented the restrictions which the militia clause places upon federal control of state forces. Three excellent articles by Alfred Avins (5, 7, 8) examine the evolution of the law of desertion. Studies by Robert Duke and Howard Vogel (52), Darrell Peck (151), Alfred Avins (10), Seymour Wurfel (208), and Robert Pasley (149) provide analyses of federal and state court review of the activities of military tribunals. An excellent article by John Kester (103) traces the development of the provision of military law which makes it a criminal offense for an officer to utter contemptuous remarks about the president or Congress, and examines the circumstances in which it has been enforced. An article by Alfred Avins (9) examines the evolution of the law governing officers' right to resign, while Robert Pasley (150) traces from the nineteenth century to the present military officials' use of the dishonorable discharge as a means of nonjudicial punishment. A study by Williams Fratcher (62) examines the growth during the nineteenth and twentieth centuries of presidential authority to make regulations concerning military justice. Works by Jack Leach (111), Joseph Duggan(51), R. R. Russell (169), and Kent Greenwalt (82) deal with the evolution of the law of conscription. Peter Karsten's tour de force, *War, Soldiers, and Combat* (100), offers a sweeping and imaginative historical analysis of the problem of war crimes.

ARCHIVES. The major source of archival material for the study of military law, martial law, and military government is the National Archives of the United States. Because of the absence of inventories for many of the record groups which contain relevant material, as well as the enormous volume of military records (particularly for the twentieth century) in the archives, it is impossible in an essay of this length to provide a discussion of the pertinent records. Scholars may obtain a general idea of the archives' holdings from *A Guide to the National Archives of the United States* (192) and the essay in this volume by Dale Floyd and Timothy Nenninger. In addition, they may obtain advice about records that they wish to consult from members of the staffs of both the Navy and Old Army Branch and the Modern Military Branch of the National Archives.

SUGGESTIONS FOR RESEARCH. Although scholars have given attention to the history of martial law and military government, there are a number of topics which merit study. We still need work on the development of the theory and law of martial rule in the late nineteenth and twentieth centuries. In the area of military government, scholars have focused far too little attention on the army's policy of "law reform" in occupied territory. Studies of military officials' efforts to rework the legal systems of Cuba and the Philippines at the turn of the century and of Japan and Germany during the post–World War II era could tell us a great deal about the attitudes, assumptions, and objectives of military and civilian policymakers. Given the dearth of scholarship on the subject and the vast amount of pertinent archival material available to researchers, scholars could also profitably devote greater attention to the American military government of Japan.

There is even greater opportunity for research on the history of American military law. We need studies—patterned after Alfred Avins's work on the law of desertion—which trace the evolution of doctrines of military law and relate doctrinal changes to social, intellectual, and political developments. We also have a great deal to learn about the actual operation of the military justice system. In fact, so little has been done in this area that we could profit from a thorough study of the functioning of the military justice during any period from the Revolution through the Vietnam War. Another topic which deserves investigation is the emergence during the years 1861-1920 of a highly-skilled, self-conscious group of military lawyers. Indeed, a study of the professionalization of military law during the late nineteenth and early twentieth centuries could contribute to our understanding of other significant changes which were taking place in military and civilian institutions at this time. Aside from Lockmiller's biography of Enoch Crowder, there are no thorough studies of the architects of American military law. Consequently, biographies of such significant figures as Joseph Holt, George Davis, and William Winthrop would fill gaps in the literature. Moreover, an area that historians have completely neglected—the military and questions of patent, tort, and contract law—offers numerous opportunities for research. Finally, scholars, regardless of whether they are interested in military law, should begin to exploit court-martial records. This rich but almost wholly neglected source could serve as the basis for studies (which would be of interest to social as well as military historians) of the values, attitudes, and behavior of military personnel.

BIBLIOGRAPHY

1. Allen, Henry T. *The Rhineland Occupation.* Indianapolis: Bobbs-Merrill, 1927.
2. Anthony, Joseph Gardner. *Hawaii Under Army Rule.* Stanford: Stanford University Press, 1955.
3. *The Army Lawyer: A History of the Judge Advocate General's Office, 1775-1975.* Washington, D.C.: Government Printing Office, 1976.
4. Ashlock, Larry Ira. "The Military Trial Judge." S.J.D. thesis, George Washington University, 1972.
5. Avins, Alfred. "Development of the Concept of Military Desertion in Anglo-American Law." *Melbourne University Law Review* 4 (June 1963): 91-110.
6. ———. "The Execution of Private Slovik and the Punishment for Short Desertion." *George Washington Law Review* 30 (June 1962): 785-805.
7. ———. 'Historical Origins of Desertion Through Dual Enlistment." *Law Quarterly Review* 78 (October 1961): 501-25.
8. ———. "A History of Short Desertion." *Military Law Review* 13 (July 1961): 143-66.
9. ———. "The Right of Military Officers to Resign: An Historical Footnote." *George Washington Law Review* 31 (December 1962): 431-61.
10. ———. "State Court Review of National Guard Courts-Martial and Military Board Decisions, 1836-1954." *Cornell Law Quarterly* 41 (spring 1956): 457-71.
11. Aycock, William B., and Seymour W. Wurfel. *Military Law Under the Uniform Code of Military Justice.* Chapel Hill, N.C.: University of North Carolina Press, 1955.
12. Baker, George T., III. "Mexico City and the War with the United States: A Study in the Politics of Military Occupation." Ph.D. dissertation, Duke University, 1970.
13. Benedict, Michael Les. *A Compromise of Principle: Congressional Republicans and Reconstruction, 1863-1869.* New York: W. W. Norton, 1974.
14. Benedict, Michael Les. "Preserving the Constitution: The Conservative Basis of Radical Reconstruction." *Journal of American History* 61 (June 1974): 65-90.
15. Benét, Stephen Vincent. *A Treatise on Military Law and the Practice of Courts Martial.* New York: D. Van Nostrand,, 1862.
16. Birkhimer, William E. *Military Government and Martial Law.* Washington, D.C.: James J. Chapman, 1892.

17. Bishop, Joseph W., Jr. *Justice Under Fire: A Study of Military Law.* New York: Charterhouse, 1974.

18. Bosch, William J. *Judgment on Nuremburg: American Attitudes Toward the Major War Crimes Trials.* Chapel Hill, N.C.: University of North Carolina Press, 1970.

19. Braibanti, Ralph J. D. "Administration of Military Government in Japan at the Prefectural Level." *American Political Science Review* 43 (April 1949): 250–74.

20. Brown, Terry. "The Crowder-Ansell Dispute: The Emergence of General Samuel T. Ansell." *Military Law Review* 35 (January 1967): 1–46.

21. Bruce, Robert V. *1877: The Year of Violence.* Indianapolis: Bobbs-Merrill, 1959.

22. Brugger, Robert. "Military Law on Trial: The Impact of the Civil War on a Jurisdictional Institution." Master's thesis, University of Maryland, 1967.

23. Cabell, Henry B. "Damnosa Hereditas: Special Courts Martial." *Military Law Review* 7 (January 1960): 145–53.

24. Callan, John F. *Military Laws of the United States.* Baltimore: J. Murphy & Co., 1858.

25. Capers, Gerald. *Occupied City: New Orleans Under the Federals, 1862–1865.* Lexington, Ky.: University of Kentucky Press, 1965.

26. Carpenter, A. H. "Military Government of Southern Territory, 1861–1865." In *Annual Report of the American Historical Association for the Year 1900,* 1:467–98. Washington, D.C.: Government Printing Office, 1902.

27. Clark, William, and Thomas H. Goodman. "American Justice in Occupied Germany: United States Military Government Courts." *American Bar Association Journal* 36 (June 1950): 443–47.

28. Coats, George Y. "The Philippine Constabulary, 1907–1917." Ph.D. dissertation, Ohio State University, 1968.

29. Coles, Harry, and Albert K. Weinberg. *Civil Affairs: Soldiers Become Governors.* Washington, D.C.: Office of the Chief of Military History, United States Army, 1964.

30. Conn, Stetson, Rose C. Engleman, and Byron Fairchild. *Guarding the United States and Its Outposts.* Washington, D.C.: Office of the Chief of Military History, 1964.

31. Cooper, Jerry Marvin. "The Army and Civil Disorder: Federal Military Intervention in American Labor Disputes, 1877–1900." Ph.D. dissertation, University of Wisconsin, 1971.

32. Cosmas, Graham. "Securing the Fruits of Victory: The U.S. Army Occupies Cuba, 1898–1899." *Military Affairs* 38 (October 1974): 85–91.

33. *Court-Martial Reports: Holdings and Decisions of the Judge Advocates General Board of Review and United States Court of Military Appeals.* Rochester, N.Y.: Lawyer's Cooperative Publishing Company, 1951.

34. Cross, Maj. Trueman. *Military Laws of the United States.* Washington, D.C.: E. de Krafft, 1825.

35. Crump, C. F. "History of the Structure of Military Justice in the U.S.,

1775–1966." *Air Force Law Review* 16 (winter 1974): 41–68; 17 (spring 1975): 55–72.

36. Daniels, Roger. *Concentration Camps U.S.A.: Japanese-Americans and World War II.* New York: Holt, Rinehart and Winston, 1971.

37. Davidson, Eugene. *The Death and Life of Germany: An Account of the American Occupation.* New York: Alfred A. Knopf, 1959.

38. Davidson, Eugene. *The Trial of the Germans.* New York: Macmillan, 1966.

39. Davis, George B. *The Military Laws of the United States.* Washington, D.C.: Government Printing Office, 1897.

40. Davis, George B. *A Treatise on Military Law.* New York: J. Wiley & Sons, 1898.

41. *Decisions of the United States Court of Military Appeals with Headnotes, Tables, Index and Parallel References.* Rochester, N.Y.: Lawyers Cooperative Publishing Company, 1951.

42. De Hart, William C. *Observations on Military Law and the Constitution and Practice of Courts Martial.* New York: Wiley and Halsted, 1859.

43. Dennison, George M. *The Dorr War: Republicanism on Trial, 1831–1861.* Lexington, Ky.: University Press of Kentucky, 1976.

44. Dennison, George M. "Martial Law: The Development of a Theory of Emergency Powers, 1776–1861." *American Journal of Legal History* 18 (January 1974): 52–79.

45. *A Digest of the Opinions of the Judge Advocate General of the Army.* Washington, D.C.: Government Printing Office, 1865.

46. Dinges, Bruce J. "The Court Martial of Henry O. Flipper: An Example of Black-White Relations in the Army." *American West* 9 (January 1972): 12–17.

47. Donihi, Robert. "Occupation Justice." *South Texas Law Journal* 1 (spring 1955): 333–58.

48. Donnell, Guy R. "The United States Military Government at Vera Cruz." In *The Charles Wilson Hackett Memorial Volume: Essays in Mexican History,* edited by Thomas Cotner, pp. 229–47. Austin, Tex.: University of Texas Press, 1958.

49. Doyle, Elisabeth Joan. "New Orleans Courts under Military Occupation, 1861–1865." *Mid-America* 42 (July 1960): 185–92.

50. Dudley, Edgar S. *Military Law and the Procedure of Courts-Martial.* New York: John Wiley & Sons, 1912.

51. Duggan, Joseph. *Legislative and Statutory Development of the Federal Concept of Conscription for Military Service.* Washington, D.C.: The Catholic University of America Press, 1946.

52. Duke, Robert D., and Howard S. Vogel. "The Constitution and the Standing Army: Another Problem of Court Martial Jurisdiction." *Vanderbilt Law Review* 13 (March 1960): 435–60.

53. Edwards, Morris O. "A Case Study of Military Government in Germany During and After World War II." Ph.D. dissertation, Georgetown University, 1956.

54. Engdahl, D. E. "Soldiers, Riots and Revolution: The Law and History of Military Troops in Civil Disorders." *Iowa Law Review* 57 (October 1971): 1–73.

55. Fairman, Charles. *The Law of Martial Rule.* 2d ed. Chicago: Callaghan and Company, 1942.

56. Fairman, Charles. *Reconstruction and Reunion, 1864–1888. Part I.* New York: Macmillan, 1971.

57. Fairman, Charles. "The Supreme Court on Military Jurisdiction: Martial Rule in Hawaii and the *Yamashita* Case." *Harvard Law Review* 59 (July 1946), 833–82.

58. Fine, Sidney. "Mr. Justice Murphy and the *Hirabayashi* Case." *Pacific Historical Review* 33 (May 1964): 195–209.

59. Foner, Jack D. *The United States Soldier between Two Wars: Army Life and Reforms, 1865–1898.* New York: Humanities Press, 1970.

60. Fraenkel, Ernst. *Military Occupation and the Rule of Law: Occupation Government in the Rhineland, 1918–1923.* London: Oxford University Press, 1944.

61. Fratcher, William F. "History of the Judge Advocate General's Corps, United States Army." *Military Law Review* 4 (April 1959): 89–122.

62. Fratcher, William F. "Presidential Authority to Regulate Military Justice: A Critical Study of the Court of Military Appeals." *New York University Law Review* 34 (May 1959): 861–90.

63. Frederiksen, Oliver J. *The American Military Occupation of Germany, 1945–1953.* Darmstadt, Federal Republic of Germany: Historical Division, Headquarters, U.S. Army, Europe, 1953.

64. Freidel, Frank. *Francis Lieber, Nineteenth Century Liberal.* Baton Rouge: Louisiana State University Press, 1948.

65. Freidel, Frank. "General Order 100 and American Military Government." *Mississippi Valley Historical Review* 32 (March 1946): 541–56.

66. Friedman, Leon. "Conscription and the Constitution: The Original Understanding." *Michigan Law Review* 67 (1969): 1493–1552.

67. Friedrich, Carl J., ed. *American Experiences in Military Government in World War II.* New York: Rinehart & Co., 1948.

68. Furman, H. W. C. "Restrictions Upon the Use of the Army Imposed by the Posse Comitatus Act." *Military Law Review* 7 (January 1960): 85–129.

69. Futrell, Robert F. "Federal Military Government of the South, 1861–1865." *Military Affairs* 15 (winter 1951): 181–91.

70. Gabriel. Ralph H. "The American Experience with Military Government." *American Political Science Review* 37 (June 1943): 417–38.

71. Gambone, Joseph. "*Ex Parte Milligan:* The Restoration of Judicial Prestige." *Civil War History* 16 (September 1970): 246–59.

72. Garner, James. "General Order 100, Revisited," *Military Law Review* 27 (January 1965): 1–48.

73. Gates, John D. *Schoolbooks and Krags: The United States Army in The Philippines, 1898–1902.* Westport, Conn.: Greenwood Press, 1973.

74. Gaynor, Charles R. "Common Law Military Offenses." S.J.D. thesis, George Washington University, 1956.

75. Generous, William T. *Swords and Scales: The Development of the Uniform Code of Military Justice.* Port Washington, N.Y.: Kennikat Press, 1973.

76. Gerhart, Eugene Clifton, *America's Advocate: Robert H. Jackson.* Indianapolis: Bobbs-Merrill, 1958.

77. Gillette, Howard, Jr. "The Military Occupation of Cuba, 1899–1902: Workshop for American Progressivism." *American Quarterly* 25 (October 1973): 410–25.

78. Gimbel, John. *The American Occupation of Germany.* Stanford: Stanford University Press, 1968.

79. Gimbel, John. *A German Community Under American Occupation: Marburg, 1945–1950.* Stanford: Stanford University Press, 1961.

80. Glasson, William Henry. *History of Military Pension Legislation of the United States.* New York: Coluumbia University Press, 1904.

81. Graber, Doris Appel. *The Development of the Law of Belligerent Occupation, 1863–1914.* New York: Columbia University Press, 1949.

82. Greenwalt, Kent. "All or Nothing at All: The Defeat of Selective Conscientious Objection." *Supreme Court Review* (1971): 31–168.

83. Griffith, William E. "Denazification in the United States Zone of Germany." *Annals of the American Academy of Political and Social Science* 267 (January 1950): 68–77.

84. Grivas, Theodore. *Military Governments in California, 1846–1850.* Glendale, Calif.: The Arthur H. Clark Company, 1963.

85. Grodzins, Morton. *Americans Betrayed: Politics and the Japanese Evacuation.* Chicago: University of Chicago Press, 1949.

86. Harris, C. R. S. *Allied Military Administration of Italy, 1943–1945.* London: Her Majesty's Stationary Office, 1957.

87. Haynes, Robert V. *A Night of Violence: The Houston Riot of 1917.* Baton Rouge: Louisiana State University Press, 1970.

88. Heller, F. H. "Military Law in the Continental Army." *Kansas Law Review* 25 (spring 1977): 353–60.

89. Henderson, Gordon. "Courts-Martial and the Coinstitution: The Original Understanding." *Harvard Law Review* 71 (December 1957): 293–324.

90. Hendricks, George. "Union Army Occupation of the Southern Seaboard, 1861–1865." Ph.D. dissertation, Columbia University, 1954.

91. Hetzel, A. R. *Military Laws of the United States.* 3rd ed. Washington, D.C.: George Templeman, 1846.

92. Hooper, Ernest W. "Memphis, Tennessee: Federal Occupation and Reconstruction, 1862–1870." Ph.D. dissertation, University of North Carolina, Chapel Hill, 1957.

93. Huie, William Bradford. *The Execution of Private Slovik.* New York: Delacorte Press, 1954.

94. Hunt, I. L. *American Military Government of Occupied Germany, 1918–1920.* Washington, D.C.: Government Printing Office, 1943.

95. Hyman, Harold M. *The Era of the Oath: Northern Loyalty Tests During the Civil War and Reconstruction.* Philadelphia: University of Pennsylvania Press, 1954.

96. Hyman, Harold M. *A More Perfect Union: The Impacts of the Civil War and Reconstruction on the Constitution.* New York: Alfred A. Knopf, 1973.

97. Israel, Fred L. "Military Justice in Hawaii, 1941–1944." *Pacific Historical Review* 36 (August 1967): 243–68.

98. Ives, Rollin A, *A Treatise on Military Law.* New York: D. Van Nostrand, 1879.

99. Jacobs, James B. "Legal Change Within the United States Armed Forces Since World War II." *Armed Forces and Society* 4 (spring 1978): 365-90.

100. Karsten, Peter. *Law, Soldiers, and Combat.* Westport, Conn.: Greenwood Press, 1977.

101. Kawai, Kazuo. *Japan's American Interlude.* Chicago: University of Chicago Press, 1960.

102. Keefe, A. J. "JAG Justice in Korea." *Catholic University of America Law Review* 6 (January 1956): 1-38.

103. Kester, John G. "Soldiers Who Insult the President: An Uneasy Look at Article 88 of the Uniform Code of Military Justice." *Harvard Law Review* 81 (June 1968): 1697-1769.

104. Kirkland, John R. "Military Occupation of the South Atlantic States during Reconstruction, 1865-1877." Ph.D. dissertation, University of North Carolina, Chapel Hill, 1967.

105. Klaus, Samuel. *The Milligan Case.* New York: Alfred A. Knopf, 1929.

106. Knopf, Richard C. "Crime and Punishment in the Legion, 1792-1793." Historical and Philisophical Society of Ohio, *Bulletin* 14 (July 1956): 232-38.

107. Kutler, Stanley I. *Judicial Power and Reconstruction Politics.* Chicago: University of Chicago Press, 1968.

108. Lane, Anne J. *The Brownsville Affair: National Crisis and Black Response.* Port Washington, N.Y.: Kennikat Press, 1971.

109. Larkin, Felix. "Professor Edmund M. Morgan and the Drafting of the Uniform Code." *Military Law Review* 28 (April 1965): 7-11.

110. Laska, Lewis L., and James M. Smith. "'Hell and the Devil': Andersonville and the Trial of Captain Henry Wirz, C.S.A., 1865." *Military Law Review* 68 (spring 1975): 77-132.

111. Leach, Jack F. *Conscription in the United States: Historical Background.* Rutland, Vt.: C. E. Tuttle Publishing Co., 1952.

112. Lermack, Paul. "Summary and Special Courts Martial." Ph.D. dissertation, University of Minnesota, 1972.

113. Lieber, G. Norman. *The Use of the Army in Aid of the Civil Power.* Washington, D.C. Government Printing Office, 1898.

114. Lindsey, Almont. *The Pullman Strike.* Chicago: University of Chicago Press, 1942.

115. Litchfield, Edward H. *Governing Postwar Germany.* Ithaca, N.Y.: Cornell University Press, 1953.

116. Lockmiller, David. *Enoch Crowder: Soldier, Lawyer, and Statesman.* Columbia, Mo.: University of Missouri Press, 1955.

117. Lofgren, Charles A. "Compulsory Military Service and the Constitution: The Original Understanding." *William and Mary Quarterly* 33 (January 1976): 61-88.

118. Macomb, Alexander. *A Treatise on Martial Law, and Courts Martial; As Practiced in the United States of America.* Charleston, S.C.: J. Hoff, 1809.

119. Magoon, Charles. *Reports on the Law of Civil Government in Territo-*

ry Subject to Military Government by the Military Forces of the United States. Washington, D.C.: Government Printing Office, 1903.

120. Malbin, Michael J. "Conscription, the Constitution and the Framers: An Historical Analysis. *Fordham Law Review* 40 (1972): 805–26.

121. Maltby, Isaac. *A Treatise on Courts Martial and Military Law.* Boston: Thomas B. Wait and Company, 1813.

122. Margulies, Herbert F. "The Articles of War, 1920: The History of a Forgotten Reform." *Military Affairs* 43 (April 1979): 85–89.

123. Marszalek, John F., Jr. *Court-Martial: A Black Man in America.* New York: Charles Scribner's Sons, 1972.

124. ———. "The Knox Court-Martial: W.T. Sherman Puts the Press on Trial." *Military Law Review* 59 (winter 1973): 197–214.

125. Maslowski, Peter. *Treason Must Be Made Odious: Military Occupation and Wartime Reconstruction in Nashville, Tennessee, 1862–1865.* Millwood, N.Y.: KTO Press, 1978.

126. Mason, Alpheus T. *Harlan Fiske Stone: Pillar of the Law.* New York: Viking Press, 1956.

127. Maurer, Maurer. "The Court-Martialing of Camp Followers in World War I." *American Journal of Legal History* 9 (July 1965): 203–15.

128. Maurer, Maurer. "Military Justice Under General Washington." *Military Affairs* 28 (spring 1964): 8–16.

129. McDermott, John Dishon. "Crime and Punishment in the United States Army: A Phase in Fort Laramie History." *Journal of the West* 7 (April 1968): 246–55.

130. Mendelsohn, John. "The Trial by Document: The Problem of Due Process for War Criminals at Nuernberg." *Prologue* 7 (winter 1975): 227–34.

131. *Military Justice Reporter.* St. Paul, Minn.: West Publishing Co., 1977.

132. *Military Laws and Rules and Regulations for the Army of the United States.* Washington, D.C. William Cooper, 1814.

133. Miller, Robert. "Who Made the Law Officer a Federal Judge?" *Military Law Review* 4 (April 1959): 39–74.

134. Minear, Richard H. *Victors' Justice: The Tokyo War Crimes Trials.* Princeton, N.J.: Princeton University Press, 1971.

135. Moore, Albert B. *Conscription and Conflict in the Confederacy.* New York: Macmillan, 1924.

136. Moore, Wilton P. "Union Army Provost Marshals in the Eastern Theater." *Military Affairs* 26 (fall 1962), 120–26.

137. Mordecai, Alfred. *A Digest of Laws Relating to the Military Establishment of the United States.* Washington, D.C.: Thompson & Homans, 1833.

138. Morgan, Edmund M. "The Background of the Uniform Code of Military Justice." *Military Law Review* 28 (April 1965): 17–37.

139. Murdock, Eugene C. *One Million Men: The Civil War Draft in the North.* Madison: State Historical Society of Wisconsin, 1971.

140. Murdock, Eugene C. *Patriotism Limited, 1862–1865: The Civil War Draft and Bounty System.* Kent, Ohio: Kent State University Press, 1967.

141. Neumann, Inge S. *European War Crimes Trials: A Bibliography.* New York: Carnegie Endowment for International Peace, 1951.

142. Nieman, Donald G. *To Set the Law in Motion: The Freedmen's Bureau and the Legal Rights of Blacks, 1865-1868*. Millwood, N.Y.: KTO Press, 1979.

143. Nobleman, Eli E. "The Administration of Justice in the United States Zone in Germany," *Federal Bar Journal* 8 (October 1946): 70-97.

144. Nobleman, Eli E. "American Military Government Courts in Germany." *American Journal of International Law* 40 (October 1946): 803-10.

145. Nobleman, Eli E. "American Military Government Courts in Germany." *Annals of the American Academy of Political and Social Science* 267 (January 1950): 87-97.

146. Nobleman, Eli E. *American Military Government Courts in Germany: Their Role in the Democratization of the German People*. Camp Gordon, Ga.: U.S. Provost Marshal General's School, 1950.

147. Nobleman, Eli E. "Procedure and Evidence in American Military Government Courts in the United States Zone of Germany." *Federal Bar Journal* 8 (January 1947): 212-48.

148. O'Brien, John Paul Jones. *A Treatise on American Military Laws*. Philadelphia: Lea & Blanchard, 1846.

149. Pasley, Robert S. "The Federal Courts Look at the Court Martial." *University of Pittsburgh Law Review* 12 (fall 1950): 7-34.

150. Pasley, Robert S. "Sentence First—Verdict Afterwards: Dishonorable Discharges Without Trial by Court Martial." *Cornell Law Quarterly* 41 (spring 1956): 545-81.

151. Peck, Darrell L. "Justices and the Generals: The Supreme Court and the Judicial Review of Military Activities." *Military Law Review* 70 (fall 1975): 1-81.

152. Perry, Thomas Sergeant, ed. *The Life and Letters of Francis Lieber*. Boston: J. R. Perry & Co., 1882.

153. Peterson, Edward N. *The American Occupation of Germany: Retreat to Victory*. Detroit: Wayne State University Press, 1968.

154. Pritchett, C. Herman. *The Roosevelt Court: A Study in Judicial Politics and Values, 1937-1947*. New York: Macmillan, 1948.

155. Prugh, George S. "Colonel William Winthrop: The Tradition of the Military Lawyer." *American Bar Association Journal* 62 (February 1956): 126-29, 188-91.

156. Randall, James G. *Constitutional Problems Under Lincoln*. 2d ed., rev. Urbana, Ill.: University of Illinois Press, 1964.

157. Rankin, Robert Stanley. *When Civil Law Fails: Martial Law and Its Legal Basis in the United States*. Durham, N.C.: Duke University Press, 1939.

158. Rasmussen, John C., Jr. "The American Forces in Germany and Civil Affairs, July 1919-January 1923." Ph.D. dissertation, University of Georgia, 1972.

159. Reel, A. Frank. *The Case of General Yamashita*. Chicago: University of Chicago Press, 1949.

160. Renner, Richard Wilson. "Conscientious Objection and the Federal Government: 1787-1792." *Military Affairs* 38 (December 1974): 142-45.

161. Rich, Bennet M. *The Presidents and Civil Disorder*. Washington, D.C.: Brookings Institution, 1941.

162. Richter, William L. "The Army in Texas during Reconstruction, 1865–1870." Ph.D. dissertation, Louisiana State University, 1970.

163. Riley, Walter Lee. "The International Military Tribunal for the Far East." Ph.D. dissertation, University of Washington, 1957.

164. Rittenhouse, John, Jr. "Courts Martial Jurisdiction over Civilians Stationed Overseas with United States Troops." *Dicta* 37 (May-June 1960): 164–83.

165. Robie, William R. "Court Martial of a Judge Advocate General: Brigadier General David Swaim." *Military Law Review* 56 (spring 1972): 211–40.

166. Robinson, William M., Jr. *Justice in Gray: A History of the Judicial System of the Confederate States of America*. Cambridge: Harvard University Press, 1941.

167. Rollman, Robert O. "Of Crimes, Courts-Martial, and Punishment— A Short History of Military Justice." *USAF JAG Law Review* 11 (spring 1969): 212–22.

168. Rostow, Eugene V. "The Japanese-American Cases—A Disaster." *Yale Law Journal* 54 (June 1945): 489–533.

169. Russell, R. R. "Development of Conscientious Objector Recognition in the United States." *George Washington Law Review* 20 (March 1952.): 409–48.

170. Rutman, Darrett B. "The War Crimes and Trial of Henry Wirz." *Civil War History* 6 (June 1960): 117–33.

171. St. Clair, Kenneth E. "Judicial Machinery in North Carolina in 1865." *North Carolina Historical Review* 30 (July 1953): 415–39.

172. St. Clair, Kenneth E. "Military Jurisdiction in North Carolina 1865: A Microcosm of Reconstruction." *Civil War History* 11 (December 1965): 341–50.

173. Scott, Robert. *An Analytical Digest of the Military Laws of the United States*. Philadelphia: J. B. Lippincott & Co., 1873.

174. Sefton, James. *The United States Army and Reconstruction*. Baton Rouge: Louisiana State University Press, 1967.

175. Sherman,, Edward F. "The Civilianization of Military Law." *Maine Law Review 22 (1970): 3*–140.

176. Sherrill, Robert. *Military Justice is to Justice as Military Music is to Music*. New York: Harper & Row, 1970.

177. Shook, Robert W. "Federal Occupation and Administration of Texas, 1865–1870." Ph.D. dissertation, North Texas State University, 1970.

178. Sibley, Mulford Q., and Philip E. Jacob. *Conscription of Conscience: The American State and the Conscientious Objector, 1940–1947*. Ithaca, N.Y.: Cornell University Press, 1952.

179. Smith, Bradley F. *Reaching Judgment at Nuremburg*. New York: Basic Books, 1977.

180. Smith, Jean Edward, ed. *The Papers of General Lucius Clay: Germany, 1945–1949*. 2 vols. Bloomington, Ind.: Indiana University Press, 1974.

181. Smith, Justin H. "American Rule in Mexico." *American Historical Review* 23 (January 1918): 287–302.

182. Stibbs, John Howard. "Andersonville and the Trial of Henry Wirz." *Iowa Journal of History and Politics* 9 (1911): 33–57.

183. Svensson, Eric H. F. "The Military Occupation of Japan: The First Years: Planning, Policy Formulation, and Reforms." Ph.D. dissertation, University of Denver, 1966.

184. Swisher, Carl B. *The Taney Period, 1836–1864.* New York: Macmillan, 1974.

185. Tarrant, Catherine M. "A Writ of Liberty or A Covenant with Hell?: Habeas Corpus and the War Congresses, 1861–1867." Ph.D. dissertation, Rice University, 1972.

186. ten Broek, Jacobus, Edward N. Barnhart, and Floyd Matson. *Prejudice, War, and the Constitution.* Berkeley and Los Angeles: University of California Press, 1968.

187. Thomas, David Y. *A History of Military Government in Newly Acquired Territory of the United States.* New York: Columbia University Press, 1904.

188. *Trial of the Major War Criminals Before the International Military Tribunal, Nuernberg, Germany: 14 November 1945–1 October 1946.* 42 vols. Nuernberg: International Military Tribunal, 1946–49.

189. *Trials of War Criminals Before the Nuernberg Military Tribunals Under Control Council Law No. 10.* 15 vols. Nuernberg: International Military Tribunal, 1949.

190. Twitchell, Heath, Jr. *Allen: The Biography of an Army Officer, 1859–1930.* New Brunswick, N.J.: Rutgers University Press, 1974.

191. Ulmer, S. Sidney. *Military Justice and the Right to Counsel.* Lexington, Ky.: The University Press of Kentucky, 1970.

192. U.S. National Archives and Records Service. *A Guide to the National Archives of the United States.* Washington, D.C.: Government Printing Office, 1974.

193. Van Aduard, Evert Joost. *Japan: From Surrender to Peace.* The Hague: Martinus Nijhoff, 1953.

194. Weaver, John D. *The Brownsville Raid.* New York: W. W. Norton, 1970.

195. Weingartner, James J. *Crossroads of Death: The Story of the Malmedy Massacre and Trial.* Berkeley: University of California Press, 1979.

196. West, Luther C. *They Call It Justice: Command Influence and the Court Martial System.* New York: The Viking Press, 1977.

197. Whiting, William. *War Powers Under the Constitution of the United States.* 43rd ed. Boston: Lee and Shepard, 1871.

198. Wiener, Frederick Bernays. *Civilians Under Military Justice: The British Practice Since 1689 Especially in North America.* Chicago: University of Chicago Press, 1967.

199. ———. "Courts-Martial and the Constitution: The Original Practice." *Harvard Law Review* 72 (November 1958): 1–49; (December 1958): 266–304.

200. ———. "The Militia Clause of the Constitution." *Harvard Law Review* 54 (December 1940): 181–220.

201. Wildes, Harry Emerson. *Typhoon in Tokyo: The Occupation and Its Aftermath.* New York: Macmillan, 1954.

202. Williams, Lorraine A. "Northern Intellectual Reaction to Military Rule During the Civil War." *Historian* 27 (May 1965): 334–49.

203. Wilson, Frederick T. *Federal Aid in Domestic Disturbances, 1787–1903.* Washington, D.C.: Government Printing Office, 1903.

204. Winthrop, William. *Military Law and Precedents.* 2d ed. Boston: Little, Brown, 1895.

205. Woetzel, Robert K. *The Nuremberg Trials in International Law.* London: Stevens, 1960.

206. Wood, Leonard. "The Military Government of Cuba." *Annals of the American Academy of Political and Social Science* 21 (March 1903): 1–30.

207. Wright, Edward Needles. *Conscientious Objectors in the Civil War.* Philadelphia: University of Pennsylvania Press, 1931.

208. Wurfel, Seymour W. "Military Habeas Corpus." *Michigan Law Review* 49 (February 1951): 493–528; (March 1951): 699–721.

209. Ziemke, Earl F. *The U.S. Army in the Occupation of Germany.* Washington, D.C.: Center for Military History, United States Army, 1975.

210. Zink, Harold. *The United States in Germany, 1944–1955.* Princeton, N.J.: Van Nostrand, 1957.

211. Zoghby, Guy A. "Is There a Military Common Law of Crimes?" *Military Law Review* 27 (January 1965): 75–108.

XXIII

U.S. GOVERNMENT DOCUMENTATION

Dale E. Floyd and Timothy K. Nenninger

HISTORY OF FEDERAL RECORDS KEEPING. For nearly 150 years the United States had no national archival institution. Each government agency was responsible for creating, maintaining, and preserving its own records. The establishment of the National Archives in 1934 sought to bring some order out of the prevailing chaos in federal records keeping. Nonetheless, some of the results (destruction, damage, disposal, and dispersal) of the previous haphazard records keeping practices remain today (8, 28, 31).

Records stored in the damp basements, dry attics, and exposed garages of federal buildings were subject to destruction and damage by water, vermin, and fire. Some extant eighteenth and nineteenth century records still show the physical effects of water damage and vermin, while fire has destroyed irreplaceable records, including a good protion of the Revolutionary War military records. The lack of uniform guidelines as to what were permanently valuable historical records, and the absence of a single qualified agency to monitor records disposition, resulted in the purposeful destruction in the past of records which today would be saved. In 1929, for instance, Congress authorized the destruction of nearly all the late nineteenth century military attaché reports—records which the War Department considered valueless because they were of no immediate operational or intelligence interest. Finally, the proprietary attitude of agencies toward their historical records is perpetuated today in the satellite archives maintained by several services. The Navy, Marine Corps, and Air Force, for instance, have retained custody of most of their World War II operational records. One result is the wide dispersal of historic records among several depositories in widely separated geographic areas. The large volume of permanently valuable military records further contributes to this dispersal; for instance, at least four major National Archives facilities have significant holdings of military records.

THE NATIONAL ARCHIVES. Distribution of Records: The permanently valuable records in the custody of the National Archives include most of the extant records of the military and naval establishments throughout much of their existence. Dating from the period of the American Revolution to the early 1960s, these records amount to several hundred thousand cubic feet. The Navy and Old Army Branch services military records through 1941 and all accessioned Navy records in the National Archives Building (33), while the

Modern Military Branch is responsible for the military (Army, Department of Defense, Air Force, and joint service) records covering World War II, the postwar years, and the cold war (17). Because the storage space available in the National Archives Building is finite, the General Archives Division at the Washington National Records Center (Suitland, Maryland) has custody of a number of series of important military records; most significantly the World War II theater, operations, and occupation records, Army intelligence records for World War II and the postwar years, and records of several Army and Navy technical, logistical, and support agencies, especially for the period from the First World War through the Second World War. The National Archives has dispersed some military records, such as those of Corps of Engineer districts and naval districts, to the archives branches in the fifteen regional Federal Archives and Records Centers (5, 82). Military records in any particular regional center generally relate to military activities in that area; thus the New York archives branch, in the records center at Bayonne, New Jersey, has records of the Brooklyn Navy Yard, the New York Engineer District, and the Third Naval District.

Content: Military records in the National Archives include those of the major army and navy policymaking and administrative entities, including the Secretary of War (and Army after 1947), Secretary of the Navy, the War Department General Staff, and the Secretary of Defense. The National Archives also has records of technical and support bureaus and services, for instance the Bureau of Ships, the Bureau of Ordnance, the Office of the Surgeon General, and the Chief Signal Officer. Additionally, records of Army field commands, tactical units, continental commands, and expeditionary forces, and of major naval operating forces are in the archives (9, 10, 21, 22, 25, 26, 29, 30, 34, 36, 38, 39).

While the value of such significant bodies of records for research in American military history is self-evident, important information on a variety of military subjects also can be found among records of civilian agencies. Over one-quarter of the papers of the Continental Congress relate to naval and military affairs during the American Revolution. Letters from George Washington and other officers among the papers contain information on the operations and administration of the Continental Army. State Department records include documentation on such topics as the military affairs of other nations, the activities of American naval and military attachés, and missions in foreign countries; and on the making of American foreign, strategic, and military policy. The voluminous records of the many wartime emergency agencies, essentially civilian, include information of interest to military historians—the War Industries Board, the War Labor Board, the War Production Board, and the Office of Scientific Research and Development are examples (3, 6).

Arrangement: In most cases, records accessioned into the National Archives retain their original arrangement and provenance. Military records, consequently, reflect the records-keeping practices and the patterns of organization of the Army and Navy (7, 18, 66). The National Archives uses the record group as the basic unit of control for records in its custody. A record group is a body of organizationally and functionally related records established with regard for the administrative history, complexity, and volume of records of the creating agency. Most record groups consist of the records of a single bureau or independent agency. Presently there are over four hundred record groups, one-quarter of which relate to military agencies or military activities.

A few examples will suffice to clarify the levels of record group arrangement in the National Archives and to delineate the wide variety of military activities documented in these records.

Record groups with titles beginning "general records," as General Records of the Department of the Navy (Record Group 80), include all the records of the office of the secretary who heads the agency as well as records of other units concerned with matters affecting the entire department or agency. The records of the Secretary of War also warrant a separate record group (RG 107). Many records of Navy bureaus and Army offices concerned with a specific administrative, supply, or technical activity are organized as record groups; for instance, the Records of the Bureau of Ordnance (RG 74), the Records of the Judge–Advocate–General (Army–RG 153; Navy–RG 125), Records of the Bureau of Supplies and Accounts (RG 143), and the Records of the Office of the Chief of Engineers (RG 77). Often such record groups include records of predecessor agencies engaged in the same or similar functions. Although the navy did not establish the Bureau of Aeronautics until 1921, the records of that bureau (RG 72) contain those of the Aircraft Division of the Bureau of Construction and Repair, the Aeronautics Division of the Bureau of Steam Engineering, and the Office of Naval Aviation, the Aviation Division, and the Aviation Section of the Office of the Chief of Naval Operations, dating as early as 1911. The Records of the Army Air Forces (RG 18) likewise include records of the Director of Military Aeronautics, the Bureau of Aircraft Production, the Army Air Service, and the Army Air Corps.

Collective record groups are another variation on the record group concept. Such record groups bring together the records of several units which have a functional or administrative relationship. Military records in this category are generally of field commands and installations. The Records of United States Army Continental Commands, 1821–1920 (RG 393) contain those of geographical department, divisions, districts, reconstruction districts, the twenty-five Civil War Union army corps, as well as of individual posts, camps, and stations. The records of overseas geographical departments, divisions, and districts, of individual overseas posts, and of such expeditions as the China Relief Expedition, the Punitive Expedition to Mexico, the Army of Cuban Pacification, the American Expeditionary Force in Siberia, and U.S. Army Troops in China, are encompassed among the Records of United States Army Overseas Operations and Commands, 1898–1942 (RG 395).

Within the record group the basic levels of control are the subgroup and the record series. Functional responsibilities of the office creating the records, and the chronological span, physical form, and filing scheme of the records are all determinants in establishing subgroups and series. Within the Records of the War Department General and Special Staffs (RG 165), for example, the records of the Office of the Chief of Staff, 1903–47, constitute one subgroup which includes further subdivisions: Provisional General Staff, Chief of Staff, Secretariat, and Deputy Chief of Staff. At the series level within the Office of the Chief of Staff is the general correspondence for 1907–17, arranged numerically; and correspondence for 1918–21, arranged by a subject-numeric scheme.

Finding Aids to Records in the National Archives: Unlike libraries, the National Archives does not maintain a central index of its holdings, but does prepare finding aids for the voluminous and complex records in its custody. Description extends from the record group level, as in the brief descriptions in the *Guide to the National Archives of the United States* (60), to the individual document level, as in special lists. A list of National Archives publications is available on request from the Publications Sales Branch (68).

Most accessioned records have been described at record group and series level in preliminary or descriptive inventories. Series descriptions in preliminary inventories are brief, seldom more than one or two sentences, and include the series title, and the chronological span, physical arrangement, and volume of the records. Descriptive inventories, which are analytical, detailed, and more accurate, will eventually replace most of the preliminary inventories. Some descriptive inventories, such as for the Records of the United States Marine Corps (RG 127) (89), contain a complete breakdown of the filing systems used in the more important correspondence series of the record group. Descriptive inventories also describe the informational content of the individual series in the record group, particularly of those series where this information is not obvious from the series title.

The publication of specialized guides relating to records on a particular topic, not tied to a single record group, is another more sophisticated level of description undertaken by the National Archives. The two guides to Civil War records, one on the Union, the other on the Confederacy, and the cartographic guide, contain much information of interest to military historians (55, 56, 58). Although dated and out of print, the *Handbook of Federal World War Agencies and Their Records, 1917-21* is still a useful source on the records and agencies of the First World War (61). The equivalent two-volume guide to the records of civilian and military agencies of the Second World War, *Federal Records of World War II,* is also out of print but remains an essential tool for understanding the bureaucratic juggernaut and the equivalent mass of records created during that war (52, 53). The recently published guides to material in the National Archives relating to Latin America and Africa contain considerable information on the records of American military involvement in those areas (57, 59).

Published proceedings of National Archives conferences are similar to the specialized subject guides. The conference volumes include scholarly papers, usually by historians who have used the records, and source papers on records relating to the theme of the conference by archivists. Of the volumes already published, those on diplomatic history, captured records, administrative history, World War II, and Indian-white relations contain information relevant to American military history (12, 13, 14, 15, 32). The forthcoming volumes on naval history, state and local history, the American Revolution, and the Army and American society will also contain information of interest to military historians.

Staff archivists have prepared over seventy reference information papers which discuss records relating to a variety of narrow, specialized topics but not limited to those from only one record group. Many of the papers are relevant to American military history, including those on wage data among the nineteenth century naval and military records, data relating to Negro military personnel in the nineteenth century, the Southeast during the Civil War, and audiovisual records relating to naval history (87, 88, 90, 91).

Still another form of delineation undertaken by the National Archives are the descriptive pamphlets prepared for each microfilm publication. These pamphlets give the arrangement and informational value of the records microfilmed, sometimes down to the document level. Significant series of military records have been filmed, such as much of the important nineteenth century correspondence of the war and navy departments. The National Archives periodically issues a catalogue of its microfilm publications (51).

Presidential Libraries. There are presently six presidential libraries administered by the National Archives and Records Service, which cover the presidencies of Herbert Hoover through Lyndon Johnson. While all six include White House records and manuscript collections related to American military history, the Roosevelt, Truman, and Eisenhower libraries are particularly rich in military documentation. Events during the incumbencies of Roosevelt and Truman and a concerted effort to collect material related to Eisenhower's military career make this so. Events in North Africa, the Mediterranean, and Northern Europe during World War II are especially well documented at the Eisenhower Library. As well as collections of the papers of many of Eisenhower's military colleagues, the library has duplicate copies of after-action reports and other operations records of a number of units that served in the European theater (23, 84).

RECORDS OUTSIDE THE NATIONAL ARCHIVES. As previously mentioned, the Navy, Marine Corps, and Air Force have retained custody of some of their archival records; the sea services at the Washington Navy Yard, the air force at Maxwell Air Force Base, Alabama. There are several excellent guides describing these records (1, 2, 35, 50, 69, 71, 72). Although the Army does not have its own archives, the Military History Institute at Carlisle Barracks, Pennsylvania, does have quasi-official records, official publications, and numerous manuscript collections as well as photographs, making it an invaluable research source for studying Army history. Several special bibliographies and guides to manuscript sources at Carlisle assist the researcher in gaining access to the institute's voluminous holdings (16, 40).

Armed forces museums and libraries, especially the libraries of military educational institutions, often have manuscript and other sources relating to the doctrinal, technological, and historical evolution of particular branches or services. The Infantry School Library at Fort Benning, Georgia, has for example, a series of "personal experience monographs" prepared by students in the 1920s and 1930s as firsthand accounts of World War I actions supplemented by historical research. Other school libraries have similar instructional materials while military museums are often depositories of rare manuscripts and publications. The Army has published a useful guide describing the mission and the holdings of its museums (11).

PUBLISHED FEDERAL RECORDS. Although as previously mentioned, some valuable original records have been destroyed over the years, a number of documentary publications have reduced the impact of this loss. In addition, such publications increase the availability of still extant records.

The War Department published compilations of documents relating to a number of American wars, including the Civil War, Spanish-American War, Boxer Rebellion, and World War I (19, 27, 41, 42, 44, 81). It also prepared collections on specialized subjects such as the medical history of the Civil War, Raphael Thian's *Legislative History of the General Staff of the Army of the United States,* blacks in the army, the Battle of Wounded Knee, the air service in World War I, and the Philippine Insurrection (20, 43, 80). Until recently the last four had only been available in typed manuscript form but they are now reproduced on microfilm (54, 62, 65, 67). An amibitious documentary publication program long has been pursued by the Navy Department, which has published compilations of documents relating to naval operations in the American Revolution, quasi war with France, war with the Barbary prirates, Civil War, and Spanish-American War (45, 70, 73, 74, 75). The State Department's Foreign Relations series, which presently covers the period from 1861 to the early 1950s, includes numerous military documents (48). Another ongoing documentary series, *The Territorial Papers of the United States,* has included documentation pertaining to the military in general and in particular contains records relating to the Second Seminole War, the Black Hawk War, and other Indian conflicts (85, 86).

The Congressional Serial Set, including published hearings and compilations of documents, has long been a useful source for information on military matters. The annual reports of the Secretary of War and the Secretary of Navy, published as congressional documents until well into the twentieth century, often contained reprinted versions of military documents. There are numerous indexes to these several kinds of publications (37, 76, 77, 78, 79).

CONCLUSIONS. Access to unpublished federal records relating to military history has been facilitated in recent years by widespread declassification. Dissemination by the military services and the National Archives of published (letterpress and microform) records has continued apace. The publication of numerous guides, indexes, checklists, and inventories describing these records has further assisted the research of military historians.

The foregoing discussion has attempted to provide some examples of the disposition, content, and arrangement of federal records relating to the military establishment. Neither this discussion nor the bibliography are meant as definitive statements on these records. The archivists and reference librarians at the institutions included on the following list can provide more definitive information on particular research subjects.

SOME USEFUL ADDRESSES

National Archives:

Navy and Old Army Branch
National Archives
Washington, D.C. 20408

Modern Military Branch
National Archives
Washington, D.C. 20408

General Archives Division
National Archives
Washington, D.C. 20409

Audiovisual Archives Division
National Archives
Washington, D.C. 20408

Center for Cartographic and Architectural Archives
National Archives
Washington, D.C. 20408

Publications Sales Branch
National Archives
Washington, D.C. 20408

Presidential Libraries:

Herbert Hoover Library
West Branch, Iowa 52358

Franklin D. Roosevelt Library
Hyde Park, N.Y. 12538

Harry S. Truman Library
Independence, Mo. 64050

Dwight D. Eisenhower Library
Abilene, Kans. 67410

John F. Kennedy Library
Columbia Point, Dorchester
Boston, Mass. 02125

Lyndon B. Johnson Library
Austin, Tex. 78705

Federal Archives and Records Centers (for each of the following, address
inquiries to the Federal Archives and Records Center Director):

Atlanta
1557 St. Joseph Ave.
East Point, Ga. 30344

Boston
380 Trapelo Rd.
Waltham, Mass. 02154

Chicago
7358 South Pulaski Rd.
Chicago, Ill. 60629

Dayton
3150 Bertwynn Dr.
Dayton, Ohio 45439

Denver
Bldg. 48, Denver Federal Center
Denver, Colo. 80225

Fort Worth
Box 6216
Fort Worth, Tex. 76115

Kansas City
2306 East Bannister Rd.
Kansas City, Mo. 64131

Los Angeles
24000 Avila Rd.
Laguna Niguel, Calif. 92677

Mechanicsburg
Defense Activities, Bldg. 308
Mechanicsburg, Pa. 17055

New York
Bldg. 22, Military Ocean Terminal
Bayonne, N.J. 07002

Philadelphia
5000 Wissahickon Ave.
Philadelphia, Pa. 19144

St. Louis
National Personnel Records Center
9700 Page Blvd.
St. Louis, Mo. 63132

San Francisco
1000 Commodore Dr.
San Bruno, Calif. 94066

Seattle
6125 Sand Point Way
Seattle, Wash. 98115

Washington
Washington National Records Center
Washington, D.C. 20409

Military Records Facilities:

The Albert F. Simpson Historical Research Center
Air University
Maxwell Air Force Base, Al. 36112

The U.S. Army Military History Institute
Carlisle Barracks, Pa. 17013

History and Museums Division
Headquarters, United States Marine Corps
Washington, D.C. 20380

Operational Archives
Naval History Division
Washington Navy Ward
Washington, D.C. 20374

BIBLIOGRAPHY

1. Agnew, James B. "USAMHRC—The Mother Lode for Military History." *Military Affairs* 39 (1975): 146–48.
2. Allard, Dean C. "Naval Historical Resources." In *International Commission for Military History: Acta No. 2,* edited by Robin Higham and Jacob W. Kipp. Manhattan, Kans.: Military Affairs/Aerospace Historian Publishing, 1977.
3. Allen, Andrew H. "Historical Archives of the Department of State." *American Historical Association Annual Report, 1894.* Washington, D.C.: Government Printing Office, 1895.
4. *American Archives . . . A Documentary History of . . . the North American Colonies; of the Causes and Accomplishments of the American Revolution. 9 vols.* Edited by Peter Force. Washington: N.P., 1837–53.
5. Angel, Herbert E. "Archival Janus: The Records Center." *American Archivist* 31 (1968): 5–12.
6. Ballentine, Robert G. "'The Territorial Papers'; A Source for Military History." *Military Affairs* 5 (1941): 241–44.
7. Bartlett, Kenneth F. "Early Correspondence Filing Systems of the Office of the Secretary of the Navy." *National Archives Accessions,* no. 58 (1964): pp. 1–11.
8. Beers, Henry P. "Historical Development of the Records Disposition Policy of the Federal Government Prior to 1934." *American Archivist* 7 (1944): 181–201.
9. Campbell, Edward G. "Use of Records of the Last War Today." *Military Affairs* 6 (1942): 63–68.
10. Cappon, Lester J. "A Note on Confederate Ordnance Records." *Military Affairs* 4 (1940): 94–102.
11. Cary, Norman M., comp. *Guide to U.S. Army Museums and Historic Sites.* Washington, D.C.: Government Printing Office, 1975.
12. Conference on Captured German and Related Records, Washington, D.C., 1968. *Captured German and Related Records.* edited by Robert Wolfe. Athens, Ohio: Onio University Press, 1974.
13. Conference on the National Archives and Foreign Relations Research, Washington, D.C., 1969. *The National Archives and Foreign Relations Research.* edited by Milton O. Gustafson. Athens, Ohio: Ohio University Press, 1974.
14. Conference on Research in the Administration of Public Policy, Washington, D.C., 1970. *Research in the Administration of Public Policy.* edited by Frank B. Evans and Harold T. Pinkett. Washington, D.C.: Howard University Press, 1975.
15. Conference on Research on the Second World War, Washington, D.C., 1971. *World War II: An Account of Its Documents.* edited by James E. O'Neill and Robert W. Krauskopf. Washington, D.C.: Howard University Press, 1976.
16. Cooling, B. Franklin, III, comp. *A Suggested Guide to the Curricular Archives of the U.S. Army War College, 1907–1940.* Carlisle Barracks, Pa.: U.S. Army Military History Research Collection, 1973.
17. Cunliffe, William H. "Archival Sources In Modern Military History."

In *International Commission For Military History: Acta No. 2,* edited by Robin Higham and Jacob W. Kipp. Manhattan, Kans.: Military Affairs/Aerospace Historian Publishing, 1977.

18. Deutrich, Mabel E. "Decimal Filing: Its General Background and an of Its Rise and Fall in the U.S. War Department." *American Archivist* 28 (1965): 199–218.

19. Eisendrath, Joseph L. "The Official Records, Sixty-Three Years in the Making." *Civil War History* 1 (1955): 89–94.

20. Farrell, John T. "An Abandoned Approach to Philippines History: John R.M. Taylor and the Philippine Insurgent Records." *Catholic Historical Review* 39 (1954): 385–407.

21. Glenn, Bess. "Navy Department Records in the National Archives." *Military Affairs* 7 (1943): 247–60.

22. Greenfield, Kent R. "Accessibility of U.S. Army Records to Historical Research." *Military Affairs* 15 (1951): 10–15.

23. Haight, David J., and George H. Curtis. "Abilene, Kansas and the History of World War II: Resources and Research Opportunities at the Dwight D. Eisenhower Library." *Military Affairs* 41 (1977): 195–200.

24. Hamer, Philip M., ed. *A Guide to Archives and Manuscripts in the United States.* New Haven: Yale University Press, 1961.

25. Huber, Elbert L. "War Department Records in the National Archives." *Military Affairs* 6 (1942): 247–54.

26. Irvine, Dallas D. "The Archives of the War Department: Repository of Captured Confederate Archives, 1868–1881." *Military Affairs* 10 (1946): 93–111.

27. Irvine, Dallas D. "Genesis of the Official Records." *Missisippi Valley Historical Review* 24 (1937): 221–29.

28. Jones, Houston G. *The Records of a Nation: Their Management, Preservation, and Use.* New York: Atheneum, 1969.

29. Leland, Waldo, G. "Historians and Archivists in the First World War." *American Archivist* 5 (1942): 1–17.

30. Lokke, Carl L. "The Captured Confederate Records Under Francis Lieber." *American Archivist* 9 (1946): 277–319.

31. McCoy, Donald R. *The National Archives: America's Ministry of Documents, 1934–1968.* Chapel Hill: University of North Carolina Press, 1978.

32. National Archives Conference on Research in the History of Indian-White Relations, Washington, D.C., 1972. *Indian-White Relations: A Persistent Paradox.* Edited by Jane F. Smith and Robert M. Kvasnicka. Washington, D.C.: Howard University Press, 1976.

33. Nenninger, Timothy K. "Sources For The Study Of Military History Among Navy And Old Army Records In The National Archives." In *International Commission For Military History: Acta No. 2,* edited by Robin Higham and Jacob W. Kipp. Manhattan, Kans.: Military Affairs/Aerospace Historian Publishing, 1977.

34. Owen, Arthur F. "Opportunities for Research: The Early Records of the Office of the Inspector General, 1814–48." *Military Affairs* 7 (1943): 195–96.

35. Paszek, Lawrence J., comp. *United States Air Force History: A Guide*

to Documentary Sources. Washington, D.C.: Government Printing Office, 1973.

36. Pease, Theodore Calvin. "A Caution Regarding Military Documents." *American Historical Review* 26 (1921): 282–84.

37. Poore, Benjamin P., ed. *A Descriptive Catalogue of the Government Publications of the United States, September 5, 1774–March 5, 1881.* Washington, D.C.: Government Printing Office, 1885.

37a. Rhoads, James B. "The Taming of the West: Military Archives as a Source for the Social History of the Trans-Mississippi Region to 1900." In *People of the Plains and Mountains: Essays in the History of the West, Dedicated to Everett Dick,* edited by Ray Allan Billington, pp. 175–203. Westport, Conn.: Greenwood Press, 1973.

38. Riepma, Siert F. "A Soldier-Archivist and His Records: Major General Fred C. Ainsworth." *American Archivist* 4 (1941): 178–87.

39. Ryan, Gary D. "Disposition of A.E.F. Records of World War I." *Military Affairs* 30 (1966): 212–19.

40. Sommers, Richard J., comp. *Manuscript Holdings of the Military History Research Collection.* 2 vols. Carlisle Barracks, Pa.: U.S. Army Military History Research Collection, 1972 and 1975.

41. U.S. Adjutant General's Office. *Correspondence from the Adjutant General, U.S.A., Relating to the Campaigns in the Philippine Islands and Porto Rico During May, June, July, and August, 1898.* Washington, D.C.: Government Printing Office, 1899.

42. U.S. Adjutant General's Office. *Correspondence Relating to the War with Spain . . . Including the Insurrection in the Philippine Islands and the China Relief Expedition.* 2 vols. Washington, D.C.: Government Printing Office, 1902.

43. U.S. Adjutant General's Office. *Legislative History of the General Staff of the Army of the United States . . . from 1775 to 1901.* By Raphael P. Thian. Washington, D.C.: Government Printing Office, 1901.

44. U.S. Army. Office of Military History. *United States Army in the World War, 1917–19.* 17 vols. Washington, D.C.: Government Printing Office, 1948.

45. U.S. Bureau of Navigation (Navy Department). *Naval Operations of the War with Spain, 1898.* Washington, D.C.: Government Printing Office, 1898.

46. U.S. Congress. *American State Papers: Documents, Legislative and Executive, 1789–1838.* 38 Vols. Washington, D.C.: n.p., 1832–61.

47. U.S. Department of the Army. *The Writing of American Military History: A Guide.* Washington, D.C.: Government Printing Office, 1956.

48. U.S. Department of State. *Papers Relating to the Foreign Relations of the United States, 1861–* . Washington, D.C.: Government Printing Office, 1862– .

49. U.S. Library of Congress. *The National Union Guide to Manuscript Collections, 1959–* . Ann Arbor, Mich. Hamden, Conn.; and Washington, D.C.: J. W. Edwards, Publishers; Shoe String Press; and Library of Congress, 1962. Subsequent volumes published by the American Library Association.

50. U.S. Marine Corps. *Marine Corps Historical Publications in Print.* Washington, D.C.: History and Museums Division, Headquarters Marine Corps, 1978.
51. U.S. National Archives. *Catalogue of National Archives Microfilm Publications.* Washington, D.C.: National Archives and Records Service, 1974.
52. U.S. National Archives. *Federal Records of World War II:* Vol. 1, *Civilian Agencies.* Washington, D.C.: National Archives and Recors Service, 1950.
53. U.S. National Archives. *Federal Records of World War II. Vol. 2, Military Agencies.* Washington, D.C.: National Archives and Records Service, 1951.
54. U.S. National Archives. *Gorrell's History of the American Expeditionary Forces Air Service, 1917-19.* Introduction by Timothy K. Nenninger. Washington, D.C.: National Archives and Records Service, 1975.
55. U.S. National Archives. *Guide to the Archives of the Confederate States of America.* Compiled by Henry P. Beers. Washington, D.C.: National Archives and Records Service, 1968.
56. U.S. National Archives. *Guide to Cartographic Records in the National Archives.* Compiled by Herman R. Friis, A. Philip Muntz, and Patrick D. McLaughlin. Washington, D.C.: National Archives and Records Service, 1971.
57. U.S. National Archives. *Guide to Federal Archives Relating to Africa.* Compiled by Aloha South. [Honolulu]. Crossroads Press, 1977.
58. U.S. National Archives. *Guide to Federal Records Relating to the Civil War.* Compiled by Kenneth W. Munden, and Henry P. Beers. Washington, D.C.: National Archives and Records Service, 1962.
59. U.S. National Archives. *Guide to Materials on Latin America in the National Archives of the United States.* Compiled by George S. Ulibarri and John P. Harrison. Washington, D.C.: National Archives and Records Service, 1974.
60. U.S. National Archives. *Guide to the National Archives of the United States.* Washington, D.C.: National Archives and Records Service, 1974.
61. U.S. National Archives. *Handbook of Federal World War Agencies and Their Records, 1917-21.* Washington, D.C.: National Archives, 1943.
62. U.S. National Archives. *History of the Philippine Insurrection Against the United States, 1899-1903, and Documents Relating to the War Department Project for Publishing the History.* Compiled by John R. M. Taylor. Washington, D.C.: National Archives and Records Service, 1968.
63. U.S. National Archives. *List of Record Groups of the National Archives and Records Service.* Washington, D.C.: National Archives and Records Service, 1976.
64. U.S. National Archives. *Navy Department General Orders, 1863-1948. Introduction by Geraldine N. Phillips. Washington, D.C.: National Archives and Records Service, 1975.*
65. U.S. National Archives. *The Negro in the Military Service of the*

United States, 1639–1886. Washington, D.C.: National Archives and Records Service, 1973.

66. U.S. National Archives. *Recordkeeping in the Department of State, 1789–1956.* Reference Information Paper no. 74. Compiled by Stephen H. Helton. Washington, D.C. National Archives and Records Service, 1975.

67. U.S. National Archives. *Reports and Correspondence Relating to Army Investigations of the Battle of Wounded Knee and to the Sioux Campaign of 1890–1891.* Introduction by John Ferrell. Washington, D.C.: National Archives and Records Service, 1975.

68. U.S. National Archives. *Select List of Publications of the National Archives and Records Service.* Washington, D.C.: National Archives and Records Service, 1977.

69. U.S. Naval History Division. *Guide to United States Naval Administrative Histories of World War II.* Compiled by William C. Heimdahl and Edward J. Marolda. Washington, D.C.: Naval History Division, 1976.

70. U.S. Naval History Division. *Naval Documents of the American Revolution. Edited by William B. Clark and William J. Morgan. Washington, D.C.: Government Printing Office, 1964–* .

71. U.S. Naval History Division. *Partial Checklist: World War II Histories and Historical Reports in the U.S. Naval History Division.* Washington, D.C.: Naval History Division, 1977.

72. U.S. Naval History Division. *U.S. Naval History Sources in the Washington Area and Suggested Research Subjects.* Compiled by Dean C. Allard and Betty Berin. 3rd ed., rev. and enl., Washington, D.C.: Government Printing Office, 1970.

73. U.S. Navy Department. *Official Records of the Union and Confederate Navies in the War of the Rebellion.* 30 vols. and index. Washington, D.C.: Government Printing Office, 1894–1927.

74. U.S. Office of Naval Records and Library. *Naval Documents Related to the Quasi-War Between the United States and France: Naval Operations.* 7 vols. Washington, D.C.: Government Printing Office, 1935–38.

75. U.S. Office of Naval Records and Library. *Naval Documents Related to the United States Wars with the Barbary Powers: Naval Operations.* 7 vols. Washington, D.C.: Government Printing Office, 1939–45.

76. U.S. Superintendent of Documents. *Catalogue of the Public Documents . . . 1893–1940.* 25 vols. Washington, D.C.: Government Printing Office, 1896–1945.

77. U.S. Superintendent of Documents. *Checklist of Public Documents, 1789–1909.* Washington, D.C.: Government Printing Office, 1911–* .

78. U.S. Superintendent of Documents. *Monthly Catalogue, United States Public Documents.* Washington, D.C.: Government Printing Office, 1895–* .

79 U.S. Superintendent of Documents. *Tables of and Annotated Index to the Congressional Series of United States Public Documents.* Washington, D.C.: Government Printing Office, 1902.

80 U.S. Surgeon's General Office. *The Medical and Surgical History of*

the War of the Rebellion. 6 vols. Washington, D.C.: Government Printing Office, 1870–81.

81. U.S. War Department. *War of the Rebellion: A Compilation of the Official Records of the Union and Confederate Armies.* 130 vols. Washington, D.C.: Government Printing Office, 1880–1901.

82. White, Gerald T. "Government Archives Afield: The Federal Records Centers and the Historian." *Journal of American History* 55 (1969): 833–42.

83. Wilcox, Jerome K. comp. *Official War Publications: Guide to State. Federal, and Canadian Publications.* 9 vols. Berkeley: University of California Press, 1941–45.

84. Zobrist, Benedict K. "Resources of Presidential Libraries for the History of Post World War II American Military Government in Germany and Japan." *Military Affairs* 42 (1978): 17–19.

SUPPLEMENT TO BIBLIOGRAPHY

85. Conference on the History of the Territories, Washington, D.C., 1969. *Conference on the History of the Territories of the United States.* Edited by John Porter Bloom. Athens, Ohio: Ohio University Press, 1973.

86. U.S. Department of State. *Territorial Papers of the United States.* Compiled and edited by Clarence E. Carter. Washington, D.C.: Government Printing Office, 1934–   .

87. U.S. National Archives. *Audiovisual Records Relating to Naval History.* Reference Information Paper no. 73. Compiled by Mayfield Bray, Franklin W. Burch, Maygene Daniels, James Trimble. Washington, D.C.: National Archives and Records Service, 1975.

88. U.S. National Archives. *Data Relating to Negro Military Personnel in the 19th Century.* Reference Information Paper no. 63. Compiled by Aloha P. South. Washington, D.C.: National Archives and Records Service, 1973.

89. U.S. National Archives. *Records of the United States Marine Corps.* Record Group 127. Compiled by Mazie Johnson. Washington, D.C.: National Archives and Records Service, 1970.

90. U.S. National Archives. *The Southeast During the Civil War: Selected War Department Records in the National Archives.* Reference Information Paper no. 69. Compiled by Dale E. Floyd. Washington, D.C.: National Archives and Records Service, 1973.

91. U.S. National Archives. *Wage Data Among 19th Century Military and Naval Records.* Reference Information Paper no. 54. Compiled by Francis J. Heppner and Harry W. John. Washington, D.C.: National Archives and Records Service, 1973.